A HISTORY OF
Mountain Climbing

Editorial Direction:
Christine de Colombel

Designed by:
Pascal Tournaire

Picture Research:
Sylvain Jouty

English-language editor:
Christine Schultz-Touge

Proofreading:
Bernard Wooding

Flammarion
26, rue Racine
75006 Paris

200 Park Avenue South
Suite 1406
New York, NY 10003

Published simultaneously in French
under the title *L'Histoire de l'Alpinisme*
Copyright © 1996 Arthaud.

ISBN: 2-08013-622-4
Numéro d'édition: 1178
Dépôt légal: September 1996

Printed in France

Library of Congress Catalog Card Number: 96-85980

A HISTORY OF
Mountain Climbing

ROGER FRISON-ROCHE
AND SYLVAIN JOUTY

Translated from the French by
DEKE DUSINBERRE

Flammarion

Paris - New York

Preceding double page:
Caspar Wolf, The Lauteraar
Glacier. Oil on canvas,
c. 1776, 54 x 82 cm. One of
the finest Alpine artists of the
eighteenth century, Wolf
(1735–1783) would first
make a sketch in oil, on
which he noted the names of
the mountains. This painting
shows the Abschwung
moraine with the
Lauteraarhorn peaks in the
distance.

Contents

OTHER MOUNTAIN RANGES

*Left-hand page, top to bottom:
Illustration from an early
manual; Jean Antoine Carrel
(seated) and A. Pession;
Catherine Destivelle on the
Planpraz Pinnacles. This
page, top to bottom: The
Everest icefall; the north
ridge of Kangchenjunga;
Reinhold Messner.*

Where does recreation end and true mountain climbing begin?

It might be said that mountaineering begins as soon as the ascent of a mountain, cliff, or secondary summit—in short, any prominent point on the globe—becomes dangerous due to altitude or climate. What is generally called mountaineering can essentially be defined by the concept of danger and the techniques devised to parry that danger. This thrilling human activity, in fact, has recently tended to become a pure sport in which the need for media coverage overshadows the aesthetic qualities formerly associated with a fine ascent.

Unlike recreational hikers, who seek relaxation and beauty above all, mountain climbers are people who enjoy vanquishing obstacles, overcoming danger, pitting themselves against nature and the elements.

There are countless casual hikers, but only a very limited number of true mountain climbers. Obviously, only an elite few will deliberately risk their lives in the firm conviction that they can dominate danger thanks to their own expertise, intelligence, solid morale, quick reflexes, and physical strength.

On the other hand, whereas recreational trekkers are forever condemned to anonymity, a mountaineer can attain notoriety. In a modern world where all that counts is the exploit—where the cult of stardom has reached fever pitch—it is entirely natural and excusable for a budding mountaineer to dream of some day making it onto the front page of the world's major newspapers, with all that this implies in terms of financial advantages and future success. Thus, an initially pure attitude has been steadily deformed ever since the day mountain climbing began to spark mass interest. Such interest is very recent, for prior to the Second World War the greatest alpine exploits were known only among climbing circles. Accounts of major feats appeared only in specialized reviews. Mountain climbing was not thought to interest the "general public." The shameless exploitation of a few

Introduction

dramatic climbing tragedies did more to popularize mountaineering than all the stimulating accounts by the likes of Guido Rey and Albert Mummery, or the moving evocations of *montagnard* experience by Tézenas du Montcel, Guido Lammer, and others.

The origins of mountain climbing go back a long way, and motivations varied widely among the people who made the first known ascents. Few of those early feats, however, were inspired by aesthetic considerations—the dominant motivation was a utilitarian one, spurred by self-interest. Early exploits were designed to win fame, promotion, notoriety, or wealth for the climber, whether soldier (the Ligurian legionnaire during the Jugurthine wars), scholar (Saussure), courtier (Antoine de Ville), or crystal seeker (Jacques Balmat).

Of these various social groups, scholars—or rather, scientists—played a considerable role. Whether geologist, botanist, geographer, physicist, or glacier specialist, intellectuals significantly contributed to the conquest of summits by conducting experiments in the field to verify their theories. Some of them, at least, combined scientific interests with an aesthetic approach, as demonstrated by the writings of Horace Bénédict de Saussure, in which learning and beauty go hand in hand.

It is probably because the motives that initially incited people to climb mountains were not devoid of self-interest that some commentators would like to date the origins of mountaineering to the founding of the Alpine Club in 1857. But that would be a serious mistake. Perhaps it would be better to say that this date represents the birth of mountain climbing as a sport, in the sense that the English originally understood the term—a disinterested activity far removed from modern athletic championships, ski competitions, and professional tennis circuits the world over, all of which also claim to be sport.

Yet it hardly matters, for ultimately there were all sorts of reasons for climbing mountains. As stated above, people were driven mainly by personal interest, though not necessarily a financial one, since the most powerful driving force was usually the desire for fame.

Above, left to right: Benoît Chamoux on the north face of Everest, at 7,350 meters; Christophe Profit soloing the west face of the Petit Dru; on the top of the Eiger after finishing the Harlin Direct route; Machapuchare at sunset. Bottom, right: Pasang Lamu, the first Nepalese woman to reach the summit of Everest.

In any case, mountaineering constitutes a type of motivation distinctly different from all the others that drove men up mountains. In fact, even as mankind thought it was conquering mountains, the mountains were conquering mankind by obliging everything to adapt to its environment. That goes not only for human and animal forms of life, but also for vegetable forms. Mountain cows are different from Normandy or Friesian varieties; bears, which live at all latitudes, adapt not only to the mountains in general but to the specific types of mountains they inhabit. As to mankind, a morphological transformation has been occurring very slowly—it is clear that the Sherpas of Namche Bazar have become perfect mountain dwellers, both in the way they have physically adapted to altitude (enabling them to live normally above 4,000 meters, i.e. 13,000 feet) and in the resources they have managed to draw from an extremely harsh nature. Human beings also live normally at these altitudes on the *altiplani* of Peru, Chile, and Bolivia; the Europeans who settled on those high lands in South America following the Spanish conquest have adapted through the centuries to the point where they, too, have become a race of mountain people.

In contrast, mountain climbing does not allow for real physical adaptation to the environment—the time scale is simply too short for it to be possible. The grandest feats of mountaineering have in fact been accomplished by men of the plains or, at the very most, of the hill country. Initially, they carried out their exploits relying only on their own devices; later they realized that they needed to replenish strength sapped by high altitudes and the lack of oxygen. So they began using oxygen apparatus that enabled them to breathe and move as though on lower terrain; then they combatted cold through special fabrics, invented purpose-built equipment, and developed new techniques. People have had to resort to their intelligence to overcome the highest peaks, which explains why climbers feel that mountains are a truly human conquest.

This is nevertheless a fragile, capricious, and extremely brief conquest, since it is never accompanied by permanent occupation of the conquered territory. People will never actually live on Mount Everest, Mount Jannu, or Mont Blanc. They may go there in a spirit of discovery and enthusiasm, but they immediately redescend to more breathable altitudes.

The conquest of mountains—particularly in recent times—has been extensively documented. Many accounts glorify mountaineering exploits, for the long history of mountain climbing is packed with all kinds of heroic deeds and sensational accomplishments.

The story of mountain climbing has already been told by distinguished participants—this book therefore offers only an overview of the history of mountaineering, one that nevertheless seeks to understand the ever-ascending (naturally!) evolution of this great passion, from its obscure origins to the advent of the grand modern sport. Furthermore, it will be seen that, however people climbed mountains and whatever their motives, a given period in the history of mountaineering has always corresponded to a distinct era of history in general—social evolution and wars have divided mountaineering's story into clear stages. Finally, the way tall mountains are conquered—mountaineering such as it has been practiced in the past and present—is inevitably revealing of the mentality of an era, land, or nation.

Logically, the history of "Alpinists" begins with the conquest of Mont Blanc in 1786. Yet even prior to the exploits of Jacques Balmat, Michel Paccard, and Horace Bénédict de Saussure, certain earlier, well-known ascents in the Alps constitute what might be called the "prehistory" of mountain climbing.

Following double page: The north face of the Matterhorn at night. The streaks in the sky are produced by the movement of stars during the long exposure required for a nocturnal photograph. The faint red point on the face itself is the bivouac lamp of Catherine Destivelle, during the first repetition, in the winter of 1994, of Walter Bonatti's historic 1965 route.

The Alps

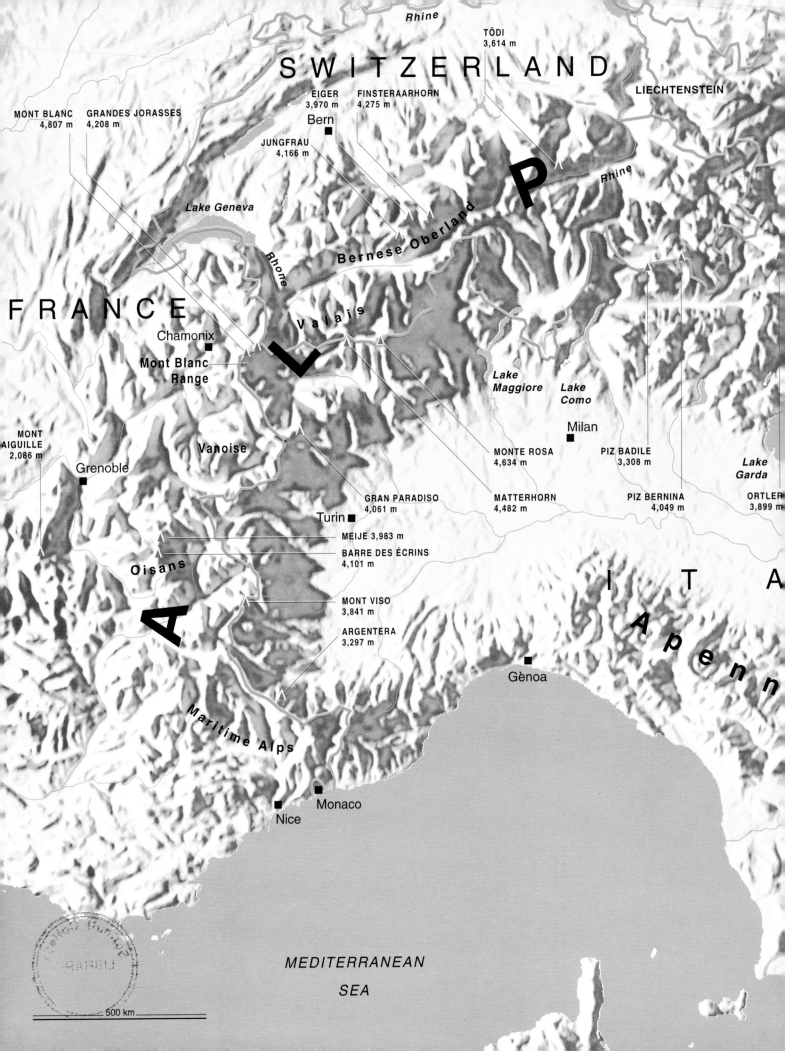

S

Karwendel

Berchtesgaden
Alps

Hohe Tauern

AUSTRIA

tztal

Dolomites

Julian Alps

SLOVENIA

GROSSGLOCKNER
3,798 m

TRIGLAV
2,863 m

MARMOLADA
3,344 m

■ Venice

CROATIA

L Y

o

n e s

SAN MARINO

ADRIATIC

SEA

Florence

■

The Prehistory of Mountain Climbing

Before there were mountaineers, the mountains may have intrigued or frightened people, but they rarely beckoned. History mentions very few people who scaled the summits — which makes their stories all the more remarkable.

As ancient texts come to light and are deciphered, the date of the earliest ascent recedes. Historians often refer to 401 B.C. during the retreat of 10,000 Greek mercenaries led by the Athenian Xenephon. But it is conceivable that in unknown, even prehistoric times, people climbed high mountains. It is hard to believe that the people of the so-called "Camunian" civilization stayed in the Camonica Valley during the Bronze Age (1500 B.C.) without ever pursuing their favorite game—deer—across the Bergamo Alps or up the easy glaciers of Adamello. Nor is it improbable that, at about the same time, the miners (or their leaders) of the Salzkammergut region climbed the imposing limestone cliffs of the Totes Gebirge in search of bear, their sacred animal.

Furthermore, there is a tendency to ignore civilizations other than our own. From time immemorial the religious peoples of the Himalayas have climbed to the high passes (if not the peaks) of sacred mountains, at surprising altitudes, to travel from Tibet to India and vice versa. Similarly, it is hard to believe that Mount Fuji, Japan's highest mountain, has been climbed only in the past few centuries. And mines in the Andes are located at such high altitudes that it is entirely probable that miners from pre-Incan civilizations searched high and far in the hope of finding a surface lode.

Yet great caution must be used in making such affirmations. Therefore, only a few precise and well-known dates will be cited here, in an effort to provide a structuring framework to the prehistory of mountaineering.

Personally, I like to date the origins of rock climbing back to the famous episode of a Ligurian soldier in the Jugurthine wars, as recounted by Sallust and cited by the delightful, witty writer Charles Gos. In 106 B.C., a Ligurian legionnaire in the troops commanded by Marius wanted to break the monotony and to improve his diet during the siege of a Berber camp, defensively situated high on a rocky cliff overlooking the Moulouya River. He therefore set off to hunt for the rock snails which were

Facing page: A chamois hunter from the Swiss canton of Glarus, depicted in an anonymous watercolor of 1816. Note the crampons and alpenstock. Left: A woodcut from Theuerdank, *a richly illustrated allegorical poem, commissioned by Holy Roman Emperor Maximilian I (1517), showing a medieval chamois hunter as a "mountaineer" with crampons on his feet.*

*Claude-Louis Châtelet
(1753–1794),* The Valley of
Chamonix and Mont Blanc.
*Oil on canvas, 96 x 129 cm.
It is possible to identify—
though with some difficulty—
the Verte-Dru group of peaks,
the Chamonix Aiguilles,
Mont Blanc, and the Mer de
Glace (known at the time as
the Glacier des Bois).*

particularly abundant in the limestone cliffs
(still considered a culinary treat today). He
started up the cliff, scrambling up chimneys,
hoisting himself above overhangs, and passing
ledges until, carried away by his enthusiasm, he
suddenly realized he had arrived at the top.
From there he overlooked the enemy camp,
which expected no attack from that direction.
The man descended, announced his discovery
to his superiors, and led an expedition back up.
He thereby became not merely a scout but a
veritable mountain guide, climbing in the lead,
forging a route, equipping it with iron stakes
and cables, and helping his comrades over the
most difficult passages.

The story does not relate whether the soldier
was later promoted to centurion. In fact, the
same scenario was subsequently replayed countless times, notably during the last Franco-

German conflict, twenty centuries later—Frendo
and his men climbed Mont Froid in 1945
(including a rockface that had been deemed
inaccessible) to take the German positions by
surprise. The Ligurian soldier also had a glorious successor during the First World War in the
person of the Tyrolean mountaineer Sepp
Innerkofler, who climbed the face of Paternkofel,
only to be killed at the summit while accomplishing his mission.

The history of mountain climbing therefore
owes much to military exploits. Yet trade relations and religious pilgrimages also merit mention. Who exactly were the people in antiquity
that crossed the passes of Lisjoch and Theodul?
Although such routes were apparently easier
then than now, this does not mean that the Alps
had less snow—to the contrary, I would guess
that the upper glaciers were so dense that they

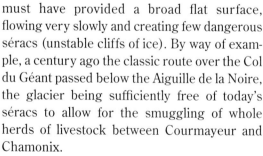

must have provided a broad flat surface, flowing very slowly and creating few dangerous séracs (unstable cliffs of ice). By way of example, a century ago the classic route over the Col du Géant passed below the Aiguille de la Noire, the glacier being sufficiently free of today's séracs to allow for the smuggling of whole herds of livestock between Courmayeur and Chamonix.

High mountains, however, had probably been climbed even before the days of the Ligurian soldier who discovered the advantages of scaling rockfaces. It is thought that Erciyas Dagi (3,916 m) in Turkey's Anti-Taurus range was climbed in the fourth century B.C. Later, Philip of Macedonia's feat of scaling Mount Haemus in the Balkans in 181 B.C. perhaps represents the first use of a mountain as a strategic observation point. The Emperor Hadrian is known to have climbed Mount Etna in A.D. 130, by which time reaching the summit was a common affair.

It nevertheless remains difficult to ascertain what induced people in ancient times to climb dangerous mountains, cross glacial cols (i.e., high passes), indeed scale steep cliffs.

In 1280, Peter III, king of Aragon, climbed Mount Canigou. According to his contemporaries, it was the highest mountain in the kingdom. Whatever the case, it was by far the most visible, making it one of those summits that irresistibly draw people. The chronicle of Peter's ascent claims that the monarch discovered a lake and a dragon at the summit—a tenacious belief found more or less everywhere in the Alps. It was perhaps to exorcise dragons that fifth-century Bishop Vallier, according to local legend, climbed the nearby 2,800-meter (9,180 ft.) mountain that now bears his name.

Left: Lauven, i.e., Slide and Cascade of Snow, Which Falls in Furious Quantities, Almost Perpendicularly from Steep Mountains, *engraving by Daniel Düringer in David Herrliberger's* Neue und Vollständige Topographie der Eydgnoszchaft (Topography of the Swiss Confederation, *1754). Top right: Portrait of Conrad Gesner, a great Renaissance naturalist who ascended Mount Pilatus in 1555. Bottom right: Another illustration from Herrliberger's* Topographie, *showing the glacier known as Rheinwaldgletscher, at the source of the Lower Rhine.*

In the fourteenth century, there were several notable exploits, including the 1307 ascension of Pilatus, a mountain that would become famous two centuries later when Conrad Gesner climbed it in 1555.

Then, on 27 April 1336, a poet worked his way up the slopes of Mont Ventoux, leaving olive groves behind, moving above the tree line, finally reaching the naked limestone forms at the top, chiseled by violent winds. It was none other than Petrarch, seized with a furious desire to reach the summit. This time, the feat concerned a real mountaineer, that is to say someone who made the climb for pleasure alone. On his return, Petrarch recorded his impressions in writing, not only with the topographic detail appropriate to a landscape, but also with the astonishing lyricism so characteristic of his day. It might be argued that Petrarch's "route description" was by far the best of its type, for it remains unequaled today.

So, at last, someone had climbed a mountain to attain inner bliss—indeed, once he had slaked his thirst for earthly visions, Petrarch continued to reflect on his act. He realized that he had completed only half his path, and that ascent meant going ever higher, toward the inaccessible. Contemplative mountaineering was born, and would last until the advent of climbing with the help of artificial aids in France, in the 1950s.

But Petrarch's climb was not merely a flight of intellect! The way he conducted and recorded it is the work of a special person. Even today, Petrarch can be counted among mountaineering's elite, and if he is more famous today for his love affair than for his ascent, it is nevertheless true that he reveals all that might have been gained had poets like Saint-John Perse and Mallarmé attempted to scale a few summits.

Another great mind, Leonardo da Vinci, climbed Monte Bo, an unspectacular summit in the Pennine Alps, in the fifteenth century. Perhaps his climb represented the first scientific ascent, given Leonardo's encyclopedic interests. This was also the period that probably gave birth to the notion of Alpine beauty, henceforth depicted in the backgrounds of paintings. Amazing portraits would be set in front of a Dolomitic landscape, while astonishing moun-

Above: Petrarch was the first writer to express feelings comparable to those experienced by today's mountain climbers. Right: An engraving from Richard Weld's The Pyrenees West and East *(1858), showing Mount Canigou, the ascent of which by Peter III of Aragon in 1280 gave rise to fabulous legends.*

tains rose above the plains of Flanders, as imagined by visionary northern artists on return from Italy!

I f Petrarch's ascent of Ventoux was aesthetic, and Leonardo's scientific, then the first ascent of a religious nature might be Rochemelon, a truly high summit (3,557 m) that towers some 3,000 meters above the monastery of Suse. At the time, Rochemelon was considered the highest peak in the Alps (in terms of relative altitude, this assessment is fairly accurate).

Boniface Rotario d'Asti wished to expiate his sins—apparently he had many for which to be forgiven—and scaled the peak on 1 September 1358, carrying a triptych of the Virgin to the summit. Ever since, the inhabitants of the valley conduct a procession each year—a pilgrimage of 3,557 meters! True enough, the southern slope of Rochemelon is a huge pile of broken rock, up which it was easy to trace a sketchy path. Furthermore, even though the French side of Rochemelon is permanently covered by a glacier, the Italian slope is soon free of snow. No matter, it is a fine mountain in any case!

Petrarch was climbing for inner bliss, Rotario d'Asti for penitence. Mountains are no longer climbed for penitence but, as French writer Jean Giono would say, the bliss endures.

The late fifteenth century produced the first example of "acrobatic" mountaineering, four centuries before Guido Rey coined the term. It was in 1492 that Antoine de Ville, a courtier to Charles VIII of France, fulfilled the king's wish by scaling Mont Aiguille, a strange tower of limestone that stands aloof from the cliffs of Vercors, above the plain of Trièves. In that feudal period, sieges of castles and strongholds were common practice, and so useful grappling techniques had been developed. Captain de Ville assessed the difficulty from a military standpoint;

for him, Mont Aiguille was simply a fortress a little larger and higher than the others. And there was little risk of boiling oil or arrows raining down upon his head. Therefore it was with the skilled use of ladders, ropes, and grappling irons—along with clever use of couloirs and ledges as he went ever higher—that the captain arrived at the summit. Once he stood on the top

Above: Mont Aiguille (depicted in Les Sept Miracles du Dauphiné, *1701) was long thought to be narrower at the base than at the top. Left: One of* Thirty-Six Views of Mount Fuji *by Japanese artist Katsushika Hokusai (1760–1849). Mount Fuji (3,776 m) is the oldest snow-capped summit with an accurately dated first ascent—the year 633.*

of the region's "seventh wonder," he discovered a flock of chamois, and was puzzled as to how they managed to get there. It is now known that chamois, ibexes, and mouflons can scramble across slick slabs inaccessible to humans—their "routes" are not the same as ours.

A similar feat was reportedly accomplished in 1555, at the Pic du Midi d'Ossau (2,900 m) by Monsieur de Candale, a gentleman at the court of Henry of Navarre. The chronicle claims that Candale's cohort came quite close to the summit with the help of hooks, grappling irons, and ladders—but such accounts are known to be full of errors. Candale also mentioned wild goats and eagles, and, in a fairly new and laudable scientific spirit, attempted to measure the altitude of the mountain.

Josias Simler and the First Overview of the Alps

The sixteenth century saw an increase in general knowledge about mountains, especially the Alps, the first major description of which was undertaken by Josias Simler. Simler's book, published in Zurich in 1574, has proven invaluable to researchers, since he used ancient texts to unearth everything that had been written about passages across the Alps, including their relative difficulty. Thanks to Simler, it is known that an

early alpine "technique" had already been devised—guides who led the way used a long, iron-tipped staff to poke for crevasses. Simler also advised wearing dark glasses against the sun, and he was aware of the dangers of vertigo and avalanches.

Since sixteenth-century exploration focused mainly on the discovery of *terra incognita* at the four corners of the globe, exploration of the nearby mountains remained the affair of a few doctors and botanists. These two professions went hand in hand at the time, since medicinal herbs were the basis of cures, and some serious climbing on steep slopes was required to attain the altitude where certain varieties of wormwood flowered.

One major event of the century went by unnoticed: the world altitude record was broken when conquistadors under Hernando Cortès climbed the 5,465 meters (17,930 ft.) of Popocatépetl in Mexico. The first ascension was made in 1520 by Diego de Ordàs with nine Spanish soldiers and a group of Indians; Francisco Montaño repeated the feat in 1522, even descending into the volcano's crater. The ascent was repeated yet again for military reasons—sulfur was needed to manufacture gunpowder.

Little more can be said of the sixteenth century in terms of landmark events that attended the birth of mountaineering. By this date, however, dangerous ascents that even today are

Above: Portrait of Josias Simler; early crampon illustrated in Ouresiphoites Helveticus *(London, 1708), a book by Swiss scholar J. J. Scheuchzer. Right: The devastating effects of avalanches, as depicted in the emperor Maximilian's* Theuerdank *(1517) and Johannes Stumpf's* Schwytzer Chronica *(1548).*

made only by accomplished mountain climbers were already being undertaken by one group of people—namely, crystal hunters. Quartz crystals were widely used for jewelry and other purposes. Since they were abundant in the Mont Blanc range, a certain number of mountain dwellers devoted themselves to this perilous search.

Several mountains were already notorious for the great quantity of crystals found on them, notably the Aiguille Verte group in the Mont Blanc range—one of the cols, or high passes, in the group is still known as the Col des Cristaux. Two peaks, Les Droites (4,000 m) and Les Courtes, were prospected right to the top, which raises the question of how many other of today's famous summits were also scaled. Crystal seekers were not concerned about reaching the top, but they almost certainly climbed many faces considered virgin today, insofar as crystal formations often nestle in the most out-of-the-way places.

The apparent abundance of crystals in those days has other important implications. Contrary to common belief, the rocky ridges and crests may have been less snowy at the time, even though an enormous glacier covered the slopes below them. In the summer of 1943, the driest summer in recent times, the snow on Aiguille Verte's Moine Ridge melted completely, which meant that even the rawest beginner could have ascended it in a matter of hours. The people in Chamonix reaped a great harvest of crystals that year—then the snows came back and the ridge was covered again in cornices of snow and garlands of ice, burying the formations that had been abruptly revealed for the brief duration of a summer.

Thus a certain group of people had long performed remarkable, if totally anonymous, mountain climbing exploits when driven by the need for resources. Subsequently—and quite naturally—these same people became the first mountain guides. It was the most famous among them, Jacques Balmat, who first climbed Mont Blanc in the company of Dr. Paccard.

Also in the sixteenth century, many hunters made a living by selling dried chamois meat (as was still done illegally in recent times in certain

isolated valleys in the Graian Alps and the Valais region). Although they were not very likely to venture onto glaciers, chamois hunters had to be sure-footed in order to follow the animals onto dizzying ledges, not to mention unstable  slopes of scree (rocky rubble) and limestone formations. When the time came, the first guides would be recruited from the ranks of these veteran hunters.

In those days, however, they were not offered the possibility of cashing in on their talent—it would be over a century before organized mountaineering began in earnest, having been only sporadically anticipated by a few striking but aleatory exploits.

Above: An 1822 engraving by J. P. Lamy shows famous chamois and mountain goat hunters John Fellmann and Gabriel Schilt in a tight spot on the Finsteraarhorn. For centuries, chamois hunting and crystal seeking were the main reasons for confronting the dangers posed by high mountains. Left: This chamois is one of the 4,000 woodcuts illustrating Johannes Stumpf's Schwytzer Chronica *(1548).*

The critical moment came in the eighteenth century. In order for mountain climbing to develop, it had to appeal to a society up till then totally devoted to the refinements of the grand European courts, and therefore hardly disposed to undertaking a wearying ascent. But when French philosopher and writer Jean-Jacques Rousseau came along, everything changed. Rousseau, a forerunner of romanticism, profoundly altered attitudes of the day by preaching the cult of nature and opening people's eyes to natural beauty. Cultivated minds were henceforth open to the idea of mountaineering and, furthermore, had at their disposal professionals long trained in seeking crystals and hunting game.

The eighteenth century was above all the one in which Mont Blanc was finally conquered. But even if that feat overshadows all others, it should be noted that in 1743 a monk from the abbey of Engelberg succeeded in climbing Titlis (3,243 m). In 1700, meanwhile, geographer Jacques Cassini had climbed Canigou and, sometime later, French explorer Charles Marie de La Condamine scaled Pichincha (4,800 m) in Ecuador in order to carry out some scientific measurements.

The crucial year was 1760. A young encyclopedist of great merit, Horace Bénédict de Saussure, arrived in Chamonix. Viewing Mont Blanc from the summit of Brévent had a determining impact on him—he decided then and there that the highest mountain in Europe just had to be climbed. He knew in that instant that his entire life would henceforth be devoted to Mont Blanc. In fact, the struggle to reach the summit took a quarter of a century (the same span it would take, 150 years later, to finally conquer Mount Everest).

Less spectacular perhaps, but equally resonant in terms of an epic gesture in the history of mountaineering, was the saga of Ramond de Carbonnières in the Pyrenees. These two great names from the same era, although inspired by very different sentiments, triggered the decisive sparks that ignited a general desire to climb, prompting people to scale mountains solely in search of knowledge.

During the troubled years of the French Revolution, it was the lesser-known Pyrenees that were scoured by a team of scientific explorers which included Dieudonné Dolomieu, the geologist who "discovered" dolomite. In 1787,

Gustave Doré painted this watercolor (cardboard, 73 x 88 cm) of the Cirque de Gavarnie. The high wall of the cirque protected access to Mont Perdu (Monte Perdido), requiring Ramond de Carbonnières to make many attempts before finding a route to the top.

Ramond, a scholar passionately interested in mountains and in scientific research, finally managed, after many attempts, to scale Mont Perdu (Monte Perdido; 3,353 m), which he thought was the highest peak in the Pyrenees. His accounts read like a mysterious and fascinating novel, for Ramond de Carbonnières, like Saussure, was a great Alpine writer, which partly explains his fame. Thanks to Ramond, much was learned, much was read, and much was retained. Yet all that should not obscure the fact that in 1797 the Pic du Midi d'Ossau was climbed by Delfau, who found a cairn when he arrived at the summit! Who could have placed it there, and when? Perhaps it was the work of Henry of Navarre's men when they accompanied Monsieur de Candale in 1555?

Meanwhile, the Deluc brothers climbed Mont Buet in 1770, but that ascent belongs to the Mont Blanc saga.

In 1779, Abbé Murith, prior at the Saint-Bernard monastery, climbed Mont Vélan (3,765 m) armed with a geologist's hammer. Murith was also a botanist, but his feat represents a true mountaineering exploit—the steep slope of snow (and ice, at times) is still formidable today.

Apart from Ramond de Carbonnières, few key names from the eighteenth century are French. The underlying reasons for this are the revolutionary disturbances of the period and the fact that neither Savoy nor the Mont Blanc range were yet part of France (Savoy became part of France permanently in 1860). So it is perhaps worth mentioning a Frenchman named Villars, who methodically explored the Oisans range between 1770 and 1787. In addition to reaching high cols (like the ones between Vénéon and Drac, or La Romanche and Guisane), Villars scaled easy summits and performed remarkable reconnaissance work.

To conclude the eighteenth century, let us turn back to 1760, when Saussure decided that Mont Blanc had to be climbed. Once finally accomplished in 1787, this ascent constituted the true advent of mountaineering as we know it. Mountain climbing had at last emerged from its prehistory, or proto-history, or, perhaps even better, its "Middle Ages," during which only a few remarkable exploits pierced long centuries of darkness.

This painting by Thomas Fearnly (1802–1842) shows the upper Grendelwald Glacier (oil on canvas, 157.5 x 195 cm). The work was painted in the artist's studio in 1838, based on an 1835 ink drawing.

To the Top of Mont Blanc, 1786

In 1786, two men reached the summit of the highest mountain in the Alps. The event created a sensation, yet was the result of a long story involving Saussure the level-headed scientist, Bourrit the passionate poet, and an enterprising group of Chamonix guides.

The twenty-five-year campaign to conquer the highest peak in Europe represents the incontestable birth of what is now called mountaineering—the art and technique of climbing the earth's high rock-and-glacier-covered mountains.

In many European languages (including, at one time, English), mountain climbers are known as "alpinists." Because the Alps were the cradle of true mountaineering, the term has come to apply to climbers of mountains all over the world, which is not the case with, say, "himalayist" or "andenist." Indeed, the Alps were an ideal terrain on which to develop advanced techniques. The entire range, and especially the Mont Blanc massif, is compact and well defined, easily reachable from the plain, and includes both rocky pinnacles and glacial domes. That is why the story of the conquest of Mont Blanc touches upon several of the mysteries that slowly kindled a new urge in human hearts—namely, stalking the summits.

Only four men were intimately engaged in the race to the top, all for different reasons. Only

three would make it. But one name among the four dominates the others in the same way that Mont Blanc dominates the Alps: Horace Bénédict de Saussure. It was Saussure who initiated the project. Next comes Marc Théodore Bourrit, a somewhat mad and visionary bard who was an authentic lover of high mountains. Both men hailed from Geneva. The former was a solid, level-headed scientist, the latter was driven by a lofty poetic temperament and a love of nature. Saussure waited twenty-five years for his moment of glory. Bourrit, who wanted everything right away, ultimately lost it all. So much for the city gentlemen.

There were two other men, who were in fact the first victors. Dr. Michel Paccard from Chamonix, son of a notary from Le Prieuré, was a sophisticated, cultivated mountain dweller who never lost his *montagnard* instincts. He made several attempts to find the right "route," yet never quite managed. That route was ultimately found by the most unexpected character, Jacques Balmat. Balmat was not a guide, was

Facing page: Climbers seeking a passage across the Crevasse du Dôme, a lithograph taken from Ten Scenes in the Last Ascent of Mont Blanc *by J. D. H. Browne (London, 1853). Ascents of Mont Blanc yielded charming and wonderfully illustrated books that are now eagerly sought by collectors. Above: A surprising engraving from an 1851 issue of the* Illustrated London News *depicting the crossing of the Bossons Glacier.*

poor, was simultaneously disinterested yet eager to cash in, and was unsparing in his efforts. And it is clear that, for this simple man, conquering Mont Blanc meant winning respect in the eyes of valley neighbors who perhaps had not taken him seriously up to that point.

Balmat was a loner, a wary crystal hunter who never divulged the whereabouts of his finds and shelters; and it is certain that in seeking crystal deposits he unwittingly accomplished technical exploits that made him the equal of the guides who were gaining fame even then—namely the Cachat and Tairraz families, tried-and-tested mountaineers who were the precursors of today's true guides.

Balmat sought fame and fortune, the former rarely occurring without the latter. Dr. Paccard, who disdained pecuniary motives, was after fame—and tended to want all of it for himself. Bourrit yearned for his mountain like a lover; but he never possessed it and his wrath disfigured the story of the conquest which, without his accounts, might have appeared quite straightforward.

Saussure, meanwhile, was driven by noble motives. For him, the ascent was a chance to resolve new problems concerning physics, biology, geology, and the study of glaciers, not to mention the effects of altitude. In Saussure's mind, Mont Blanc was already the ideal obser-

vatory he would in fact build several years later on the Col du Géant. When a person's goals are that lofty, money and honors no longer count—and arrive on their own precisely because they have been spurned.

That, then, is the quartet of players who would entertain the valley of Chamonix for a quarter of a century.

A quarter of a century is a long time for something that seems so simple today. But it should be recalled that everything still had to be invented. The pioneers had neither rope, nor ice ax, nor crampons, much less techniques for crossing snow-covered glaciers. Not many people even approached Mont Blanc itself; crystal seekers scoured the Mer de Glace basin, and a few chamois hunters must have pushed as far as the Montagne de la Côte and the foot of the needle-like peak, or aiguille, known as Aiguille du Goûter. Nor did guides show much interest in the affair at first. For most of them, climbing Mont Blanc was a question of earning a bit of money. They only really began to address the question when Saussure announced a cash bonus for the first one to reach the summit. At that point rivalry and competition provoked sneaky, underhanded struggles—everyone wanted to be the first to the top.

Above, left to right: Title page of the first volume of the work by Horace Bénédict de Saussure, published in 1779; the compass used by Saussure; portrait of Saussure by Jens Juel.

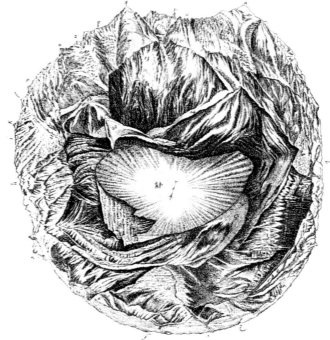

Given all the rivalry, it is hard to know which aspect of the conquest deserves most admiration. Perhaps it was Saussure's tenacity and detachment, his primary concern to get a barometer to the summit, that is to say to make scientific measurements. Saussure simply waited patiently, rarely getting involved in the teams of scouts that he inspired among the local specialists. Saussure clearly thought of himself as a great captain, sending his couriers ahead, preparing the route, only advancing himself once victory was assured. He displayed, perhaps, just one human failing, that of minimizing Dr. Paccard's exploit, to the greater benefit of Balmat. In Saussure's eyes, the local doctor's role was of value only insofar as it permitted a true scientist to reach the summit.

Twenty-five Years of Effort

These days, it might seem unthinkable to wait twenty-five years for somebody else to pave the way. Saussure's withholding of himself until the final assault now seems strange. Yet not only was there no question of waiting for him to be party to the first ascent, he did not even make the trip until the third time—he first insisted on a second ascent by his own guides, confirming that Balmat's route could be repeated.

Bourrit's attitude, meanwhile, however silly, was nevertheless endearing. Fascinated by the mountain, physically incapable of assuming the harsh climb awaiting him above, he was nevertheless carried to the summit in his imagination. He never ceased pushing and spurring on the others!

The main players in the conquest have now been presented. But there were others, whose names have not gone down in history books, who made attempts so determined that they inevitably contributed to the final victory. First there was Pierre Simond, who awakened Saussure's passion by taking him up the Brévent. Then there were Jean-Marie Couttet, Cachat the Giant, Jean-Pierre and Victor Tairraz, Grand Jorasse, and Cuidet the chamois hunter. Each of them had ideas on how to get to the top and each sought his own route, as did Jean-Nicolas Couteran, Victor Tissay, and Michel Paccard.

Such boldness, combined with authentic knowledge of the mountains, is amazing today. Techniques and materials were already being refined. The coarse cloth of the men's suits was heavy but warm, and they wore felt gaiters, greased wool sweaters, heavy shoes cut from the most solid of leathers. Such garb was of course the basic dress of mountain folk, modified in terms of detail but retaining the virtues of warmth and dryness. Two centuries later, this

A true mountain enthusiast, Marc Théodore Bourrit (shown here in a portrait by Saint-Ours) produced the first circular panorama, titled Circular View of the Mountains seen from the Summit of the Buet Glacier.

View of the Valley of Chamonix, *by Marc Théodore Bourrit (gouache and white chalk). An engraved reproduction of this painting was used to illustrate volume III of Bourrit's* Nouvelle Description des Glacières, Glaciers et Amas de Glaces du Duché de Savoie *(1785).*

dress would still be worn for high-altitude routes through snow. The long, metal-tipped alpenstock, however, would disappear with the arrival of rope and ice ax, which is too bad, for an alpenstock was used above all for "glissades," a controlled slide down a steep slope of hard or soft snow. It was an ideal tool for snow, and nothing better has yet been found for a rapid descent down a truly steep couloir, or gully; it was also useful when descending rubble and scree. During the twenty-five-year assault on Mont Blanc, certain types of ice ax began to appear, most of which were just hatchets attached to long handles. Other pioneers used a geologist's hammer to carve footholds in the ice. Yet if few advances were made in ice ax technology during the eighteenth century, that was above all because mountain climbers of the day strictly avoided the passages where it would have been necessary—slopes of hard, fresh ice, and sharp ridges. It might be supposed that if Balmat had known how to use an ice ax, he would have climbed the ridge known as Arête des Bosses without a second thought during his extraordinary attempt of June 1786.

The conquest of Mont Blanc was a veritable expedition, requiring camps and bivouacs. These were of two kinds. A true bivouac meant passing the night alone on the rocks, with nothing more than warm clothing, braved by mountaineers who embarked on the adventure confident of their solid endurance. Sometimes a fire might shorten long nights, and sometimes blankets were carried (to places like Pierre Ronde and Montagne de la Côte), but most of the time a scout could not be encumbered with unnecessary weight. Organized camps, however, were another matter entirely, and required many porters. When Saussure climbed, he was accompanied by a veritable suite of porters and servants—it was inconceivable that a distinguished gentleman of the day would sleep like a ground hog in some hollow rock! Saussure's dignity, perhaps more than his comfort, called for such measures.

One of the most decisive events in the conquest of Mont Blanc was Balmat's unplanned but deliberate bivouac on the snowfield of the Grand Plateau at 3,900 meters (12,800 ft.), on

the night of 9 June 1786. Until that time, no guide or mountain dweller had spent a night on a glacier—convinced that they would be frozen to death, they had never dared to attempt it. Instead, crystal hunters and guides always sought exposed rock, however uncomfortable, on which to pass the night. This meant that if they ventured any distance onto a glacier, they always arranged to be back on terra firma by nightfall (as demonstrated by Jean-Marie Couttet and Cuidet the chamois hunter on the Dôme du Goûter, and Pierre Simond on the Col du Géant). They would sleep on moraines, on boulders, or on islands of rock thrusting up above the glacier. Thus on the route up Mont Blanc, the only three outcrops of rock before the Grand Plateau were utilized: Montagne de la Côte, the Grands Mulets, and the Heureux Retour. So when Balmat descended after having spent a night on the glacier, he was newly confident of two things: he had found a route to the top, and a night on snow was not lethal. Henceforth, he feared nothing!

Up till that moment, everyone had been groping in the dark. When Bourrit arrived for the first time in Chamonix and set eyes on Mont Blanc, he expressed amazement that people had not already made every attempt to climb it. It was a revealing observation. In fact, in the first half of the eighteenth century, Mont Blanc served mainly as a luminous backdrop to Geneva and the Enlightenment philosophers. It only acquired its present name in 1742, when Pierre Martel drew up the first map of the valley and established place names; what had been previously labeled on vague maps as "glaciers" or "Cursed Mountain" was given the simple, merited name of "White Mountain" (Mont Blanc). Yet even once Mont Blanc was baptized, no one considered climbing it.

I t was on 17 February 1740 at Conches, near Geneva, that the architect of victory was born—Horace Bénédict de Saussure. The Saussure family was in tune with the spirit of the times, and appreciated nature, plants, and minerals. Under the influence of Albrecht von

Top left: The Mer de Glace as Seen from Montenvers (Chamonix), a lithograph from Jean DuBois's Souvenirs de la Suisse (Geneva, 1828). Bottom left: An engraving of the Bossons Glacier by Samuel Birmann. Above right: Portrait of Michel Gabriel Paccard, painted by L. A. G. Bacler d'Albe in 1788.

This original sketch by Paccard (top), rediscovered just a few years ago, is of crucial importance, for it clearly indicates the role played by the doctor in the conquest of Mont Blanc by showing the care with which he studied his route. This find does not, however, diminish the role played by Jacques Balmat, pictured above in his old age, after the king of Sardinia, accorded him the right to call himself Balmat du Mont Blanc.

Haller and his uncle, the botanist Charles Bonnet, Horace learned to enjoy mountain outings, climbed the easy summits around Geneva, traversed the wonderful high meadows of the Savoy foothills, and finally scaled Môle, a perfect vantage point for studying the Mont Blanc group. He learned the rough feel of limestone on Mont Salève, and experienced the delicate intoxication and euphoria provoked by pure mountain air. Above all, he acquired a strong desire to approach the giants, snow-capped all year long, that occupied the horizon to the east.

Saussure was twenty when, traveling alone, he stopped to visit the glaciers of Chamonix, guided by Pierre Simond, an agile little man who led him intelligently, showing him everything necessary for a good knowledge of surrounding mountains. As befitted his rank, Saussure lodged with the local priest. He was rich and not stingy with his gold louis. Taking him into the hills was a pleasant task because Saussure was a sturdy walker and paid well. Yet he might have merely passed through Chamonix, never to return, like so many others. Fortunately, that was not the case.

Simond and Saussure climbed to the top of Mont Brévent, a modest (2,525 m) but well-placed mountain. It is opposite Mont Blanc, at just the right height to reveal the entire range in its true proportions. Seen from Brévent, Mont Blanc is not squashed by the distance and the verticality of its slopes (as it is when seen from Chamonix). The summit of Mont Blanc continued to rise as the young Saussure and his guide mounted the precarious Bel-Achat path. When they arrived at the top, the giant opposite them suddenly rose on its base, noble, imposing, of haughty proportions, finely balanced in mass and volume. This vision was the revelation of Saussure's lifetime. That white mountain, towering over Europe, had to be scaled. And he would stimulate the interest necessary to achieve it.

Although young, Saussure seems to have had a psychologist's flair. Or perhaps he knew what money meant to Chamonix folk. He not only advertised a reward of two guineas to the first person to find a route to the top, he even offered to pay a daily fee to those who made unsuccessful attempts. Saussure kept his word and, for twenty long years, financed a succession of attempts on the summit.

One aspect of his behavior seems significant. The reward was offered to the person who discovered "the route," which suggests that

Saussure reserved the right to be the first person to take that route.

Viewed with a twentieth-century mentality, it seems surprising that the young Saussure, who was a steady hiker and far from infirm, did not participate in the search directly, did not commit himself physically, did not mastermind the attempts himself. Imagine a legendary modern climber like Lionel Terray sitting in an office, sending guides and mountaineers to Jannu for years, waiting for a telegram announcing they had found a route, then jumping onto a plane just in time to be the first man on the summit. But Saussure was an aristocrat of the day, a rich man who felt that the groundwork was unworthy of his rank; he would just be wasting precious time that could be devoted to other projects. Ultimately, Saussure made no distinction between his own servants and the guides he paid; at the very most, the latter occupied a higher rung on the domestic ladder. Nor, of course, did Saussure think that Mont Blanc had truly been climbed until the ascent was made by a gentleman.

Two Guineas for Attempting an Ascent

Perhaps Saussure's offer to Simond of two guineas for attempting to find a route merely reflected a wish to link his name to a worthy undertaking; perhaps he never seriously thought of attaining the summit himself. That urge would, in fact, only take hold of him little by little. But as the years slipped by without results, that urge increased, becoming a passion, the supreme goal of his life. So even back then, apparently, it was dangerous to flirt with mountains—they had already learned how to steal a man's soul.

Thus the word went around Chamonix that a wealthy Genevan client of Simond's was offering a reward to anyone who could find a route up Mont Blanc. Several attempts were made, but they proved fruitless. The truth is that these early attempts were not very earnest.

Simond and his companions tried heading up the Mer de Glace. This "sea of ice," when viewed from below, seemed to rise right up to the highest shoulders of the mountain; Chamonix guides, accustomed to taking the path from the Talèfre cirque, where crystals were found in abundance, assumed that the route up the mountain must pass via this long white valley. It was also the path to the Col du Géant, already partly explored. The trailblazers of the day, however, probably ran straight into the barriers known as Combe Maudite and Aiguilles du Diable. Simond then tried to pass via the Bossons Glacier; chamois hunters knew vague passages through the alder scrub covering the escarpments on Montagne de la Côte, but above that was a *terra incognita* of ice!

Furthermore, the guides were already being kept busy taking travelers to see the Mer de Glace. Custom was good, profitable, and not dangerous. So what was the point of taking a long shot at success, particularly if a guide had

Left to right: Three Mont Blanc guides from the heroic era. Marie "The Bird" Tournier, the last of Saussure's guides; Cachat "the Giant," who guided Saussure during his stay on the Col du Géant, shown here in front of the Grands Charmoz in an engraving by Karl Weibel; Joseph-Marie Couttet, nicknamed "the Captain of Mont Blanc," who led thirteen ascents to the summit.

a family to feed? That required a pioneer spirit, someone to spur men onward when money no longer sufficed. From his house in Geneva overlooking Mont Blanc, Saussure impatiently dreamed of reaching the summit, but never thought for a moment of spurring the quest through his own physical effort. This meant that the guides merely kept things ticking over—which is only human, if hardly heroic.

Fifteen years went by without results. The reconnaissance missions did not even come up with proposed solutions. It seemed hopeless.

Yet a poet had entered the lists a few years earlier. Marc Théodore Bourrit, also from Geneva, was a writer, musician, and artist. As a poor man, however, he had to find a steady income in order to pursue his interests. The post of cantor at the cathedral of Geneva suited him perfectly in this respect. All his spare time was spent in the mountains.

Bourrit was born in 1739, making him one year older than Saussure. Like Saussure, Bourrit's enthusiasm for the Alps came in a revelation around 1761. This time the blinding flash occurred on the summit of Voirons, a wooded outcrop overlooking Lake Geneva. Unlike Saussure a year earlier on Brévent, Bourrit's relationship with Mont Blanc was not a marriage of convenience, from which passion emerged slowly but surely. His was love at first sight, an impetuous, demanding desire that would make Bourrit the most unbridled lover the mountain has ever known. Ardent, imaginative, and willing to commit himself physically, Bourrit traversed the Alps from that point onward, climbing easy summits. Seven times he ascended the Buet, that unique belvedere scaled by the Deluc brothers in 1770. From that high perch, stretched out on a limestone slab now named after him—the Cantor's Table—Bourrit would contemplate and admire Mont Blanc, seeking possible itineraries along the glaciers, up the white and silent hollows, over the dazzling domes where his imagination carried him.

Two engravings by George Baxter, illustrating John MacGregor's 1855 ascent, are among the most charming ever published. The left one shows the party leaving the Grand Mulets, while the right depicts the Mur de la Côte.

Unlike Saussure, Bourrit wanted to climb the mountain himself right from the start. But he would be the only protagonist who never made it. He displayed a braggadocio that was thoroughly endearing; he could be childish, indeed pushy, yet his imagination was greater than his determination. He dreamed a lot, agitated a great deal, but would not persevere when the least difficulty arose. And yet without Bourrit, the conquest of Mont Blanc might have taken many additional years.

The First Serious Attempt

For fifteen long years, from 1760 to 1775, the attempts made by guides and mountain folk around Chamonix, spurred by Saussure's reward, produced almost no results. Then suddenly, on 13 July 1775, around eleven o'clock at night, a team of locals decided to go for the summit. The party was composed of Michel and

François Paccard, the scholarly Jean-Nicolas Couteran, and the agile Victor Tissay. The account of this attempt has come down to us via Bourrit, who enthusiastically transcribed the picturesque and, indeed, keenly observed details of the ascent as recounted by Couteran.

The climbers ascended Montagne de la Côte at night by following a customary route along the right edge of the Taconnaz Glacier. Then they moved onto the Bossons Glacier, traversing the Junction via the Grands Mulets and the Petit and Grand Plateaux, ultimately arriving at a fairly high point that seemed to be slightly above the Grand Plateau. At first they thought they were close to the summit, but then realized they had misjudged the distance. So they decided to descend, for none of them wanted to spent the night on the glacier. Exhausted, one member of the party fell into a crevasse on the way down. Finally, they returned to Chamonix twenty-two hours after setting off, having accomplished a feat that, though extraordinary, would not be followed up.

Eight years went by.

Faithful to his word, Saussure continued to encourage new attempts but never took part personally. In contrast, Bourrit went all out by advocating, encouraging, and provoking assaults. Finally, in 1783 three guides from Chamonix decided to renew the attack on the itinerary explored eight years earlier by Couteran and his companions. They were led by one of Saussure's guides, the highly intelligent and determined Jean-Marie Couttet (an able commander, Couttet would subsequently make dogged assaults on the summit, and came second only to Balmat as hero of the story of conquest). With Couttet went Joseph Carrier and a man of Herculean stature named Lombard, but known as Grand Jorasse.

The weather started out as wonderful, but it turned into a scorching day. At the Grand Plateau, altitude sickness struck Grand Jorasse who, like Hercules slain, lay down in the snow and fell asleep. Although close to the Col du Dôme, they were obliged to turn back. The unknown malady that had overcome the stoutest of them alarmed everyone.

They returned to the valley and broke the news.

Saussure despaired, and nearly gave up in discouragement. Fortunately, the manic, visionary Bourrit took up the torch. In a key move, he decided to head an expedition himself. Up to that point, only guides had risked their necks. If a "city slicker" did the same, they reckoned, there must be something to it.

That same year, Michel Paccard organized two reconnaissance missions—one via the Mer de Glace, the other by Tête Rousse. This detail alone reveals the doctor's intelligence. He was convinced that it was pointless to continue climbing the Glacier du Géant which, contrary to common belief, did not flow down from Mont Blanc but was irremediably separated from it by the Brenva sink. On the other hand, Paccard noted that the long ridge of the Aiguille du Goûter rose steadily and harmoniously in successive stages from the Col de Voza to the Dôme du Goûter. A

route to the summit might lead from there. Paccard reconnoitered that side, getting as far as Tête Rousse. Whether it stemmed from Bourrit's suggestions or from Paccard's own initiative, the idea was a new one.

Also in 1783, Bourrit teamed up with Paccard, whom he recognized as a worthy rival. Nor was he mistaken. Unfortunately, this initial attempt via Montagne de la Côte was doomed to failure. Bourrit never even set foot on the glacier, for a storm arrived and they had to retreat in the face of bad weather.

People were learning that Mont Blanc could not be approached with impunity. Three experiences drove the point home: in 1775, Couteran fell into a crevasse; in 1783, Grand Jorasse suffered from sunstroke and altitude sickness (and everyone else from greater or lesser degrees of snow blindness); and the last attempt had been foiled by bad weather.

Nevertheless, 1783 was a year in which serious efforts were undertaken, even if they got no higher than the attempt made eight years earlier. The Col du Dôme seemed to be a critical threshold, hard to breach.

The next attempt, on 17 September 1784, focused on the Aiguille du Goûter, at Bourrit's initiative. Perhaps he chose the route himself, but it is highly probable that the idea came from Cuidet and Gervais, two chamois hunters from La Gruvaz. They claimed to have reached the summit of the aiguille, which is entirely possible given the enthusiasm of chamois hunters hot on the tracks of their prey. Furthermore, chamois have a tendency to climb ever higher, and the ridges of the Aiguille du Goûter are kid's play for a chamois.

Bourrit started out from Sallanches, with a mule driver and his dog. He was accompanied by Cuidet and Gervais themselves, as well as by the two famous Chamonix guides Couttet and Grand Jorasse (the very ones who, the previous year, probably reached the Col du Dôme via the Grands Mulets).

No efforts were spared in those days. The caravan set out from the village of Bionnassay on

Another Baxter engraving of MacGregor's ascent shows the climbers celebrating their arrival at the summit of Mont Blanc with champagne.

the evening of 16 September, crossing the wilderness of Pierre Ronde by night, arriving at the little glacial plateau of Tête Rousse on a cold dawn. As Grand Jorasse and Gervais helped Bourrit with his gear, Couttet and Cuidet swiftly scaled the lower buttresses of the Aiguille du Goûter. Bourrit wanted to follow, but allowed himself to be talked out of it. In fact, the two climbers were determined to go as far as possible. So Bourrit followed them with his gaze, watching them disappear over the peak of the aiguille. In his mind's eye he accompanied them across the mysterious, icy plateau of the Dôme du Goûter. Bourrit and his companions, however, headed back to Bionnassay.

The two men did not return to the chalet until eleven o'clock on the night of 17 September, exhausted after a hike that had lasted nearly thirty hours. They were nevertheless in high spirits. This time, they claimed, the route to the summit had been found. In fact, they reached an altitude of 4,360 meters (14,300 ft.), where the Vallot Hut is now located, at the foot of Grande Bosse. They might even have carried on if they had not been terrorized by the sight of the setting sun, dropping to the horizon like a stone with unfamiliar swiftness. They would not have spent the night on the glacier for anything in the world—they only felt safe on rock.

In September, the sun begins to set early, which means that the two men took only four hours or so to get down to the chalet at Bionnassay from the foot of Grande Bosse. The trip takes at least as long—if not longer—today, which says a great deal about their skill at moving across snow and rock. From every point of view, the men who conquered Mont Blanc were great guides and formidable *montagnards.*

Bourrit was beside himself with joy. He wrote to Saussure, pressing him onward. But Saussure was methodical in nature, and wanted to prepare for every eventuality. He also wanted to prepare his scientific instruments—the ascent was pointless for him if he made no observations.

The next attempt was therefore scheduled for the following year, 1785. According to testimony, the season was unpromising, plagued by rain and snow.

The ever cautious Saussure had his regular guides, Pierre Balmat and Couttet, confirm that the planned route was in good condition. On 5 September, Couttet, now accompanied by Jacques Balmat, had climbed the Aiguille du Goûter and moved onward until a violent hailstorm forced them to turn around. A major snowfall blanketed the mountain, so it was not until 12 September that the caravan set out.

This time, Saussure came along himself, with all his equipment, his many fragile instruments, and a full team of seventeen guides and porters.

Bourrit and his son joined Saussure. Couttet, Pierre and Jacques Balmat, and their loyal team of locals constituted the lead party. The night was spent at the foot of the Aiguille du Goûter, where Bourrit had a little stone shelter built for himself. Saussure began taking measurements, while Couttet went to reconnoiter the initial path up the couloirs of the aiguille, to facilitate the next day's start.

The caravan rolled into action at six o'clock the next morning. The snow was deep and powdery, becoming deeper as they climbed. After three hours they had to stop, due to the heat. Pierre Balmat tried to forge a path to the summit of the aiguille, but returned to say that continuing would be dangerous and that, at any rate, the abundance of fresh snow on the upper plateaux would make progress impossible. It was a wise decision.

Retreat ensued. Saussure spent a second night at Tête Rousse, while Bourrit returned to Bionnassay that very evening.

That was Saussure's first contact with high altitude climbing, and he seemed to appreciate the technique employed at the time. He climbed between two guides who firmly held an alpenstock at each end, forming a barrier between him and the precipice.

At last, the decisive year of 1786 arrived.

The experiments of the previous year had been rewarding. It was realized that two routes could lead to the summit: one via the Bossons Glacier (also called the Vallée Blanche route), and another via the Aiguille and Dôme du

Above: This delightful engraving, titled Breakfast on a Bridge of Snow, *served as the frontispiece to John Auldjo's* Narrative of an Ascent to the Summit of Mont Blanc *(1827). Facing page: A color lithograph of the crevasse on the Mer de Glace, from Elijah Walton's* Peaks and Valleys of the Alps *(London, 1867).*

Goûter. The Aiguille route arrives at the current site of the Vallot Hut, and there is no doubt that if Cuidet and Couttet had reached that spot by midday instead of dusk they would have persevered! Meanwhile, the Col du Dôme had certainly been reached via the Bossons Glacier. But it was not clear which route was quicker. Each had its supporters, and so it was decided that two teams would set out on the same day, 8 June 1786. Couttet and Pierre Balmat were to spend the night in a cabin at Pierre Ronde, while François Paccard and Joseph Carrier would

Aiguille de Bochard 1337 T — Aiguille Verte 2100 T — Aiguille du Dru 1947 T — Aiguille des Charmaux 1647 T — Aiguille de Crepon — Aiguille du Plan 1892 T — Aiguille du Midi 2009 T — Sommet du Mt Blanc 2436 T — Dôme du Goûte 2130 T — Aiguille du Goûte 1980 T

Glacier des Bois — Glacier des Bossons

HÔTEL DE LONDRES & D'ANGLETERRE
tenu par Victor Caurraz
Journeaux français & anglais — on reçoit des Pensionnaires
On parle a l'hotel francais, anglais & allemand.

strike from the summit of Montagne de la Côte.

However, just as they were setting out from the foot of the mountain on 7 June, Paccard and Carrier saw a young man descend—haggard, frozen in icy garments, famished, and, it seemed, at the end of his strength. It was Jacques Balmat who had spent two days and two nights on the upper glaciers and snowfields, alone, in the hope of finding a route. History does not record just how far he got, but a guess can be based on the fact that the very next day he headed straight for what would become the first passage to the top.

The conversation between the three men was a little sharp. Balmat was not fooled by the others' claim that they were after mountain goats. He well knew the reward offered by Saussure, and he hotly coveted it. After all the effort he

Interest in Mont Blanc dramatically increased the popularity of Chamonix, where hotels began advertising themselves on fine Bristol cards like the one above.

had just made, losing the recompense to others seemed cruelly unfair. The men parted, and Paccard and Carrier climbed confidently, reassured; Balmat had always been a maverick, but after the physical effort he had just made, they could sleep peacefully at the top of Montagne de la Côte, secure in the knowledge that no one could catch up with them.

They were mistaken about Jacques Balmat. In the long history of mountaineering, only a few outstanding individuals merit comparison with him: Jean-Antoine Carrel on the Matterhorn; Hermann Buhl on Nanga Parbat; Walter Bonatti on the Petit Dru. He who had just spent two dreadful bivouacs on the meager rocks poking above the ice (probably the Grands Mulets or the Heureux Retour) had scarcely arrived home when he changed, dried himself, warmed up, ate, filled his sack with "vittles" and set out again. He climbed Montagne de la Côte himself, interrupting Carrier and Paccard's dreams of victory by awaking them in the night.

His arrival was less than welcome, but nothing was to be done. The three men would continue the ascent together.

Traveling up the Bossons Glacier, the trio arrived at the Col du Dôme long before Couttet and Pierre Balmat. The issue was resolved: the glacier route was by far the shorter, and it was decided that future attempts would follow it. Then the team attempted to go higher. The Arête des Bosses was just ahead, but the ridge turned out to be so sharp and razor-thin, between two precipices the likes of which the climbers had never seen, that everyone retreated—except for Jacques Balmat, clearly made of sterner stuff than his mates. They watched for a while as he gingerly advanced along the sharp edge of hard snow, then lowered himself to straddle it, slowing his progress considerably. At which point his companions headed back down, purely and simply abandoning Jacques.

Was that a betrayal? Not really, for their attitude has to be understood in context: Jacques was used to being in the mountains alone (at the time, climbers did not rope themselves together for safety), and so it did not seem as though leaving Balmat to seek a route on his own constituted any special danger. Nor, for that matter, did they feel that they would be able to help him if he encountered trouble. The experienced guides probably thought, with a bit of contempt, "Balmat's quick! He'll catch up." They could not see the point of all that effort—it was obvious he would not make it to the top. Maybe they thought that another setback would take the edge off Balmat's pride. At any rate, they left his sack and headed down.

And that is when Jacques Balmat came into his own.

He did, indeed, have to climb back down the ridge—very carefully. He must have found the snow extremely hard, perhaps covered with fresh ice. In fact, Durier has suggested that if the ridge had been blanketed in new, deep snow, as occasionally happens, Balmat would have made it to the summit—an opinion I share. But on that day in 1786, the arête was less than pleasant to climb. Balmat came back down. He noted with irony that his companions had already left. But that suited him. It was only four o'clock in the afternoon, so he descended as far as the Grand Plateau, then started up "his" route. It was a route that, without having said a word to anyone, he had already tried. The first time, he had been unable to cross the bergschrund (or series of crevasses), but now he found the snow very hard. (This reinforces the theory that the Arête des Bosses would have required a great deal of step cutting, whereas the ice ax had not yet been invented.)

On studying Mont Blanc with an eyeglass from the top of Brévent, Balmat had sensed that climbing the snowy slope to the right of the Rochers Rouges might lead to the top. That is where he now headed. Despite his youth, he displayed a mature experience of snow and he was obviously sure-footed. Since it would have been too dangerous to angle across the face in an effort to join the upper slopes to the east, he headed straight up, cutting little holds with the iron tip of his alpenstock.

Thus he arrived above the Rochers Rouges; just ahead, a gentler, safer slope led toward the summit. But already he could see Courmayeur in Italy—an extraordinary moment of victory! It could be argued that from that moment Mont Blanc had been tamed. Unfortunately, a spherical cloud known as the "dunce cap" had clamped down on the mountain, and Balmat did not know

exactly where the summit was. He decided to head back down. Step by step, he redescended the gigantic ladder of ice. Night caught up with him, and he knew that a large crevasse awaited below. Suddenly, he took the most heroic decision of his career—he would spend the night on the glacier, something that had never been done. Without realizing it, Balmat expanded the range of tactics for conquering Mont Blanc. He proved that a night on a glacier was not lethal.

But what a night! A cold sleet fell, and Balmat had no bivouac gear. He spent the night sitting on his leather sack, clapping hands and stamping feet, not letting himself fall asleep, demonstrating amazing will power. Altitude and fatigue drove him closer to a sleep from which he would never awaken. It was his fourth consecutive night outdoors—two on the rocks in his previous attempt, one climbing the mountain from below, and now this one!

In the morning, he briefly considered heading back up, for victory was in his grasp. He no longer had the strength, however, and could hardly see. He headed back down into the valley, went home, ate, shut himself in the barn and slept for twenty-four hours.

Balmat kept his attempt secret.

One day, he learned that Dr. Paccard had decided to mount a new expedition. Paccard was a dangerous rival; he had already conducted several reconnaissance trips, was affluent, and enjoyed a considerable reputation. Jacques Balmat sensed that if he made the ascent entirely on his own, no one would believe him. The whole valley would be against him out of jealousy, and everyone else out of spite. On the other hand, if he climbed with Paccard, he had an unimpeachable witness, whose word no one would doubt.

Balmat went to Paccard, and told him about the route. Paccard certainly had a great deal of respect for Balmat, since he was drawn to the adventurous nature of the young man, born in

Above: Engraving depicting an accident near the Tacounag Glacier, from the Illustrated London News *in 1855. Following double page: Map of the Mont Blanc massif drawn up by Eugène Viollet-le-Duc in 1876.*

1762 (when Saussure first launched the idea of climbing Mont Blanc). He knew that Balmat did not lie, would not dither, and would not seek to string out the attempts in order to make the whole affair last longer. Balmat, as a needy husband and father, certainly hoped for financial reward, but what counted most was success. Maybe he would have earned more had he confided nothing to Paccard and immediately proposed the ascent to Saussure. On the other hand, not having completed the final leg, perhaps he wanted to be sure there was no chance of failure—he had to be absolutely certain before he took Saussure along. He wanted the reward for himself, obviously. But most of all he wanted to prevent it going to others, who merited it less than he.

The two men saw eye to eye. Paccard devoutly wished to climb Mont Blanc. He reckoned that the success of a local man would redound to the credit of the whole valley, and he proved to be right. Perhaps Paccard was never really captivated by mountains themselves, given that Mont Blanc was his unique mountaineering exploit; subsequently, he preferred to follow family tradition and pursue the comfortable life of a wealthy notary public. On the other hand, the fact that ten years after the ascent, he married Jacques' sister, Marie-Angélique Balmat, proves the two men's mutual esteem. People sought to drive a wedge between them, but Paccard and Balmat never really fell out.

Returning to their first ascent, it was on 7 August 1786 that they started up the familiar path to Montagne de la Côte. They took a blanket, provisions, some light scientific equipment, and alpenstocks, but had neither rope nor ice ax.

They bivouacked at "Balmat's lair," then started out again at 4 a.m. There was a good deal of fresh snow, and Balmat showed signs of

Engraving of an "incident" that occurred during a descent from Mont Blanc, within sight of the valley of Chamonix. Taken from Ten Scenes in the Last Ascent of Mont Blanc *(London, 1853) by painter J. D. H. Browne, who had made the forty-second ascent to the summit the previous year.*

fatigue. As a loyal team member, the doctor took part of his load. Given the strenuous efforts already made by Balmat, it is not surprising that he should suffer a lapse in strength, which, in any case, would prove to be of short duration. Much has been made of this incident, however, to give most of the credit to Paccard.

They followed the familiar itinerary as far as the Grand Plateau. Then, to reach the summit of the Rochers Rouges, Balmat acceded to Paccard's opinion and they took a route to the left of one he had forged earlier (called a "variation" in today's terminology). Paccard was in great shape, to judge by the active part he played in the ascent—working hard, scaling the Rochers Rouges and Petits Mulets, taking samples, giving orders to Balmat. It was not one of Jacques's better days, and he was terribly anxious: one of his children was dying, and he had promised his wife to return that same day. Paccard was determined to push on. They indeed made it to the top of Mont Blanc, but on the very day Jacques's little child died. Balmat obviously had a heart, for just when he was about to taste victory after having risked everything to reach the summit, he had only one desire—turn back as soon as possible to be with his wife in what must be the cruelest moment a mother can ever experience, the death of her child.

Nevertheless, it was getting late. A gust of wind carried Paccard's hat into Italy. The two men did not climb the final, broad slope side by side nor one behind the other, but each in his own fashion. Paccard went straight ahead, Balmat made a detour. Finally they were both at the summit at 6:23 p.m. on 8 August 1786.

Some historians claim that Paccard, exhausted and half-blind, collapsed in the snow one hundred meters from the final goal, and that Balmat came down from the summit to help the doctor to the top. It is impossible to know for sure.

In a famous affidavit, signed by Jacques Balmat in 1787 to put an end to a controversy started by Bourrit, the guide paid homage to Paccard, giving him credit for organizing the expedition, acknowledging the help he provided. That should have killed the legend, but legends die hard.

Balmat or Paccard? It is better simply to say Balmat *and* Paccard, both of whom have merited the admiration of generations of mountaineers. Why is it that every first ascent, every remarkable conquest, is sullied by sterile polemics? Why should such a noble activity be so belittled by accounts, criticism, and judgments motivated by hatred, jealousy, and spite?

Whatever the case, Mont Blanc was beaten! Dr. Paccard's exploit was trumpeted throughout the Alpine world (which in those days was limited to Geneva and Switzerland). Meanwhile, Saussure was preparing his own ascent. A tinge of resentment—the only apparent weakness in his otherwise generous nature—led Saussure to minimize Paccard's feat and magnify Balmat's.

The subtle distinction was that Balmat was merely a guide, so far as Saussure was concerned, and his ascent therefore meant little to history. On the other hand, the success of Dr. Paccard—a man of some standing—killed Saussure's hope of being the first amateur to stand on the summit of "his" mountain.

His resentment did not last long, apparently. Saussure was already concentrating solely on his own ascent. Paccard's scientific observations had been very vague, and everything remained to be done. Since such observations were the sole valid justification for an ascent in those days, Saussure would in fact be accomplishing a "first," for which he had campaigned for twenty-five years, formerly paying out of his own pocket and now with his own sweat. But all his efforts were to be rewarded at last, since a route had been found. Once found, the route merely had to be climbed.

Jacques Balmat thus passed into the background. Everyone's attention focused on Saussure's attempt. In composing his party, Saussure had instructed that it include "Jacques Balmat, who was the guide for Dr. Paccard's expedition." Already the distinction was being made. Balmat was to be used, paid for his knowledge, for "his" route. Hence a misconception about the roles of guides and amateurs was born. Some people have taken this idea very far, assuming that once a guide is paid everything has been bought, including merit and fame. All the guide gets is money! This is pathetic hypocrisy, for no one has ever pointed out that payment of a guide precisely represents a recognition of that guide's superiority in this domain,

an admission that a guide is crucial to an ascent that could never have been made otherwise. It therefore follows that, in addition to money, mountaineers owe their guides recognition. But prejudices die hard.

In exchange for fame, Paccard paid Balmat an ecu—the going price for an outing in those days.

Saussure's Scientific Ascent

To return to Saussure and his ascent, it was on 18 August 1786 that he arrived in Chamonix and learned of Paccard and Balmat's triumph from the innkeeper, Jean-Pierre Tairraz. It was Tairraz who advised Saussure to hire Balmat as head of the expedition

The caravan spent the night of 20 August on the summit of Montagne de la Côte, but was beaten back by snow and foul weather. The attempt was postponed until the following year. This delay enabled Saussure to make extensive preparations, for example measuring the exact altitudes of Geneva and Chamonix with a barometer, starting from the sea coast.

Determined to place all the odds in his favor in 1787, Saussure had Balmat repeat the feat of 1786. It was only on the third attempt on 5 July 1787 that Balmat reached the summit in the company of Cachat (alias the Giant) and Alexis

Above: Engraving from Sir Charles Fellows's Ascent to the Summit of Mont Blanc *(1827) showing a tricky passage across a crevasse.*

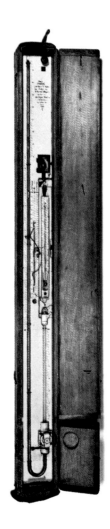

Horace Bénédict de Saussure's barometer, made by another great high-altitude explorer, Jean André Deluc. Personal effects from Saussure's 1787 ascent of Mont Blanc.

Tournier. On his return, he went to see Saussure in Sallanches and announced the good news. Saussure was seized with enthusiasm and headed over to Chamonix.

But the weather did not clear until 1 August, when he finally set out. His large expedition consisted of eighteen guides (including Balmat) and a substantial amount of equipment (a folding bed, tent, collapsible wooden ladders for crossing crevasses, and the indispensable scientific instruments). Thus the early days of Alpine exploration entailed porters, the installation of camps, and regular liaisons—which would also be the case later in the Himalayas.

On the first day, the party got no further than "Balmat's lair" on Montagne de la Côte. As with any major expedition, merely getting under way took a long time (loads have to be distributed, roles have to be assigned), and it was not until 6:30 in the morning that they began weaving through the séracs and crevasses of the Junction. At the Grands Mulets, where Saussure initially thought he might halt, Tairraz had built a shelter of stone; but Saussure

decided to press on, and they took the now classic Petit Plateau route to the Grand Plateau, at an altitude of 3,900 meters (12,800 ft.), where Jacques Balmat had spent the first recorded night on a glacier.

Fear was still rife within the party—the men were afraid that the glacier would open beneath them during the night. But everything went well and, on 3 August, the caravan negotiated the final difficulties. The snow on the slope sweeping up to the Rochers Rouges was hard that day, and they successfully reached the ridge leading to the summit.

It is worth describing the basic techniques then in use. Climbers did not rope up—the individualism of those pioneers has already been mentioned—even on glaciers. Everyone had to trust in himself, in his own sure-footedness and knowledge of the glacier. On this particular ascent, the presence of a scientist implied the use of a long pole held by two guides, forming a railing for the traveler. The first time up, Balmat had used the point of his alpenstock to cut steps. This time, a small hatchet was used

(called a *pioulette* in the local dialect, origin of the French term for ice ax, *piolet*). Properly used by mountain veterans, the hatchet hollowed steps comfortable enough to allow Saussure to climb the glacier in his nail-studded walking shoes.

As they mounted higher, the hard snow gave way to deep snow, probably the remains of earlier snowfalls that had not packed. They were obliged to carve a path through cold, powdery, unstable snow, which was liable to collapse in an avalanche. But they were sufficiently numerous for the task, and soon they reached the upper dome, where they briefly rested before setting off again.

From there to the summit took two hours, which may seem long today. But Saussure was no longer young and, suffering from the thinning oxygen, he staggered with each step. Finally, he reached the summit for which he had yearned for a quarter of a century. He trampled the spot, to use his own words, in a sort of fury. Then, once the rage had passed, he got down to work. He conducted many experiments, using a barometer to calculate the height of Mont Blanc, which he declared to be 2,450 French fathoms (15,626 ft.), a remarkably accurate figure when it is realized how erroneous barometric measurement is even today, and how difficult it is to triangulate without an absolutely precise point like sea level.

The caravan then very carefully descended the steep, avalanche-prone slope. They probably took an enormous risk by attempting the ascent on what was only the second day of fine weather. Fortunately for them, there had been so much snow that the avalanches had already occurred on the Petit and Grand Plateaux by the time they arrived. Later, Dr. Hamel would not be so lucky.

They spent that night on the first rocky outcrop they encountered, now known as the Heureux Retour, an ideal site at 3,700 meters. They had no desire to repeat a night on the glacier, and anyone who has ever bivouacked on glaciers—feeling the snow and ice shift underneath, hearing invisible crevasses crack, awakening to all those mysterious "plops" and

Saussure's ascent to the summit of Mont Blanc, after an engraving by Muller. The impact of Saussure's ascent was amplified by the numerous copies made of these engraved scenes, sometimes with minute variations.

sounds that accompany the slow movement of glaciers—will appreciate their terror.

Continuing the descent on the fourth day, Saussure's team found that the glacier had changed, and used the ladder to cross crevasses. Novices were taught the "glissade" technique of sliding downhill, using the alpenstock as a brake, which saved a great deal of time. By 9:30 a.m. they were at the crest of Montagne de la Côte. When they entered the village of Le Prieuré, they were greeted as great victors.

Thanks to the measurements he carried out and the exploratory character he gave to his ascent, Saussure inaugurated the era of true mountaineering, which, with just a few exceptions, would long be identified with the scientific study of mountains.

Above: The ascent of Mont Blanc remained a prestigious affair throughout the nineteenth century. Every successful ascent merited the awarding of an official certificate by Chamonix's Compagnie des Guides. Facing page: An ascent made by Mademoiselle d'Angeville, depicted in a lithograph by Baumann.

Bourrit was not so lucky, for he never made it to the summit of Mont Blanc himself. His moodiness—what today we might call his nervous breakdowns—led him suddenly to give up, for no reason, at the slightest obstacle. Guides were therefore not inclined to include him in a party. Bourrit turned to the Col du Géant, making the second traverse of it in 1787, after Exchaquet and his guides.

Saussure continued to trek across the Alps, his most productive accomplishment being his long sojourn on the Col du Géant in 1788. He spent sixteen consecutive days on the high pass, at an altitude of 3,350 meters, staying in a small stone shelter that he used as an observatory. When Saussure died in 1799, he left behind substantial writings of literary and historical, as well as scientific, value.

Jacques Balmat continued to explore the Alps. He was an exceptional man, and was never a true guide in the precise sense of the term. He was too whimsical, in fact, too much of an "enthusiast." In total, he scaled Mont Blanc six times: the first with Paccard in 1786, twice in 1787, again in 1788 with Woodley, once more twenty years later during the first female ascent by Marie Paradis (who worked at the Grands Mulets Hut), and, finally, a last ascent in 1817 at the age of fifty-seven. He was known to have died in the horseshoe-shaped cirque called Fer à Cheval while hunting for gold in the recesses of Mont Ruan and Mont Tenneverge, but the exact nature of his death remained a mystery for many years. In fact, it was not all that unnatural, for long afterwards it was learned that he had quite simply fallen. Balmat had died while mountain climbing, like the true *montagnard* he had been all his life.

Dr. Paccard increased his wealth, living a rich bourgeois life at the foot of the mountains, totally leaving behind the adventurous exploit of his youth. There are many modern figures similar to Paccard, famous climbers who have leapt forth like a spark, illuminating mountaineering history for a brief moment, only to extinguish soon. The most famous of them was perhaps "Ryan the comet."

As the eighteenth century came to a close, however, new Alpine feats would progressively shape the nature of mountaineering.

Everything started with Mont Blanc, which, fourteen years after the first ascent, became a regular climb conducted with the help of a company of guides that already boasted a quarter century of experience. They perfected their equipment, which henceforth included rudimentary crampons, an ice ax (still in the form of a hatchet, however), and the use of rope, in addition to poles at certain critical passages (although their rope handling was probably neither very efficient or precise).

With the exception of Mont Blanc, however, people were still seeking a way up mountains as the nineteenth century dawned.

Scientific Mountaineering

Scientists, armed with barometers and hammers, followed in Saussure's wake, scouring peaks and glaciers. Although not yet a sport, mountaineering was no longer pure exploration.

The conquest of Mont Blanc enabled Saussure to establish the main stages leading to the discovery, exploration, and ascent of the world's mountains. Prior to Mont Blanc, there had been a few isolated feats when people scaled famous mountains for reasons of faith, aesthetic inspiration, science, or pride. But twenty-five years of struggle to tame Mont Blanc yielded the rudimentary techniques of mountain climbing and permitted development of very different conceptions of mountaineering. Saussure was thus the first true promoter of a scientific mountaineering expedition. His success with Mont Blanc foreshadowed the great expeditions to the Himalayan range a century and a half later, in which the active part was played by professional climbers under the leadership of a scientific explorer.

Guides thus began training for their profession. Every step higher on the route to the summit called for new equipment and led to new discoveries. Climbers came to learn about crevasses, the risk of avalanches, the various qualities of snow. Equipment was modified, the future ice ax

was tested. People began using ropes, the first crampons were invented, dark glasses prevented snow blindness. All of these techniques would be of great use to future climbers.

If Saussure was the first scientific mountaineer, Paccard was the true sporting amateur, the first person to climb without a guide, as proved by his own search for a route up Mont Blanc, his spirit of initiative, and his competence. By the time he teamed up with Balmat, Paccard had already proved himself. He was a man who climbed "for no reason," for the thrill of reaching a goal, of triumphing over himself. And perhaps to flaunt his ego a little. But that hardly matters, for those same reasons would henceforth motivate all mountain enthusiasts.

That makes for two groups of climbers—scientific mountaineers who descended directly from Saussure, and mountain enthusiasts. For nearly fifty years, the latter were found only on Mont Blanc. They were not interested in discovering new peaks. Mont Blanc was glamorous, and climbing it constituted a somewhat

Facing page: The frontispiece from Naturhistorische Alpenreise (Natural History Travels to the Alps, *Solothurn, 1830) by Franz Joseph Hugi shows the scientist and his team scaling a wall of the Bärenwand in order to reach the foot of Jungfrau in Switzerland. Engraved by Dietler after a drawing by Martin Disteli. Above: Johan Rudolf Meyer, the conquerer of the Jungfrau.*

exalted feat. Climbers delighted in returning to the valley as conquering heroes, welcomed by the sound of cannon fired in their honor and escorted to the hotel by a swarm of admiring young women.

Saussure's descendants, in contrast, were more efficient. It was they who, in the name of science, climbed major summits in the first half of the nineteenth century, exploring not only the Alps but also the Caucasus, Himalayas, and Andes.

Pure enthusiasts popped up here and there, but they were the exception. Their turn came later, during the golden age of mountain climbing, a decade during which most of the major Alpine peaks were scaled.

Taking things schematically, first there was Mont Blanc, an experimental site where methods, material, and personnel were put to the test. Then came other summits, chosen on the basis of scientific or geographical interest. Finally, the main summits having been reached, it became a question of attacking the ridges, then the faces, and then the spurs. One by one, the "final Alpine problems" were resolved. A stage of groping was followed by steadily increasing challenges, requiring the invention of artificial aids and advanced techniques.

The long period between 1786 and 1854, preceding the golden age of major conquests, was characterized above all by a few men of great integrity, driven by the thirst for scientific knowledge. They realized that the mountains offered them an ideal natural laboratory for studying minerals, plants, and animals, as well as the biological reactions of humans in varying climates and latitudes. The late eighteenth century had been marked by the work of Ramond de Carbonnières in the Pyrenees, and of Louis Agassiz and Edouard Desor in the Bernese Oberland. Carbonnières would only go up Mont Perdu in 1802, but that same year Cordier reached a high cleft on Maladetta (Monte Maladito) and, the following year, scaled Tenerife Peak. Agassiz and Desor became famous for their remarkable research into glacier movement. They were among the first to spend weeks on the Aar glaciers, and the spot where they built their first shelter of stones, near

Louis Agassiz and Edouard Desor, two great Swiss naturalists famous for their exploration of the Bernese Oberland and the scientific study of glaciers.

Grimsel, entered Alpine history under the name of "Hôtel des Neuchâtelois."

The early nineteenth century, however, was above all the era of earth scientists. They were everywhere, but since they were interested primarily with the results of their research, little is known about the ascents they made. Many mountains were thus climbed without the exact date of the first ascent being recorded. It is known that Balaitous was climbed in 1825 by Peytier and Hossard, and that Captain Durand scaled one of the summits of Pelvoux in 1830. In the major non-European ranges, Alexander von Humboldt attacked Chimborazo.

Mountaineering in the early part of the century was the affair of just a few men, but they sufficed to mark their era and pass on the torch. A monk named Placidus a Spescha, from Disentis, clearly had an alpine calling—his mountain climbing career extended from 1788, the year he climbed Stockhorn, through 1793 (when Oberalpstock and Urlaun were scaled), to 1824, when, at the age of seventy-two, he made an attempt on Tödi! Another cleric, Franz Altgraf von Salm, distinguished himself in 1800 by ascending Grossglockner (3,798 m). Also at that time, Archduke John of Austria ordered the siege of Ortler (3,800 m), repeating the process of Mont Blanc all over again; the chamois hunter Joseph Pichler would take the geologist Gebhard up it in 1804.

It is highly probable that Saussure's writings reached Austria, enabling his imitators to benefit from his long experience. Thus a shared technique spread throughout the Alps. Anyone who hoped to climb such summits needed to be not only hale and hearty, but also have plenty of pluck and the help of local people. There was a brief appearance of pure mountaineering in the years 1811 and 1812, a rare phenomenon anywhere other than Mont Blanc, when the Meyer brothers from Aarau made their remarkable Alpine explorations. They scaled Jungfrau (4,166 m) in 1811 and attacked Finsteraarhorn (4,275 m). Some commentators claimed they reached the summit, others say they stopped just below, thereby awarding conquest of the culminating point of the Oberland to Leuthold and Währen. Jakob Leuthold and Johannes Währen served as guides to Franz Joseph Hugi, the most important Alpine writer after Saussure, who, in 1829, nearly reached the summit of Finsteraarhorn himself. Hugi traversed numerous high passes and glacial summits, and therefore is rightly considered a pioneer.

Naturalists were everywhere, including Oswald Heer on Piz Palü and Piz Linard in 1835, and Johann Coaz on Piz Bernina in 1850.

If few French names are to be found in that group, it may be due to reasons mentioned above—the upheavals of the French Revolution and imperial wars oriented French youth toward more bellicose careers. Nevertheless, the young scientist Jacquemont explored the Himalayas from 1829 to 1832, reaching an altitude of 5,500 meters (18,000 ft.).

In 1813, Maynard made the first ascent of Breithorn, one of the major peaks over 4,000 meters (13,000 ft.). It is worth noting that he was accompanied by Jean-Marie Couttet, a veteran of the Mont Blanc campaign and the finest ancestor of all guides. A few years later, Couttet would survive the accident that hit Dr. Hamel's Mont Blanc expedition of 1820.

Among the pioneering naturalists and scientists of the day, special mention should be made of Dr. Friedrich Parrot, a German scholar. He notably trailblazed in the Pyrenees, which he covered from one end to the other. In 1811, he was in the Caucasus, attaining the altitude of 4,200 meters on the slopes of Kasbek. By 1817 Parrot was back in the Pyrenees, drawn there by Ramond de Carbonnières's influence, conducting a vast "barometer campaign" that took him to every summit. By reaching the top of Maladetta (3,350 m), Parrot broke the record established on Mont Perdu. As late as 1829, he scaled Ararat in Turkey.

In 1837, Cazaux and Guilhembet made the first ascent of Mont Vignemale (3,298 m), while in 1842 Tchihatcheff and his guides managed to conquer Aneto, or Nethou (3,404 m), the highest peak in the Pyrenees.

Finally, a list of outstanding names should include James D. Forbes, a veritable Alpine explorer, scholar, geologist, and writer. As worthy heir to Neuchâtel climbers Louis Agassiz and Edouard Desor, his long career took him all

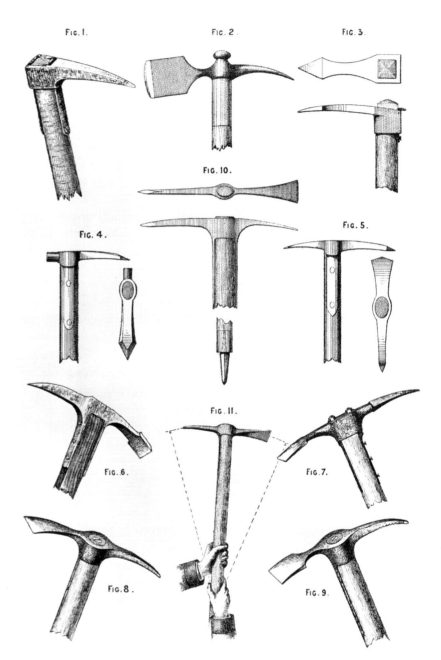

across the Alps; even if he made no famous ascent himself, he explored the range, studying topography and toponymy, drawing up maps and diagrams, recording many valuable itineraries. He made a full exploration of the Oisans region in 1839 and 1841, and is credited above all with the famous High Route in the Valais massif, carried out in 1842. He proved to be one of mountaineering's most useful pioneers.

Major dates in the history of mountain climbing often revolve around one single mountain that incarnates the hopes and aspirations of a

Plate showing ice axes used by pioneering mountain climbers, including Almer (1), Coolidge (6), Kennedy (7), and Pilkington (11). Fig. 2 was a Chamonix model, fig. 3 was designed by Leslie Stephen, and fig. 4 was recommended by the Alpine Club.

generation. Just as the latter half of the eighteenth century was the era of Mont Blanc, the first half of the nineteenth century featured the conquest of Monte Rosa, Europe's second highest peak. Later, the battle of the Matterhorn epitomized the golden age of mountaineering and heralded the final, Himalayan period, marked by the ultimate victory over Everest.

The story of Mont Blanc was straightforward. A learned gentleman, Saussure, offered a reward to locals from the valley of Chamonix, who were already used to scrambling over the mountains, in order to spur them to find a route to the summit. It took them twenty-five years. Everything happened in a single valley, from a single side of the mountain, as though Mont Blanc had only one face—the north face as seen from Geneva.

The Conquest of Monte Rosa, 1855

Two scenes of ascents in the Pyrenees, from the Album du Guide Jam. *The summit of Balaitous is shown on the left, the chimney of Mont Vignemale is on the right.*

The conquest of Monte Rosa was another story. Although it was being reconnoitered at the same time as Mont Blanc, the first climbs met with little notoriety. In 1778, Beck and Vincent from Gressoney apparently climbed to the high pass known as Lisjoch (4,200 m), a legendary col

between Monte Rosa and its imposing neighbor, Liskamm. Then, in 1789, Saussure himself, flushed with his victory over Mont Blanc, made a reconnaissance trip to Monte Rosa, although he never followed it up.

Monte Rosa, in fact, never drew crowds—in today's terms, it simply was not a winner. Unlike Mont Blanc, it wasn't *the* highest. Nor was it visible from the plains, or from a big city. Viewed from the Piedmont to the south, it blended into the snowy wall of the Pennine Alps, presenting no striking feature. From the north, meanwhile, it remained downright invisible; furthermore, the path to it from Zermatt's Visp Valley was hardly known. Yet the mountain existed, and was known to inhabitants of the valleys to the south, both Piedmont and Aosta. The strange, divergent valleys of Gressoney, Alagna Valsesia, and Anzasca, although south of the Alps, are inhabited by German-speaking people. There is therefore a linguistic unity ringing Monte Rosa, like the unity of the French language around Mont Blanc.

Although outsiders and plain dwellers showed little interest in Monte Rosa, the inhabitants of Gressoney and Alagna displayed a great deal more. Monte Rosa, it must be said, is not a single, majestic pyramid like Mont Blanc, but is

simply the highest fragment of the very high Pennine chain. Where does Monte Rosa actually begin? To be accurate, it starts from the Theodulpass and runs to Monte Moro. Liskamm is almost as high as Monte Rosa, and Dom (Mischabel) to the north also approaches the same altitude, constituting a veritable "Oberland" of glacial giants, the highest tip of which is difficult to discern.

At first, all the action took place on the southern slope. Since there was little ice, and the permanent snowfields ended high up, access appeared straightforward. Seen from the southern valleys, it looked as though easy, airy ridges would take climbers very high.

In Gressoney and Alagna, numerous hunters of chamois and mountain goats knew how to approach the giant. As at Mont Blanc, they became the first guides. Leading citizens of the valleys were driven by the simple desire to scale the mountain; the disinterest of their motives added to the elegance of their attempts. There may have even been a little mysticism in their search. A tenacious legend, which might well have a scrap of truth to it, asserts that long, long ago it was easy to cross the Lis Pass (4,200 m), and that on the other

side was a fabulous, prosperous valley. In fact, all that was to be found on the other side was the village of Zermatt (also called Praborgne), a few wretched chalets, and the remnants of a backward, uncivilized population. As to the story about crossing the pass, it is backed up by a similar one about crossing the Theodulpass, which perhaps suggests that at one time the retreating glaciers left an easy passage through the rounded, scattered rocks left behind. That could have created a kind of bridge, around 1500 B.C., between "Camunian" and other Bronze Age civilizations.

But returning to Monte Rosa, it was in 1778 that Beck and Vincent reached the Lisjoch but went no further. They were followed by Saussure. Then, in 1801, Dr. Pietro Giordani, a physician from Alagna Valsesia, reached an altitude of 4,000 meters (13,000 ft.) on a nearby summit that now bears his name.

As with Mont Blanc, a long period then passed before renewed attempts were made. Meanwhile, as described above, mountaineering techniques were developed and refined by repeated ascents of Mont Blanc.

Failing a Saussure, Monte Rosa needed a Dr. Paccard or a Jacques Balmat. The man who dominated the initial attempts on the summit

Left: The first ascent of Gross Venediger on 3 September 1841, in a lithograph by Kürsinger. Led by Anton von Ruthner, the ascent party included no fewer than thirty-nine people. Right: A portrait of Placidus a Spescha, a humble monk from the abbey of Disentis and a great explorer of central Switzerland.

*Markus Pernhart
(1824–1871),*
Grossglockner Seen from
Hohenwartscharte. *Oil on
canvas, c. 1857, 58 x 74 cm.
The painting strongly
idealizes the summit of
Grossglockner, which is less
daunting in real.*

was a forestry inspector from Gressoney, with the Germanic-sounding name of Zumstein. In association with the now famous German climber Dr. Parrot, he nearly reached the 4,000-meter mark. In the following year, he tried again in the company of one Vincent, the son of the pioneer who made the first reconnaissance trip. They would seem to have constituted another Paccard-and-Balmat team.

In 1819, Vincent reached the lesser peak (4,215 m), now known as the Vincent Pyramid. The same year, he repeated the climb with Zumstein. The accounts state that they were familiar with rope techniques but decided not to use them, judging it too risky on an icy ridge where one man's slip would inevitably drag the other down.

In 1820, having familiarized himself with high-altitude slopes, Joseph Zumstein attacked

the true summit. He managed to get a foothold in the upper glacial cirque, accompanied by the two Vincent brothers and the ageing Beck (who had accompanied Vincent senior back in 1778). They were then joined by assorted guides and hunters, constituting a veritable expedition. A bivouac was set up in a crevasse at 4,200 meters, substantially bettering Saussure's record on the Grand Plateau. The next day they followed a sharp ridge of ice, attaining what they thought was the highest point, which is now called Zumsteinspitze (4,570 m).

But Monte Rosa is a long, sinuous terminal ridge with tricky clefts that define five distinct summits. Zumsteinspitze was not the highest. Even today, a complete traverse of Monte Rosa's five points constitutes a tough mountain route; the audacity of the pioneers appears all

the greater when their rudimentary equipment is compared to modern devices. Zumstein scaled his summit again in 1821 and 1822, while in the same year of 1822 Colonel von Welden reached the point known as Ludwigshöhe (4,350 m).

Although the rush of exploratory expeditions was over, Monte Rosa's highest summit remained unconquered. It should be pointed out that this summit actually overlooks other valleys, mainly Anzasca, and, furthermore, has one of the sheerest cliffs seen anywhere in the Alps. Having scaled the points facing their own valley, the men of Gressoney and Alagna seemed satisfied with their achievements.

Twenty years passed. Mountaineering entered a dormant period—the great scientists died one by one, whereas the great sportsmen had not been born yet. In 1842, Father Gnifetti, the priest of Alagna, decided to pursue

attempts to scale the highest summit. He reached a point dubbed Signalkuppe (4,560 m). But he was still some ten meters below Zumstein's record. The true summit was, in fact further north.

Suddenly, the direction of attack changed. Up till then, with the exception of the terrifyingly sheer east face overlooking Macugnaga, all attempts had been made from the south. Now bold climbers approached the north slope, in Switzerland, which was completely covered in glaciers. By this time, advances in Alpine exploration in the Valais region had led to greater knowledge of glaciers. In fact, starting in 1847, mountaineering would evolve with extraordinary rapidity.

That was the period when Forbes was traversing the High Route in Valais, and it is unfortunate that he never attacked Monte Rosa himself.

Above: The first attempt to ascend Grossglockner by Cardinal von Salm in 1799, depicted in a painting by Joseph Hermann. He was accompanied by a suite of no fewer than sixty-two people. Following double page: Hugi and his companions in the Rottal district of Switzerland (oil on canvas, 60 x 81 cm). Painter and caricaturist Martin Disteli (1802–1844) accompanied Hugi in his Alpine travels, producing extraordinary "visual documents" such as this depiction of the Lauterbrunnen Breithorn.

For once, though, it was two Frenchmen who launched the new period of conquest. One was Victor Puiseux, a professor of science at the University of Besançon, who continued the tradition of great naturalists; the other man was Dr. Ordinaire. Leaving from Zermatt, they climbed the Gorner Glacier as high as Silbersattel, situated to the north of the highest ridges.

In 1848, however, Puiseux turned his attention to Mont Pelvoux, leaving it to others to pursue "Operation Monte Rosa," as it might be called today. That same year, guides Melchior Ulrich, Mattias Zumtaugwald, and Johannes Madutz, on their own, scaled an icy rockface that presented great difficulties, reaching a point now thought to be the Grenzgipfel

The upper cirque of Mont Vignemale, a vista painted in watercolors by Franz Schrader in 1875.

(4,631 m). The true summit to their west was only a few meters higher—4,634—but would defy attempts to scale it for another seven years. In 1849, Ulrich's attempt from Nordend ended in failure, and in 1851 Grenzgipfel was reached by the Schlagintweit brothers. But Dufourspitze, the real peak (4,364 m), was only conquered in 1855.

The golden age of mountaineering was about to dawn. It assumed a new image as the scientific motivation for climbing mountains faded, and the sporting challenge of conquering peaks grew. It was the British who were behind this evolution, setting the aristocratic tone that would survive in the western Alps right up to the Second World War. Rich British amateurs would hire one or several guides and

rack up as many peaks over 4,000 meters ("4,000ers") as they could.

The final phase of the conquest of Monte Rosa, then, was led by a new generation of climbers with new principles. In 1854, the brothers James and Christopher Smyth, along with Thomas Kennedy, reached Ostspitze (4,633 m) and thought they were on the highest summit. But the true summit, Dufourspitze, only fell the following year, on 1 August 1855, when guides Ulrich Lauener, Johannes Zumtaugwald, and Mattias Zumtaugwald led the Smyth brothers, Charles Hudson, John Birkbeck, and E. J. Stephenson to the top.

These names signal the end of a long, dark period and the beginning of a decade-long revolution, in the course of which the main Alpine summits would tumble one after another in an unprecedented rush.

Meanwhile, the final point on Monte Rosa, Nordend (4,612 m), succumbed only on 26 April 1861, when the British climbers Thomas and Edward Buxton and John Cowell, led by the famous Chamonix guide Michel Payot, managed to scale it. It had taken a full eighty years from the date of the first attempt to finally complete the total conquest of Monte Rosa. Even the highest Himalayan peaks, in the next century, would not hold out so long.

But things would now move fast, very fast. Fortunate were the climbers who lived between 1850 and 1865—between them they bagged all the "4,000ers." It was to be the golden age of mountaineering.

The Golden Age of Mountaineering

The conquest of the most "inaccessible" summit should have been a resounding victory. But it ended in tragedy: four dead, including an English peer. The golden age of mountaineering drew to a close in tragic, yet epic, fashion.

It was truly a golden age. With the exception of just a few major summits, everything was still there for the picking. Just think of it: between 1863 and 1865, nearly one hundred principle summits were scaled by a handful of mountaineers, usually British, and their guides. It was not yet a question of difficult routes, of ridges or north faces—the main thing was to conquer a virgin peak. The scientific conception of mountaineering that had motivated pioneers a half century earlier had slowly faded. The only remaining representative of that approach, in fact, was the famous John Tyndall, a brilliant Irish physicist who made the divorce between scientists and straightforward climbers spectacularly clear when he resigned from the Alpine Club (the first and most elite of mountaineering clubs, founded in 1857).

The concept of science was replaced by that of pastime. In this respect, mountaineering during the Victorian era was a privileged sport reserved for a wealthy elite, like polo and cricket. This set the tone in the western Alps until the worldwide upheaval of 1914. Only the western Alps were affected, however, for in Bavaria, Austria, and the Tyrol, mountain climbing adopted a more public image, inspiring enthusiasts from all social categories.

In the eastern Alps, mountaineering was associated with a Nietzschean philosophy alien to aristocratic British circles.

Furthermore, eastern mountaineering remained outside of the mainstream (perhaps because its practitioners were recruited from large populous towns like Innsbruck, Munich, Vienna, Linz, Salzburg, Bolzano) and did not publicize its activities a great deal. Its accomplishments were known only indirectly. For seventy-five years, therefore, it was British mountaineering that dominated international mountain climbing, defining the rules, methods, and spirit. That very spirit restricted the recruitment of members. Although their statutes may have been less strict than those applied by the Alpine Club, the Club Alpin Français, the Club Alpino Italiano, and the Schweizer Alpen Club

Facing page: Ferdinand Hodler, Ascent, *panel II, 325 x 180 cm. A vestige of two large frescoes showing the 1865 ascent of the Matterhorn. Above: Cover of Theodor Wundt's* Das Matterhorn und seine Geschichte *(History of the Matterhorn, Berlin, 1896), one of the first books devoted to the peak.*

carefully screened potential members. Candidates had to be sponsored by a member, and required good references. Social status meant a great deal.

British mountaineering, which dominated the entire golden age from 1854 to 1865, entailed climbing with professional guides. The climber–guide team was viewed as an association of honorable men. A famous climber, having found a local mountain dweller whose character matched his own, would employ that same guide throughout his climbing career. This gave birth to the technique of roped climbing, which entailed not only the use of rope between two climbers, but shared attitudes and movements, complementary action on the part of the two members, each developing his particular strength.

British climbing parties thus produced extraordinary guides. A brief aside here, concerning guides, may prove useful to an understanding of the rapid history of Alpine climbing that follows. The last great guide of the preceding era, Jean-Marie Couttet, had been surpassed. New names came to the fore. Whereas the Mont Blanc and Monte Rosa periods were dominated by men from Chamonix (who benefited from terrific training thanks to multiple ascents of Mont Blanc, yet who were not considered French, Chamonix remaining part of the Duchy of Savoy until 1860), it was the Swiss valleys that began to provide famous guides. The British colony found that the character of Swiss guides was closer to its conception of mountaineering. A guide from Chamonix would be deliberately testy and bossy by nature, whereas a Swiss guide with the same technical skills would have a better idea of what might be called customer service. All the Swiss guides were extraordinary climbers. Most were

Christian Almer was perhaps the greatest guide of the early period of mountaineering, and was still active at age sixty-five. Here he is shown aged seventy, on his golden wedding anniversary in 1896, which he celebrated by taking his wife (aged seventy-one) to the summit of the Wetterhorn.

either shepherds or chamois stalkers, crystal hunting being a Chamonix specialty. Given the structure of the Swiss Alps, with their well-defined, snowy peaks, they excelled on routes over snow and ice, or what would today be considered a mixed rock-and-glacier route. Mont Blanc guides, on the other, became great rock climbers. Specialization tended to follow geographic origin, although there were major exceptions—it was the Swiss who forged the greatest rock routes up Mont Blanc! Chamonix guides of the day were content to take clients up well-known sites.

It was therefore the British who, once they had decided to devote their holidays to this new game, first codified the pointless if wonderful struggle between humans and peaks. In conquering the Alps, they displayed all the thoroughness and tenacity for which they are famous.

The English suddenly discovered the mountains on learning of Saussure's ascent of Mont Blanc. It is probable that, in their desire to be pre-eminent everywhere, they regretted not having thought earlier of this form of domination. But it would not take them long to catch up! On 9 August 1787, just six days after Saussure, the fourth ascent of Mont Blanc was made by Colonel Beaufoy; the fifth ascent, in 1788, was also made by an Englishman. The first French ascent, by the count of Tilly, would have to wait fifty years.

In just a few years, there were over one hundred British climbing enthusiasts. These leisured, wealthy climbers were all able to organize and finance the expeditions that the times required. And above all, thanks to their athletic fitness and outstanding endurance, they were able to make the most of the work of their guides. That, ultimately, was what completely changed the face of mountaineering and produced an exceptional string of victories.

From 1854 to 1865, all the tallest summits of the Alps were scaled, with one exception—Meije, which would only fall eleven years later under the assaults of Pierre Gaspard senior and junior, accompanying Boileau de Castelnau. Attempting to list every conquest would be beyond the scope of this book. It is worth pointing out, however, that the golden age ended with the first ascent of the Matterhorn. The conquest of that majestic mountain notably entailed lethal consequences that left British mountaineers mourning for a long time—it would take them roughly a decade to get over the shock.

It might also be expected that, having conquered all the summits, the British thought that the job had been completed. But later Albert Mummery would come along, and everything would start all over again in a more modern fashion, with advanced techniques that remained in use right up to the First World War. It was an era of difficult challenges, tricky ridges, direct routes, sheer rockfaces. Heralding techniques fifty years in the future, what Guido Rey called acrobatic mountaineering took a foothold in the eastern Alps.

The Matterhorn accident, which cost the lives of Michel Croz, Robert Hadow, Reverend Charles Hudson, and Francis Douglas, had an enormous impact. A polemic arose, fanned by journalists and cartoonists. Already in 1820, the avalanche that struck Dr. Hamel's expedition on Mont Blanc had drawn general public attention to the mountains. Tragedy often generates energy. It is undeniable that the French ascent of Annapurna in the Himalayas, the first peak over 8,000 meters (roughly 26,000 ft.) to fall, received so much publicity because it took a dramatic turn—one which nonetheless produced fertile lessons and results.

Hamel's accident had provoked a virtuous reaction on the part of the guides' guild, or Compagnie des Guides, in Chamonix. The former route below the Rochers Rouges was declared off-limits in favor of the Corridor route. This latter route, which led to the Bosses route above, was very long, but at least the avalanche victims did not die in vain, because important lessons had been learned.

The Matterhorn disaster, meanwhile, resulted in a new technique. Today's climbers are struck by the casualness of the way mountaineers formerly roped themselves together. As a matter of fact, there was no real rope technique for rock

climbing at the time: safety ropes would be affixed as handrails, and poles and ladders were employed. That eight climbers descending the Matterhorn were all tied to the same rope—or rather, two ropes of differing strength—seems horrific today. Even those who have done that fatal route now equipped with cables shudder at the thought of the heterogeneous party—experienced climbers and complete beginners—linked by such a fragile thread on the icy gneiss

of the Matterhorn's "Shoulder." The fact that Whymper was able to anchor the survivors is a testimony to his cool-headedness. The accident long weighed on Whymper's mind. In any case, from that tragic day onward, tying so many climbers to the same rope was apparently proscribed. Parties would include three, or at most four, climbers roped together. It was also realized that one technique was appropriate to scaling a rocky cliff, while another was needed on a less steep but heavily crevassed glacier. The next generation would refine such techniques.

But to return to the main conquests of the golden age, it was in 1854 that Kennedy and the Smyth brothers scaled Monte Rosa's Ostspitze. That same year, Alfred Wills and his guides

Two of Edward Whymper's illustrations for John Tyndall's Hours of Exercise in the Alps *(London, 1871). Left: Saving a porter on the Aletsch Glacier. Right: Ascending the Lawinen Thor. Scientist Tyndall and artist Whymper rivaled one another to be the first to the top of the Matterhorn.*

Above, left: The Blanc
Glacier and the Barre des
Ecrins, scaled by Whymper's
party in 1864, in a
watercolor by Ernest Hareux
for Daniel Baud-Bovy's La
Meije et les Ecrins
(Grenoble, 1907). Above,
right: Melchior Anderegg and
Leslie Stephen. Bottom, right:
Michel Croz, the famous
Chamonix guide, sketched
by Whymper.

climbed the Wetterhorn, their expedition being overtaken just near the summit by a little shepherd carrying a fir tree, who obviously intended to be the first to the top. The young man was named Christian Almer, and would become one of the great guides of his day, notably partnering William Coolidge.

In 1855, there was a double first on Mont Blanc: the Smyth brothers, Kennedy, Hudson, and Ainslie not only made the first ascent of Mont Blanc via the Saint-Gervais route, they were also the first climbers to do it without guides.

Without making an exhaustive list of all the firsts in that glorious era, a few key summits indicate the development of mountaineering. The conquest of Weisshorn, in 1861, redounded to the credit of the famous scientist John Tyndall, who reached the top (4,512 m) via the east ridge in the company of J. J. Bennen and Ulrich Wengen. The glamorous Weisshorn had already repulsed two serious attacks, by Leslie Stephen in 1859 and Matthews in 1860 (led by the famous guide Melchior Anderegg and Johann Kronig).

British mountain climbers did not limit themselves to the Valais region, they also "traveled" with their guides. It was in 1864, after many other "4,000ers" had been

climbed, that A. W. Moore and Edward Whymper scaled the Barre des Ecrins (the culminating point of the Oisans range), guided by Christian Almer and Michel Croz (practically the only French guide of the day who could equal or even surpass his Swiss counterparts).

That same year, mountaineering reached a new grade of difficulty in pure rock climbing with the first ascent of the rocky peak known as the Zinal Rothorn (4,223 m) by Leslie Stephen, Craufurd Grove, Melchior Anderegg, and his brother Jakob. Scaling Rothorn presented a serious challenge over broken rock and mixed terrain, foreshadowing the future ascents of Meije and Grépon. Stephen was not only Britain's most distinguished mountain climber, he was also a talented writer.

His *Playground of Europe* provided a superb rationale for British mountaineering as a supreme pastime or diversion for aesthetes, rejecting any scientific or philosophical justification (perhaps out of modesty).

The leading guides were Melchior and Jakob Anderegg, Christian Almer, and Michel Croz. Their names were associated with the conquest of the principal summits, guiding a handful of brilliant British climbers— Tyndall, Bonney, Ball, Wills, Hudson, Smyth, Moore, Kennedy, and Whymper.

Before discussing the exploits of the year 1865—the most glittering of the decade—it is also worth mentioning Stephen's fine victory over Bietschhorn (3,953 m) with Johan and Anton Siegen and Joseph Ebener, as well as the first ascent of Aletschhorn (4,182 m) in 1859 by F. F. Tuckett, P. Bohren, and Chamonix guide Victor Tairraz. Tairraz, Croz, and François Devouassoud personified the high professional calling of Chamonix guides.

The year 1865 was marked above all by the Matterhorn. But that event towers so high above all others that it constitutes a chapter in the history of mountaineering all by itself. It will be discussed below. The same year, meanwhile, saw the conquest of highly challenging summits that presented a series of difficulties quite superior to the glacial pyramids of the Valais range. For instance, on 29 June Whymper climbed the Aiguille Verte (4,121 m) with Christian Almer and Franz Biener. Whymper's usual guide, Michel Croz, did not want to let down another client who had booked him that day, which speaks for Croz's integrity when one realizes what victory over the finest summit in his home valley would have meant to the guide.

Croz took his revenge on 5 July by guiding English climbers George C. Hodgkinson, Hudson, and Kennedy, accompanied by Michel Ducroz and Peter Perren, to the top of the Aiguille Verte via the ridge, or arête, known as the Moine.

Back on 24 June of that year, Whymper was the first to climb the Grandes Jorasses (4,184 m), in the company of Croz, Almer, and Biener (a finely composed trio of guides, one coming from Chamonix, the other from Grindelwald, the third from Zermatt). The highest peak of the Grandes Jorasses (4,208 m) would be scaled in 1868 by Walker, with Melchior Anderegg and Johann Jaun.

Also in 1865, the Aiguille de Bionnassay fell to Buxton, Grove, and MacDonald, climbing with Jean-Pierre Cachat and Michel Payot, the latter winning fame somewhat later when he succeeded in forcing the first passage up the southern slopes of Mont Blanc.

On 14 July 1865, the very day that tragedy struck the Matterhorn, one of the greatest mountaineering exploits to date was accomplished in the Mont Blanc range by Moore and Matthews, along with Frank and Horace Walker, guided by Jakob and Melchior Anderegg. The party left Courmayeur in Italy on the 14th, bivouacked on the left flank of the Brenva Glacier, attacked the great rocky spur and then the steep glacier culminating in the Col de la Brenva. Jakob Anderegg had to cut countless steps into the slope. Given the date, lack of crampons, and rudimentary techniques of the day, it was quite a feat!

In addition to conquering high summits, the great routes of the future were already being traced. In 1864, Leslie Stephen, R. S. MacDonald, and Craufurd Grove climbed the southwest ridge of Jungfrau with the Anderegg brothers and Johann Bishoff. On 29 August 1865, Reverend George and Sir George Young inaugurated the era of north face climbing by traversing the north face of Jungfrau via the now classic Guggi route, guided by Christian Almer (naturally), Hans Baumann and Ulrich Almer.

One exploit from 1866 merits stressing—the ascent of Mönch via Wengernalp, a fine north face route by the Swiss climber Edmund von Fellenberg, accompanied by Christian Michel and P. Egger. Up till then, all the major firsts in the western Alps had been made by British parties—at last, a Swiss citizen broke with tradition and claimed a first for himself!

While those heroic struggles were underway in the west, P. Grohmann was trailblazing in the east. It was Grohmann, a fine figure of a pioneer, who truly explored the Dolomites, making many ascents in the Hohe Tauern, attacking the Tyrolean campaniles, and racking up numerous firsts including Marmolada, Cristallo, and Tofana. This eminent explorer produced remarkable descriptions and guide books. Despite his solid contributions, he lived somewhat in the shadow of the golden

Above: Augustus William Moore, one of the earliest members of the Alpine Club. Left: Melchior Anderegg, as drawn by Edward Whymper.

Above: An illustration from the book by Fellenberg and Roth, Doldenhorn und Weisse Frau *(Koblenz, 1863). Right: Four pioneers of Swiss mountaineering, photographed c. 1880—Dübi, Aeby, Studer, and Fellenberg. The latter two had founded the Schweizer Alpen Club in 1863.*

age. Mountaineering in the eastern Alps only really began with Paul Grohmann. A pioneer, it was Grohmann who really discovered the Dolomites. He made a number of distinguished first ascents. Grohmann also founded Austria's climbing club, the Osterreichischer Alpen Verein, in 1862, later promoting the joint German-Austrian Deutscher und Osterreichischer Alpen Verein, the largest climbing association in the world today in terms of numbers.

This short list of some of the outstanding feats of the golden age of mountaineering has digressed from the conquest of the Matterhorn. It is time to return to that tale.

Just as the conquest of Mont Blanc could be summed up as the story of two men—Jacques Balmat the crystal hunter and Horace Bénédict de Saussure the scientist, whose association miraculously gave birth to mountaineering—so

the tale of the Matterhorn features two names: Jean Antoine Carrel and Edward Whymper. Carrel the bersagliere, or marksman, was more hunter than guide, more smuggler than peasant, while Whymper was a modest artist and engraver whose swift, dramatic mountain-climbing career would open the tightly closed doors of one of the elitest clubs in Victorian England—the Alpine Club.

Saussure, a highly talented writer, left a literary account of his conquest. Whymper, in contrast, left sober, spare, sincere reports of his ascents, devoid of all romantic exaggeration, reflecting the truth and revealing the personality of his characters. It would have been possible to carefully reconstruct the details of the conquest of the Matterhorn by comparing Whymper's account with those of other great climbers of the day, but this task has been made redundant by the great

Italian writer Guido Rey, who was bewitched by the magic mountain and wrote a marvelous book on the heroic battle conducted against that haughty summit. Admiration for the book's literary qualities is matched only by Rey's profound sensitivity and the reliability of his references. Thanks to Rey, it is is possible to understand the harsh Whymper–Carrel duality; what had seemed inexplicable now seems clear.

Just as Jacques Balmat had a personal, intense passion for mountaineering and an ardent desire to scale Mont Blanc—even to the extent of going it alone—so Jean Antoine Carrel considered the Matterhorn—known locally as "La Becca"—to be his personal property. Carrel felt that conquering the Matterhorn was the business of local people! Because he was treated like a servant or porter, because his strong, independent personality was so underestimated, and because it was not understood that he could accept only a leading role, the conquest of the Matterhorn was delayed by several years. At any rate, logically it should have fallen into the hands of Tyndall and his Swiss guides.

A strange analogy can be drawn between the behavior of the mountain folk who conquered Mont Blanc and the famous guides of the Matterhorn period. The former contented themselves with taking travelers to familiar cols and peaks; attempts on the summit of Mont Blanc were carried out half-heartedly, and success would never even have been envisaged without the prospect of a reward. A century later, the attitude toward the Matterhorn was scarcely different, even though leading guides had by then conquered major Alpine summits. The greatest climbers had declared the mountain invincible, and top-notch guides like J. J. Bennen and even Christian Almer tried to dissuade their clients. Other, more fruitful climbs beckoned, and guides were paid by the expedition. There seemed little point in wasting time on a cursed peak when guides could be crossing the Alps from valley to valley, treated as lords of the mountain. A failed attempt on the Matterhorn could only damage a guide's reputation. In both instances, the ultimate victors were men with nothing to lose: the poor and solitary Balmat on

Top: The summit of Weisse Frau during the first ascent led by Edmund von Fellenberg and Abraham Roth in 1862, as illustrated in their Doldenhorn und Weisse Frau. *Above: Swiss naturalist Edmund von Fellenberg (1838–1902).*

Mont Blanc, and Carrel, driven by a mystic, almost religious, passion toward the huge pyramid of gneiss barring the narrow valley known as Val Tournanche.

Both Saussure and Balmat were indispensable to the conquest of Mont Blanc. They persevered for twenty years and were rewarded with success. Whymper, however, played a different role on the Matterhorn. Although he was one of the driving forces, he was not the main one. Whymper met his equal in Carrel, who was no mercenary. For Carrel, the thrill of conquest was more important than financial reward. He dearly wanted victory for himself and for his country. He was ferociously jealous of foreigners who paraded into his poor, undeveloped little valley as conquering heroes. Whymper nevertheless had qualities that seem superhuman, however hackneyed that term may be these days. For some strange reason, Whymper has always seemed like a mature, middle-aged man, although in fact he was just twenty when he began his campaign and a still-young twenty-five when he succeeded. Today, climbers that age are hardly taken seriously. Imagine a young, twenty-five-year-old man deciding, on his own, to climb an unknown "8,000er"! All things considered, it comes down to the same thing.

Carrel was older, had fought for the unification of Italy, and was therefore a veteran battler.

Whymper, meanwhile, was probably driven by the ambition to escape from his modest status of engraver. (His childhood could perhaps be summed up by the laconic comments in his diary, such as the entry for 24 September 1857: "Cut up wood. Drew diagrams, etc. etc. The same everlasting filthy round day after day, one day not varying at all from the other.") He and Carrel would face off against one another for five years, spurred by the same ambition to scale the Matterhorn. Both, in their own way, were loners—that is what would ultimately bring them closer. On many occasions Whymper found himself without guides, without porters, abandoned by all except perhaps the poor hunchback of Val Tournanche, one Luc Meynet, an extraordinary, modest, courageous, humble, determined, and, above all, faithful soul. And on equally many occasions Carrel set off alone, sensing an approaching threat when parties of famous climbers were spotted in Breuil or on the hilly pastures of Giomein.

The strangest chapter in the story is the final victory. After ten years of struggle and defeat, a very mixed party (alas!), put together by Whymper in desperation, struck out along the overlooked Hörnli Ridge. The team was led by a guide who was not from the area, and who was making his first attempt on the Matterhorn—yet they arrived at the summit in a matter of hours.

These three illustrations by H. G. Willink for Clinton Dent's Mountaineering *(London, 1892) give a good idea of the climbing "ambiance" during the heroic era.*

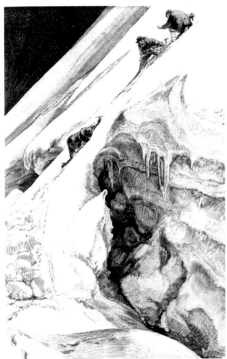

Victory, then, went not only to Whymper but also to Michel Croz from Chamonix, the biggest revelation of the day after Almer and Melchior Anderegg. A strange party, formed in haste, won an easy victory only to end the greatest day in mountaineering history with the most horrible of tragedies.

Taming the Matterhorn, 1865

The first attempt on the Matterhorn was made from Italy. And for nearly ten years without interruption, all subsequent attempts were launched from there. Yet now that it is known that the easiest route leads up the Hörnli Arête on the Swiss side, it might be wondered why that side of the mountain facing the Zermatt Valley sparked so much admiration for its fine, architectural lines yet so little action from climbers. Perhaps it was because the nearby presence of some one hundred peaks over 4,000 meters provided sufficient scope to British mountaineers of the golden age. Even though they all recognized the attraction of conquering the Matterhorn, they all quickly described it as impregnable. This assessment, coming from the most renowned and experienced enthusiasts, when combined with the lack of enthusiasm on the part of professional guides, endowed the north face of the Matterhorn with a

kind of mysterious aura that suited it perfectly. And perhaps that aura suited the mountaineers themselves, insofar as it fed their dreams—they knew full well that as long as the Matterhorn loomed high, untouched and unconquered, there would always remain something for which to strive.

Over on the Italian side, things looked different. The times were propitious to conquest—a veritable *rinascimento*, or Italian renaissance, was taking place. The sense of patriotism was growing every day. The foundations of national unity had been laid, and Italy's current and future leaders, all from Piedmont and Lombardy, keenly coveted the mountains garlanding the new northern borders of the kingdom. Scaling such mountains was a patriotic duty reflecting the need to assert ownership.

In the dark, wooded valley of Val Tournanche, local folk were raised on mysterious legends, all of which seemed to penetrate the ice and rock of "La Becca," that strange fortress of gneiss blocking the path northward. Shepherds, farmers, and hunters had more or less approached the base of its fantastic southern face, measuring the height of the wall, listening for hours on end to the fall of avalanches or the eternal rocketing of stones that sometimes sparked at night along the side of the mountain. Born into that legendary setting, local folk unconsciously wanted

Left: The vast crevasse at the foot of Mont Blanc, as illustrated in William Adams's Mountains and Mountain Climbing *(1883). Center and right: Two illustrations from Dent's technical manual,* Mountaineering, *from the pen of H. G. Willink.*

to climb the mountain. And the most ardent of them all was perhaps a young seminarian from Val Tournanche, Abbé Aimé Gorret, a peasant-priest and faithful listener to the accounts of Canon Carrel, a resident of the valley who was yet another of those contemporary thinkers motivated by the desire to scale mountains in order to observe nature and the stars.

The first serious attempt was made in 1857. Gorret joined up with two robust hunters from the valley, Jean Antoine Carrel, the notorious bersagliere, and J. J. Carrel, who was more thoughtful and level-headed. They climbed a point to the west known as the Tête du Lion, and from there gazed beyond the harsh, narrow gap separating them from the ridge of the Matterhorn. There they contemplated the staggered rise of towers, spurs, and rockface streaked with couloirs down which boulders tumbled continuously.

That same year Gabriel Maquignaz and Victor Carrel followed in their footsteps, discovering a steep couloir that linked the Tête du Lion to the Matterhorn. They reached the Col du Lion and scaled the snowy chimney up to the ridge, attaining an altitude of 3,450 meters. But the top was still over 1,000 meters above them!

In 1858, the famous British climber Thomas Kennedy looked the Matterhorn over, only to convince himself of its invulnerability. Anyone who looks at it from below would be of the same opinion: three sides of the famous pyramid drop into terrible voids on the north face, while the fourth wall, which appears more attractive and overlooks the high pastures of Giomein, was equally hostile (and would be one of the last to be scaled).

In 1859, V. Hawkins went to investigate and claimed that ascent was possible from the Italian side. His guide was the famous J. J. Bennen.

In the year 1860, everything would change. Hawkins returned to Breuil with the scientist Tyndall and his guide Bennen. They also hired J. J. Carrel as porter. Bennen did not disguise his contempt for Carrel, so when Hawkins showed signs of fatigue in the chimney, Carrel was left behind with him while Tyndall continued upwards with Bennen. They got as high as 3,900 meters.

The same year, Parker made an attempt via Hörnli, convinced of the accessibility of that ridge, but his companions did not seem enthusiastic about the route.

That was when a young, twenty-year-old artist arrived in Val Tournanche and saw the Matterhorn. It was none other than Edward Whymper, a talented draftsman commissioned by a London publisher

A talented artist, Edward Whymper (right) depicted the cream of mountaineering society at Zermatt in 1864, including Leslie Stephen (seated left, with a pipe), A. W. Moore (to the right of Stephen, slightly bent), John Ball (standing, foreground, with alpenstock in hand), William Matthews (standing, hand on hip), John Tyndall (standing, hand open), Alfred Wills (arms crossed), and Lucy Walker. The four guides on the right are Franz Andermatten and Peter Taugwalder Jr. (seated), with Jean-Joseph Maquignaz and Peter Perren (standing).

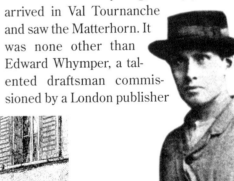

to draw and engrave the famous Alpine landscapes that were so fashionable at the time. In short, he was a forerunner of modern reporters, whose attitude and audacity he shared—he wanted to be the first everywhere, and would do whatever it took to succeed. Furthermore, he realized that a project should never be abandoned halfway, because the interest aroused would inevitably generate rivals. But above all, when confronted with the Matterhorn and its pure forms, thrusting ridges and pyramidal shape, Whymper realized that he had found "his" mountain. It was his to conquer, his life's goal!

Much ill has been spoken of Whymper. He was apparently hard and cruel. But was he always like that? Or did he suffer the psychological effects of the tragedy that cast a pall over his victory? All those who waged battle alongside or against him acknowledge the chivalrous side of his nature. For example, he was the first to congratulate those who succeeded; and he made his tent available to Tyndall, sparing the latter precious time and unnecessary weight on the Lion Ridge; and when he finally triumphed, his first thought was sadness and affection for Jean Antoine Carrel who, less lucky that himself, was not among the victors (even though Carrel, on whom Whymper thought he could count, had abandoned him to join the Giordano team, a semi-official Italian expedition organized by a government minister, Quintino Sella). None of that affected Whymper's character. Only one thing changed it—the sorrow and pain of the accident that tarnished his victory, an accident for which he felt, to a greater or lesser extent, responsible. Finally, the affection that he showed toward Luc Meynet, the hunchback who was his most faithful companion, is clear proof of Whymper's kindness.

Whymper first went to the Alps in 1860. But he was so gifted and had so much endurance that, after just one summer of climbing, he acquired enough feathers in his cap to be admitted to the Alpine Club the following year. It was a great distinction and right from that date he became, in a way, the leader of British Alpine mountaineering.

It has been claimed that Dr. Paccard, the hero of Mont Blanc, was the first amateur to climb without a guide. Whatever the case, Whymper's solo attempts and those done in the company of a sole porter clearly demonstrated once and for all that "where there's a will, there's a way." It was perhaps his audacity and will to climb that so impressed his peers and, even more surprisingly, inspired another exceptional figure in the form of Carrel the bersagliere.

Three illustrations by Whymper. Below, right: A hasty descent from the Aiguille du Midi, published in the Alpine Journal, vol. 5 *(1870). Below, left: Rockfall on the Matterhorn, which threatened Whymper himself. Above: A vignette from Whymper's most famous book,* Scrambles Amongst the Alps.

The famous Swiss painter Ferdinand Hodler produced two vast frescoes loosely based on the Matterhorn tragedy. Unfortunately, these cumbersome works were cut up, and only fragments remain. Shown here is the third panel of The Ascent, *measuring 245 x 145 cm.*

Whymper got his first glimpse of the Matterhorn in 1860; he returned in 1861 having decided not to rest until victory was his. In that year of 1861, Parker would make another attempt on the Hörnli Ridge, returning after having climbed to an altitude of 1,500 meters. In Zermatt itself, Parker's attempts were not taken very seriously. But on the other side, in Val Tournanche, the winds of battle were blowing. Tyndall, having just scaled Weisshorn, arrived in Breuil. Whymper made haste to get the jump on Tyndall, who was a very dangerous rival. When Whymper tried to hire Carrel's services, the latter refused—it was a head-on clash. Obviously the great Carrel did not want to allow anyone else to find the first route to the top; perhaps he was also presumptuous enough to think he was the only person able to so do. In those days there were many Swiss guides in Breuil, which had no tradition of local mountain guides in the sense the profession is now understood—people like Carrel and Maquignaz went into the mountains when they damned well felt like it, and they generally preferred to hunt chamois or smuggle contraband or quite simply cut hay rather than accompany tourists up the Theodulhorn. So Whymper turned to Swiss guides; Taugwalder was well known, but reluctant to make the attempt. Whymper ultimately set out with a makeshift guide who turned out to be more of a hindrance than a help. The British mountaineer spent the night in his tent on the Col du Lion, and made it up the chimney the next day, but then had to descend.

Jean Antoine Carrel, who had refused to accompany Whymper for money, had meanwhile formed his own personal team and, with J. J. Carrel, preceded Whymper up the mountain. They reached the highest known point to date, about 4,000 meters, some 100 meters above Tyndall's mark the previous year. Jean Antoine Carrel carved his initials there, almost taunting Bennen and warning Whymper: lest they expected him to take a back seat, he was born to lead!

The following year, 1862, the battle raged furiously between Tyndall and Whymper on the one hand and Carrel and the Swiss guides on the other. The year began with a strange winter attempt on the Hörnli Arête by Thomas Kennedy in the company of Peter Perren and Peter Taugwalder, during which they reached an altitude of 3,300 meters, slightly above the current location of the Hörnli Hut. Then, on 7 July, Whymper set off with his friend MacDonald, Johann Zumtaugwald, Johann Kronig, and the faithful hunchback Luc Meynet. They bivouacked on the Col du Lion, but were overtaken by a storm and were obliged to turn back.

On 9 July, Whymper, Carrel, Pession, MacDonald, and Meynet headed back up to the Great Tower; Pession was taken ill, and they had to retreat. The ridge yielded ground grudgingly. Yet even if progress was disappointing, at each attempt tricky passages were improved, preparing the way for future routes. Intrigued by Kennedy's attempt, Whymper went to Zermatt and had a look at the Hörnli Ridge; deciding it could not be scaled, he returned to Val Tournanche where he discovered that no guide would or could join him—they were all out hunting or mowing hay. The fine weather would not last much longer. Even Luc Meynet left him in the lurch. The local  people, however modest, had the same attitude as Jacques Balmat or Moutelet. Their most precious possession was their freedom—freedom of movement, of action, of thought.

By 18 July 1863, Whymper wearied of waiting. He set off alone for the Col du Lion, where he spent an unforgettable night. He reached the Great Tower, at 4,000 meters, but on returning he fell on an icy slope and seriously wounded his head. He returned to Breuil.

On 23 July, Jean Antoine Carrel agreed to climb with Whymper. Carrel was impressed with the young foreigner's courage and, if it had not been for the difference in nationality that meant victory might go to the English at the expense of the Italians (and, more to the point, of the folk from Val Tournanche, who were the rightful owners of the Matterhorn), then Carrel might well have committed himself to Whymper body and soul. On this

The Matterhorn, which was the emblematic peak of mountaineering's golden age, generated a great deal of imagery. This postcard shows two Zermatt guides in front of the mountain.

Above: Jean Antoine Carrel, photographed above in old age, was almost as determined as Whymper to scale the Matterhorn. He died of exhaustion on that very peak in 1890, at the age of sixty-one, after having safely guided home his client, an Italian named Sinigaglia. Right: Mountain boots featuring nailed soles similar to those used during the heroic era.

attempt, Whymper and Jean Antoine Carrel were accompanied by César Carrel and Luc Meynet—they managed to get beyond the Great Tower but were driven back by bad weather. On 25 July, the Carrels abandoned the team, while the faithful Meynet remained with Whymper, who managed to get past his own highest point (4,100 m) before turning back once more.

He planned to make one last attempt that year. But to his surprise, on returning to Breuil he discovered that Tyndall, his powerful rival, was organizing a large expedition and had monopolized all the guides. Tyndall set out with the famous Bennen as lead guide, plus Anton Walter, and Jean Antoine and César Carrel, hired as porters. What a shame that Tyndall did not appoint Jean Antoine to pave the way. If he had, the Matterhorn would probably have fallen that year. On the other hand, how could Tyndall have offended Bennen, his faithful Bennen, who had led him to the top of Weisshorn and so many other "4,000ers."

Indefatigable, Whymper climbed back up to his tent, which he had left

at the Great Tower, an altitude of nearly 4,000 meters. There he awaited Tyndall, offered him use of the camp, and then redescended, in an extraordinary gesture of fair play on the part of a man described as harsh, indeed nasty. Instead, it is Tyndall's sense of fair play that could be questioned here: why did he not invite Whymper to climb with him?

Tyndall reached the largest prominence on the Lion Ridge, the point at 4,258 meters now known as Tyndall Peak. Seen from below, it appears to be one of the summits of the Matterhorn. But a narrow and deep cleft separates it from the mountain's final slope. The great Bennen hesitated, shilly-shallied, procrastinated. When Tyndall asked Carrel for an opinion, he received the haughty reply, "Ask your guides—we're only porters!" If Carrel had been willing that day, there is no doubt that the Matterhorn would have fallen, all the more so if Tyndall had taken aboard Whymper, the tall loner with the steely gaze.

The expedition turned around. That was the last attempt for 1862.

Things quieted down in 1863. Whymper continued his tour of the Alps, scaling numerous summits, before returning to Breuil. First he completely circled the Matterhorn in the company of Jean Antoine Carrel, but gleaned little new information. So he set out once more with Jean Antoine and César Carrel, Luc Meynet, and two porters, only to be halted by a snowstorm that hit the Matterhorn at an altitude of 4,000 meters. Although the storm was unusually violent, seen from the valley it appeared to be just a cloud that capped the summit for two days.

That was Whymper's last attempt via Breuil.

Another attempt from the Italian side, however, was secretly being planned in great detail. During a preparatory meeting in Turin early in 1863, Quintino Sella and Bartolomeo Gastaldi practically founded the Club Alpino Italiano, whose first official meeting would be held on 23 October of that same year. Sella was not only a great mountaineer, he was also a prominent politician in the newly unified Italy. He instructed his friend Felice Giordano to organize an expedition to the Matterhorn. Giordano went to Breuil, where he sounded out Jean Antoine Carrel about contributing to the Italian effort. He did not have much trouble convincing Carrel of patriotic duty. Carrel was always faithful to his word, however; once given, he would never go back on it. And when he did not feel like guiding, he refused. That is why he sometimes climbed alongside Whymper, and sometimes alone. But he was constantly active, constantly in the forefront, perhaps allying himself with his adversary the better to size up the competition.

So in 1864, under Giordano's direction, the mountain was equipped—certain passages were made easier, everything was prepared. Giordano thought that by recruiting stonecutters from Val Tournanche, who were skilled at driving iron pins into rock, the main obstacles could be overcome. He was not wrong—the Maquignaz brothers became the masons of the Matterhorn.

The decisive year was 1865. It began with an unexpected foray, featuring an angled line of attack conceived by Christian Almer, Whymper's number one guide. This time, Whymper made full preparations: in addition to Almer, he hired Michel Croz from Chamonix and Franz Biener from Zermatt, as well as the hunchback Meynet to carry the tent. Almer's unusual itinerary was supposed to take them up a couloir on the southern face to the Furggen Arête, then across the east face to the Hörnli Ridge. Fortunately, falling rocks put an end to the scheme right at the outset, below the Col du Breuil. Almer did not try to disguise his opinion that there were many more interesting mountains to climb. Croz, meanwhile, had contracts back in Chamonix. So the team broke up, or rather returned to Chamonix, where Whymper made the first ascent of the Aiguille Verte and Croz the second.

At that point, things began accelerating. Giordano had not been wasting his time in Breuil. He knew that Whymper was his main adversary, and he organized an expedition scheduled to leave on 11 July. Jean Antoine Carrel had committed himself to Whymper until the

10th, but disengaged himself from the commitment on the grounds of bad weather. There was nothing underhand about Carrel's maneuver, so I am inclined to accept it, as did Whymper, who bore no grudge against Carrel. The arrangement with Whymper was over a year old, Carrel was sworn to the greatest secrecy by the Italians and, without being given a specific date, was asked to be ready at a moment's notice.

Giordano's expedition was minutely planned. All the guides and *montagnards* in Val Tournanche were hired. By the time Whymper got wind of Giordano's imminent departure, there was not a single guide left. Whymper was seized by a kind of panic—Giordano had stacked all the cards in his own favor and, by taking Carrel, who knew the whole route right up to the gap at Tyndall Peak, was assured of success. Whymper had to act fast, and at that point fate intervened. In Breuil, Whymper met a young and distinguished British mountaineer, Lord Francis Douglas. Douglas and his guides left with Whymper for Zermatt on 12 July.

Above: In The Ascent of the Matterhorn, *Whymper related how he fell during a solo attempt on the Matterhorn, which he miraculously survived. Ropes were used with a certain reluctance by pioneering climbers, since as well as saving lives a rope could drag others to their death, as would later happen on the Matterhorn. Left: A bowline knot, still used today.*

Giordano's men had already been at work on the Matterhorn for three days. They were advancing slowly but surely. Everything had been planned, the camps organized, the difficult passages made easier. The important thing was to get Giordano or even—supreme honor—Sella himself to the top, and Carrel did not want to leave anything to chance. Just as Balmat had preceded Saussure to the summit of Mont Blanc to be certain of getting his client up there, so Carrel would go to the top first to prove the feat possible.

Giordano, who followed the progress of his countryman through a telescope, leapt with joy when he suddenly saw men on the highest peak, on 14 July. It had to be Carrel! Giordano sent a victory telegram to Sella.

He suffered a cruel disappointment, alas, the next day when his "victors" returned in defeat. While they were still on the Shoulder, Carrel and his companions were intrigued by shouts and stones coming from the summit—on lifting his gaze, Carrel recognized Whymper's white trousers. Disappointed, sickened, and disgusted, Carrel had no will to carry on. He headed straight down without stopping and buried his despair in his hayloft in Avouil.

Giordano displayed great strength of character. In the valley, he convinced people that nothing was lost, that the Matterhorn still had to be conquered from the Italian side. Of course, they were still in the dark about the tragedy on the Zermatt side. Carrel had nevertheless collapsed—these days, he would be diagnosed as having had a nervous breakdown, and with good reason!

So the gentle Abbé Aimé Gorret, who made the first attempt back in 1857, returned to the fore. He marshaled everyone's energy and on 16 July launched another expedition led by J. A. Carrel, J. B. Bich, and J. A. Meynet. With the exception of Carrel, most of them were new to the Matterhorn. But faith drove them onward. They bivouacked at the foot of the Tower, then crossed over to the snowy Zmutt slope before reaching the upper ridge via the Corridor. At that point, Carrel once again demonstrated decisive leadership—realizing that all of them would never make it to the top, he decided that Abbé Gorret and Meynet would wait there, while the others carried on. Soon they were at the summit. It was 17 July 1865.

There was no doubt in the valley this time. The Matterhorn had been conquered!

Only then did news of the first ascent, from the Swiss side, begin to arrive, simultaneously filling the Italians with sadness and a kind of pride. Because it was a local expedition that, with no outside aid, no "foreign" help, had found the safest route. It seemed obvious that no one would ever scale the Zermatt face again.

What exactly happened, then, on the Hörnli Ridge on 14 July? Whymper arrived in Zermatt on the evening of the 12th, accompanied by Lord Douglas and his guides, Taugwalder and son (known as "old Peter" and "young Peter"). There they found Almer, although due to a previous engagement he was unable to join them. On the other hand, Whymper was also delighted to find at Zermatt his favorite guide, Michel Croz from Chamonix, with whom he had climbed the Grandes Jorasses and the Ecrins. Croz was accompanying an excellent English mountain climber, Reverend Charles Hudson, as well as a young novice, Robert Hadow, whose only experience was an ascent of Mont Blanc that had proved his ruggedness. There was no question of Douglas or Hudson giving up their guides or abandoning their plans. Whymper had no choice: if he wanted the guides, he would have to accept their clients. He had confidence in Douglas and Hudson. But Hadow had just as much claim to Croz as Hudson, and Whymper religiously respected prior commitments. So Hadow would come along. After all, he would be the only novice on the team.

On 13 July, they bivouacked high on the Hörnli Arête, the lower part already being familiar to the Taugwalders. The next day, Croz took the lead. As a determined climber in the prime of his life, he was spurred by what he thought he perceived as a quick route to the top. With great energy he urged the team upward. Climbing on the Hörnli Ridge turns out, in the end, to be easy from a technical standpoint—but everything depends on the condition of the terrain. Dry, it is a relaxed climb to 4,300 meters, just above the Shoulder; icy, it is very dangerous. Generally, conditions are such that ice only forms above the point where the ridge rises for the final thrust to the top, forcing climbers to shift to the north face. From a technical point of

The Fall, *panel I,
326 x 160 cm. One of the
remaining fragments from
Hodler's immense diptych,
freely based on the
Matterhorn tragedy.*

view, more difficult rockfaces had already been climbed at that time, for example the Zinal Rothorn.

Croz, who had already demonstrated incomparable class on all kinds of terrain, had recently accomplished some of the finest Alpine firsts ever. He hardly had to stop and seek his route over the Shoulder, skirting around overhangs by the snowy couloirs on the north face.

They reached the summit at 1:40 p.m. on 14 July. Victory was so swift and easy that they were stunned. It was a major and unexpected triumph for Croz. There where Almer, Bennen, and so many others had failed, he had dared and succeeded!

The Matterhorn has twin peaks. The slightly lower, Italian one is linked to the higher Swiss peak by a snowy ridge. Whymper immediately thought of Carrel and Giordano, and ran along the virgin ridge to verify that it was as yet untrodden by human steps. From there he could see, on the Shoulder below, his adversaries and climbing companions, whom he nevertheless liked and admired. Whymper and others shouted, waved Croz's blouse like a flag, and tossed stones. Down below, the others saw and understood.

It was time to descend. On the way up, everything had gone well, and even though the exact order of march was not recorded, it is probable that the physically fit Hadow, carefully monitored by his companions, climbed without too much difficulty. But descending was another matter. The first 100 meters presented a steep slope of rock covered with snow or ice, and little foothold. On the way up, Croz's glacier experience enabled him to cut the steps that they would use again for the descent.

But how would they proceed? Three men stood out—the exploits of Croz, Hudson, and Whymper put them in a class above the others, including not only the novice Hadow but also the Taugwalders, somewhat obscure guides more accustomed to the Theodul than to dangerous climbs. Whymper, as head of the expedition, assumed his responsibility—he would descend

last. Why Whymper, when normally a guide would go last? Probably because, apart from Croz, he was the most confident. Croz would go first, leading the descent. Those who know the Hörnli Arête can testify to how difficult it is to find a passage on the immense ridge. A great deal of experience is required, and the path would have to be prepared. It was right that Croz assume that role. It might seem surprising that Hadow and Hudson were not immediately flanked by the Taugwalders, but perhaps Whymper thought Hudson provided better backup for Croz.

In those days, rope technique was in its infancy. Familiarity with long glacial routes had accustomed mountaineers to roping numerous climbers together, which slowed progress and hindered rock-face climbing. It now seems certain that the Taugwalders possessed inadequate skills, although their reactions at the moment of the accident were good and worthy of the finest professionals, since they perfectly anchored their ice axes. If only the rope had not snapped.

The expedition, then, was making its long, dizzyingly steep descent. It arrived at about 100 meters below the summit, where two outcrops of red gneiss forced them to angle across the bluff on the north face. Even today, if safety cables had not been installed, this passage would still be considered difficult, indeed dangerous. It is not hard to picture the long line of the team, roped together: Whymper last, some 40 meters (130 ft.) above his companions; below him were the two Taugwalders, father and son, and below them came the three Englishmen, Lord Douglas, Hudson, and the novice Hadow; at the bottom of the human ladder was the indefatigable Michel Croz carefully cutting steps into the ice, directing the feet of young Hadow, who seemed very ill at ease.

Tragedy struck in an instant. As Croz turned his back to study the rest of the route, Hadow suddenly lost his footing and slid into Croz, knocking him over. The two men sailed into the void. Hudson and Douglas desperately gripped the rock, but were plucked off the cliff one after the other. High above, Whymper heard the shout and realized there had been a fall—he instantly anchored his ice axe, and old Peter did likewise. There was a brief jolt, then nothing.

Two moving vestiges of the Matterhorn tragedy. Top: Michel Croz's tombstone. The inscription to the "faithful, stout-hearted guide," composed by Whymper himself, refers to "a brave and devoted man loved by his companions and esteemed by travelers." Bottom: Whymper's drawing of the snapped rope.

The rope had snapped between young Peter and Douglas. The four unfortunate men below dropped into the dreadful void of the north face.

Victory was transformed into wretched defeat.

The two Taugwalders were overcome with shock. Whymper dug deep into his indestructible energy to find the strength to lead the retreat. It was indeed a long and difficult retreat that he had to conduct. During the descent they apparently experienced an optical effect called the Brocken phenomenon: against the shadow of the Matterhorn cast to the east, they saw a mighty arch, or fogbow, flanked by two dreadful crosses in the sky. But perhaps it was just the shadow of the survivors themselves, cast by the sun and enlarged by refraction against the low ceiling of clouds.

Violent polemics broke out from all sides. The Taugwalders were unfairly criticized for the fact that the rope linking them to Douglas was weaker and therefore more liable to break. The slander would follow them all their lives. For Whymper, aged twenty-five, it was the end of a glorious career that would probably have continued for a long time. Whymper responded to his detractors—most of them members of the Alpine Club—with a noble letter in which he reported the strict, unembellished truth. It contains the despairing phrase that provides a glimpse of the true substance of his character: "A moment of negligence can destroy a lifetime of happiness." In fact, from that day, his life seemed over. As a mountaineer, he organized distant expeditions, exploring the Andes with Carrel, his friend and rival, and going to the polar regions. Then he gave up climbing. But not the mountains. Having become gloomy, at age sixty-six he married a woman aged only twenty-one—it was not a happy marriage. Every summer, Whymper toured the Alps, scrupulously correcting the guides he published.

In 1911, Whymper passed through Grindelwald, where he made his peace with William Coolidge, the temperamental mountaineer with a thousand ascents to his name. On arriving at Chamonix, Whymper went to bed and, feeling death approach, locked himself in his room, forbidding anyone to come near. He died alone, like a noble animal in the wilderness, perhaps still hearing in his head the last word shouted by Michel Croz the instant he plummeted: "Impossible!"

Following the disaster, a curse seemed to cling to the Hörnli Ridge. Giordano spent seven days on the Italian slopes of the Matterhorn without managing to reach the top. In 1867, Craufurd Grove made the second ascent via the Italian ridge, in the company of Jean-Antoine Carrel, Bich, and Meynet; Jean-Joseph Maquignaz made the third and fourth. Finally, in 1868, the famous Tyndall made the first crossing from Breuil to Zermatt, shattering the spell cast by the tragic arête and, in the same year, the reverend Julius M. Elliot, Joseph Marie Lochnatter, and Peter Krubel of Zernatt made the second ascent.

The golden age had come to a close. There remained just one major peak to scale—Meije. It would hold out for another ten years. But meanwhile, climbers were already beginning to focus on new, technically difficult challenges.

The Matterhorn accident, which cost the life of an English lord, made a huge impression on public opinion, as reflected in this lithograph, which was drawn by Gustave Doré and printed by Eugène Cicéri, two of the greatest illustrators of the day.

Mountaineering without Guides, 1865–1914

Of all the major Alpine peaks, only the Meije remained unconquered. Climbers, however, began attacking the Alps' sheerest cliffs and steepest ridges from one end of the range to the other, progressively developing appropriate techniques.

The long period during which mountaineering techniques were developed and increasingly difficult routes were climbed might, in fact, be called the Mummery era. Coming twenty years after his predecessors of the golden age, Albert Frederick Mummery initiated long rock routes that even today remain great classic ascents. Furthermore, Mummery was indisputably the founder of mountaineering without guides, which prior to that time had been the prerogative of a few brilliant individuals like Paccard and Whymper. Unlike these latter two, who made just a few solo climbs, Mummery (who had learned the exceptional art of rock and glacier climbing from his famous guide, Alexander Burgener) set out on difficult exploits not only without a guide, but in the company of other amateurs. It should not be forgotten, however, that between his arrival in the Alps in 1872 and his first guideless ascent of the Grépon in 1892, he benefited from twenty long years of tough lessons dispensed by that bearded giant, Burgener.

The half century dominated by the giant shadow cast by Mummery is hard to divide into specific epochs; from a technical standpoint, there was less difference between Mummery's first ascent of the Grépon (1881) and Young and Knubel's conquest of the same aiguille via the east face (1911) than there was between the major accomplishments of the golden age and the conquest of the Grépon. During the golden age, of course, all the main Alpine peaks were scaled, the lion's share of the French Alps from Mont Blanc to Mont Viso having been bagged by Croz, Whymper, Hudson, Walker, and Almer. Ultimately, however, it should be realized that these were long routes over mixed terrain or, very often, purely snow routes. Rock climbing was avoided and, despite the clear poverty of ice and snow techniques, the latter routes were always preferred over pure rock. It was a time when dozens of hours were spent cutting steps one by one, when Herculean guides took turns in the lead (for example Jakob Anderegg who cut steps for Melchior Anderegg).

Facing page: Climbing Cima Undici, *a painting of the Dolomites by mountaineering artist E. T. Compton. Compton's works were often designed to be reproduced in books and periodicals, which is why many of them are handled in tones of gray or bistre. Above:* Pierre Gaspard, *a watercolor by Ernest Hareux for Daniel Baud-Bovy's* La Meije et les Ecrins *(Grenoble, 1907).*

In contrast, everything began to change between 1865 and 1870. The natural process leading to modern mountaineering had been triggered. To sum up briefly, first the highest peak, Mont Blanc, was conquered, followed a long time later by most of the other major "4,000ers" (the only one remaining in 1865, the Meije, was primarily a rock route). Once the summits had been tamed, newer and more difficult routes were forged, like the ridges of the Matterhorn or the glacier faces of those same summits. Soon everything, or almost everything, had been scaled. Climbers turned to secondary peaks, the ones overlooked by the previous generation; it was the great era of the aiguilles above Chamonix. Then history repeated itself on those same secondary summits—virgin ridges, untried couloirs, untouched rockfaces. The rocky pinnacles along the way, known as "gendarmes," were of course ignored; Mummery thought the famous Aiguille de Roc on the route up the Grépon was little more than a negligible outcrop, which would hardly be the opinion of the great climbers who later delighted in scaling it. Thus the importance of the summit steadily declined, but not the difficulty. Climbers ultimately wound up attacking simple rocky needles named Etala, Père Eternel, Ravanel, Mummery. Yet for a long time several enormous virgin pillars and tough north faces withstood attack—these were the "final great problems"

posed by the Alps. They would only fall with the spread of aid techniques to the western Alps.

That is why it is essential to point out that, toward the end of the nineteenth century, climbers in the eastern Alps developed what they called acrobatic mountaineering, appropriate to the limestone Alps in the north and the peaks of the Dolomites. That is where mountaineers began using pitons for protection, then stirrups, and finally the use of lightweight shoes with friction soles (first of felt, then of rubber). Already highly advanced in the east by the early twentieth century, the technique of using pitons was practically unknown in the western Alps, where it would not appear until around 1930. When applied to sheer granite faces, it led to new conquests.

The Mummery era was also characterized by the obsession of the last climbers of the golden age to find new fields of action. For that generation, which valued the "summit" over a given route or face, Europe had become too small. Hence as techniques continued to develop, so did exploration of the major mountain ranges outside Europe. First climbers went to the Caucasus, and then—like Whymper—to the Andes, to the Himalayas, to New Zealand, and to the Rockies. Major

The northeast face of Monte Rosa (below), the vastest face in the Alps, was climbed as early as 1872 by Ferdinand Imseng (right), guiding English climbers Taylor and Pendlebury.

expeditions had sensational success in Alaska and Africa. And at the end of that period the constant desire to go ever higher returned once again, when sights were finally set on Everest.

But a great deal of ground still had to be covered between Whymper's tragic conquest of the Matterhorn and the attempts on Everest.

The first major exploit of that period was the 1872 ascent of the east face of Monte Rosa, the prodigious Macugnaga abyss, by the Reverend Charles Taylor and brothers Richard and William Pendlebury, led by Ferdinand Imseng. One hundred years later, despite improved techniques—the use of ultra-light crampons, handy ice axes, nylon ropes, and purpose-made shoes—the east face was still considered one of the century's major challenges. Imseng was thus a great precursor.

The year 1872 was important for another reason: it was the year Mummery entered the scene. Later he would meet the bearded guide from the Saas Valley, Alexander Burgener, and would hitch his career to that exceptional man. Mummery slowly "broke himself in" by scouring the Alps from Oberland to Valais with Burgener, making numerous ascents. His day of glory would come later.

Meanwhile, the last pioneers of the golden age carried on even as newcomers "repeated" their firsts, which would enable the eccentric American minister, Reverend William Coolidge, to haughtily claim that, although not the first, he had certainly been the second man at the top of all the Alps!

For the first time, meanwhile, a French climber would stand out from the pack—Henri Cordier. The fact that he was French was in itself unusual, for France had not produced brilliant mountaineers up to that point. Above all, however, Cordier's conception of mountaineering was fifty years ahead of its time. Getting to the top of an easy, secondary summit, even if virgin, did not interest him in the least. He was only twenty at the time. Perhaps he had a foreboding that he would die stupidly at twenty-one when a snow bridge over a torrent collapsed beneath him as he was returning from a reconnaissance trip to the Meije. It was 1875, and Cordier was climbing with the Englishmen Maund and Middlemore, who had assembled a remarkable team of guides, all from Switzerland, including Jakob Anderegg (the best step cutter of his day), Kaspar Maurer, Johann Jaun, and Andreas Maurer. The Aiguille Verte had been scaled ten years earlier, but Cordier decided to attack it from the north face: a couloir of ice, a spur of icy rock, séracs. By succeeding, Cordier laid claim to the first great north face route. That same year, Cordier and his guides traced a direct route up the north face of Les Courtes, and the next year conquered Les Droites. Then he headed for the Meije, where he died. His was a strange fate.

Two of the greatest exploits in the 1870s. Bottom left: The north face of the Aiguille Verte, climbed in 1875 by the Frenchman Henri Cordier, the Englishmen Maund and Middlemore, and the guides Kasper Maurer, Johann Jaun and Andreas Maurer. Bottom right: The Meije, the last great Alpine summit to be conquered. It was scaled in 1877, by Boileau de Castelnau and the guide Pierre Gaspard.

Cordier's impetus had no immediate sequel. But climbers were becoming bolder and bolder, and 1877 was a great year marked by two major feats. First, the Meije, the "last great peak" was conquered. Then British mountaineer James Eccles, a worthy climber from the golden age, and his guide Michel Payot explored the south flank of Mont Blanc, opening a remarkable route from the Brouillard Glacier to the base of Innominata ridge, then finally joining the Peuterey Arête above the Grand Pilier d'Angle. Payot had to cut steps into the ice for seven and a half long hours in order to finally conquer Mont Blanc from the south. The climbers then made it down to Chamonix in only three hours, which says a great deal about their physical endurance and their glacier skills.

The first ascent of the Meije, coming long after those of Rothorn and Matterhorn, marked a new stage in rock techniques. One year later, in 1878, the Grand Dru was scaled by British mountaineer Dent, in the company of guides Alexander Burgener and Kaspar Maurer. Although twenty-one meters higher than the Petit Dru, from which it is separated by a projecting bar, the Grand Dru was set to the rear; hence, when viewed from Chamonix, the smaller peak capping the elegant pyramid of granite seemed to be the true summit. Jean Charlet from Chamonix, after a solo attempt in 1876 during which he not only got quite high but gained fame for the first use of a rope to "rappel" (or abseil) back down, accomplished the first ascent in 1879 along with two other Chamonix guides, Prosper Payot and Frédéric Folliguet.

But the period belonged to Burgener. The previous year, he had climbed the Grand Dru. Among his clients was Mummery, a young and brilliant athlete, a thoroughbred Brit—sophisticated, humorous, and full of enthusiasm for the "game" of mountaineering that he had discovered back in 1872.

Mummery was a pure climber. He brushed aside all scientific and poetic pretexts, and perceived mountaineering primarily as a struggle, an unrivaled game that required total commitment. The accounts he left behind are nevertheless highly seductive; although the emotion is restrained, his sensitivity emerges from beneath the varnish of his biting wit, and his friendship with the bearded Burgener was clearly profound. As a great skeptic, Mummery was modest about his feelings and seemed to enjoy understating his own fine qualities. He nevertheless conducted, first with Burgener and later as leader himself, what was nothing less than a revolution in the art and manner of climbing mountains. He also helped shape climbing attitudes into their current form. Mummery was a great, indeed very great, precursor of the present.

The famous Burgener–Mummery team got off to an impressive start in 1879 by making the first ascent of the Matterhorn's Zmutt Ridge, a famous "nose" of black rock poking over the grim Teifmatten abyss. The following year, they forged the extremely exposed Col du Lion glacier route, during which Burgener broke the handles of two ice axes while using his lumberjack's strength to cut steps.

In 1880, the Mummery–Burgener–Venetz party climbed the Grands Charmoz, the first of

Facing page: Increased interest in mountaineering meant that difficult passages were being equipped by 1875. This painting by Ernst Platz shows the normal route up Zugspitze, the highest peak in the German Alps, which was fitted with iron stakes and cables. Below: Alexander Burgener (left), guide to Albert Mummery (right), seen climbing the famous crack that now bears his name, in a historic photograph taken by Lily Bristow in 1893.

Above: The "normal route" up Meije is probably the most difficult of all the major Alpine summits from a technical standpoint. These watercolors by Ernest Hareux, published in Daniel Baud-Bovy's La Meije et les Ecrins (Grenoble, 1907), illustrate the key passage.
Right: Boileau de Castelnau, who gave up mountaineering soon after conquering the Meije.

the Chamonix Aiguilles. It was pure, dizzying rock climbing, enabling Burgener to test his porter Venetz by sending him into difficult passages—given his skill at climbing barefoot, Venetz was dubbed "the Indian." During that first ascent, in fact, all three climbers took off their heavy boots; Mummery scaled the granite cracks and chimneys in his socks. That same summer, Burgener and Mummery climbed the Y-Couloir on Aiguille Verte in record time, starting from the Charpoua Glacier.

The year 1881 was the year of the Grépon. In the Chamonix Valley, the Grépon had a reputation for impregnability. For years, guides and mountaineers had probed for a weak point in the fortress. Then Mummery, Burgener, and Venetz suddenly entered the lists. Their conquest of the north peak was followed, a few days

later, by that of the true summit, constituting the greatest exploit of the whole fifty-year period. Their traverse of the Grépon Arêtes remains a prototype of sustained, difficult, athletic, and vertiginous rock climbing. The crux sequence, the famous Mummery crack, is still considered a classic example of fissure climbing. Over one hundred years later, the Grépon Traverse is still a route that inspires respect.

With his conquest of the Teufelsgrat on Täschhorn, Mummery set his seal on all the great rock routes. Nothing he undertook has subsequently been downgraded much on the scale of difficulties, despite Mummery's own joking comment about the difficulty of an ascent—in ten years he claimed that the Grépon went from being "the most difficult climb in the Alps" to "an easy day for a lady," which was clearly an

exaggeration. His book *My Climbs in the Alps and Caucasus* remains one of the finest mountaineering books ever written, and was bedside reading for climbers for nearly half a century.

Meanwhile, Mummery had left for the Caucasus, where he racked up major successes, to be discussed later. Then he returned to the Alps and, thanks to his experience, began a remarkable series of great ascents "without guide," during which he himself led three or four British partners. Sometimes with his wife, sometimes with G. Hastings and Norman Collie, his most faithful climbing companions, he scaled several peaks: Grands Charmoz in 1892 (that same year he signally failed on the north face of the Aiguille du Plan); in 1893, the first ascent of the Grépon without guide and, above all, the first ascent of the Dent du Requin. After

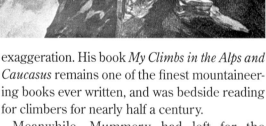

other, equally remarkable exploits, in 1894 he led his party up Mont Blanc via the Brenva Glacier, demonstrating his profound ice skills, acquired during his expeditions to the Caucasus. Mummery would end his brilliant life and career on Nanga Parbat in the Himalayas in 1895, a pioneer right to the end.

It was thanks to Mummery's impetus that the conquest of secondary but difficult Alpine peaks continued, primarily on rock routes. Although Mummery's outstanding qualities overshadowed brilliant climbers like his faithful British companions, two other names constantly appear in the annals of *fin-de-siècle* Alpine mountaineering: Emile Rey and William Coolidge. Rey, a famous guide from Courmayeur, was the "man of a hundred firsts." Even as he climbed countless secondary, rocky spires, Rey

Above: Two more passages on the Meije traverse, illustrated in watercolor by Hareux. On the left is Cheval Rouge, on the right is the sharp Doigt de Dieu Ridge showing Grand Pic and the plunging void of the south face. Left: Henri Duhamel, Boileau de Castelnau's rival in the conquest of the Meije, went on to play a major role in bringing skiing to the Alps.

blazed several highly elegant routes up the southern face of Mont Blanc and was notably the first to climb the Peuterey Arête, after having scaled Peuterey's Aiguille Noire and Aiguille Blanche and the Dames Anglaises (whose garland of granite is the most impressive feature of Mont Blanc seen from the Italian side). Rey sometimes managed to match Burgener's feats, repeating the ascent of the Zmutt Ridge on the Matterhorn.

Coolidge, meanwhile, was an American mountaineer who spent his whole life in the Alps. Along with his aunt, Miss Brevoort, and his dog Tschingel (after whom an Oberland col is named), Coolidge climbed all the peaks from Piz Bernina to the Oisans. He was the most complete of the explorers of the Oisans range, having scoured every sector and indefatigably climbed every summit, teaming up with Christian Almer and later Almer's son, Christian junior. Coolidge ended his days in his Grindelwald chalet opposite the Eiger, snuggled up against the limestone foothills with which he fell hopelessly in love as a young adolescent, heralding his Alpine calling.

The period from 1900 to 1914 was one of sta-

bilization. Great guides flourished in Chamonix and Zermatt, often the offspring of conquering pioneers. But the former were generally content to lead their clients up already-known, if difficult, routes. That was the era of the Simonds and Ravanels in Chamonix, the Perrens, Bieners, and Zurbriggens in Valais. Several names nevertheless stand out: Joseph Ravanel from Chamonix, Franz Lochmatter and Josef Knubel from Sankt Niklaus in the Visp Valley, and Angelo Dibona from the Dolomites.

Mountaineering clients can often bring out a guide's greatest qualities, and thus professional fame sometimes involves an element of luck. Emile Fontaine enabled Joseph Ravanel, called "Red," to demonstrate his worth on the Sans Nom Arête of the Aiguille Verte, on the Ravanel and Mummery needles, and on the famous "Z" that makes it possible to go from the Petit to the Grand Dru without external aids. Similarly, Guido Mayer was certainly responsible for the brilliant career of Dolomite guide Angelo Dibona in the western Alps, where his resounding successes on the southeast ridge of the Dent du Requin, the south face of Meije, and the aiguille that now bears his name in the Oisans, anticipated modern mountaineering by some forty years.

The years from 1910 to 1914, dominated by the strong personality of Franz Lochmatter, the most accomplished guide of the day, were distinguished by two famous climbing teams. The first party comprised Lochmatter (plus his brothers Gabriel and Josef) and the Irish mountaineer Valentine Ryan. The second, equally bril-

Above: A 1901 study in pencil and chalk by mountaineering artist Ernst Platz. Right: Miss Meta Brevoort and the dog Tschingel, two faithful climbing companions to American mountaineer William Coolidge. Far right: E. T. Compton's drawing of Ludwig Purtscheller, cutting steps in 1893.

liant team was composed of Josef Knubel and the British mountaineer Geoffrey Winthrop Young. But what a difference there was in character and method when it came to the Alpine careers of these two incomparable teams, simultaneously active in the Alps.

Ryan is known to have been a cold, haughty, arrogant character, who passed through the Alps like a "comet," during four seasons in which he achieved admirable exploits. But Ryan put himself entirely in his guides' hands—he disliked carrying a knapsack and never wielded an ice ax (cutting steps being a chore, he paid his guides to do it). His attitude was a long way from the affectionate Burgener–Mummery collaboration. Hands in his pockets, but endowed with admirable endurance, he followed his guides without ever taking the least part in determining the route. His talent as a climber was nevertheless indisputable, as testified by the record times taken on the east faces of the Chamonix Aiguilles.

It was in 1905 that the Ryan–Lochmatter team made the first ascent of the Grépon via the east face, taking a route no longer used today, toward the Trou du Canon. In 1906, what Lochmatter declared to be their greatest feat took place on the east ridge of the Aiguille du Plan, where they opened a route that is now known as Ryan Ridge. This majestic, demanding route on rock remains a significant ascent even today.

Still in 1906, Ryan and Lochmatter teamed up with Young and Knubel to climb the south face of Täschhorn, the critical overhang being scaled in desperation by Lochmatter, who truly outdid himself that day. At the same time that Ryan was accomplishing his feats in a brief, four-season career, Young and Knubel were also making sensational ascents. While Lochmatter was clearly the mentor who conceived, directed, and executed the Lochmatter–Ryan ascents, the relationship between Young and Knubel was a different matter. Young was the soul of the team, drawing up plans, choosing routes, thrusting forward the extraordinary climber he had uncovered in the person of Josef Knubel, a modest guide from Sankt Niklaus endowed with transcendent qualities. Young himself was a brilliant figure, of pleasant disposition, and not inclined merely to fol-

low—he often acted as lead climber. He therefore needed a flexible, easy-going partner, and despite his unflagging friendship with Franz Lochmatter, Young realized that the great guide's professional and personal qualities would not tolerate relegation to second climber. Nor would Young himself consent to remain in second position for long.

As for Knubel, he merits credit for the brilliant route he traced in 1911 on the east face of the Grépon, exactly one year after the first ascent had been made. Traversing, at just the right level, the large slabs that had thrown

Above: E. T. Compton's painting of the Vajolet Towers in the Dolomites (oil on canvas, 138 x 93 cm), one of which was conquered in 1877 by the young Georg Winkler. Bottom, left to right: Guide Sepp Innerkofler; climber Hermann von Barth, shown here horrified by the pitons that invaded the Alps after the First World War; Georg Winkler, who died aged eighteen.

Lochmatter off course, he reached the Balfour Gap and completed the ascent via the crack that now bears his name.

Young's credentials are nevertheless dazzling, notably including the Weisshorn and Zinal Rothorn. His finest accomplishments came in the year 1911. On 9 August, in the company of Humphrey Jones and Dr. Karl Blödig (who scaled every single "4,000er" in the Alps, without exception), Young and Knubel made the first ascent of the Brouillard Arête on Mont Blanc, followed by the first descent of the Hirondelles Arête of the Grandes Jorasses, and the first route along the west ridge of the Col des Grandes Jorasses to the summit—a difficult, rocky climb.

As the great worldwide conflict of 1914 began brewing, an era of mountaineering drew to a close. The war would leave a lasting scar in the climbing world, for many mountaineers fell in the defense of their countries. Young was wounded in one leg but, thanks to extraordinary determination and unflagging faith, took up serious climbing again, scaling "4,000ers" in Valais.

During the period from Mummery to Young, a new technique was being forged in the eastern Alps, where pure rock climbers were pitting themselves against apparently impregnable limestone and dolomitic cliffs. Several of these Tyrolean, Bavarian, and Austrian climbers appeared in the western Alps from time to time and it was one of them, Angelo Dibona, who demonstrated that their techniques were well ahead of the outmoded ones still being employed in the west.

Pitons, metal spikes with an eye through which a rope can be passed, were not used in the western Alps. Certain great climbers, like Ryan, gave up on the east ridge of the Grandes Jorasses rather than use pitons in the Rey Fissure. Aid techniques had of course already been used on the imposing aiguilles: guide Joseph Simond

from Chamonix had used a crossbow to fire a rope over the sharp summit of the Aiguille de la République; in 1882, the Sella brothers conquered the Dent du Géant (where Burgener had failed) by using pitons from bottom to top, thanks to help from the Maquignaz brothers, those mason-guides from Breuil who had already placed cables on the Matterhorn. But the standard use of pitons with an eye through which a big steel clip-hook (or "carabiner") could be snapped, in order to hold the rope in case of a fall, was completely unknown.

And yet that was precisely the new technique which would enable mountain climbing to progress. The last remaining problems posed by the Alps were finally resolved thanks to the application of methods developed by Bavarian and Tyrolean climbers. But prior to discussing that stage, it is worth taking a look at what actually happened over by Kaisergebirge, Gesäuse, and the Dolomites.

The second half of the nineteenth century was a period of remarkable increase in the number of mountain climbers in the eastern Alps. Guides and amateurs from towns in Bavaria and Austria—Munich, Linz, Innsbruck, Salzburg, Vienna—were romantic, determined, ingenious aficionados of the mountains, roaming them tirelessly. They accomplished resounding feats on summits that did not draw British climbers, who preferred the taller "4,000ers" to the west. Eastern climbers, faced with the strange, twisted, ravined mountains of the limestone Alps to the north and the Dolomites to the south, were the first to confront vertical walls, minute handholds, awesome overhangs. So right from the start their technique differed from the one used by climbers to the west. They developed a purely acrobatic style, although it was much later that the Italian writer Guido Rey first used the word "acrobatic" for climbing.

In fact, rope techniques remained pretty basic in the rock routes up the Swiss and French Alps: the leader would climb the length of the rope, until he arrived at a platform or spot where he could secure those who followed by passing the rope around a spike of rock. Shoes had nailed soles

Above: This vignette from an old manual shows how the art of climbing managed to develop even prior to the invention of modern protection techniques. Right: Emil Zsigmondy, who died on the south face of the Meije. Facing page: Tragedy on Mont Blanc, *an engraving from* Le Petit Journal, *a periodical that delighted in such disasters.*

The South Face of Duranno,
*a painting by Rudolf
Reschreiter. Prior to the
widespread use of pitons and
carabiners, climbers favored
fissures and chimneys, as
shown here and in the
vignette on the facing page.*

and Burgener did not hesitate to take them off to get up slabs or difficult chimneys. Ice axes had long handles, suitable for cutting steps in a glacier or icy couloir, but impossible to carry in difficult rock climbing situations.

On the vertical limestone walls or in the Dolomites, these western techniques soon proved inadequate. But it was not until the grand period of 1910 to 1914 that rock climbing equipment and techniques were overhauled from top to bottom.

Prior to that date, remarkable men had already proved the worth of the German and Austrian schools of climbing, such as those that emerged from Munich (whose field of action was Kaisergebirge and Wetterstein), Vienna (centered on the Inn gorges, the Gesäuse, with walls over 1,000 meters high), and in the Dolomites, where outstanding guides made rock climbing a specialty. The mountaineers could easily be mixed and matched, since in no other region was there so little difference between guide and client—Innerkofler, Piaz, von Barth, and Purtscheller were like peas in a pod despite their different backgrounds. Tita Piaz accomplished many firsts all alone; Hermann von Barth climbed Karwendel without a guide; Ludwig Purtscheller, as skilled on ice as on rock, was the first to ascend the Cima Piccola di Lavaredo; the young, romantic Georg Winkler went to the very top of the Vajolet Towers; Zsigmondy would be one of the great pioneers on the Meije, losing his life in an attempt via the southern face. Heinrich Pfannl, Paul Preuss, and Hans Pfann enjoyed resounding careers, and Pfann even climbed the Peuterey Arête without a guide!

But their exploits were little known in the western Alps. They were suspected of using shameful methods—of planting pitons with metal rings into the rock! Which is exactly what they did. But to understand their new technique, it must be realized that on limestone or dolomitic cliffs, finding a rocky spike to use as anchor is often impossible, and the steeper the rockface, the greater the distance between potential belay stances. The Austro-German climbers therefore found new solutions to these specific problems.

But it was not really until after 1910 that eastern techniques diverged permanently from the ones used in the Mont Blanc and Valais regions. It was in 1910 that Oscar Eckenstein invented light crampons that could be easily carried in a backpack while climbing rockface, and then taken out and used for passages up icy couloirs. Similarly, he advocated short-handled ice axes. The same year, the Tyrolean guide Hans Fiechtl, who was the theorist of the new school, invented pitons cast as a single piece (i.e., with an eye at one end rather than an attached ring); they were lighter, easier to employ, and were convenient to use with the carabiners invented by Otto Herzog from Munich. Pitons and carabiners provided climbers in the eastern Alps with a new system of protection. There was no longer a need to find a spike of rock since a piton could be hammered into a crack in the middle of a rock wall. By placing pitons at regular intervals, the length of "unanchored" rope between the lead climber and the second was considerably reduced. Furthermore, until that time mountaineers climbed in heavy shoes with nails in the sole; Tita Piaz and Sepp Innerkofler made their first great rock climbs in such footwear. Then Hans Kresz invented lighter shoes with felt soles, called *manchons* (grips), which would reign for thirty years until the arrival of hardened rubber soles.

The tools were being invented, but the technique needed developing. That was the role of Hans Fiechtl, who acquired incomparable mastery in rope handling. He invented a horizontal rapelling (or abseiling) method, known as a pendulum, making it possible to traverse smooth slabs for distances unequaled to that

Below: Heinrich Pfannl from Austria, one of the great nineteenth-century "guideless" climbers. He made the first "clean" ascent of the Aiguille du Géant, eschewing the safety cables placed on the mountain by the Maquignaz brothers in 1888.

date. Fiechtl had a particularly gifted pupil named Hans Dülfer, who applied the principles of horizontal traverse to successfully climb the east wall of Fleischbank in 1912, followed in 1913 by the enormous crack in Fleischbank, now known as Dülferriss.

Obviously, even prior to Dülfer, born climbers like Venetz, Knubel, and Red Ravanel used friction climbing and layback techniques, but no one had yet defined the grand climbing principles that now constitute the basic techniques taught in rock-climbing courses. The strength of German climbers lay precisely in the fact that

not far from their cities they could reach cliffs that served as veritable training grounds. (The systematic teaching of climbing techniques did not begin in France until 1936, the year André Ledoux and I founded the first private school of mountaineering in Chamonix. But the school had to close two years later given the hostility of guides and leading mountaineers, for once united in their opposition. Ice and rock climbing, in those days, was not something one learned—it was a question of experience or supernatural gift!) Dülfer's analysis of the opposition of forces and the distribution of the

Top left: Hans Fiechtl, who pioneered the use of pitons. Bottom left: This photo of Paul Preuss lead-climbing the west face of Totenkirchl in Austria gives a good idea of his skill and audacity. Far right: A gouache by Ernst Platz (1908) showing the risks taken by climbers prior to the use of pitons—a fall by the lead climber would have been catastrophic.

climber's weight and balance led to the development of the "layback" technique (known in French as *dülfer*) in which the feet push in one horizontal direction while the hands pull in the opposite horizontal direction, permitting an upward traction that is far less unpleasant than chimney climbing.

These principles of piton protection and layback traction were first applied by Angelo Dibona, the remarkable guide from Cortina, and his faithful clients and companions, the Mayer brothers. On 25 May 1910, Dibona tested the new method of piton protection on the Gesäuse,

and in 1911 he and the Mayer brothers scaled the north wall of Lalidererwand.

From that point onward, the major rockface problems in the northern limestone Alps were swiftly overcome, and most of the now classic routes in the Dolomites were opened.

Then the First World War broke out.

Innerkofler was killed, the Mayer brothers went bankrupt. Still, it could be argued that climbers of the Bavarian school already possessed a sufficient lead over others to guarantee their future dominance in mountaineering's final international scrambles.

Late nineteenth-century mountaineering artists illustrated now-forgotten aspects of climbing. Today no climber would dream of descending the nearly vertical, grass-covered face of Höfats with ice ax and crampons, as depicted by Ernst Platz (far left). On the other hand, O. Linnekogel's drawing of the Dülfer route on Fleischbank (top) and the hand-over-hand technique illustrated in Dent's manual (bottom) seem perfectly modern.

Climbing between the Wars, 1918–1939

It was the era of "final problems" posed by the Alps—those murderous, invincible north faces that rebuffed the assaults of the finest teams. The Matterhorn, the Grandes Jorasses, and the Eiger were the most dreaded of all.

Wars obviously trigger profound changes in human society. And these changes in attitude and behavior even have an impact on the way people appreciate and climb mountains. New trends have emerged after each cataclysm, affecting the population—some nations are crushed, others are lulled by affluence. If France was almost totally absent from the the vast conquest of the Alps during the golden age, that was above all due to the political instability and revolutionary climate that led to the fall of the Second Empire and the founding of the Third Republic. Once calm returned, France produced top-notch mountaineers like Duhamel, Castelnau, and Fontaine.

As mentioned earlier, on the eve of the First World War British mountaineering was at its height, having imposed its aristocratic, Victorian approach on all the mountain ranges of the world. Yet it has also been pointed out that in the eastern Alps new rock climbing techniques were being forged, based on the use of pitons, carabiners, and stirrups, which made it possible to overcome difficulties that had long seemed insuperable.

Unfortunately, the cataclysm that rocked Europe from 1914 to 1918 prevented the blossoming of these new techniques. It was only after the war ended and borders were reopened that the Austrian and German climbers could apply their methods to the western Alps. The Munich school felt ready to attack the final problems in the Alps; at the same time, political developments like the rise of Nazism in Germany and fascism in Italy encouraged the heroic glorification of youth, ready to sacrifice itself for the honor and glory of its country. The totalitarian nature of the regimes made it easy to channel youthful energy, and it is certainly true that fascism and Nazism gave young people access, via mountaineering schools, to the joys of mountain climbing. The same phenomenon occurred in France during the dark years of the German occupation, when a movement called Jeunesse et Montagne (Mountain Youth) was founded; once the war was over, the purest representatives of contemporary French mountaineering sprang from that movement.

The enthusiasm of German youth for the mountains might suggest that it was interested

Facing page: Just before and after the First World War, mountaineers began attacking the steepest of rockfaces, as documented by artist E. T. Compton, himself a worthy climber. Above: Anderl Heckmair, the Bavarian guide who participated in the first ascent of the notorious north face of the Eiger, the most murderous mountain of the interwar period.

only in public exploits and demonstrations of superhuman superiority. While that may have been true of certain individuals, it should not be forgotten that, long before 1914, mountaineering was the passion of mountain peoples living in Bavaria, the northern and southern Tyrol, Salzkammergut, Carinthia, Styria, and even Vienna. The allied victory in the First World War meant, among other things, that Italians gained access to the southern Tyrol, which became a province of Italy. They thereby acquired the unparalleled playground of the Dolomites, producing an absolutely remarkable flowering of Italian mountaineering in the space of just a few years.

Whereas British mountain climbing stagnated, France underwent a marked revival. In the end, the birth of a movement depends on just a few individuals: there had been Whymper and Mummery, Paul Preuss and Paul Güssfeldt; henceforth there would be Solleder and Lauper, Comici and Cassin, Welzenbach and Merkl. In France, the founding of the Groupe de Haute Montagne (GHM), an elite club in terms of rules and recruitment, brought together the finest of those who climbed "without a guide," and rapidly became the most envied of all mountaineering clubs. The founders were brothers Jacques and Tome de Lépiney, Paul Chevalier,

and Henry Bregeault, soon joined by Jacques Lagarde and Henri de Ségogne.

By attacking the great Alpine problems which, up to that point, had always been resolved thanks to the help of remarkable professional guides, the members of the GHM gave France a leading role in the development of non-professional climbing. The only thing to regret is that they obstinately advocated the purest tradition of British and Swiss mountaineering, which, by overlooking developments in the eastern Alps, slowed the evolution of French mountain climbing by ten years.

During that period in France, two professionals stood out from the crowd—Armand Charlet and Alfred Couttet (dubbed "Champion"). These two exceptional beings were as different as could be in terms of character and approach. Charlet came to the attention of the younger members of the GHM, who admired his exploits when still an amateur. He boasted versatile skills on ice and mixed terrain, as well as being a terrific rock climber. If, during his youth, he had been exposed to eastern Alpine methods, he would certainly have become the finest climber anywhere. Highly attached to the Mont Blanc range, he reinvigorated climbing

Right: Jacques de Lépiney, a founder of the elite Groupe de Haute Montagne, initially closed to guides. Far right: Armand Charlet the greatest guide of his generation, an unequalled master on both ice and rock.

there by turning exceptional routes into classic climbs, and by accomplishing numerous firsts.

Couttet was older and, having fought in the First World War, was weakened physically. It was not until 1923–24 that he was able to climb again. But once under way again, he had a great career. He was naturally drawn to rock climbing, and in addition had an inventive, eclectic mind. His curiosity led him all across the Alps, and he was familiar with every mountain range of Europe, from the Sierra Nevadas to the Tatras. He made frequent trips to the Dolomites, where he noted the use of felt-soled rock shoes (which he introduced at Chamonix), pitons, and carabiners (which he immediately had the Simond firm in Les Bossons begin to manufacture). Couttet had many firsts to his credit, including countless acrobatic little aiguilles, like the Doigt de l'Etala and the Capucins du Requin. He also made major second ascents (République, Deux Aigles). And he guided Miss Fitzgerald on the first complete traverse of the Grandes Jorasses from the Col des Jorasses to the Col des Hirondelles. Couttet should above all be credited for being the first French guide to advocate the systematic use of training cliffs, which he encouraged by cleaning up the Gaillands cliff and opening practice routes that are still used today.

Charlet was known for his exploits, such as taking every imaginable route up the Aiguille Verte and, above all, his incredible 1928 conquest of the Nant-Blanc face of Pic Sans Nom, in partnership with his colleague, the guide Camille Devouassoux. Meanwhile, having climbed every needle on the Diable one by one, Charlet guided Myriam O'Brien and Robert Underhill on a complete traverse of the Aiguilles du Diable, with the help of porter Georges Cachat. It is worth noting that in 1928 Charlet was still unaware of pitons; he used the more risky ice ax anchors and, faithful to his great forerunner and idol Franz Lochmatter, Charlet boldly "free climbed" what were exceptionally long pitches at the time.

In 1927, guides Adolphe and Henri Rey from Courmayeur, along with Evariste Croux, joined the ranks of the finest professional climbers of the day by making difficult routes up the Jorasses and Innominata. Also in 1927, Graham Brown and Frank S. Smythe lent new luster to British mountaineering by forging new routes on the Brenva side of Mont Blanc, notably the Red Sentinel and Major routes. These were remarkable climbs, yet were accomplished using techniques that had not progressed in thirty years.

Above: Hans Lauper, the Swiss climber who scaled the northeast face of the Eiger in 1921. Left: The Brenva slope of Mont Blanc, up which British climber Graham Brown traced three famous routes in 1927—the Red Sentinel, the Major, and the Via della Pera.

Above: Brothers Franz and Toni Schmid arrived from Munich by bicycle and proceeded to conquer the north face of the Matterhorn in 1931. Facing page: The north face of the Matterhorn, composed of mixed ice and rock terrain, is now considered to be less difficult than the other great north faces—yet it remains the most elegant. On the left is the Hörnli Ridge (the line of the "normal route" from Zermatt) and on the right is the bulging Zmutt Nose.

Admiration for the British school marked the style of Hans Lauper, who dominated Swiss mountaineering during that period. Lauper attacked most of the north glacier faces in the Oberland, where he opened a number of remarkable routes, his finest achievement being the 1932 ascent, with Zürcher and guides Alexander Graven and Josef Knubel, of the northeast face of the Eiger. In 1931, Genevan climbers Greloz and Roch successfully climbed the north face of the Triolet.

Meanwhile, new mountaineers were beginning to challenge the traditional approach to climbing in the western Alps. As early as 1923, the Bavarian mountain climber Welzenbach used ice pitons, thereby scaling, with his partner Merkl, numerous north faces in the Bernese Oberland. Welzenbach remained Lauper's main rival until 1933.

However, the moment had arrived when the last three big challenges of the day could—or should—be confronted: the north face of the Matterhorn, the north face of the Eiger, and the north face of the Grandes Jorasses. These three problems were ultimately resolved by new arrivals to the scene.

The use of pitons was beginning to spread. The resounding conquest of the northwest face of Punta Civetta in 1925 by Emil Solleder and Lettenbauer revealed the possibilities of the new technique. The Germans had used pitons moderately, of course, but the technique still enabled the climbers to scale the 1,200 meters (4,000 ft.) of reputedly impregnable wall. The same methods led, in 1929, to victory over the south pillar of Marmolada.

In 1930 came the first great achievement due to the use of new methods in the Mont Blanc region. Brendel and Schaller scaled the southern ridge of the Aiguille Noire, representing a whole new level of difficulty in rock climbing. People were beginning to realize that the new techniques would considerably extend the limits of the "possible".

In 1931, taking advantage of heavy snow that held the rocks in place, Toni and Franz Schmid climbed the north face of the Matterhorn, meeting little resistance. Only the Grandes Jorasses and the Eiger held out. Those battles would be a lot tougher.

Also in 1931, a great star appeared in the mountaineering firmament. It shone for a long time, a beacon of human boldness. That star was Italian mountaineer Emilio Comici. To the great benefit of Italian mountaineering, Comici was not only a remarkable climber but also a peerless teacher. The Bavarian technique was already well developed, but it was Comici who perfected the method and gave it its current form. Furthermore, Comici accompanied his achievements with a concern for elegance and aesthetics that lent an almost perfect form to his routes. His famous phrase was that a route should be "straight like a falling drop of water!" He applied it in 1931 to the Civetta by tracing the most direct route, *la direttissima*. And he did not simply "straighten" known routes by linking them with several connecting pitches, as is too often done today. Comici's *direttissime* were great new routes from beginning to end. Comici thus inaugurated the sixth degree of difficulty, the highest rating on the Bavarian scale.

But the world's first sixth-degree climber thought he could do better. So in 1933, he attacked the north face of the Cima Grande di Lavaredo, an overhang for 220 meters (700 ft.). Steiger and Paula Wiesinger had managed to scale only eighty meters of it. Comici climbed it using "aid" techniques—stirrups, swings, hanging bivouacs (affixed to the ceilings of overhangs). It was an entirely new universe "beyond the vertical," as French climber Georges Livanos would later put it so well.

Also during that period, in Comici's wake there emerged an excellent school of climbers from the Dolomites. Names that would become famous began cropping up in chronicles, as the exploits of Riccardo Cassin, Gino Soldà, and Giusto Gervasutti became known. Having trained on limestone peaks, these climbers would apply their methods to major challenges in the western Alps.

Thus in 1934 Gervasutti and Lucien Devies climbed the northwest face of Olan, some 1,100 meters high. In 1935 Pierre Allain and Raymond Leininger conquered the north face of the

Climbing techniques of the 1930s as illustrated by a German manual. Left: A rope traverse to negotiate a smooth slab. Right: Protection techniques—the second climber, at the belay stance, wraps the rope around his shoulder, while the lead climber protects himself from a potential fall by driving pitons into the rock. In those days their lightweight rock boots usually had felt soles.

Drus, even as Gervasutti and Devies tamed the north face of Ailefroide. (These were also the years when the conquest of the north face of the Grandes Jorasses was underway; it will be discussed later as a key example of the achievements of the interwar years.)

Victory over the north face of the Drus brought to the fore a group of climbers who epitomized a new spirit. Quietly, during several years, they had been preparing for their exploits by training intensively on the boulders in the forest of Fontainebleau, outside Paris. Practicing on Lilliputian boulders just a few meters high caused smirks in some circles, but the Parisian mountaineers developed muscles and fingers of steel, as well as a virtuosity of style that surpassed in difficulty the highest ratings of the day. These climbing exercises were also accessible to all, thereby encouraging mass participation in French mountaineering, which until that time had been somewhat limited to the affluent classes. The leader of the Fontainebleau school was Pierre Allain. He had his own ideas about mountain climbing, and dared to pronounce the word competition, which had been hypocritically censored from all accounts of exploits. And yet what had been taking place in the preceding years if not a veritable sporting competition between nations, a

competition in which a pure love of mountains, while perhaps still strong among a few individuals, was inevitably relegated to the background? Allain and his disciples were among the first climbers to break the "sixth-degree" barrier. Their fingers of steel and their exceptionally bold free climbing would certainly have taken them even farther in racking up new victories if war had not intervened once again.

Not, however, before another major difficulty was vanquished: the north face of Piz Badile, an imposing granite chute. It was scaled by Italian climbers of the Lecco school—henceforth, all great climbers would emerge from one of the great Alpine training grounds—namely Riccardo Cassin, Gino Esposito, and Vittorio Ratti, who drew Valsecchi and Molteni in their wake. The latter two had incautiously undertaken a challenge too tough for them, and would die of exhaustion in the blizzard that struck during the descent.

By 1939, war was nigh. But it did not prevent Ratti and Vitali from conquering the west face of the Aiguille Noire by using aid techniques to overcome the notorious granite overhang.

Meanwhile, the remaining problems posed by the Alps were finally being resolved: the north face of the Eiger and north face of the Grandes Jorasses. It is worth dwelling on both of these

resounding exploits, which brought the conquest of the Alps to a kind of close. They sum up the technical progress made in mountaineering techniques that made such victories possible.

The North Face of the Grandes Jorasses

Bounded to the east by the Col des Hirondelles and a ridge of the same name, and to the west by the Col des Grandes Jorasses and the Mont-Mallet Glacier, the north face of the Grandes Jorasses forms a two-kilometer frontier between France and Italy. The imposing wall rises 1,200 meters (4,000 ft.) above the Leschaux Glacier to the highest peak, Pointe Walker (4,208 m), and some 1,000 meters to the central summit, Pointe Croz Spur (4,108 m). Between the Walker and Croz spurs leading to their respective pinnacles, a large central couloir, usually of hard ice but constantly bombarded by falling rocks, seemed to present a possible route up. Farther west, is a third pinnacle, Pointe Young (4,000 m), but its location on the edge of Mont-Mallet Glacier placed it beyond the routes sought by climbers.

It was in 1907 that the famous team of Geoffrey Winthrop Young and Josef Knubel made the first known attempt on the north face, perhaps with little conviction, given the usual tenacity of that incomparable pair—presumably they were led there by a simple sense of curiosity. Similarly, Valentine Ryan and Franz Lochmatter had unsuccessfully attacked the north face of the Drus three years earlier. For those kings of free climbing, who eschewed any use of pitons, such walls held no appeal. In 1911, on the other hand, Young, Humphrey Jones, and Knubel would make the first complete traverse of the Col des Grandes Jorasses to Pointe Walker, climbing hard, fifth-degree passages on the 4,000-meter pinnacle.

For the people in Chamonix, the north face of the Grandes Jorasses epitomized "impregnability." It was constantly in view from Montenvers, that rendezvous of the international mountaineering set. Climbers often approached it on their way to the Couvercle or Leschaux huts and some climbers must have dreamed of scaling it, they also must have realized that they were dreaming. Not merely vertical but actually overhanging, the kilometer-high granite cliff was rarely "in good condition": on only a few days per year, during the dry summer, would the rocks shed their film of ice—which merely increased the danger of falling rocks.

It was in 1928 that the first serious attempt was made, by the famous Chamonix guide Armand Charlet, who seemed to have shrugged off

Other typical 1930s images from the same manual, with, on the right, a detailed shot of equipment used at the time: harness, loops of hemp rope, steel pitons and carabiners, wooden stirrups, and hammer. Following double page: The north face of the Grandes Jorasses and the Leschaux Cirque as seen from an airplane, with the fine Périades Aiguilles in the foreground.

superstition and dared to think that the terrible wall might prove vulnerable. He was seconded by a young guide from Courmayeur, Evariste Croux, and his experienced "clients": Zanetti, Rand Herron (who would be killed by a fall from the Great Pyramid in Egypt), and Gasparetto.

Charlet benefited from youthful boldness. Backed by mountaineering circles, and especially by the GHM, he had already accomplished numerous exploits and his resounding victory on the Nant-Blanc face of Pic Sans Nom ranked him among the best—some people said he was *the* best. But Charlet respected the traditions of his elders; he did not trouble himself with pitons, ignored the potential of carabiners, was able to free climb pitches of over thirty meters in nail-soled shoes with no protection and, when the overhang became too extreme, used risky ice axe holds. Above all, he was the best crampon climber of his day.

It has been asserted that he was the only French guide at the time capable of making an attempt on the Grandes Jorasses. But that overlooks the fact that between 1928 and 1935 another Chamonix guide was enjoying his heyday—Couttet "the Champion," the finest rock specialist. In 1930, on that very same Grandes Jorasses, he made the first complete traverse from the Col des Jorasses to the Col des Hirondelles, in the company of Miss Fitzgerald and Anatole Bozon. He specialized in short but extremely difficult rock climbs; he was also skillful at throwing a rope, which enabled him to tri-umph over the Doigt de l'Etala, République, and Deux Aigles, of which he made the second ascents. Unlike Charlet, who operated exclusively in the Mont Blanc area and made his name on mixed ice and rock routes, Couttet traveled a great deal; as pointed out earlier, he learned how to use pitons and carabiners in the Dolomites, which he introduced into France along with notions of how to teach climbing techniques.

So why did Couttet not enter the lists? Quite simply because of his "clients." For a guide, and especially for a guide in those days, the first and foremost priority was to build up a clientele. The second priority was to keep it. Couttet had a rich, notably American, clientele that included some great mountaineers, like the Washburn brothers, Edwards, and Miss Fitzgerald. To avoid disappointing them, one day he declined to accompany Prince Leopold, heir to the Belgian throne. Couttet was haughty and proud—like Charlet, for that matter. They were two extraordinary figures. And it is conceivable that had they teamed up to solve the problem of the north face, they would have succeeded without much difficulty, given Charlet's confidence in rocky "crampon" terrain and Couttet's virtuosity on smooth slabs and cracks. But it was inconceivable, at the time, for two such lively rivals to team up. Like Franz Lochmatter, both were not only lead climbers but also expedition leaders— they decided on the climbs and routes to be undertaken by the clients. Furthermore, at that

One man more than any other embodied the flair of Dolomite climbers—Emilio Comici from Trieste. These shots illustrate his mastery of both free and aid climbing.

time, the spirit of pure enthusiasts was not shared by guides, except perhaps for Charlet, who was influenced by his relationship with the members of the GHM. And yet Couttet already displayed that spirit in another fashion: he willingly took along youths from the valley to teach them the routes. But he also saved the exploits for his clients.

I also feel—as I frankly told my friend and mentor Charlet himself—that his inexplicable retreat after various unsuccessful attempts cannot be explained by poor weather alone! I think that after his rapid, far-reaching reconnaissance climb in 1935 with Fernand Bellin, he could have gone on and finished before the gathering storm broke. The two men were the fastest in the region on difficult terrain, and would have measured up to task. Once certain of victory, however, Charlet, ever the astute guide, probably hoped to save this resounding accomplishment for one of his clients, just as Carrel had done on the Matterhorn.

From 1928 to 1934, Charlet made five unsuccessful attempts on the Grandes Jorasses. So it is hardly surprising that no other French climber tried an ascent where the best among them had failed. And yet, if only Pierre Allain . . .

The 1928 assault by Charlet's team enabled them to reach the base of the Walker Spur. On the first try, they opted for the most direct route. Unfortunately, the granite wall is relentlessly vertical—they were unsettled by smooth slabs with no apparent holds, by cracks longer than anything they were used to confronting.

On 1 July 1931, a Munich team made its appearance. Anderl Heckmair was not only an eminent rock climber, but also had formidable crampon skills. With a clear disregard for the obvious danger, he and his partner Kröner attacked the central couloir of ice between the two spurs. They reached a point 100 meters above the bergschrund, then retreated. On 8 August, Brehm and Rittler also headed up the central couloir. They were killed by falling rocks; Heckmair and Kröner, on their second try on 13 August, found the lifeless bodies of their companions, and turned back. That same year, Toni Schmid, who conquered the north face of the Matterhorn, also made an attempt, once again via the central couloir and base of Walker Spur.

Victory over the famous north face came to resemble an international competition in 1932, a year of numerous attempts. First there was Bratschko, then guides Binel and Crétier accompanying Boccalatte and Chabod, all from Valle d'Aosta; then came guides L. Carrel and P. Maquignaz with Benedetti and Crétier; and finally two more attempts by Armand Charlet, the first with P. Dilleman, the second with Couturier. But none of these various attempts got any further than the foot of the base, for, with the exception of the Munich climbers, none of them were familiar with the piton technique being developed in the Dolomites.

Far left: The famous Tre Cime di Lavaredo, featuring, from right to left, Cima Ovest, Cima Grande, and the Punta di Frida/Cima Piccolissima/Cima Piccola group. Left: Riccardo Cassin working on the notorious fifty-meter traverse between two rows of overhangs during the first ascent of the north face of Cima Ovest in 1935.

In 1933, Otto Welzenbach went to examine the north face, without result. But that was the year great progress would be made, thanks to a reconnaissance climb up the central spur by two Italian mountaineers, Gervasutti and Zanetti. They reached an altitude of 3,500 meters but were overtaken by a storm before reaching the central snow field on the Croz Spur, yet came away convinced that the feat was henceforth possible. Less high and less difficult—although presenting passages rated grade V in difficulty—the central spur could, indeed, be "free" climbed; despite the sheer verticality of certain slabs, it was within reach of great western climbers like Charlet.

On 5 July 1934, Charlet attacked once more, but this time he ignored the Walker Spur and followed Gervasutti's itinerary. He was climbing with Robert Greloz from Geneva, famous for the first descent from the north face of the Petit Dru. They reached the height of 3,600 meters, then made a sudden and rather inexplicable retreat—Charlet was reportedly halted by the smooth slabs just below the snowfield. On 9 and 10 July, Raymond Lambert and Loulou Boulaz from Geneva made an unsuccessful attempt on the same central spur. On 28 July, Meier and Steinauer followed Lambert's route up the left side of the large couloir, swept by falling rocks—no luck.

Finally, on 30 July 1934, a full-scale attack was mounted on the central spur, henceforth recognized as offering a possible route to the top. That day, German climbers Haringer and Peters, who bivouacked the previous night halfway between the towers and the central snow field, were overtaken by Chabod and Gervasutti, who had no intention of abandoning victory in the route he had discovered. Another Austrian team was also making an attempt, though with little hope of success. Finally, sensing the threat, Charlet and his colleague Fernand Bellin, a veritable rockface acrobat and an amazingly swift climber, set out that same day and soon overtook everyone, reaching 3,500 meters by noon. Just then, foul weather threatened. Given the swiftness of Charlet and Bellin, it might be regretted that they did not

push on, reaching the ridge before the really bad weather hit. However, only the mountaineer actually confronted with a given problem is competent to judge—their decision was probably the fruit of wisdom. The other parties followed suit and turned back, except for Haringer and Peters, who displayed a sovereign contempt for danger and death by carrying on. That evening they reached the snowfield, having detected a passage in the fissured slabs—difficult, perhaps, but within the reach of climbers like Bellin and Charlet.

On the 31st, the storm completely closed over the mountain, bringing snow, fog, and cold. The two Germans turned back. Haringer was killed, and Peters alone returned on 2 August, having spent five days and four nights on the face. But he brought back a valuable secret, for he had found a solution to the crux sequence and knew that victory was now within his grasp.

The summer of 1935 was therefore decisive. Peters teamed up with his compatriot, Meier, and the two attacked the central spur once more on 29 June. But they were not alone.

French mountaineers Frendo and Chaix, who had long hovered around the north face, spent the night at Leschaux where, unsurprisingly, they bumped into Genevan climbers Robert Greloz and André Roch, who had also entered the lists. But luck was not on their side. Greloz, who was already familiar with the first few hundred meters of the face, was out front. Idiotically, he dislocated his shoulder; Frendo and Chaix demonstrated a sporting attitude by giving up on their attempt to help Roch get his partner back down the slope.

Peters and Meier pursued their climb up the central spur. Peters was on familiar territory, and came across the rusty pitons he had planted the previous summer. That evening, the two men bivouacked on the summit.

It was then that two other parties, unaware of the German victory, simultaneously attacked the central spur on 1 and 2 July. First there was Raymond Lambert and the courageous Loulou Boulaz, both from Geneva, followed by the indefatigable Chabod and Gervasutti. They soon realized that the Germans had preceded them.

Above, left: The Aiguille du Dru. The Allain route up the north face followed the borderline between sun and shadow. Top right: The boulders at Fontainebleau enabled Allain to acquire unmatched climbing skills. Bottom right: Pierre Allain and Raymond Leininger on their return from the conquest of the Drus.

The Walker Spur has become a classic climb. Seen from a helicopter is the crux sequence up a ninety-meter dihedral (corner) on a fine summer's day—the climbers have to line up!

But both teams managed, after a bivouac, to get very near to the summit of Pointe Croz, accounting for the second and third ascents of that route, repeated yet again on 7, 8, and 9 July by Austrians Toni Messner and Ludwig Steinauer.

Once the central spur was conquered, it seems there was a certain respite. Two years would pass before anyone seriously considered attacking the Walker Spur. In fact, although the north face had indeed been ascended, the finest, most original, most direct route—leading to the 4,208-meter Pointe Walker—remained absolutely virgin, all attempts having halted at the base of the granite spur. But Walker Spur could only be scaled by mountaineers with solid piton skills.

Nevertheless, it could have fallen to French climbers. In 1937, Pierre Allain and Édouard Frendo arrived at the foot of the rocks and seriously studied possible routes up them. On 1 August, Allain and Raymond Leininger, who were not only highly refined and athletic climbers, having trained at Fontainebleau, but also decent piton technicians, finally got past the lower band of slabs and climbed a thirty-meter. crack—graded VI in difficulty—with the help of numerous pitons. Above that point, the rocks were covered in ice, and the climbers unshrewdly decided to wait for better conditions. They felt confident that victory would be theirs, because there were no other specialists in the western Alps who could overcome the difficulties they had encountered. Since they were primarily rock climbers, they preferred a dry wall. Whatever the case, they were truly the first to have overcome the lower barrier of the Walker Spur.

That same day, three heavily laden climbers from Lecco—Cassin, Esposito, and Tizzoni—descended the Géant Glacier heading in the direction of Leschaux. They had absolutely no experience of the western Alps. On the other hand, Cassin was considered to be one of the leading specialists in high dolomitic walls, notably tracing a bold route up the north face of Cima Ovest di Lavaredo. Above all, he also made the dramatic first ascent of the northeast face of Piz Badile, a granite peak in the

Bregaglia Valley. His familiarity with using pitons on granite—technically quite different from use on limestone and dolomite—was a valuable asset for Cassin.

But what really made the difference between Cassin and Charlet or Allain was not the climber's intrinsic virtuosity, but rather the spirit in which the rockface was attacked. Guides from Chamonix had difficulty envisaging bivouacs on the face, just as they avoided carrying a heavy load. Charlet, Couttet, and Bellin were extremely rapid—they attacked and either succeeded or failed, but whatever the outcome they immediately returned to the valley. They took only the bare necessities with them, carrying neither pitons, carabiners, nor warm bivouac garments, preferring to walk through the night rather than halt. Thus Fernand Tournier spent a whole night climbing down the south face from the Col du Fou to the Envers des Aiguilles rather than bivouac on the spot. But this attitude was no longer shared by the likes of Pierre Allain, who, as an amateur, could afford to take his time, not having clients waiting below. Allain nevertheless still followed the western approach to a given wall or face, which entailed finding a weak point, skirting difficulties, angling upwards—just as his great predecessors such as Ryan, Lochmatter, and Knubel had done on routes up the Mer de Glace face of the Aiguilles.

Cassin, on the other hand, came from the realm of sheer verticality. He was in the habit of craning his neck as far as it would go to discern a path over imposing overhangs. It mattered little whether the sheer verticality continued for 300 or 1,200 meters; the method of attack was always the same—climb straight up, driving pitons where necessary, not seeking to skirt left or right. The necessary equipment was hauled along, including bivouac material.

The three Italians, then, attacked the Walker Spur directly. Ignoring the route taken first by

Top: Riccardo Cassin on the cliffs above Lecco. Bottom, left to right: Gino Esposito, Riccardo Cassin, and Ugo Tizzoni returning from the Walker Spur, 7 August 1938.

Charlet and then by Allain, which was never more severe than a grade IV rating, they climbed straight up the edge of the spur along a fissure seventy meters long, graded VI (but rarely followed since then). They installed their first bivouac above that point. Then, with a highly precise sense of their route, they continued to angle very slightly along the edge, scaling many passages graded V and VI. In certain spots, layers of ice covered the granite slabs, on which they used the same piton technique. Things went well on 5 August and they bivouacked again above the notorious pendulum traverse that makes retreat impossible in the event of difficulty or bad weather. They were two-thirds of the way up the spur. That is precisely where the structure and icy condition of the rock incite climbers to seek a passage to the right, that is to say in the upper part of the central couloir, for the spur is composed at that point of a long series of gray and black slabs covered with a thin layer of ice, barred by apparently impassable overhangs. But Cassin was not mistaken in thinking that the route lay in precisely that direction, that he had to get back to the edge of the spur at all costs, and not be tempted by an apparently easy exit. Even today it seems an amazing decision, especially after the dramatic escape via the terribly sheer slopes to the right which was made in 1946 by Lionel Terray and Louis Lachenal.

Cassin and his team bivouacked on the summit on the night of 6 August. They were back in Courmayeur by the 7th.

They came, they saw, they conquered. It was a magnificent, flawless victory, representing the triumph of a technique that would henceforth be as appreciated in the western Alps as in the east. Cassin had just demonstrated that nothing was impossible and that granite, contrary to common belief, was as amenable to pitons as limestone. Their route would not be repeated until 1945, by Édouard Frendo and Gaston Rébuffat.

In the meantime, war had broken out again.

In 1937, Mathias Rebitsch (seen above in the Hinterstoisser Traverse) and Ludwig Vörg, after spending 112 hours on the face, were the first climbers to descend the Eigerwand alive.

The Northwest Face of the Eiger, 1938

The northwest face of the Eiger—or Eigerwand—is one of the most sharply hewn faces in the limestone Alps to the north. The base is over one and a half kilometers long while the cliffs rise nearly a mile high, forming the side of a regular pyramid that curves slightly inward at the center where a network of thin couloirs meets several snowfields. Everything else is steeply vertical, even overhanging.

An early attempt on the Eigerwand, in 1929, came to a swift end. The hour had not yet struck and even though the northeast face of the imposing pyramid had been scaled in 1932 by Hans Lauper, Josef Knubel, and Alexander Graven, a kind of taboo hung over the great northwest face of limestone, darkened by water from melting snow. Depending on the year, it could be covered in layers of ice or bombarded by rocks loosened by a thaw. The rather shattered rock is not conducive to climbing, for nowhere does it offer serious holds and, even though never extremely difficult from a technical standpoint, the route is always highly exposed given the difficulty of driving pitons and establishing protection. I have solicited the reactions of several mountaineers who have climbed the northwest face, including Lachenal, Terray, Rébuffat, and Leroux, and all agree that climbing the Eiger is unpleasant. Aversion apparently grows after having made the ascent, and there is no desire to repeat the feat. Weather conditions are everything on this immense face: if the cliff is dry, the climbing is easier but the objective dangers increase in the middle sector; if the cliff is snowy or icy, the climbing becomes dangerous and extremely tricky. With this type of ascent, it is very difficult to grade the degree of difficulty—every ascent is a unique case, and cannot be compared to others.

Munich climbers Max Sedlmayer and Karl Mehringer were the first, in 1935, to make a serious attack on the gigantic face. They started almost straight below the summit. During the day of 21 August they reached the base of a bulging wall and, after having started up it, bivouacked at around 2,900 meters just below the overhangs, which they would spend all the

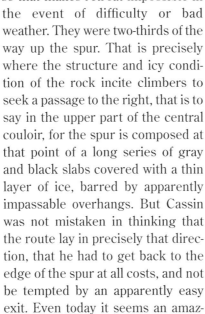

*The north face of the Eiger.
The Hinterstoisser Traverse
is located right at the line
between shadow and sun, on
the rocky wall forming the
base of the second snowfield
(which is in full sun at the
center of the face).*

Historic photos of the first ascent of the Eigerwand. Left: Fritz Kasparek on the first snowfield. Right: A belay on the ramp.

next day surmounting. Exhausted, they spent another night on the first snowfield. It was a very cold night which must have hit them hard, for the next day they made slow progress, bivouacking in the upper part of the second snowfield. The fourth day, the face was shrouded in fog, but when a hole briefly opened observers in Kleine Scheidegg spotted them just reaching the third snowfield, at an altitude of 3,200 meters. They were never seen again.

Although this tragic failure made a big impression on people, it proved nothing. The extremely slow progress of the two men in the middle section was hard to explain. Experienced mountaineers thought—rightly—that things became complicated higher up, where the cliffs steepened again and the icy couloirs converged on a snowfield called "the Spider," a focal point for all the falling rocks but the only possible route.

Nevertheless, in 1936 other German mountaineers renewed the attack. They were all young, excellent climbers on rock, though not necessarily on ice. Once again, however, the Eiger was covered in snow. They went ahead, driven by an irresistible force; it was a crucial year for the Nazis, who were hosting the Berlin Olympic Games. The over-excited Hitler Youth racked up exploit after exploit, and this great first ascent had to be claimed for the fatherland! In referring to the deaths on the Eiger, one of these youths even claimed: "Giving one's life that way is the most perfect of transgressions."

The climbers readying themselves at the foot of the Eiger were Herbst, Teufel, Andreas Hinterstoisser, and Toni Kurz from Berchtesgaden (the Führer's favorite retreat), plus Edi Rainer and Willy Angerer from Innsbruck. While waiting for the best conditions, Herbst and Teufel warmed up on a secondary north face, which they successfully scaled; but a fall during the descent killed Teufel and seriously wounded Herbst. In normal times, the other climbers would have cancelled their attempt after such an accident. But to the contrary, it seemed to have stimulated the desire to conquer at any cost. The Munich and Tyrolean climbers teamed up, henceforth linking their fates.

On 12 July, given the tragic outcome of the previous year's attempt, the attack was launched farther to the right, toward the Rote Fluh. Right away, Hinterstoisser found a weakness in the armor—they rose quickly, only to halt at the foot of impossibly steep slopes. But they were already higher than the rocky central band that had cost their predecessors a whole day's work. As a worthy heir to Dülfer, fully mastering the eastern Alpine technique, Hinterstoisser employed horizontal rappels to make an angled traverse as far as the first snowfield. All subsequent attempts would follow this route and the pendulum sequence was dubbed the "Hinterstoisser Traverse" after its initiator. But every coin has a flip side: once the traverse was complete and the climbers had recovered the ropes, their line of retreat was cut off. They shrugged off the risk, however, and continued to climb. Angerer suffered a head wound from a falling rock, but by the evening of the first day they had already reached an altitude of 3,200 meters, covering in one day what had taken Sedlmayer and his partner three.

On the second day, the fog closed in. Progress was slow. Although good on rock, the climbers were less experienced on ice. From the valley they could sometimes be glimpsed thanks to a break in the fog, and it was realized that tragedy was brewing: at the rate they were going, they would never make it to the summit. They would have to turn back.

Rescue efforts were already being organized. But on the third day, they were seen continuing up to the base of the upper neck where Sedlmayer and Mehringer had disappeared. Only then did the young climbers give up. The wounded Angerer had to be slowly lowered by his companions. A fifty-meter passage between the two snowfields took four hours. They reached Sedlmayer's second bivouac. The weather worsened. They descended toward Rote Fluh and arrived at the edge of the smooth sheer slab they had traversed earlier by using the artifice of an angled downwards rappel. Climbing back up it was impossible. They were trapped.

Just when things seemed desperate, a guard from the Jungfrau railroad made voice contact

On the upper part of the face, four climbers were hit by bad weather, making the final pitches on snow-covered rock extremely tricky.

with them through the window of a small tunnel used to evacuate material. He thought they were home free. But when, several hours later, the worried guard called again, he was answered by anxious cries for help—a heavy storm had risen. Some two hundred meters separated the climbers from the opening: on one side was life, on other, death. But between the two was the notorious "Hinterstoisser Traverse."

The alarm was raised. Swiss guides, who had sworn never again to become involved in hopeless attempts, forsook their oath and thought only of the human lives at stake. They exited by the Eiger Station window and, through the blizzard, managed to get within 100 meters of the unfortunate lads. Only Toni Kurz was still alive. The blizzard deepened, night fell. The guides retreated to their tunnel, returning to the same spot the next day. Kurz was still alive, standing on a tiny outcrop. Hinterstoisser had fallen, Angerer died of cold, and Rainer was dangling, strangled by the rope.

Kurz still had enough strength to tie ends of rope together and toss it to the guides, who thereby managed to get ropes, pitons and carabiners to him so that he could descend by rappel. Unfortunately, he attached himself to the rope by looping it through a carabiner. And the awful tragedy was that the carabiner could not slide past the knot tying the two ropes. His descent was blocked in mid-air! Kurz made a last, desperate struggle, as snow fell all about him. Then, suddenly, he hung lifeless on the end of the rope.

Thus ended the first great tragedy on Eiger.

That year, the local government in Berne outlawed any ascent of the Eigerwand. It was understood that Swiss rescue teams would no longer go into action under any circumstances. The decree was revoked at the request of

These two photos of the same spot near the top of the Eiger's second snowfield were taken fifty years apart. Right: Ludwig Vörg. Far right: Pierre-Alain Steiner during a winter ascent.

renowned mountaineers. As to rescue missions, the same story always repeats itself. Every time they are needed, rescue teams go into heroic, fraternal action. Twenty-one years later, a rescue mission on the Eiger resulted in the largest ever international gathering of rescuers and succeeded in saving the Italian climber Corti from death.

German attacks on Eigerwand were renewed in 1937, despite moral disapproval and strong opposition from Swiss mountaineering circles. A great deal of publicity was guaranteed to anyone who camped at the foot of the dreaded face, and many amateurs took advantage of the fact to have their names bandied about.

Alongside all the phonies, however, were two remarkable mountain climbers from Munich, Mathias Rebitsch and Ludwig Vörg. They meticulously prepared their ascent. During one preparatory climb, they equipped the one-way traverse, which they officially dubbed "Hinterstoisser." After three weeks of poor weather, they set out once again. Thanks to their familiarity with the route and the ropes they had left in place, they bivouacked beyond the traverse. The next day, they attacked the mid-level snowfields. Vörg possessed remarkable glacier skills and both men were all-round, highly fit mountaineers. Yet they were slowed considerably by difficulties on the ice and by the water cascading down the couloirs. A second attempt led them above to the right of the highest, fatal point reached by Sedlmayer, when a break in the fog suggested that worse weather was on the way. After a second bivouac, they turned back and tirelessly worked their way down the snowfields, reaching the first bivouac above the Hinterstoisser Traverse. They still hoped that the weather might break in their favor. But at any rate they were confident, for they had done preparatory work on the traverse

and, thanks to those basic precautions, were certain they could redescend. Which is what they did the next day, having spent 112 hours on the cliffs.

Their attempt was the first to be conducted by resolute, confident climbers skilled in all mountaineering techniques on both ice and rock, and for whom an ascent of the northwest face of the Eiger would not depend on luck or the sublime inspiration that drove their unfortunate young compatriots ever higher. At any rate, their return demonstrated that retreat was possible for highly experienced climbers. Although the attempt by Rebitsch and Vörg was unsuccessful, it meant that the Eigerwand was henceforth ripe for the picking.

And yet in 1938, two Italians, Menti and Sandri, would die at the fateful altitude of 3,200 meters, that is to say at the foot of the unconquered upper third of the rockface, composed of 650 steep meters of slope hollowed in the middle by the Spider snowfield.

In July of that year, however, just a few weeks after the tragic failure of the Italians, two teams of climbers from Munich and Vienna entered the lists. The Munich mountaineers were Anderl Heckmair (a veteran known not only for a failed attempt on the north face of the Grandes Jorasses, but also for brilliant achievements on rock and ice) and Ludwig Vörg, Mathias Rebitsch's partner, who had already climbed two-thirds of the face and returned to tell the tale. From Vienna came Heinrich Harrer (who would subsequently spend seven extraordinary years climbing in Tibet) and Fritz Kasparek.

At first, the two parties climbed independently. But as Harrer and Kasparek were climbing up the wall toward the second snowfield, Heckmair and Vörg, who had turned back the evening before, started back up again and caught up with the Viennese climbers somewhere around the third snowfield. From that point on the two teams roped their fates together. They reached the Sedlmayer point and then, heading left, discovered a passage called the Ramp, a chimney-couloir that offers access to the upper slope, just as the Hinterstoisser Traverse was the key to the mid-

level snowfields. They bivouacked, wet and frozen, at 3,400 meters, which represented a major feat for Heckmair and Vörg, who had climbed the whole way in a single day.

The next day, they encountered severe difficulties on the upper slope, for the cold night had transformed the day's torrents into over-

hanging blocks of ice. They finally reached the Spider, the last snowfield below the couloirs leading to the summit. Avalanches crashed down, nearly sweeping them away. Kasparek was injured. They managed to get above the Spider, and bivouacked on the sheer rockface, hanging from pitons.

Two days later, on 24 July 1938, after having struggled with desperate energy through a snowstorm and against successive avalanches, they reached the summit around 3:30 p.m.

The northwest face of the Eiger had fallen.

Not until after the Second World War would additional attempts to scale that formidable face be made—some successful, some not.

The four conquerors of the north face of the Eiger on their return. Facing page: Climbing the final snowfield.

The French to the Fore, 1940–1960

New equipment, different ideas—postwar mountaineering

proved that no wall could resist the march of pitons.

It also showed, in the Alps, that the realm of the unknown

was constantly shrinking.

The interwar period had demonstrated the indisputable merits of Austro–German–Italian climbers and of the eastern school of mountaineering, which involved the use of pitons not only for protecting the climber in case of a fall, but also as a "means of progression" on vertical walls. It also meant improved equipment—ropes, pitons, and, above all, boots.

It was just before 1939 that Vitale Bramani developed his famous boots with hardened rubber soles that had a tire-tread grip. Bramani initially designed them as ski boots for winter mountaineering, but their use swiftly became general. At the outbreak of the Second World War these "Vibram" soles were still unknown in France. Instead, very light, sneaker-like shoes—developed notably by Pierre Allain—were worn for rock climbing.

These, however, were totally inappropriate for hiking on mixed terrain. It was only from 1945 onward that the use of shoes with hard rubber soles, usable on both ice and rock, became widespread.

Starting in 1950, after the great Himalayan experiments and wartime research, nylon ropes finally replaced the ones made of hemp. Nylon meant lighter, thinner, stronger ropes and, above all, increased flexibility in snow, ice and wet conditions. Prior to that point, bad weather made rope maneuvers more dangerous because cold and moisture would make hemp stiff and heavy. With nylon, those problems were a thing of the past.

Heavy, uncomfortable garments were also relegated to history. Military technology paved the way for ultra-light down jackets, windbreakers, hoods—outfits that made it possible to withstand bivouacs at high altitudes.

As new, lighter, and stronger alloys appeared, progress was also made in the manufacture of ice axes and crampons. Specific mountaineering techniques and technology henceforth existed in all spheres, particularly that of equipment.

So what exploit would profoundly mark the coming period? The "last remaining problems" had all been resolved: the northwest faces of the

Above, left: The 1965 death of Lionel Terray on the cliffs of Vercors shocked the French public, as witnessed by the cover of the popular weekly magazine, Paris Match. *Facing page: Gaston Rébuffat, French mountaineering's finest ambassador, displays his talents on the Aiguille du Midi.*

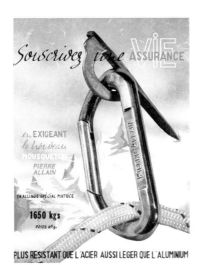

Aiguille Noire and the Eiger, the north faces of the Grandes Jorasses, the Matterhorn and Piz Badile had all been scaled. Climbers had gone "beyond vertical" in the Lavaredo group in the Dolomites, as they also had in the limestone peaks to the north, including Kaisergebirge, Salzkammergut, and Gesäuse. In fact, the truth is that the great feats of the day occurred beyond the Alps—the dominant postwar exploit was the Himalayan conquest of Mount Everest (8,848 m; 29,028 ft.) on 29 May 1953 by Sir Edmund Hillary and Sherpa Tenzing Norgay, three years after victory over the first "8,000-meter" peak, Annapurna.

But the logical culmination of the history of mountaineering on the highest peak in the world can only be appreciated by taking a look at the past. I have deliberately avoided discussing mountain ranges other than the Alps up till now, yet they too underwent slow and steady exploration. Starting with the golden age of mountain climbing around 1860, the history of their conquest can be compared, with a slight time lag, to that of the Alps, the scale of altitude rising by about 1,000 meters at each step: 4,000 meters (13,000 ft.) in the Alps; 5,000 meters (16,400 ft.) in the Caucasus; 6,000 meters (19,700 ft.) in the Andes and Alaska; 7,000 meters (23,000 ft.) in the Himalayas. Another golden age of mountain exploration occurred between 1950 and 1960, when thirteen of the fourteen "8,000ers" were conquered; the last (and lowest), Shisha Pangma (or Gosainthan, 8,013 m), having remained virgin for four additional years

solely by virtue of its geographic position in a distant corner of Tibet, which was diplomatically off-limits to Westerners.

The tale of these explorations will be recounted later, after the history of the Alps has been brought to a close with an account of the exploits that marked the final phase of conquest.

One day, just for fun, André Contamine decided to draw up a list of ascents made in the Alps between 1945 and 1960 that were superior in difficulty to grade VI (including aid climbs). He managed to fill over fifty pages with his dense handwriting. His list illustrates the inevitable oversights—most of them deliberate—in the somewhat broad fresco painted here, where only ascents of extraordinary length or difficulty have been discussed, plus those involving marked technical improvements or shifts in the approach to mountaineering (solo climbs, winter climbs, etc). The evolution in the psychology and philosophy of mountaineers seems much more important to me than the ascents actually made (the latter being a function of the former).

Between 1920 and 1940, only German, Austrian, or Italian climbers succeeded in making great climbs that required pitons—ignorance of the technique had caused the French to fall behind. But France would miraculously make up for lost time by experiencing its own golden age. During that magnificent period, it can be unchauvinistically asserted that French mountaineers suddenly became

the best in the world thanks to their technique, their well-trained instructors, and their enterprising spirit.

How did the miracle occur?

Once again, it was a question of war. Its terrible upheavals stirred the masses, excited youth, and glorified nationalist sentiments. It was the victory of 1918 that inspired impatient young Frenchmen, now demobilized, to glorify the pioneers of the Groupe de Haute Montagne. And, in contrast, it was defeat that spurred the mad, determined resolve of Austro-Germans on the great Alpine peaks; and it was once again war that sparked a revival in Italy by awarding it the Dolomite range, over which battle had raged for five years. Similarly, it was the defeat of France in 1940 that allowed France to rise from its ashes and forge a new generation of youth. This apparent contradiction was all too real.

France was occupied. Only a fraction of its population carried on the war from abroad. French youth had to endure everything—restrictions, the German occupation, difficulty in traveling outside of authorized zones. People in the southeast were stuck in the Alps, while for everyone else the mountains would remain a fond memory until the Liberation came. That was when the attraction of non-mountainous training sites became obvious; it was the great period of Fontainebleau, where climbers honed their skills. The discovery of the famous cliffs at Saussois in Burgundy encouraged the development of aid climbing and the use of pitons and stirrups. In the south, climbers practiced at Caroux; in Marseilles, the seaside Calanques cliffs proved propitious, turning out climbers such as Gaston Rébuffat and George Livanos. In Nice, Le Baou de Saint-Jennet produced Gurekian, the Vernets, Jean Franco, Claude Kogan, and her husband. But perhaps the most important development took place in the Alps with the creation of a paramilitary youth movement, Jeunesse et Montagne (Mountain Youth). Founded by General Faure, it was designed to discreetly help Air Force officers keep fit beyond the investigative reach of armistice committees.

Jeunesse et Montagne centers sprang up everywhere: Chamonix, Pralognan, in the Tarentaise and Oisans regions. Young people were recruited for a kind of national service, which in fact turned out to be the systematic practice of mountaineering. Remarkable and readily accepted discipline mobilized their latent strength and youthful energy, channeling that strength and spirit toward battle with the mountains. Mountaineering thus played a key human role. Twenty years later, it became apparent that the majority of great French mountaineers had belonged to the Jeunesse et Montagne movement, where they had been trained by excellent guides and ski instructors.

Thus the forced idleness of the occupation placed French youth in a privileged position. Everywhere else in the world, young people were busy fighting the war, whether German, Austrian, Italian, British, or Russian. The paradox was that the men of the vanquished nation, while awaiting their revenge, forged their mountaineering skills and thus managed to catch up

Above, left to right: An ad for Vibram soles of hardened rubber, invented by Italian climber Vitale Bramani; Gaston Rébuffat; Rébuffat posing for a photographer.

with their counterparts in the eastern Alps. Training cliffs produced good climbers, for they made it easier to acquire the right technique and make the first moves in difficulties graded V+ or even VI.

Jeunesse et Montagne's broad recruitment also enabled it to reach diverse sectors of French society, which meant that young city dwellers discovered a new calling. Most of them, in fact, would remain faithful to the mountains, and their systematic training often made them eminent mountaineering teachers and technicians.

Few major exploits were achieved during the war years, however. Food rations and travel in an occupied country were both strictly limited. In August 1944, Jean and Jeanne Franco made the first ascent of the south pillar of the Ecrins, not only pulling off an admirable feat but also forging a wonderful route that would become a classic (perhaps the finest honor a mountain climber can receive). At Chamonix on 17 August 1942, Fernand Tournier, Authenac, and Vitrier scaled the southwest face of the Aiguille Mummery along a very difficult route.

Once the war was over, however, new challenges beckoned.

In fact, the first thing to be done was to repeat the classic conquests. Significantly, the second ascents of the Walker Spur of the Grandes Jorasses, the north face of the Eiger, and the west face of Aiguille Noire de Peuterey were all made by French climbers.

The party that made it up the Walker Spur came from mixed backgrounds. Edouard Frendo was a veteran who climbed truly fine routes in the Oisans region, yet had been unsuccessful in his attack on the Grandes Jorasses. He nevertheless took his revenge from 14 to 16 July 1945 by teaming up with Gaston Rébuffat, who had trained on the Calanque cliffs and become a leading theorist of aid techniques. "The hardest thing," Frendo later told me, "was making climbs like that when the only food in your sack was cold, boiled potatoes." Those were the days of food rationing.

In 1946, the third and fourth ascents of the Walker Spur were the work of two French teams. The first was composed of veteran Pierre Allain and his young Fontainebleau climbers—René Ferlet, Jacques Poincenot, and Guy Poulet. The second team was another of those brilliant tandems that glittered like a bright star in the mountain sky: Louis Lachenal and Lionel Terray. It was they who, in 1947, also made the second ascent of the north face of the Eiger.

In 1948, Gaston Rébuffat and Bernard Pierre bagged the second ascent of the northeast face of Piz Badile, requiring two bivouacs. (The following year, Lachenal and Terray pulverized the speed record by making the sixth ascension of the same route without a single bivouac.) Then

Left to right: Three great French climbers from the postwar period, all of whom died young: Louis Lachenal (fell into a crevasse in the Vallée Blanche in 1955); Lionel Terray (fell off a cliff of the Vercors in 1965); Jean Couzy (struck by a rock in the Dévoluy range in 1958).

in 1949, Rébuffat and Pierre made the second ascent of the west face of the Aiguille Noire de Peuterey, following Ratti and Vitali's route.

These eloquent accomplishments suddenly revealed the existence of an unrivaled French school of mountaineering. Another golden age was dawning. It was essentially the product of two things—training cliffs and the systematic organization of recreational activities that enabled many youths to spend time in the mountains. The Groupe de Haute Montagne (GHM), meanwhile, which should have spurred admiring imitation in the prewar period, had in fact been limited by an overly restricted social recruitment and an old-fashioned amateurism that deliberately rejected professionals, which relegated it to somewhat academic honors. The GHM had locked the best climbers of the day into mistaken theories and had remained aloof from the major developments of modern mountaineering. It might even be argued that had it not been for Lucien Devies, who was on friendly terms with Gervasutti and therefore familiar with eastern Alpine methods, France would have clung to the aristocratic phalanx of the early days. It would never have nurtured those individuals who have shaped modern French mountaineering, those climbers who even today are still leading the movement.

A list of names would have to include all the professional monitors from Jeunesse and Montagne, plus those from the Mountaineering College in Les Praz, and finally the National Ski and Mountaineering School, from Jean Franco to Maurice Herzog via Lachenal, Terray, Contamine, and Rébuffat. My apologies for skipping over at least fifty other names, especially the monitors ably headed by Armand Charlet, who managed to "produce" all those future professionals.

For the postwar period was marked above all by the emergence of a new category of mountaineers; it was henceforth the professionals who directed operations. Recruitment was broadened—a previously closed guild like Chamonix's Compagnie des Guides admitted the likes of Terray, Lachenal, and Rébuffat, and would later admit Leroux and Desmaison. But the training the new guides had received pushed them in a new direction, namely the organization of foreign expeditions and the exploration of mountain ranges the world over. This trend would be capped by the French conquest of the world's first "8,000er," Annapurna, on 3 June 1950.

It was thanks to these mountaineers that amazing feats were accomplished, such as the smashing success of the Makalu expedition and the technically admirable exploit of the conquest of Jannu. Party leaders were

Left: Celebrating their conquest of the west face of the Drus are (left to right) Guido Magnone, Lucien Bérardini, Adrien Dagory, and Marcel Lainé. Right: Bérardini after the ascent—note the harness made of hemp.

henceforth physically implicated in their expeditions—not only did they organize them, but they took part in the assault teams. They therefore provided both brains and brawn and, thanks to their personal experience, could succeed where pure theorists had once failed.

Finally, another important difference was that guides were now allowed to have their say. Previously, they were more or less considered to be a tool that could be used as desired; the fact that they received wages meant that they were treated as inferiors. It was finally understood that when seeking the best, it was wisest to turn to professionals. Only professionals had undergone the intensive training and daily practice that lead to conditioned reflexes; only professionals had honed the absolutely precise techniques enabling them to move very fast over difficult terrain or rockfaces (seven times out of ten, it is speed that determines the success of an expedition or even a simple climb).

This development does not mean, however, that the great "amateurs" of the day should be overlooked. There was Maurice Herzog, the admired leader of the Annapurna expedition (who would have been a peerless guide had he not been drawn to politics and glamor). And there was above all Jean Couzy, the best all-round amateur mountaineer, simultaneously thoughtful and bold, one of the few to measure up to professionals in every sphere.

Alongside these mountaineering successes, however, a psychological deformation of climbers' attitudes was occurring. As I have argued elsewhere, there developed a mania for exaggerated use of pitons, an exclusive love of rock accompanied by a disdain or dread of snow and ice, and an overwhelming focus on the exploit itself. Mountain climbing would no longer be practiced for the interior joy it brings, but merely to make the front page of the newspapers. The only thing considered worthy was the exploit for its own sake; discussions turned solely on levels of difficulty. This attitude had its drawbacks. First of all, pitons were being used excessively—one summer,

nearly five hundred pitons were counted on the face of the Grand Capucin, that is to say nearly one per meter! In contrast, climbers like Franz Lochmatter, Armand Charlet, and Alfred Couttet had free-climbed pitches over thirty meters long in nailed-soled shoes—without the security of pitons.

Little by little, the field of action shrank. The number of remaining challenges diminished, reduced to a few overlooked pillars or to the rectification of classic routes. Although Comici's

doctrine was still being applied—"straight like a falling drop of water"—it only entailed minor ironing out of routes on places like the north face of the Meije, the Cordier Spur of the Aiguille Verte, and the Frêney Pillar.

These digressions are not meant to imply that mountaineering existed only in France. Once borders were reopened after the war, the Italians, Germans, Austrians, and, finally, the British entered the lists again.

Thus in 1951 two young Italians, Walter Bonatti and

Above: Gaston Rébuffat in the dihedral (corner) of the northeast face of Piz Badile during the second ascent. Right: Three stamps on the theme of mountaineering from the Republic of San Marino.

Luciano Ghigo, pulled off the extraordinary ascent of the east face of the Grand Capucin du Tacul in the Mont Blanc range. The east face of that veritable pillar of granite is partly overhanging; like every exquisite form in the mountains, the pillar would subsequently be ascended many times despite its extreme difficulty.

In 1952, the west face of the Petit Dru was climbed twice, first by French mountaineers Guido Magnone, Lucien Bérardini, and Adrien

Dagory, then by Marcel Lainé. All were from Paris, and all had trained on the Saussois cliffs. Magnone applied expedition techniques to the Petit Dru for the first time, carrying equipment and forming teams. His victory had a great impact and, once the face was equipped, the route could be climbed in a single go.

But pride of place inevitably goes to the magnificent route forged by Walter Bonatti up the southwest pillar of the Petit Dru from 17 to 22 August 1955, alone and with no outside help. This prodigious solo ascent was the product of intelligence, determination, and technique. It had been well thought-out and executed by the

guide who, within a few years, would become the world's leading climber.

Continuing with the repetitions of big Alpine challenges, guides Michel Bastien and Pierre Jullien would repeat Gervasutti's famous route up the Grandes Jorasses. In 1950, Anderl Heckmair, who had tamed the Eiger, was at last able to climb the Walker Spur.

New names emerged, future stars that would shine in the ten years to come—young Swiss climbers like Asper and Bron from the

Androsace Club in Geneva (the most elite alpine club in the world: forty members elected not only on the basis of their accomplishments but also for their *montagnard* spirit and camaraderie) took over where Roch, Greloz, Marullaz, and Dittert had left off, notably by scaling the Grand Capucin in 1956. Later, Michel Vaucher would be the youngest Himalayan specialist to reach the top of an "8,000er," namely Dhaulagiri.

The Italian Dolomites produced climbers like Ghedina, Maestri, Mauri, and Oggioni, while Bonatti and Gobbi steadily demonstrated their great class in the western Alpine ranges.

Above, right: The east face of Grand Capucin, scaled by Bonatti in 1951. Above, left: Bonatti bivouacking during the first ascent of this face.

Above, right: Walter Bonatti signing the Charpoua Hut log book (top) after returning from his historic ascent (bottom) of the southwest pillar of the Petit Dru.
Above, left: The state of Bonatti's bag after having been hoisted up the length of the face.

British climbers returned gradually. Mountaineering had taken on a new tone in Britain, where the war had also changed attitudes. Victorian-style mountain climbers led by guides had been replaced by young people who had trained on the cliffs of the Lake District and Scotland, and then ventured into major undertakings. Excellent rock climbers, they tended to embark on highly risky attempts. Some, like Joe Brown, Chris Bonington, and Don Whillans, solved extremely complex problems, like the west face of the Blaitière after a rock slide had completely "erased" Allain's route and totally "renewed" the face. Even more impressive was their first ascent of the Frêney Pillar in 1961, followed the same day by the French team Jullien, Pollet-Villard, and Desmaison.

One other French exploit is worth stressing, for it helps to illustrate the evolution of French techniques. In 1951, Marseille climbers Livanos and Gabriel, who had climbed exclusively on the Calanque cliffs but were reputed to be the finest practitioners of aid techniques, climbed Cima su Alto, one of the highest and most difficult faces in the Dolomites, thereby ranking themselves alongside the best eastern specialists in a single blow.

The last major problems posed by the southern flank of the Mont Blanc group were attacked in 1957. Walter Bonatti and Toni Gobbi, both guides, climbed the Grand Pilier d'Angle and continued up the Peuterey Arête. One by one, all the spurs on the south face were scaled, the last being the famous Frêney Pillar, where one of the most tragic episodes in the history of mountaineering occurred in July of 1961. Bonatti and Oggioni, guiding Italian climber Gallieni, and the French team of Mazeaud, Kohlmann, Guillaume, and Vieille, were surprised by bad weather on the lower third of the pillar. During the ensuing retreat (led with desperate energy by Bonatti), Vieille and then Guillaume died of exhaustion, soon followed by Oggioni, who was coming down last in order to

aid descent of the difficult Grüber Rocks. Finally, almost in sight of the hut, Kohlmann went mad and died of exhaustion in turn.

On 5–7 August 1961, Pierre Jullien, René Desmaison, and the Italian Piussi had to turn back just fifty meters from the summit, due to a loss of material and bad weather; thanks to a heroic retreat, they were able to regain the Gamba Hut. Shortly afterwards, victory was achieved by British climbers Chris Bonington, Ian Clough, and Don Whillans, along with the Polish climber Dlugosz on 27–29 August. They arrived at the top just two hours ahead of Jullien, Pollet-Villard, Desmaison, and Piussi, who recovered the equipment left in place by the first team. Thus on a single day, mountain climbers from four different countries managed to scale a spur whose main attraction was to pose problems of aid climbing at an altitude of over 4,000 meters.

The Frêney Pillar was certainly not worth four deaths. Times had truly changed since the days when Michel Payot and James Eccles sought a path up the totally virgin south face of Mont Blanc, managing to reach the top by a route that says a great deal about their *montagnard* instincts, their knowledge of rock and ice, and their technical skills at a time when crampons were unknown and pitons not even envisaged.

This change in mountaineering attitudes— provoked, of course, by the fact that all the highest peaks had been scaled and all the great routes climbed—produced a burst of amazing if minor exploits between 1955 and 1960. They merit mention, if only to indicate the degree of difficulty that mountaineers had attained in the realm of pure climbing. As early as 1958, a direct route was forged up Cima Grande di Lavaredo by Germans Brandler, Hasse, Lehne, and Löwe, using expansion pitons. They replenished their supplies by lowering a basket on a rope.

Better, in 1959 three teams—Swiss, Italian, and French—attacked the north face of Cima

Chris Bonington's party reaches the foot of the four pillars of Frêney in 1961. The central pillar with its final shaft (La Chandelle) is the one in the middle of the photo, seemingly the highest.

Above: Two scenes from the first ascent of the Frêney Pillar—a tricky passage (left) and Chris Bonington and Don Whillans (with his inevitable cap) at a bivouac (right). Right: After the tragedy on Frêney, Pierre Mazeaud leaves the hospital on Walter Bonatti's back.

Ovest di Lavaredo almost simultaneously, each one looking for the *direttissima* route. Three teams were assembled: the Swiss Weber and Schelbert; the Italians Bellodis, Franceschi, and Michielli; and French climbers Desmaison, Mazeaud, Kohlmann, and Lagesse. Targeting the most direct route, they completed the ascent in six days and five nights (6–11 July), including several bivouacs seated on a swing dangling from the sheer face! Apparently a crowd of several thousand spectators with binoculars watched the exploit from the hut—good business for the hut's caretaker!

Also that year Lacedelli, the famous "squirrel" from Cortina, climbed the northwest face of the same peak in five days. Time was no longer of the essence. Still in 1959, a direct route up the south face of Torre Trieste was scaled in five days, requiring the use of 450 pitons, including 150 expansion bolts. It was a record at the time. But not for long.

"The era of the finite has dawned," wrote Lucien Devies long ago, in reference to the conquest of Everest. But the history of mountaineering, like history itself, is an eternal recommencement. Once Europe's "playground" had become as densely populated as a city square, the rest of the whole wide world beckoned. The next step—in perhaps a not-so-distant future—will be the mountains of the moon and Venus!

Faster transportation has shrunk the world considerably. Back in 1935, I had to trek for seventeen days (seven of them on camel) to reach the Hoggar range in southern Algeria. By 1960 climbers were heading regularly to the Hoggar; a half day in a plane, a few hours in a jeep and there they were at the foot of Garet, ready for a week's climbing during Christmas or Easter break, then back to work the following Monday. Similarly, the Cordillera Blanca in Peru became a familiar field of action for private expeditions. Other small expeditions mounted by clubs or groups of friends attacked the lesser Himalayan peaks. In short, after the conquest of the Alps, the other great ranges of the world would be conquered. Those conquests merit a section of their own, which entails turning the clock back half a century. Before

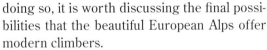

doing so, it is worth discussing the final possibilities that the beautiful European Alps offer modern climbers.

New scope for action arrived with the advent of winter climbs, no longer applied exclusively to snowy peaks and glaciers, but also to major rockfaces. Not that winter mountaineering is all that new: in 1872, Mont Blanc was climbed by Isabella Straton and Jean Charlet, her guide and future husband (the story goes that it was at the top of Mont Blanc, in trying to warm his client, that the future conqueror of the Petit Dru also warmed her heart). And the first winter traverse of the Matterhorn was made in 1882.

But it was not until the period between 1920 and 1940 that much more important winter exploits were racked up—Pierre Dalloz on the Meije in 1926, Armand Charlet, and André Roch on the Grépon and the Drus in 1928, Charlet and myself on the Aiguille de Bionnassay, also in 1928. That same year, Erwin Schneider scaled the south face of Mont Blanc even as Swiss, German, and Italian mountaineers were climbing other Alpine peaks, including La Dent Blanche and the Weisshorn.

When activity revived between 1945 and 1960, even bolder feats were undertaken. The Swiss won attention on the west face of the Matterhorn, then on the Peuterey Arête. Italian guides Toni Gobbi and Henri Rey deliberately confronted major rock challenges like the south ridge of Aiguille Noire in 1949, while Gobbi and Arturo Ottoz climbed remarkable routes on Mont Blanc, like the Major route in 1953.

In France, Desmaison and the methodical and surprising Jean Couzy scaled the west face of the Drus up to its junction with the north arête, then redescended by the same route. In 1960, René Desmaison, Michel Payot, and Fernand Audibert, three guides from Chamonix, made the first winter ascent of the notorious northwest face of Olan in the company of Jean Puiseux, thus proving that a major Alpine problem could be successfully tackled even in winter.

A still greater exploit was the first winter ascent of the north face of the Eiger in 1961 by German climbers Toni Hiebeler, Toni Kinshofer, and Anderl Mannhardt, along with the Austrian W. Almberger. They accomplished it in two separate stages, thanks to a rendezvous with the famous evacuation tunnel (the first part was climbed in late February, the second stage from 6 to 12 March). This ascent sparked a lively polemic at the time, which was hardly

Above, left: Three routes on the north face of Cima Ovest di Lavaredo. To the right is the Couzy route forged by René Desmaison, in the middle is the Swiss route, and on the right is the 1935 Cassin route. Above, right: René Desmaison negotiating the overhanging sections of Cima Ovest.

justified, since a remarkable precedent for that very method had been established by the first ascent of the southwest face of the Drus (also accomplished in two stages only later joined together).

Early 1963 was marked by another remarkable feat: Bonatti and his partner Cosimo Zapelli made the first winter ascent of the Walker Spur of the Grandes Jorasses, which required six bivouacs between 25 and 30 January.

Given the exceptional weather conditions in the winter of 1964, several parties attacked the most prestigious peaks. During the week of 6–14 January alone, three winter firsts were chalked up. In the Mont Blanc range, three young guides from Chamonix—Georges Payot, Gérard Devouassoux, and Yvon Masino—scaled the north face of the Drus in three bivouacs (two on the rockface, one at the summit). At the same time, Chamonix guides Fernand Audibert and Claude Jacoux completed the long and tricky traverse from the Grands Montets to the Aiguille Verte. Finally, in the Oisans region, Parat and Chèze, from Lyon, made the first winter ascent of the difficult northwest face of the Ecrins, bivouacking four nights.

All those climbers, like Bonatti a year earlier, descended via a normal route. But in winter those normal routes were covered in deep snow, presenting significant dangers that required solid experience on mixed terrain and underscored the very serious nature of such exploits.

Winter ascents of towering rockfaces thus became increasingly fashionable. They demanded additional skills of climbers—rock specialists, for instance, could only succeed if they acquired excellent crampon and step-cutting techniques. Furthermore, the tough climate called for perfect equipment, without which any attempt would be suicidal. Difficult rock becomes several degrees harder under icy or snowy conditions; a climber who easily passes a grade V+ sequence when the rock is dry would have real trouble in a grade IV route covered in ice. Winter mountaineering therefore produced a

Karl Blödig (top) and Guido Lammer (bottom), two great forerunners of solo mountaineering.

distinct rise in the level of difficulties that had to be overcome.

Amazing prowess was thus displayed in the northern limestone Alps and in the Dolomites, notably Fritz Kasparek's exploits on the Gesäuse and Fleischbank. It was during winter firsts that the name of Hermann Buhl came to the fore, a startling climber if ever there was one. Bonatti, Mauri, Buhl, Rainer, Kasparek, Brunhueber, and Wiegele attacked everything that looked impossible. According to Kasparek, the toughest winter climb ever made was the Hochtor on Gesäuse, which he accomplished in 1941.

But another way of transcending limits—or at least of greatly increasing danger and difficulty—is to climb difficult peaks all alone. Even before Bonatti's amazing feat on the pillar of the Petit Dru, many famous climbers had thrown caution to the winds and made solo climbs. In the footsteps of Guido Lammer, Paul Preuss, and Hans Dülfer, all of whom were active prior to the First World War, came modern climbers like Edy Stofer (French), Fritz Hermann (Austrian), Richard Hechtel (German) and Zapparoli (Italian), not forgetting Dr. Karl Blödig, a mountaineer in his seventies, who conquered the Brouillard Arête with Josef Knubel and, in 1932, completed his collection of "4,000ers" by making a solo ascent of the Argentière slope of the Col Armand Charlet, descending by the same route. Finally, in 1937 Emilio Comici climbed the north face of Cima Grande, prefiguring Bonatti's exploit.

The recent period has brought new names to the fore. One prestigious, romantic name worth remembering is that of Hermann Buhl, who made a solo ascent of Schusselkar, the southeast face of Fleischbank and the northeast face of Piz Badile, capping it all with the 1952 ascent of the notorious east face of Watzmann not only alone, and in winter, but also by *night*! After that, you may as well pull up the ladder—or rather, stirrups—behind you.

Cesare Maestri, an Italian climber from the Dolomites, racked up impressive solo ascents of the Solleder route on Punta Civetta and, above all, in 1953, the southwest face of Marmolada, an exploit surpassed only by Walter Bonatti's first extraordinary ascent, in six days, of the southwest pillar of the Petit Dru.

Does that mean there is nothing else to accomplish, nothing else to seek from the Alps? Not counting the significant number of winter firsts still to be made—and strongly discouraging solo climbs for all but truly rare beings of exceptional endurance, technique, and audacity—I feel that the true field of action has shifted beyond the Alps, where ninety per cent of the routes remain to be traced (with the exception of the Caucasus and the Peruvian

ago, exceptional natural beauty unknown to city dwellers.

That beauty includes an unreal halo over a landscape of peaks and summits, a flaming sunset seen from a hut, a night spent listening to the song of the earth chanted by falling rocks, sliding avalanches, and grumbling torrents; and it includes the understanding that a harsh struggle up dizzying ridges or sheer rockfaces has no meaning if it does not lead to a better apprecia-

Andes, which have already been extensively explored).

But since not everyone can travel so far, wisdom would counsel a return to healthier notions of mountaineering, to a view of climbing as a highly committed but nevertheless non-competitive sport. It can provide the physical and mental regeneration sought by modern populations, requiring a mind sufficiently clear to be able to appreciate, as people did fifty years

tion, once back in the valley, of the sweetness of human life on this earth. Only then will young people never tire of climbing and reclimbing the old routes, becoming so experienced that the word "difficulty" becomes meaningless. Only then will they find their own truth everywhere, on snowy ridges as well as sheer walls. When I say everywhere, I mean everywhere—providing they are in the mountains. Because in the end, it is a question of loving the mountains.

Gaston Rébuffat demonstrates all the subtleties of aid climbing in an overhang on the south face of the Aiguille du Midi.

Endgame?

Several summits are now climbed in a single day, solo, in winter. Famous peaks are densely crisscrossed with routes. As the twentieth century comes to a close, the Alps definitely seem too small for aficionados of the sport to which they gave birth.

In 1964, the conquest of the Alps seemed to be drawing to a close once again. All the major faces had been scaled. Obviously, there were a few overlooked walls, a few "winter firsts" to claim, some "direct" routes to forge and solo climbs. But it became clear that all of that would soon be accomplished. There was no longer a "last remaining problem," that is to say an invincible face that cruelly repelled all assaults, as the north face of the Eiger had done in the 1930s. Everyone realized that pitons, stirrups, double ropes—in short, aid climbing—could overcome the most dramatic overhangs and the slickest slabs.

Perhaps Walter Bonatti sensed this lassitude. It is striking that he decided to end his career at the age of thirty-five, in 1965, with a symbolic flourish: the first solo winter ascent of a direct route up the north face of the Matterhorn, one hundred years after the initial conquest of that emblematic summit. First, winter, solo—the three dimensions of postwar mountaineering would be combined on a mythical peak. It was a way of saying, with great elegance, that a certain form of mountain climbing was bowing out with Bonatti.

In fact, those who followed Bonatti at first seemed to be sharing the scraps of a diminishingly bountiful repast. This led to a search for the steepest of walls, even if there was little logic in scaling them, proving that the summit now mattered less than the ascent itself. Significant in this respect was the bold route opened in 1969 by Alessandro Gogna and Leo Cerruti on the Zmutt "Nose," that steep rise on the north face of the Matterhorn. Less direct that Bonatti's route, it went out of its way to be difficult. Since then, two other routes have been traced on this narrow portion of the face! Because the increased abilities of modern climbers strictly limited the number of mountains liable to give them real trouble, everyone wanted to leave a mark on the really tough ones—the prestigious north faces of the Eiger, the Matterhorn, and the Grandes Jorasses have changed radically in the past thirty years. Where only one or two routes formerly existed, there are now five (the Matterhorn), ten (the Eiger) or twenty (the Grandes Jorasses)! It hardly needs to be pointed out that not all of these routes have left a lasting mark on their times.

Facing page: Todd Skinner and Paul Piana bivouacking in their "portaledge" during the ascent of The Great Canadian Knife in the Canadian Rockies. International cross-fertilization in the 1960s brought American techniques to the Alps. Left: A spring-loaded cam device wedged into a crack provides protection where classic pitons are useless.

Major Winter Ascents

In the mid-1960s, it nevertheless seemed important to complete the winter conquest of the Alps. While the major faces had already succumbed, there were still some tough items outstanding. In winter, pure difficulty counts less than isolation, length, and the danger of approach and descent. In this respect, the winter ascent of the central pillar of Frêney (René Desmaison, Robert Flematti, 1967) represented a key moment and degree of "commitment" rare for the Alps, given its isolation, altitude, and the tragedy of 1961, which was still in everyone's minds. The period would conclude with two achievements that pushed these developments

The equipment used by Bonatti (bottom) on his solo route up the Matterhorn, compared to the gear used thirty years later (top) by Catherine Destivelle on the second ascent of the same route.

to an extreme. First there was the winter ascent of the entire Peuterey Arête by two teams in 1973—a French party composed of Yannick Seigneur, Marc Galy, Louis Audoubert, and Michel Feuillerade, and a party from Valle d'Aosta, Arturo, and Oreste Squinobal. Then there was the winter ascent of the last of the great walls conquered prior to the war—the northwest face of Ailefroide, in the Ecrins range. Given its isolation, the climb was a major undertaking, successfully accomplished by Pierre Béghin with Olivier Challéat, Pierre Caubet, and Pierre Guillet on 19–23 February 1975. From the Eiger in 1961 to Ailefroide, it took less than fifteen years to scale, in winter, all the great rockfaces conquered in the 1930s.

To increase difficulty, the best thing to do was follow Bonatti's example: trace a new route in winter. Before him, a first winter "superdirect" had been forged up Cima Grande in 1963, but that "Saxon Route" (Rainer Kauschke, Gert Uhner, Peter Siegert) was unfortunately of debatable validity, given the prodigious resources employed, excusable only by the novelty of the idea.

For a goal of a quite different scope—a direct route up the north face of Eiger—the same tactics were used in 1966 by two teams, one Anglo-American and one German, initially in competition but ultimately in collaboration. The successive installation of safety ropes and camps made the enterprise resemble a Himalayan expedition. The limits of the method were revealed by the death of the American climber John Harlin, the victim of a safety line that snapped. These "Himalayan siege tactics" would continue to be employed in the Alps, but came under increasing criticism. When, in 1971, the Swiss mountaineers Hans Berger and Hans Muller made a winter ascent of the north face of Les Droites, rightly considered the most difficult glacier route of the day, many people thought that a "lighter" technique could and should have been used.

A light expedition, however, is demanding, risky and highly committed. In the winter of 1971, René Desmaison and the young guide Serge Gousseault tried to forge a remarkable route between the Shroud and the Walker Spur of the Grandes Jorasses, but Gousseault died of exhaustion high on the slope, and live media coverage of his death throes led to a tortured debate.

This carefully staged bivouac
shot is intended to illustrate
Bonatti's winter route up the
north face of the Matterhorn.
Note the teddy bear.

Louis Audoubert (above, left) and his companions during the first winter ascent of the magnificent Peuterey Arête.

Desmaison would complete the route two years later, with Michel Claret and the Italian climber Giorgio Bertone. And yet theirs was a long way from being the last route opened on the north face of the Grandes Jorasses. That great face seems to sum up recent developments in mountaineering, with routes such as Louis Audoubert's "Directe de l'Amitié" (1974), Slavko Svetičič's "Manitua" (1993), and the direct route up the Croz Spur

opened by Jean-Christope Lafaille, not to mention the central couloir (Japanese route, 1972) and the Colton-McIntyre ice gullies (1976).

Advances in Glacier Technique

Of all the "firsts," the most important was also one of the oldest—the big icy slope up the Grandes Jorasses, called the Shroud, which the

best teams of the 1960s attacked in vain, unable to overcome the imposing lower ice gullies. It finally fell in January 1968 to René Desmaison (undoubtedly the finest "post-Bonatti" climber), accompanied by Robert Flematti. This remarkable first ascent pushed contemporary possibilities to their limits. And yet just nine years later, Jean-Marc Boivin from Dijon repeated the route, alone, in the astonishing time of two hours and forty-five minutes! In the meantime, obviously, a technical revolution had occurred. The new technique did not emerge at Chamonix, but rather in the modest mountains of Great Britain; there the winter is harsh, and ice-covered rockfaces offer truly tough mixed routes. In accomplishing these winter ascents which, although short, require total "commitment," Scottish mountaineers developed new ice axes that dif-

René Desmaison (above, right) in 1973 forging a superdirect winter route up the Grandes Jorasses, with Michel Claret and Giorgio Bertone (above, left).

fered from the equipment used in the Alps. Hamish MacInnes, a Scot, was the first to manufacture ice axes with metal handles in 1964. The blade of the axe was angled to provide a better anchor. Meanwhile, German manufacturer Salewa marketed adjustable crampons. Crampons with twelve points had been invented by Laurent Grivel as early as 1934 to aid in frontal progression, but had not been used systematically. In 1966, Americans Tom Frost and Yvon Chouinard invented rigid crampons that were even better suited to steep walls of ice. Then ice screws began appearing. These innovations

made it possible to attack increasingly vertical ice slopes head on. In France, Armand Charlet's traditional approach was still official doctrine—a lateral progression using all the points of the crampons, a technique suited only to slopes of average steepness. It was several years before the technical "dam" finally broke, thanks to the resounding first ascent of the north couloir of the Petit Dru.

Once again, the Drus Couloir presented an obvious route that the finest teams had repeatedly failed to complete. It was only at Christmas 1974 that success came to Walter Cecchinel and Claude Jager, using ice axes and crampons made specially for Cecchinel by the Chamonix-based manufacturer Simond. This ascent represented a conclusive victory for the frontal technique, employing the forward points on crampons and axes with angled blades. Ice axes would continue to evolve, becoming ever shorter and more curved in order to make progression easier, even

Putting the John Harlin Direct route up the north face of the Eiger in 1966 required the hollowing out of several ice caves.

on vertical cascades of ice. By the 1980s, such "gear" had little in common with the ice axes of the 1960s. Previously unthinkable routes suddenly became conceivable. The situation was not limited to the Alps, for easier contact and travel meant that mountaineering developments were henceforth worldwide. Thus on Mount Kenya, the Diamond Couloir had repelled all assaults until the U.S.–Kenyan team of Phil Snyder and S. Thumbi Mathonge conquered it in 1973. Meanwhile, the "final problem" in New Zealand's Southern Alps, the Caroline Face of Mount Cook, had succumbed to Gough and Glasgow in 1970, and swiftly became a classic route.

The same thing occurred with notorious ice routes in the European Alps. The most famous route of the 1970s had nevertheless been inaugurated long before the Shroud or the north couloir of the Drus, namely the north face of Les Droites, climbed in five days by Maurice Davaille and Philippe Cornuau in 1955. It was a pioneering route whose novelty was scarcely perceived at the time, even though the few early followers were all obliged to bivouac several times. Climbing the Davaille route was long considered a major accomplishment, and its ascent remained obligatory for serious climbers until it was dethroned by even tougher ice routes.

Attacking Cascades and Ice Gullies

A new concept of climbing emerged. The Davaille route had followed the classic approach by searching for the best itinerary up a vast face; but advances in equipment made it possible to envisage new types of routes inconceivable to the previous generation of mountaineers, namely up nearly vertical ice gullies and even bands of séracs (unstable ice cliffs). Up to that point, the few routes up extremely sheer slopes involved either cutting steps into the face or employing numerous ice screws. The new concept was epitomized by the Supercouloir on Mont Blanc du Tacul, a route up a thin shaft of ice flanking the Gervasutti Pillar, climbed in 1975 by Patrick Gabarrou and Jean-Marc Boivin.

Given this impetus, mountaineers began concentrating on previously overlooked ice gullies. They discovered them in the most unexpected

The conquest of the north couloir on the Drus by Walter Cecchinel and Claude Jager represented a key date in the development of ice techniques. Seen here, one of the first times the route was repeated. Following double page: The Supercouloir on Mont Blanc du Tacul, another major ice route, here repeated by Patrick Gabarrou sone twenty years after the first ascent.

Patrick Gabarrou, known for his many new routes, seen here working on the Notre-Dame Icefall, one of the many ice routes he forged.

places, such as the southern, sunny face of the Grandes Jorasses, where, in 1978, Italians Giancarlo Grassi and Gianni Comino traced the Hypercouloir route entirely on ice. Comino, who also made the first solo ascent of Supercouloir (1978), began specializing in an even stranger type of ascent by climbing straight up the most forbidding—and dangerously unstable—bands of séracs. He was killed in 1980 while tracing a particularly risky route up the enormous séracs separating the Major from the Poire on the Brenva slope up Mont Blanc. Subsequently—and fortunately—Comino had few imitators.

Glacier specialists turned to a field of action equally thrilling but less dangerous—the waterfalls that, at middle attitudes, freeze into cascades of ice in the winter. Given their generally modest height, limited degree of commitment, and often easy access, they provide useful training and practice for the major glacier routes, much as cliff climbing can refine rock technique for mountain ascents.

Californian Influence

Another revolution, though of lesser scope, was occurring at the same time. This time it concerned rock techniques. Once again, the technique basically originated in the United States and Great Britain, which moreover illustrates a highly important characteristic of mountaineering in the past thirty years—cross-influence between various countries has come into full play, minimizing local particularities and rendering a strictly regional history impossible. Starting in 1960, Alpine mountaineering would be influenced by what was occurring on the other side of the world, in California.

Indeed, French mountain climbers received a shock when a small gang of Americans turned up in Chamonix and proceeded to scale, in turn, a new direct route some 600 meters high up the west face of the Drus (dubbed La Directe Américaine by the French, climbed by Gary Hemming and Royal Robbins, 1962), the south face of the Fou (one of the rare remaining virgin faces, by Tom Frost, Stewart Fulton, John

Harlin, Gary Hemming, 1963), and a super direct route (Direttissima) up the west face of the Petit Dru (John Harlin, Royal Robbins, 1965). These three routes represented a level of difficulty, notably in terms of aid climbing, that surpassed anything done in the Alps up till then.

The Californians brought to Europe not only their talent, but also pitons of chrome molybdenum, and other strangely shaped devices in aluminum called "bong bongs" (replacing unreliable chocks of wood), and razor-thin "rurps" (for "realized ultimate reality pitons," developed by Chouinard and Frost in 1960). Photos also arrived of the strange, vertical world of Yosemite, with its geometric structures and soaring, fissureless slabs hundreds of feet high.

The Yosemite walls, especially the one called El Capitan, are much more compact than those in the Alps. Climbing them largely requires the use of aid techniques and, for smooth slabs, the use of "bolts" (equivalent to the expansion pitons used in Europe, for which a hole must first be drilled). The man behind Californian climbing was John Salathé, a metalsmith originally from Switzerland, who made the first "American" pitons in the 1950s.

But the ageing Salathé did not participate himself in the real breakthrough, namely the forging of the first route up El Capitan, the highest cliff in Yosemite (3,000 ft.). The route, up a spur called the Nose, required eighteen months of effort, forty-five days of climbing, 675 pitons, and 125 bolts before Warren Harding and his companions reached the top in 1958. On learning of this unfamiliar type of ascent, Alpine mountaineers were left speechless.

Subsequently, techniques for climbing California's "big walls" became increasingly specialized, entailing pulleys to hoist sacks, safety ropes, bivouacs in dangling hammocks. Aid climbing reached a level of sophistication unmatched elsewhere. In 1968, Royal Robbins remained alone for ten days on Muir Wall, the first great solo ascent in Yosemite. In 1970, observers were staggered by the twenty-eight consecutive days spent on the cliff (without assis-

The Italian climber Giancarlo Grassi, a remarkable ice specialist, was killed in an accident on Monti Sibillini in 1991.

tance and with only fifteen days of supplies) by Warren Harding and Dean Caldwell to conquer the Wall of the Early Morning Light. This endurance record has never been beaten, but two years later Charlie Porter spent nine days alone opening Zodiac, a route requiring a new rating of difficulty in aid climbing (A5). Meanwhile, ascent times were accelerating—the Nose, which around 1980 still required several

The Dolomites offered plenty of scope for action. The route up Cima Grande opened by Comici, for instance, skirted the imposing over-hangs directly below the summit. In 1958, Saxons Lothar Brandler and Dietrich Hasse traced a route unequalled anywhere in the world in terms of going "beyond vertical," to use Georges Livanos's felicitous expression; even Yosemite was the realm of the vertical, not of

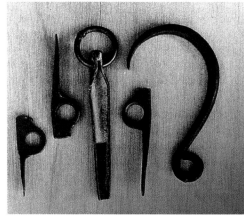

overhangs. Their example was swiftly followed—by the next year, two routes were traced up the even greater bulges project-ing from the north face of Cima Ovest; the route, dedicated to Jean Couzy by René Desmaison and his companions (requiring 350 pitons, of which only thirty were expansion pitons), was exceptional in its length and the commitment required—after the first few pitches, it is no longer possible to retreat by rap-pelling down the rope.

Such routes have their own logic—mountaineers use aid techniques and expansion pitons only when they cannot do other-wise. In the 1960s, the Italians launched the fashion for "tech-nological" routes, that is to say aid routes almost entirely based on expansion pitons driven into the densest walls, as typified by the Maestri route up Roda di Vael, as well as those opened by Mirko Minuzzo on Cima Grande

Top left: John Salathé and Ax Nelson after climbing Lost Arrow Chimney, Yosemite. Top right: Pitons and hooks made by Salathé. Bottom left: Warren Harding, one of the Californian "rebels." Bottom right: Gary Hemming. Facing page: A passage on the northwest face of Half Dome, Yosemite.

days to accomplish, was climbed by Peter Croft and Dave Schultz in 1991 in the astonishing time of four hours, forty-eight minutes and *ten seconds*. What precision!

The Era of Superdirects

Whereas the influence of American techniques was marked on the granite peaks of the Mont Blanc range, the primarily limestone eastern Alps had not awaited the arrival of Americans in order to push "aid" climbing much further than Comici, Bonatti, or Guido Magnone had done.

and Torre Venezia. The routes were indeed *diret-tissime*, but at the expense of what might be called a certain contempt for the rock—340 expansion pitons were driven into Cima Grande for some 500 meters (1,600 ft.) of rockface!

In 1968, a powerful voice rose in protest against such practices—that of Reinhold Messner, a young climber from the southern Tyrol who already had some major ascents under his belt. Messner claimed that superdi-rects had killed off the idea of the "impossible" in mountaineering. For him, bolts eliminated the true exploit, because they made it possible to

*Above, left: The young
Reinhold Messner during an
ascent of the Walker Spur on
the Grandes Jorasses. Above,
right: Jean-Claude Droyer
making the first free ascent of
the Comici route on Cima
Grande di Lavaredo.*

climb anything. He suggested that they be banned, and his opinion was soon shared by all. As late as 1974, Doug Scott could still write that, "bolts are not necessary on limestone." Today, however, they are found on limestone cliffs throughout France!

"Clean" and "Free" Climbing

Such comments raised the idea of an "ethics" of mountaineering, a notion already present when Mummery declared that the Dent du Géant was "absolutely inaccessible by fair means." The main concept behind this ethics was that the means should be appropriate to the ends. Whereas bolts are appropriate at Yosemite and safety ropes acceptable in the Himalayas, those practices should be banned in the Alps. Similarly, oft-repeated classic routes should not be over-equipped with protective gear. But, as happens every time a critical principle is introduced, some people want to make it absolute. It was queried, for instance, whether pitons are really necessary at all.

The challenge to pitons came partly from Great Britain, where, for historical reasons, they were used with great reluctance. Instead, climbers would try to anchor their rope on stones jammed into cracks; a little later the stones were replaced by the nuts of industrial bolts. A similar technique, employing knots of rope, had been used since the turn of the century on the sandstone towers around Dresden in Saxony. The first specially manufactured climbing "nuts" and "rocks" (of plastic or metal) only appeared on continental Europe in 1969. They were followed by wedges that created a camming effect, leading in the U.S. to Ray Jardine's 1974 invention of "friends," spring-loaded cam devices that could take the impact from a fall in previously "unprotectable" places, like fissures with obtuse angles.

The new methods of protection present few drawbacks yet offer a significant advantage. Whereas pitons were hammered forcefully into the rock and steadily damaged it, "natural" devices only go into action in the event of a fall. It was discovered with amazement that they can replace old-fashioned pitons in almost all situations.

Two key dates are worth mentioning: in Yosemite, the first ascent of the Nose without hammer and pitons was made by Yvon Chouinard and Bruce Carson in 1973; in the Alps, a route up the west face of the Petit Dru, equally free of ham-

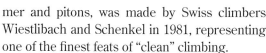

mer and pitons, was made by Swiss climbers Wiestlibach and Schenkel in 1981, representing one of the finest feats of "clean" climbing.

At the time it seemed as though pitons, especially bolts, were doomed to extinction. But the opposite occurred. Even as clean climbing was developing, another apparently convergent—although, in fact, contradictory—trend was spreading fast: "free" climbing.

Free climbing was born on the training cliffs, and involves the idea that a route has been fairly climbed only when *nothing but rock* is used as a means of progression. Free climbing therefore makes a strict distinction between anchors (used only to halt a fall) and artificial aids (any piton, nut, or friend used as an artificial hold or point of rest).

For advocates of free climbing, it went without saying that all the old routes completed using aid techniques needed to be free-climbed sooner or later. This entailed, obviously, a significant increase in difficulty. In 1977, Jean-Claude Droyer "freed" the historic Bonatti route on Grand Capucin using only nine points of aid or rest; he followed with the Comici route up Cima Grande. It was up to the next generation of climbers to demonstrate that even the most forbidding routes formerly scaled artificially could henceforth be climbed without using pitons as holds. Thus the Buhl and Maestri routes on Roda di Vael in the Dolomites were freed in 1980 by Hans Mariacher and Alberto Campanile, respectively. Benoît Grison repeated the exploit on the Directe Américaine up the Petit Dru in 1981. But the big year was 1983: the south face of the Fou and the last aid passages on the Grand Capucin were overcome by Eric Escoffier and the Superdirect on the Drus fell to Marco Pedrini from Switzerland, who furthermore used nuts exclusively. In Yosemite progress was a little slower, given that the large, monolithic slabs that had required bolts were recalcitrant to free techniques. They were only "freed," for that matter, when the holes originally made by pitons became progressively large enough to be used as providential hand-holds. The Salathé Wall was scaled without the use of artificial aids by Todd Skinner in 1988, capped in 1993 when the Nose—*the* Yosemite route—was freed by the American woman climber Lynn Hill.

At the same time, however, the increase in difficulty deliberately sought by partisans of free climbing meant that occasional falls were

Above, left: Eric Escoffier. Above, right: Kurt Albert filmed by Gerhard Baur during the first free climb of the forbidding overhangs on the Swiss route up Cima Grande di Lavaredo.

inevitable, whereas classic mountaineers had felt that any fall was an error or fault.

This shift in attitude was made possible by improved protection equipment. Nylon ropes had been available since the end of the Second World War, but it was only with comfortable sit-harnesses, developed by Don Whillans in 1970, that long, repeated falls became bearable. But only if the piton held, of course! Originally, the routes on what had been called "training cliffs" were protected, as in the mountains, by hammering pitons into the rock. As the number of climbers skyrocketed, this technique became untenable, which led to the idea of cementing permanent bolts into the wall.

The Bolt Revolution

In the meantime, however, free climbing had led to a radical change. On the limestone cliffs religiously explored by free climbers, it soon became clear that bolts made it possible to trace routes completely independent of cracks or fissures. It was in the Verdon Gorge in France—a site halfway between training cliff and mountain wall, typical of the challenge sought by free climbers in the 1970s—that the discovery was perhaps most striking. When Jacques Perrier

opened a route called "Pichenibule" in 1978, its long diagonal traverses were designed primarily to create a highly aesthetic sequence of moves across slabs that neither nuts nor pitons could protect. If Messner's principles had been respected, such routes would never be climbed.

Up in the high mountains, forgers of new routes took note. Not only did they adopt bolts, but by 1980 they began taking rock drills along! Michel Piola in the Mont Blanc range, the Rémy brothers in Switzerland, and Jean-Michel Cambon in the Oisans region all made a specialty of these modern routes that make such delightful climbing for rock lovers—*committed* rock lovers, that is, since most of these routes are technically quite demanding.

Not all mountaineers, however, responded to the siren song of modernity. In Italy, climbers like Enzo Cozzolino were determined to continue forging routes "in the old style," without bolts or even nuts. Cozzolino, from Trieste, was known for the extreme, sustained difficulty of his routes, and died on Civetta in 1972 at the age of twenty-four. In Austria, Albert Precht opened some five hundred routes without the use of bolts. In general, the eastern Alps remained more traditional than France and Switzerland.

The use of "expansion bolts" made it possible to attack compact slabs where neither pitons nor nuts could provide protection. Here Pierre-Alain Steiner is opening a route (Une Gueule du Diable) on the Envers des Aiguilles.

In these countries, improved technique, the use of bolts, sustained physical training, and so on, all contributed to a remarkable decade of rising levels of difficulty, not only on walls of average scope, like the south face of the Aiguille du Midi or the east face of the Grand Capucin, but also on the highest faces. Two highly reputed routes marked the 1980s through their combination of sustained, extremely difficult and exposed passages (whether climbed free or with artificial aids)—"A Travers le Poisson" on Monte Marmolada in the Dolomites, by Czech climbers Igor Koller and Jndřich Šustr (1981); and "Divine Providence" on the Grand Pilier d'Angle, by Patrick Gabarrou and François Marsigny (1984). Both routes underwent the same evolution; when first ascended, they included a few passages of aid climbing, but several years later were "freed" by other climbers (Hans Mariacher for "Poisson," Alain Ghersen and Thierry Renault for "Providence").

Unexpectedly, the number of new routes created each year has not diminished. To the contrary, the very concept of new route has changed. In the past, a new route had to be autonomous, finding its own logical path up a reasonably independent portion of the face. Now it suffices to offer fine new sequences of moves, regardless of whether or not the route parallels existing itineraries. This means that the only logic followed by the most recent routes is quite simply to avoid previous ones. Thus, it is certainly possible to open even more new routes, probably more difficult ones, in the same way that climbers on training cliffs seek out the most forbidding overhang. But whether intentional or not, this dense mesh of paths shrinks the dimensions of the great faces by multiplying the number of escape routes.

Trailblazers have scoured the mountains to find overlooked faces, and have found them without too much trouble, insofar as today's mountaineers are less concerned about whether a route leads to a summit or not, as long as it affords some fine climbing. Looking at mountains from this new perspective has profoundly altered, in a mere matter of years, the way that various ranges are frequented. The hut at Envers des Aiguilles, formerly little used, has become wildly popular as the cliffs overlooking it have been systematically explored. At lower altitude, formerly unknown climbing zones are springing up all over, even when they culminate in slopes of grass or scree. It hardly matters any

In the 1980s, climbers sought out overlooked faces. Left: Making a route up the wonderful limestone of Wendenstock in the Titlis range, Switzerland. Center: Czech climber Igor Koller during the first ascent of a new route on Marmolada. Right: François Marsigny making the first ascent of "Divine Providence" on the Grand Pilier d'Angle.

more, since climbers can always rappel down. This new exploration of verticality has taken diverse forms in the Verdon Gorges, the superb granite routes up the Dôme de l'Eldorado, and the magnificent limestone walls of Wendenstock.

The upshot is that the summit has lost its symbolic importance, to the benefit of a specific route and its difficulties. The challenge has become instead a question of successfully negotiating the crux, or key sequence. The nature of many routes has also been changed by new material, if only by equipping a quick and easy rappel where once climbers had to carry heavy crampons and ice axes to make a long and complex descent. This has lent a certain blandness to many routes that were once "great classics," compounded with the reassuring possibility of helicopter res-

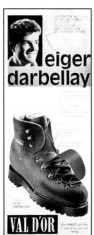

cue (a fairly recent option, since the first airborne rescue was carried out on the north face of the Eiger only in 1971).

This blandness is probably the price to pay for the increasing difficulty of more recent routes, where, even at high altitudes, certain climbing passages are given a numerical grade of 7a or higher (Alpine grade VI+; US Class 5.12), a level of difficulty only attained on training cliffs as recently as 1977. This development goes against the commonly held idea that there is henceforth a total separation between mountaineering and pure rock climbing. It is now necessary, though by no means sufficient, to have very good rock skills in order to be a good mountaineer. The mountaineering of the 1950s has broken down into various specialties: rock climbing (itself subdivided into different approaches—bouldering, cliffs, artificial walls, etc.), ice cascades, Himalayan climbing, and mountain skiing. This diversity implies not only multiple skills, but also the perfect mastery epitomized by solo ascents.

The Development of Solo Ascents

One of the most striking phenomena of contemporary mountaineering is the extraordinary development of solo ascents. Climbing alone is

a venerable tradition, associated with names like Preuss, Comici, and Winkler. However, during the 1960s, solo climbs were most unusual, reserved for an elite that only practiced them in moderation. These days, talented mountaineers consider a solo ascent to be as normal and natural as climbing with a partner.

The question was how to surpass the two great masters of the 1950s, Hermann Buhl and Cesare Maestri. In 1963, Michel Darbellay from Valais showed the way by scaling the north face of the Eiger on his own, just after an aborted attempt by Bonatti. Then the west face of the Petit Dru succumbed to René Desmaison in 1965, while the Walker Spur fell to Italian mountaineer Alessandro Gogna in 1968. Above all, in 1969 Messner made a solo ascent of the two routes then considered to be the toughest in the Alps: on rock, the Philipp-Flamm route up Punta Civetta; on ice, the north face of Les Droites (in only eight and a half hours, whereas all previous parties had taken over two days). In the next few years, most classic routes were the target of first solo climbs, such as the Directe Américaine on the Petit Dru (Jean-Claude Droyer, 1971), the Frêney Pillar (Georges Nominé, 1971), and the complete Peuterey Arête, the longest route in the Alps (René Desmaison, 1972).

Subsequently, solo climbing "took off." Ascents of famous routes became more numerous even as recent, more difficult routes fell to a sole climber only a few years after being opened. Enthusiasts then competed to compound the difficulty, either by making a solo ascent under winter conditions, or by forging a new route all alone (following in Bonatti's footsteps in both instances), or by doing several climbs one after another (called "marathon linkage"), or even by combining all of the above in one exploit!

Renato Casarotto made some remarkable solo winter ascents starting in 1984: the north face of Pelmo, the Andrich-Faé route up Punta Civetta, the Cozzolino dihedral (corner) on Piccolo Mangart in the Julian Alps, the east face of the Grandes Jorasses. Casarotto went on to string together several solo winter routes one after another: the Ratti-Vitali route up the Aiguille Noire de Peuterey, the Gervasutti route on Gugliermina, and the Frêney Pillar on Mont

Preceding double page: Jean-Christophe Lafaille on the face of Frêney during his linkage of two new solo routes in 1991. Above: Michel Darbellay posed for an ad after making the first solo ascent of the north face of the Eiger in 1963.

Blanc (1982). Climbers who opened new routes all alone include Catherine Destivelle on the Petit Dru, Slavko Svetičič on the Grandes Jorasses, and, well before everybody else, the Czech mountaineer Thomas Gross, who took eighteen days in 1975 to trace a new route up the west face of the Petit Dru, accompanied by—his guitar. The first winter solo openings included Marc Batard on the Petit Dru, Jean-Christophe Lafaille on the Grandes Jorasses, and the American Jeff Lowe on the Eiger (1991). Finally, Lafaille capped it all with successive solo winter firsts when tracing two new routes, on the Grand Pilier d'Angle and the central pillar of Frêney (1991).

One feat among many others illustrates the mastery acquired by solo mountain climbers: in 1990, the Slovenian mountaineer Slavko Svetičič took

symbolize the mortal risks taken by mountaineers. Assuming that a good, "theatrical" target has been chosen (Drus, Eiger, Jorasses), there is no faster road to fame than a solo ascent.

The very concept of a "completely solo" ascent, however, is somewhat contradicted by media coverage. Despite the lack of a rope, is an ascent truly done "alone" when the climber is followed second by second by a helicopter with which he or she is in constant radio contact? Should the climber fall, the outcome is obviously the same, but in the event of some other incident, observers would be criminally guilty of refusing to save someone in mortal danger if they offered no aid. Hence when Eric Escoffier broke an ice axe during his ascent of the north face of the Grandes Jorasses, a helicopter provided a

only twenty-seven hours to climb the Harlin Direct route up the Eiger which, when first opened a mere fourteen years earlier, had required siege tactics, ten climbers, and nearly a month of effort!

But twenty-seven hours is a long time, it might be objected, compared to the three hours it took France's Christophe Profit to scale all 1,000 meters of the Directe Américaine in 1982, or the four hours and fifty minutes required by Thomas Bubendorfer from Austria to make it up the classic route on the Eiger in 1983—records that still stand today. But, like all virtuoso performances, these exploits require a lot of rehearsal, and are carried out on well-known itineraries whose difficulties are quite reasonable given the current standards of contemporary climbers.

One—though not the only—reason for the popularity of solo ascents is that they attract more media attention than any other feat, because they

replacement. Some mountain climbers got the message, and they now climb "solo" in complete solitude, which has the drawback of denying them the fruits of media success.

A New Game—Marathon Linkage

Stringing routes together in a marathon linkage, or "enchaînement," has become a phenomenon as striking as solo ascents. Since it now takes only a few hours to scale the tallest faces, why not link them together? To suggest that marathon linkage is a new phenomenon would be historically inaccurate, however. As early as 1895, for example, Ludwig Norman-Neruda and Rudolf von Arvay climbed the four existing routes up Punta Cinque Dita (or Fünffingerspitze) in the Dolomites in only five hours and forty-five minutes. But up until the 1970s, such

Four of the world's major solo climbers (from left to right): Georges Nominé, Alessandro Gogna, Christophe Profit, and Slavko Svetičič.

In 1983, Austrian climber Thomas Bubendorfer made a superfast solo ascent of the north face of the Eiger; he is seen here in the upper part of the second snowfield, one of the crux passages on that magnificent face.

Alain Ghersen soloing the ninety-meter dihedral (corner) on the west face of the Drus during his 1990 linkage of the Robbins–Hemming route (La Directe Américaine, Petit Dru), the Walker Spur (Grandes Jorasses), and the Peuterey Arête (Mont Blanc).

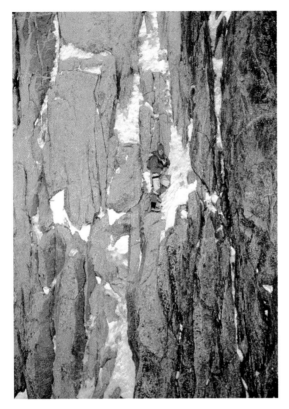

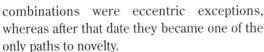

combinations were eccentric exceptions, whereas after that date they became one of the only paths to novelty.

In 1961, a surprising exploit—incomprehensible at the time—heralded the future. Belgian climber Claudio Barbier scaled the five north faces of Tre Cime di Lavaredo in a single day: the Cassin route on Cima Ovest, the Comici route on Cima Grande, the Preuss route on Cima Piccolissima, the Dülfer route on Punta di Frida, and the Innerkofler route on Cima Piccola. Not only did Barbier demonstrate an uncommon mastery of climbing skills, there was also a certain logic in deciding to link these five historic, neighboring routes. The starting signal for the modern series of linkages was given by Nicolas Jaeger in 1975, when he successively climbed the Grand Pilier d'Angle and the central pillar of Frêney. Then, in 1978, came Marc Batard, who scaled the Major route, descended the Red Sentinel, and finally climbed back up Mont Blanc via the Brenva Spur. Such feats proliferated in the 1980s: the south face of the Fou and the Directe Américaine on the Dru by

Christophe Profit (right) made a splash by successfully linking three of the great north face routes—the Grandes Jorasses, the Eiger, and the Matterhorn. He is seen above during his trilogy, on the Walker Spur (Grandes Jorasses).

Patrick Béhault and Jean-Marc Boivin (1982); Directe Américaine and Bonatti Pillar by Eric Escoffier and Daniel Lacroix (1982); Directe Américaine and Walker Spur by the same team (1984), the four pillars of Frêney one after another by Christophe Profit and Dominique Radigue (1984). And all of that in a single day.

The marathon linkage of different routes can be evaluated from various angles—that of difficulty, that of intrinsic logic, that of length, and even that of symbol. Since routes are numerous, their potential permutations are even more so. Barbier's 1961 series, for instance, seemed natural. Much less logical, though highly symbolic, was the "trilogy" that won so much media coverage for mountain climbing in the 1980s: the north faces of the Matterhorn, the Eiger, and the Grandes Jorasses. They had been Heckmair's "three final Alpine problems." Yvano Ghirardini had already climbed all three in the course of a single winter; in 1985, Profit managed to scale them all in a single day by being helicoptered from one face to another (and by climbing the Grandes Jorasses via

the Shroud, a much quicker route than the Walker Spur). In 1987, Profit repeated his performance, this time in winter, and opting for the Croz Spur, in just forty-two non-stop hours. Even more surprising, if even less logical, were exploits like Alain Ghersen's 1990 ascent of the Directe Américaine, the Walker Spur, and the Peuterey Arête. Downright bizarre was Ghersen's 1987 linkage, thanks to a car and the highways, of an extremely difficult boulder passage at Fontainebleau near Paris with a crag route at Saussois in Burgundy, followed by the Peuterey Arête in the Alps. Hans Kammerlander and Hanspeter Heisendle, on the other hand, opted for bicycles when "linking" the north face of Ortler to the north face of Cima Grande. Climbing routes in series is far rarer outside the Mont Blanc range, not because other ranges are less conducive to it but because the whole concept is tied to media coverage that insists on focusing on the "well-known" summits around Mont Blanc. Although Thomas Bubendorfer's 1988 ascent of five major Dolomite routes was heavily (overly?) covered by the media, that

was not the case in 1990 when Manrico dell'Agnola and Alcide Prati climbed the Solleder and Philipp–Flamm routes in the same day, even going so far as to descend on foot. Nor was much attention paid when, in December 1993, Christophe Moulin took five days to link solo winter ascents of the two most austere faces in the Oisans range, namely the north face of Meije and the northwest face of Ailefroide.

Among more recent linkages, German climber Frank Jordan rendered explicit homage to precursor Claudio Barbier and to the entire history of the Dolomites when, in fifteen hours, he completed the Cassin route up Cima Ovest, the Preuss route up Piccolissima, and the Brandler route up Cima Grande. His feat focused on the famous Tre Cime, covered three different periods of mountaineering, and honored three great mountain climbers—an almost perfect symbol. When it is realized that Brandler was originally an artificial aid route that had only recently been "freed," Jordan's ascent without rope or artificial hold emerges as a thoroughly remarkable feat.

Left: Jean-Marc Boivin, one of the leading lights of French mountaineering in the 1980s. Above, left: The versatile Boivin demonstrates his rock skills. Above, right: Christophe Moulin performed some fine marathon linkages in the Oisans range.

Mountaineer Skiing

Outside the highly academic milieu of pure rock climbing, modern mountaineers have become extremely versatile athletes. In 1994, at age twenty-eight, the Italian Simone Moro was the first to have combined the ascent of an "8,000er" with a passage graded 8b (Alpine VII, U.S. 5.13). Pedrini, meanwhile, who died young, was one of the first to test bungee jumping. Heini Holzer was Reinhold Messner's climbing partner before going on to become one of the most brilliant advocates of "extreme skiing." As to paragliding, most of today's mountaineers practice it. There are no longer any rigid divisions between mountaineering activities.

The person who exemplifies that trend is indisputably Jean-Marc Boivin. His sequence of exploits on the Matterhorn in 1980 typifies his conception of mountaineering—he descended the east slope on skis, made a solo ascent of the north face, and then jumped from the summit in a hang-glider! He was also the first to take off in a paraglider from the top of Everest (1988) and has performed some of the finest exploits of extreme skiing.

Extremely difficult descents on skis became popular in the 1970s, giving mountaineering a new dimension. Obviously, remarkable runs had already been made in the past, especially taking into account the nature of the equipment used. As early as 1939, André Tournier skied down from the top of the Aiguille d'Argentière via the Milieu Glacier (400 meters at a 40° gradient).

But the great initiator of extreme mountain skiing was Sylvain Saudan from Switzerland. He made a name for himself in 1967 by being the first to ski down the Spencer Couloir on the Aiguille de Blaitière, at a 51° gradient. It was an impressive feat, even though this descent has now became classic. The following year, Saudan repeated the exploit on the Gervasutti Couloir of Mont Blanc du Tacul and the Whymper Couloir of the Aiguille Verte. Saudan was no longer alone—in 1969, Austrian mountaineers Kurt Lapusch and Manfred Oberegger skied down the north face of Gross Wiessbachhorn (roped together!), perhaps being the first to attack a 60° slope. In 1971, Serge Cachat-Rosset was the first to ski down the now classic descent of the northeast face of Les Courtes. Two years later, Cachat-Rosset pulled off a highly coveted descent: the Couturier Couloir of the Aiguille Verte. But he was set on the summit by helicopter, a debatable technique, whereas Heini Holzer, from the southern Tyrol, preferred to climb to the top before skiing down the Brenva Spur of Mont Blanc via the Güssfeldt Couloir.

The risks of this new activity were underscored when Holzer fell to his death on Piz Roseg (Graubunden, Switzerland) in 1977. The accident did not discourage other skiing mountaineers, however. That same year, Daniel Chauchefoin skied down the northeast face of Les Courtes via the Austrian route, a truly serious glacier itinerary that includes passages at gradient of 65° and has not, up till now, been repeated. Extremely difficult descents on skis are dangerous entreprises limited to the few. They are also governed by the necessarily ephemeral conditions on the mountain. It is a question of knowing how to seize the opportunity presented by these conditions; summer climbers up the southeast face of the Moine, for instance, follow an entirely rock route, and yet Boivin skied down it, in 1987. Two years later, Boivin descended the Nant-Blanc slope of the Aiguille Verte, while "extreme snowboarding" came of age when Bruno Gouvy descended the Couturier Couloir. A chapter seemed to come to a close when Jérôme Ruby snowboarded down the Shroud of the Grandes Jorasses, a route that had been a mythical ascent just fifteen years earlier!

The new generation of mountaineer-skiers, like the Italian Stefano De Benedetti and Frenchman Pierre Tardivel, have shown that the conquest of the Alps on skis is far from over, and that modest summits, when snow-covered, can still offer a vast terrain for adventure.

"Extreme skiing" is a spectacular new form of mountaineering, promoted by the likes of Pierre Tardivel (above, left). Facing page: Tardivel descending the north face of Mont Dolent.

Women Mountaineers

Until a relatively recent date, few truly top-notch mountaineers were women. More importantly, feats that would have gone unnoticed if performed by a man were considered an exploit if accomplished by a woman—for a long time, all the "female firsts" entailed a woman climbing in second position behind a man, whereas men had to be lead climber for an exploit to count!

The name of the French climber Simone Badier nevertheless merits mention, for in the 1970s she was lead climber up almost all the prestigious Alpine routes (the south face of the Fou, Walker Spur, etc.), and was probably one of the first women to climb regularly.

Being lead climber means acting as a guide. The first woman guide was Gwen Moffat from Britain, back in 1953, but it was a long time before her example was imitated on the continent (Moffat subsequently became a successful author of mountaineering novels). In France, it was Martine Rolland who broke the taboo in 1983, quickly followed in other Alpine countries. Now Chamonix's prestigious and very conservative Compagnie des Guides has Sylviane Tavernier as one of its members. At the same time, the competence of the finest women mountaineers has risen markedly, especially in terms of high risk activities—solo ascents, winter climbing, forging new routes, and Himalayan expeditions are no longer the sole prerogative of men, even if they still outnumber women.

It is only recently that the most dangerous category of mountain climbing, solo ascents, has been undertaken by women, although not as recently as some people think. As early as 1978, Beverly Johnson climbed the Dihedral Wall of El Capitan in Yosemite solo. That same year, two teams of Polish women—Wanda Rutkiewicz, Irena Kesa, Anna Czerwinska, and Krystyna Palmovska—made a winter ascent of the north

Catherine Destivelle has deservedly become one of the most famous women mountaineers of the day. She is seen here forging a new solo route on the granite face of the Petit Dru, an almost unique exploit in the annals of women's mountaineering.

face of the Matterhorn. Polish women, notably Rutkiewicz, would later play a decisive role in the feminization of Himalayan mountaineering.

None of these exploits received much attention. The same could not be said, however, of *the* female mountaineer of the 1990s, Catherine Destivelle, whose solo ascents symbolized a new era. She opened a new route up the west face of the Petit Dru in 1991, then made the first woman's solo winter ascent of the north face of the Eiger in 1992, then the Walker Spur the following year, and finally the rarely climbed Bonatti route up the Matterhorn. Other women were hard on Destivelle's heels, however; during the summer of 1993, British climber Alison Hargreaves climbed solo the Shroud on the Grandes Jorasses and the north faces of the Matterhorn, the Eiger, Piz Badile, Cima Grande, and the Petit Dru, that is to say the six classic north faces of the prewar era celebrated by Gaston Rébuffat in his book, *Starlight and Storm*. As might be expected, solo climbs by women have increased in the past few years: Swiss mountaineer Evelyne Binsack climbed the Lauper route up Eiger (1994), Anne Grete Nebell from Norway climbed the Rimmon route up Trollryggen (1995), and Japanese climber Yuka Endoh vanquished the Zodiac on El Capitan in Yosemite (1992, in what was in fact the second woman's solo ascent, Sue Harrington having been the first eight years earlier).

It is nevertheless worth distinguishing two types of situation. When Destivelle made her solo winter ascent of the north face of the Grandes Jorasses, it represented a feat that several men had already accomplished—forget the gender, and it is no longer a first. When, on the other hand, Czech climbers Zuzanna Hofmannová and Alena Stehlíková made the first winter ascent up the British route on the north face of Piz Badile, it was quite simply the first winter ascent ever. Similar, and much more important, was the first "free" climb of the Nose of El Capitan by Lynn Hill

from America in 1993—for the first time, an exploit long coveted yet never achieved by the finest male climbers had been accomplished by a woman. As far as mountaineering goes, differences in performance between men and women will probably continue to shrink.

Right: Wanda Rutkiewicz (standing), Irena Kesa, Anna Czerwinska, and Krystyna Palmovska after making the first women's winter ascent of the north face of the Matterhorn. Below: Sylviane Tavernier, the first woman accepted into the prestigious Compagnie des Guides in Chamonix.

The Public Face of Climbing

Histories of mountain climbing, whatever the type, all make the same mistake of failing to distinguish between rare exploits and mass activity. After all, mountaineering would not exist without its institutions (guide corporations, mountain rescue services, climbing clubs). Guides do not make a living from exploits, but from their numerous anonymous clients. And mountaineering has changed for common mortals just as much as for celebrities.

Mass mountaineering is now typified by two trends, which happen to be contradictory. On the one hand, the technical level of climbers has risen; a practiced mountaineer today will not shrink in fear before a passage graded VI, which only yesterday was considered the ultimate in difficulty. But this rise in standards has led to new demands—people are no longer willing to hike several hours to reach a few pitches of fine rock climbing. The increasing number of bolted routes reduces mountaineers' experience of using pitons, of seeking an itinerary, of advancing into the unknown, even as it induces a some-

times fallacious sense of "security." Modern routes favor zones where the rockface is finest, making many people forget that 99 percent of any mountain, as Rébuffat claimed of the Matterhorn, is "a sublime heap of rubble." In other words, the purely qualitative alpine atmosphere has taken a back seat to quantifiable climbing feats, favoring an attitude of pure consumerism based on figures.

To exaggerate somewhat, it could be said that the mountaineering "public" now chooses either modern, well-equipped routes on fine rock, or the easy normal routes up famous mountains (sometimes little more than trekking). Everything in between the easy slope and the vertical wall—that is to say everything that was formerly the delight of classic mountain climbing—no longer attracts many people. But every trend comes full circle, as recent history has demonstrated. If Messner had been told back in 1975 that just fifteen years later people would be opening new and magnificent routes with the aid of an electric drill, he would probably have been highly skeptical. In the near future, perhaps, people will rediscover the charm of long, hard-to-follow routes where every spike of rock looks the same, where the difficulty of a ridge remains an unknown factor, where a chilly bivouac may be required while awaiting dawn. In short, the great mountains as they really are most of the time, offering the simple pleasure of finding—or losing—one's way.

By making the first free ascent of the Nose on El Capitan, Lynn Hill from the United States pulled off an exploit unsuccessfully attempted by many men mountain climbers.

Other Mountain Ranges

Greenland

BAFFIN
ISLAND

ALASKA

Arctic Circle

MCKINLEY
6,194 m

NORTH

AMERICA

ROCKY MOUNTAINS

MONT BLANC
4,807 m

E

PYRENEES

SIERRA NEVADA

MOUNT WHITNEY
4,417 m

ATLAS

ATLANTIC

Tropic of Cancer

HOGGA

OCEAN

A F

PACIFIC

Equator

CHIMBORAZO
6,310 m

HUASCARAN
6,768 m

OCEAN

ANDES

ANDES

SOUTH

AMERICA

Tropic of Capricorn

ANDES

ACONCAGUA
6,960 m

ANDES

PATAGONIA

FITZ ROY
3,375 m

Antarctic Circle

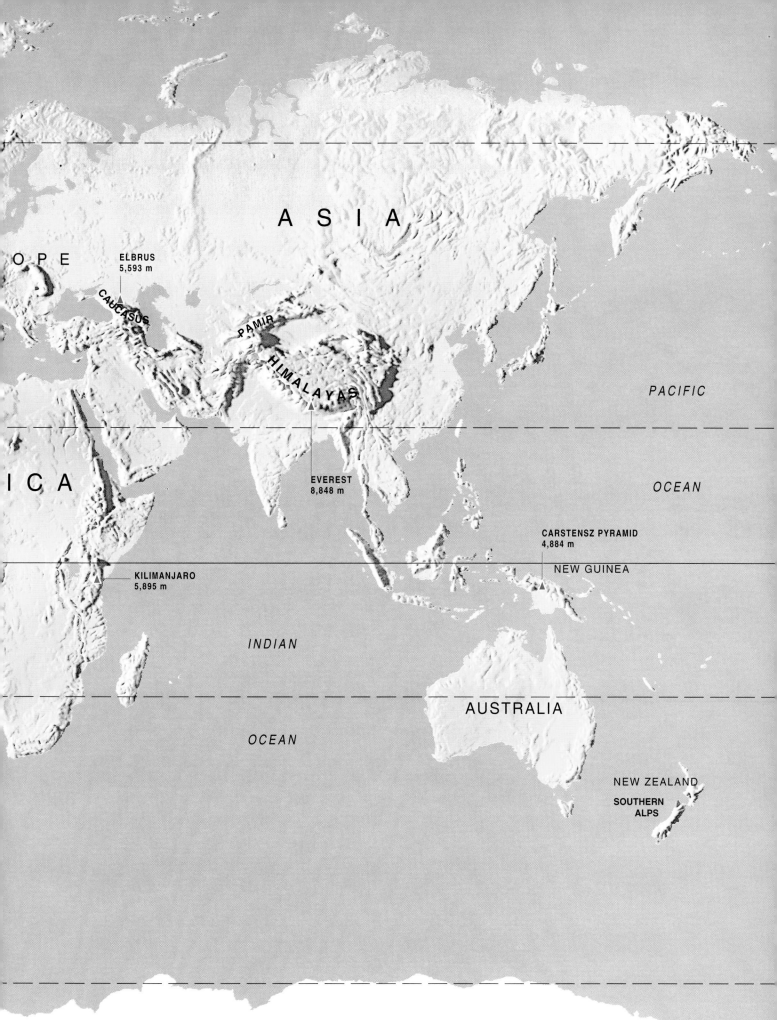

ASIA

OPE

ELBRUS
5,593 m

CAUCASUS

PAMIR

HIMALAYAS

PACIFIC

ICA

OCEAN

EVEREST
8,848 m

CARSTENSZ PYRAMID
4,884 m

NEW GUINEA

KILIMANJARO
5,895 m

INDIAN

AUSTRALIA

OCEAN

NEW ZEALAND

SOUTHERN
ALPS

ANTARCTICA

From One Range to Another

Early expeditions outside of Western Europe—from the Caucasus to New Zealand via Africa and the Andes—served as training grounds for mountain climbers.

Traveling back in time to the year 1865, the golden age of Alpine conquest was coming to a close—every great summit except the Meije had been conquered. Mountain climbers were already beginning to attack new problems. For some, mountaineering was entering a purely sporting, purely disinterested phase, as climbers began tracing new routes up peaks already scaled, minutely exploring each face and each ridge. These same mountaineers would then scale secondary summits—secondary in terms of altitude, that is, for in general the lower the peak the more difficulties it presented—and subsequently went from secondary peaks to ridges, pinnacles, and pillars. Eventually they arrived at the point where they were attacking, say, a previously overlooked gendarme (rocky prominence) on a ridge.

This new form of mountaineering did not satisfy everyone, however. The great British climbers, who had explored the Alps immediately, began seeking new fields of action. They found them in distant lands, thereby inaugurating the second phase in the history of mountaineering, namely the exploration of the world's other mountain ranges.

Mountain climbers of the day had to rely on their own financial resources to fulfill their ambitions, which naturally favored the English climbers of the Victorian era. Occasionally, a princely family might also display an interest in exploration, as demonstrated by the duke of Abruzzi's admirable accomplishments. This period would last until the First World War, which provoked upheaval in the social equilibrium right across the world.

Later, expeditions would be financed by clubs, geographical societies, and even governments, yet what was remarkable was that the members of those expeditions all came from mountaineering circles. Once they had proved their worth, mountain climbers tended to become explorers; it was rarer for explorers to become mountain climbers.

Regardless of the period, the likes of Whymper, Mummery, Freshfield, the duke of Abruzzi, Eccles, Graham Brown, Smythe, Allain,

Left: Poster for a film about the Norwegian expedition that made the first ascent of Tirich Mir, in the Hindu Kush.
Facing page: By going beyond the Alps, mountaineers discovered peaks that were not only higher and wilder, but were also still wreathed in mystery.
Pages 166 and 167: The north slope of Mount Everest.

Merkl, Welzenbach, Lambert, Dittert, Joe Brown, Schneider, Harrer, Heckmair, Terray, Lachenal, Rébuffat, Franco, Contamine, Magnone, and the Jeunesse et Montagne team accomplished extraordinary exploits in the Alps before moving on to the Himalayas or the Andes. The same comment applies to Italians such as Bonatti, Gobbi, Rey, and Lacedelli, not to mention Maestri and Mauri, as well as the great lone climber, the Austrian Hermann Buhl. Even when history was being made elsewhere, it was being made by mountaineers already famous in the Alps, with the exception of a few climbers like Fynn, Hillary, and the New Zealanders, whose southern exploits did not reach European ears.

As to professional guides, the great names of the golden age, whether from Switzerland, Chamonix, or Italy, also pioneered the exploration of other ranges—Devouassoud, Blanc, Carrel, Croux, Petigax, Ollier, Zurbriggen. They were succeeded by Lochmatter and, more recently still, Lambert, Franco, Rébuffat, Terray, Lachenal, Bouvier, Leroux, Coupé, Desmaison, and Pollet-Villard, all of whom lent luster to the profession of guide by forthrightly demonstrating their competence not only as mountaineering technicians but also as expedition leaders, as did their Italian counterparts such as Bonatti, Gobbi, Lacedelli, Rey, and Maestri.

Yet of all the professionals who deserve mention in the early chapters of this phase of mountain climbing, two names stand out. First of all there was François Devouassoud, guide to Douglas Freshfield and his companions, who explored the Caucasus, Armenia, and the Himalayas, as well as a number of little-known ranges. Devouassoud acted as a veritable "Sirdar" (chief) in the Indian sense of the term. Above all, however, the greatest guide was Matthias Zurbriggen from Macugnaga, successor to the great Ferdinand Imseng on the east face of Monte Rosa, although an explorer by predilection. Zurbriggen went everywhere—to the Himalayas as early as 1892 with Conway's Karakoram expedition, then back again for another twelve years with the Workmans all across the Himalayas, but not before having won fame for his first, solitary ascent of Aconcagua in the Andes in 1896, not to mention his solo ascent of Mount Cook, the highest peak in New Zealand, in 1894. Zurbriggen was a veritable explorer of summits. He remained unequalled for a long time, until Lionel Terray came along. Terray was another man capable of organizing, leading, and making the ultimate decisions required of a large, modern mountaineering expedition.

Although these explorations could be presented in a more or less chronological order, it

Below, left: Douglas Freshfield, one of the first to explore the Caucasus and the Himalayas. Below, right: The Caucasus range, on the fringe of Europe, with summits over 5,000 meters high. In the center is Ushba.

seems preferable here to discuss them range by range. Familiarity with most of the figures involved makes it possible to situate the relevant milieu and period correctly. Yet it is worth noting the general scale of altitudes across the various ranges. In the Alps, the highest summits rise above a threshold of 4,000 meters (13,000 ft.); in the Caucasus and in Africa, the threshold is 5,000 meters (16,400 ft.), rising to 6,000 meters (19,700 ft.) in the Americas, and reaching 7,000 meters (23,000 ft.) in the Himalayas, Pamirs, and Tien Shan. Finally, fourteen peaks on the planet, in the Karakoram and Great Himalayan Ranges, rise above 8,000 meters (26,250 ft.).

The Caucasus

Once the great battle in the Alps was over, it quite naturally occurred to the conquerors to turn their attention to the nearest non-Alpine mountain range. At that time, although practically unknown, the Caucasus was still part of the European sphere.

The pioneer in the Caucasus was Douglas Freshfield from Britain. More than just a climber, Freshfield was an explorer who had journeyed through mountain ranges from the Alps to the Balkans and Asia Minor prior to heading for the Caucasus with his faithful friends Moore and Tucker, and, above all, his guide and friend François Devouassoud. If, at other points in this book, I have succumbed to the temptation to criticize the behavior of British mountaineers toward their guides (for having placed guides in a marked state of subservience), then I should stress here the sincere, lifelong friendship linking Freshfield and Devouassoud, a friendship concretized by the laconic phrases on Devouassoud's tomb in Chamonix.

In 1868, Freshfield, Devouassoud, and their companions climbed the two main peaks of the central bastion of the Caucasus: Kasbek (5,043 m) and, above all, the east summit of Elbrus (5,593 m), the highest point in the Caucasus.

Freshfield did not, however, reach the truly highest point. Elbrus is an easy giant, a former volcano terminating in twin, rounded summits; on the day they climbed it, a thick fog masked the west summit, making verification of altitude impossible. But although the west peak (5,629 m) was climbed in 1874 by Walker and Gardiner with their guide Knubel, the total absence of difficulty on either of the snowy domes suggests that, had there been no mist that day, the conscientious Freshfield and his companions would normally have gone to the top of the true summit.

Below, left: Freshfield's Caucasus party. Freshfield is seated right, while standing behind him is the Chamonix guide François Devouassoud. Below, right: Two Russian mountaineers in front of the refuge on the normal route up Elbrus.

The central Caucasus includes five peaks over 5,000 meters. Two of them were climbed during the first expedition, but there still remained Shkhara (5,184 m), Dykh-Tau (5,198 m) and Koshtan-Tau (5,145 m). Shkhara was climbed in 1888 by Cockin, accompanied by Ulrich Almer and G. Roth, and in the same year the famous Mummery, with Heinrich Zurflüh as guide, made the first ascent of Dykh-Tau. It was in 1889 that Woolley and Jossi conquered Koshtan-Tau, the last "5,000er."

Other British, German, and Italian expeditions would follow. Vittorio Sella, the remarkable Italian photographer, returned with beautiful images. Most of the conquerors were accompanied by famous guides, almost all of whom were Swiss—Almer, Knubel, Zurflüh, Graf, Furrer, and so on. Thus Ushba, the finest, if not the tallest of peaks—the Matterhorn of the Caucasus—was scaled as early as 1888 by Cockin, with Christian Almer Jr., while the traverse of Ushba's two summits was accomplished in 1903 by the Germans Pfann, Distel, and Leuchs.

The Soviet revolution would put a damper on the growth of moun-

Above: Chimborazo (6,310 m) was long thought to be the highest peak on the planet. Right: The naturalist Alexander von Humboldt climbed its slopes in 1802 to become "the highest man in the world."

taineering in the Caucasus for many years. In the interwar period, the door was opened a crack for several privileged expeditions of Germans, Swiss, and Britons, as well as for one French expedition, led by Jacques Lagarde and three other members of the Groupe de Haute Montagne (GHM). Although there were no "5,000ers" left to scale (at least via classic routes), a new form of mountaineering was coming into fashion, namely the traverse of long ridges. Here the Caucasus provided some remarkable ridge routes, which required veritable expeditions sometimes lasting more than a week. The 1931 traverse of the Bezinghi Arêtes, starting from Shkhara, required a German team to bivouac six times in ice caves along a route that never descended below 4,300 meters (14,000 ft.). In 1936, Germans Frauenberger, Radistchnig, and Peringer completed, in two stages, the terrific itinerary from Dykh-Tau to Koshtan-Tau, which includes four "5,000ers" and six peaks over 4,500 meters! The route was repeated, in a single go, by Soviet mountain climbers Abolakov and Miklashevsky in 1938. The traverse from Wologata to Karangom, meanwhile, was made in 1934 by the famous Swiss climber Lorenz Saladin (the explorer of the Tien

Shan mountains) and Walter Frei, with their guides Otto Furrer and Hans Graf, and the Soviet climber Sharlampiev.

But war intervened again. Silence and isolation reigned behind the iron curtain. During that period, Soviet mountaineering restructured and reorganized itself. The Russians rejected the most brilliant individuals in favor of mass mountain climbing, a doctrinal but efficient approach thanks to massive recruitment followed by a selection process within the various Soviet youth groups. The Soviet system nevertheless produced some rather extraordinary results. They had to "reinvent" mountain climbing techniques, given that they lagged so far behind European experts. On the other hand, they managed to produce truly strong teams that accomplished impressive exploits in the realm of long traverses across the Caucasus and the use of bivouacs. Whereas swiftness seemed to be the prerogative of Western climbers, Soviet mountaineering in the Caucasus retained all the features of grand expeditions, which would enable Soviet climbers to shine when it came to the highly difficult climatic conditions on the "7,000ers" of the Pamirs and Tien Shan.

After having been a goal of distant exploration, the Caucasus became a training ground for the people of the USSR, just as the Alps pro- vided practice for Western European mountain climbers, who then set off for the world's other mountains.

The Western Hemisphere: The Andes

It might have seemed more logical to begin in the time-honored order by discussing North America first, followed by South America, but in the realm of exploration the Andes indisputably take precedence over the Rockies, if only in historical terms. It was Edward Whymper, conqueror of the Matterhorn, who brought the Andes to the attention of mountaineers. He was not the first pioneer, however, since that title goes to the botanist Charles Marie de La Condamine for his attempts on Chimborazo, the highest volcano in Ecuador, as early as 1740. La Condamine was succeeded by Alexander von Humboldt, who managed to get higher up the slopes of the volcano in 1802.

Chimborazo (6,310 m; 20,702 ft.), a perfect volcano, rises above the high plateau of the equatorial Andes, overlooking a whole set of lofty volcanic peaks. It does not present any particular mountaineering difficulties, apart from altitude. Whymper reached the summit in 1880 following methodical reconnaissance. He

Above, left to right: A drawing by Whymper to illustrate his ascent of Chimborazo in 1880; Miss Annie Peck, an American feminist who scaled one of Huascarán's two summits in 1908; Huascarán in Peru.

accomplished the ascent in the company of his great rival on the Matterhorn, guide Jean Antoine Carrel, and together they also climbed the second highest volcano, Cotopaxi (5,897 m), first conquered back in 1872 by mountain climbers Reiss and Escobar.

It might be regretted that Whymper did not choose mountains worthy of his talent. Imagine what a mountaineering expedition by Whymper and Carrel to the Cordillera Blanca or Aconcagua would have yielded! But it should be pointed out that, at the time, Chimborazo was thought to be the highest summit in the Americas, and it was only logical to climb it first.

However, an ascent made in 1877 had gone by almost unnoticed. Illimani (6,480 m) in the Bolivian Andes was climbed by a picturesque international party composed of the Frenchman Charles Wiener, the Peruvian Ocampo, and the

Russian Grumblow, who reached the central peak. The south peak was scaled in 1888 by Sir Martin Conway and his guides from Val Tournanche, including the famous Maquignaz brothers.

The Andes stretch from north to south for some 5,500 miles along the South American continent, from Colombia to the Antarctic regions. They therefore run through a great variety of climates, exaggerated by the presence of the tropical pressure cooker of the Amazonian rain forest followed, further south, by the dry Argentinean pampas. Snowfall patterns also differ greatly: while snow can be found at an altitude of around 4,600 meters at the equator, it does not start until 6,000 meters in the drier Andes to the south. The cordilleras in Peru, meanwhile, present highly contrasting slopes depending on whether they face west

(dry) or east (humid). Thus the finest section of the Andes, although not the tallest, is the magnificent Cordillera Blanca group in Peru, comprising dozens of peaks over 6,000 meters high, capped by wonderful glaciers.

For the same geographical and climatic reasons, methodical mountaineering exploration of the range would have to await the modern era. The challenges posed for climbers are in fact very difficult, and could only be met with very modern techniques of ice and rock climbing.

The Andes, then, yielded a somewhat strange phenomenon. Very early attempts, usually successful, were made on the main summits, especially the highest, via the easiest route. This pioneering period began immediately after the golden age in the Alps and continued into the dawn of the twentieth century,

resulting in the conquest of the three great kings of the Andes: Chimborazo to the north in 1880; Aconcagua to the south in 1897 (6,960 m); and finally Huascarán in the middle in 1908 (6,768 m).

Subsequently, the period from 1930 to 1940 featured incredible activity on the part of Austro-German and Swiss mountain climbers, who conquered a good many peaks over 6,000 meters in the notorious Cordillera Blanca. Lastly, the recent period has seen the completion of exploration and conquest of the most difficult summits, both in the Cordillera Blanca and in Patagonia, a period consolidated by the first ascent of the south face of Aconcagua by a French party and by another victory, also French, over Mount Fitz Roy in Patagonia.

To return to the pioneers, Aconcagua, on the edge of the dry Andes of Chile, was commonly

Above, left: An early depiction of Cotopaxi, an Andean peak scaled as early as 1872. Above, right: The Franco–Belgian expedition to the Cordillera Blanca, with (left to right) René Mailleux, Raymond Leininger, Claude Kogan, Jean Guillemin, and Georges Kogan.

thought to be over 7,000 meters high (23,000 ft.) and it was therefore natural that climbers dreamed of conquering the culminating point in the western hemisphere (the latest triangulations peg it at 6,960 meters). Thus Paul Güssfeldt attacked it as early as 1883, coming to within 400 meters of the summit.

Then came a British expedition that included Edward Fitzgerald and Stuart Vines, accompanied by the famous Matthias Zurbriggen from Macugnaga. They laid siege to the north face of Aconcagua. (To avoid any misunderstanding, not only are the seasons reversed in the southern hemisphere, so is the exposure of slopes—so attacking the north face of Aconcagua in January, as Zurbriggen did, would correspond in the northern hemisphere to climbing a south face in July.) On 14 January, after climbing with difficulty up screes and easy but exhausting

snowfields, Zurbriggen reached the summit alone, his companions having abandoned the ascent due to altitude sickness. Not until Hermann Buhl reached the top of Nanga Parbat would another of the world's highest peaks be conquered by a solitary climber.

Then, on 13 February of the same year, Stuart Vines made the second ascent of Aconcagua, accompanied by the faithful porter Nicola Lanti, recruited back in Macugnaga by Zurbriggen. Finally, to terminate the campaign, Vines, who clearly seemed to adapt best to altitude, climbed Tupungato (6,550 m).

It is interesting to note that even today just a small minority of climbers who tackle Aconcagua actually reach the summit, most falling victim to altitude sickness. The reason for this remains unknown, since other, higher mountains have been scaled without climbers

suffering from the thinness of the air. I think the cause of the problem lies in the very lack of difficulty of the normal route up the mountain—climbers attempt the ascent without previously acclimatizing themselves by a stay at high altitude, as they would do, say, in the Himalayas. They climb too swiftly, without precautions. The same thing occurs on all the easy ascents like Mont Blanc and Elbrus. The climbers who explored the Cordillera Blanca, which is almost as high, only failed to reach the top due to technical difficulties; the fact that they spent time in base camps over 4,000 meters high would seem to support this theory of indispensable acclimatization.

After Chimborazo in the northern Andes and Aconcagua to the south, there remained the highest central peak, Huascarán (6,768 m) in the Cordillera Blanca in Peru. Although the

facts have been disputed—above all because of intense women's rivalry—it would seem that the first ascent was made in the month of August 1908 by an American, Miss Annie Peck. And although anecdote holds that she managed to arrive only by being hoisted onto the stout shoulders of her two guides from Zermatt, R. Taugwalder and Gabriel Zumtaugwald, it is certain that she at least made it to the north peak (6,655 m). Unfortunately, Miss Peck assigned her mountain the somewhat fanciful altitude of 7,300 meters, which conveniently made her "the highest woman in the world." The record was held at the time by Mrs. Fanny Bullock Workman who, on one of her several trips to the Himalayas, had climbed one of the peaks of Nunkun, judged to be 7,200 meters high. Furious at having been bested, Bullock Workman had a triangulation made of

Above, left: The summit of Quitaraju, with the Alpamayo pyramid in the distance. Above, right: Claude Kogan and Bernard Pierre on arrival at the summit of Salcantay.

Situated at the very southern tip of the Andes, the snow-capped Monte Sarmiento was attacked by Sir Martin Conway as early as 1898, but only succumbed in 1956.

Huascarán, at her own expense, and thereby reclaimed her title. Strangely, she failed to take the opportunity to have her own peak checked—the one she climbed with her porter, Ciprien Savoie, was not the real Nun, but a buttress called Pinnacle Peak, measuring 6,930 meters!

At the southern tip of the Andean range there stands, though much less high, the Patagonian Cordillera. From a polar landscape rise the granite towers of Hielo Continental, the biggest glacier cap on the continent. The tallest peaks in the area barely surpass 3,000 meters; one of them, Cerro Sarmiento (2,184 m), overlooks the glacial desert of Tierra del Fuego. In 1898, Sir Martin Conway and his guides from Val Tournanche, the Maquignaz brothers, made an attempt but halted 500 meters below the summit. It would remain the only attempt in those southern latitudes for a long time, since not until the mid-twentieth century would that range be explored anew.

Meanwhile, mountaineering in the Andes underwent another period of exploration, extremely brilliant this time, between 1930 and 1940. That was when an Austro–German expedition, composed of Borchers, Bernhard, Hein, Kinzl, and above all, Hoerling and Schneider, made ascents that brought the Cordillera Blanca to the attention of the entire world. In the 1932 season alone, the team successively climbed Huandoy (6,396 m), Artesonraju (6,025 m), Hualcan Central (5,645 m), Janaraju, Huascarán South (6,768 m) and East (6,550 m), and finally Nevado de Copoa (6,188 m).

This slew of conquests could only mean that German and Austrian climbers were particularly inspired and well in advance of their times. Indeed, in those days the major mountaineering powers were obsessed by the conquest of Himalayan summits, enviously watching Great Britain slowly advance, stumble, and relaunch its attack against the highest summit in the world, Everest. Andean summits of 6,000 meters seemed insignificant compared to the 8,000 meters of the Himalayas. But Erwin Schneider's team seemed to have understood that, while the time had come to practice mountain climbing beyond Europe, certain ranges like the Cordillera Blanca offered a field

of action comparable to the Alps, that is to say in conditions that call for Alpine techniques as opposed to Himalayan techniques. Furthermore, Peru was within reach of private expeditions.

So the expedition returned in 1936. Schneider and Awerzger climbed Nevado Champara (5,749 m), Quitaraju (6,100 m), Pucahirca (6,100 m), Siula (6,350 m), and Nevado de Ressac (6,040 m). And another team went back again in 1939, this time composed of Rohrer, Schmid, Schweizer, and Brecht, scaling Contrahierbas (6,036 m), Hualcan (6,125 m), Tocclaraju (6,032 m), Palcaraju (6,274 m), Ranrapalca (6,162 m), and Nevado Chinchey (6,222 m).

In 1934, a strong Italian expedition explored the Andes in Chile and Argentina, climbing numerous peaks over 5,000 meters and participating in the attack on Tronador (3,470 m), a steep and difficult mountain on the northern end of the Patagonian group. It represented an ideological target for the German and Italian teams of the day, highly motivated as they were by totalitarian politics.

Nevertheless, it was not until calm returned after the Second World War that exploration of the Andes was completed. This entailed the systematic conquest of secondary peaks, of tough faces, and of new routes up known summits, following the same pattern as the history of mountaineering in the Alps.

It was in 1948 that a group from Akademische Alpenclub in Zurich—Lauterburg, Schmid, Sigrist, Szepessy, and Marmillod—successively climbed Pucaraju (6,259 m), Pucaranra (6,145 m), Cashan, Carhuac, and Nevado Bayo. The years 1950, 1951, and 1952 represented a new golden age in the conquest of the Andes. More and more private expeditions were organized. And there were local "Andenists" like Ramirez, who frequently climbed with the European teams. Thus in 1950 Ramirez and Szepessy together scaled Cerro Victor.

It was in 1951 that two sensational victories were claimed by private expeditions. In June and July, a small Franco-Dutch team organized by geologist Tom de Booy and his compatriot Egeler, headed by Lionel Terray (a veteran of

The formidable granite wall of Mount Fitz Roy, seen from its snowy shoulder. The original French route followed the sunny slabs above the climbers.

That same year also saw the conquest of Alpamayo (6,120 meters), described as "the most beautiful mountain in the world." Imagine the Matterhorn completely covered in ice—a perfect pyramid. A Franco–Belgian team laid successful siege to it in August, and the summit was reached on 13 August by the Belgian climber Jongen, French mountaineers Georges Kogan and Raymond Leininger, and guide Maurice Lenoir.

On 18 August two French women, Claude Kogan and Nicole Leininger, made the second ascent of Quitaraju (6,100 m) and were the first women's team to reach the summit. They were followed by Jongen, Leininger, Fortunato, Georges Kogan, the Mailleux brothers and Dr. Guillemin; the same expedition also climbed Nevado Pisco (6,000 m).

The ascents of Alpamayo and Huantsan launched the idea of bold glacier climbing, which would subsequently be applied in all its rigor by Lionel Terray, who became *the* man in Peru.

The year 1952 was the year of the Italians and Germans, who explored the Cordillera de Vilcabamba and attacked its highest summit, Ausangate (6,550 m), the property of Italian settler Lomellini. The team of Ghiglione, Bolinder, and Rebitsch climbed the five peaks of Ausangate one by one without, however, reaching the highest point, which was conquered in 1953 by Harrer, Wellekamp, and März.

On 5 August of the same year, a French team composed of the courageous woman climber Claude Kogan and Bernard Pierre, in the company of members of two private American expeditions—Fred Ayres with George Bell and Graham Matthews with David Michael—made the first successful ascent of Salcantay, one of the finest summits in the Cordillera de Vilcabamba. The spirit that reigned among these small private expeditions appears as a refreshing relief to the bitter and sometimes underhand struggles between the major national expeditions to other mountain ranges.

Alpamayo, Salcantay, and Huantsan had succumbed—there were hardly any major "firsts" left to conquer. The hardest ascent of all, however, which for years would remain the most

Annapurna), attacked one of the finest peaks in the Cordillera Blanca, Huantsan (6,397 m), scaling both summits via the north arête. This time, it was no longer a question of a relatively easy mountain—Huantsan presents ice obstacles that, in any other mountain range, would be unscalable. But Terray discovered the "plasticity" of tropical ice and dared attack slopes steeper than the most vertiginous couloirs in the Alps. In the Andes, a gradient of 70° is common. On the other hand, step cutting is easier and ice axes can be driven home for protection. These crucial factors would also be exploited in the conquest of Nevado Pongos (5,713 m).

difficult climb in the world, was made on 2 February 1952 in the southern part of the Patagonian Cordillera. There the incredible Mount Fitz Roy (3,375 m) rises like a jet of pure granite above the glacier cap of Hielo Continental, plunging toward the dry pampa to the east. It is an inaccessible peak whipped by the strongest winds on earth. No camp could withstand such wind. The French expedition was thus forced to bivouac in ice caves. Using artificial aids and countless pitons, Terray and Guido Magnone finally managed to reach the summit—the most difficult mountain on earth had fallen.

Then, in 1954, another French expedition accomplished an outstanding and highly envied feat by making the first ascent of the south face of Aconcagua (6,960 m), representing 3,000 meters of extremely difficult rock and ice climbing. The undertaking by young French mountaineers Bérardini, Denis, Dagory, Lesueur, Paragot, and Poulet lasted seven days and ended in terrible storm conditions; the cost of victory, as at Annapurna, was very serious frostbite on the hands and feet of several members of the team.

From that date onward, however, the eyes of mountaineers have turned above all to Patagonia, where extraordinary towers of granite stand to attention above the ice. Antarctic-type expeditions were required in order to explore Hielo Continental and mount attacks on the final challenges in that polar landscape.

Meanwhile, other feats were being accomplished in the central Andes, notably the Cordillera Blanca and the Cordillera de Vilcabamba. Peru experienced a new golden age—not of the Incas this time, but of mountain climbers. Difficulty, rather than the summit, was henceforth the goal of the operation. Furthermore, the mountains were becoming more accessible as local porters gained experience and as immense glacier peaks became the targets of teams attempting to conquer virgin slopes and arêtes. In 1956, it was Terray once again who climbed the extremely difficult peaks of Chacraraju (6,150 m) and Taulliraju (5,830 m), with their steeply inclined glaciers and icy granite walls, accompanied by Martin, Davaille, and Sennelier.

In 1962, fresh from his victorious assault on Jannu in the Himalayas, Terray returned to scale the east face of Chacraraju, the first great glacier face in the range to be conquered, comparable to the north faces of the Alps. The period of exploration was coming to a close, the era of application had begun.

At the northern tip of the Andes in Colombia, the 5,000-meter sentinels of Sierra Nevada de Santa Marta dip their toes into the warm Caribbean sea. These major glacier peaks were explored notably during the period from 1939 to 1945 by mountaineers from many different countries.

Two major conquests of French mountaineering in the 1950s: the pyramid of Fitz Roy (above) and the vast south face of Aconcagua (following double page).

Alaska and the Rocky Mountains

A double chain of rocky mountains extends all the way from Alaska to the Mexican plateau, crowned in the north by major peaks that constitute the highest summits in North America—Mount McKinley (6,194 m; 20,320 ft.) and Mount Logan (5,951 m; 19,524 ft.). It is also in that region that the biggest glaciers in the world are located, like Malaspina Glacier and Leconte Glacier, which run right down to the sea. The unusual degree of snowfall caused by Pacific currents and precipitation continues into British Columbia and the northwestern United States. Then, as the Rockies continue further south, glaciation lessens and massive summits become more distinct, diminishing the impression of blank wilderness.

If Canada and Alaska are excluded, the history of mountaineering in North America is primarily a record of high but easy summits—sixty-seven are over 14,000 feet high (4,270 meters). All were scaled long ago, and some were even climbed by pioneers pushing west. However, it would be unfair not to mention the long trip through the Rockies taken by British mountaineer James Eccles and his guide Michel Payot, which in fact constituted veritable exploration of a land still dangerous during that great period epitomized by "westerns."

It was a botanist, Ed James, who scaled the first known "14,000 footer," Pikes Peak (4,310 m; 14,110 ft.), in 1820. Then, in 1842, Fremont climbed a fine 14,000-foot mountain that now bears his name, Fremont Peak. In 1848, Powell scaled Longs Peak (4,345 m; 14,256 ft.). But the most striking ascent seems to have been that of the loveliest mountain in the United States, the Grand Teton (4,197 m; 13,770 ft.), climbed in 1872 by Lanford and Stevenson. The highest peak in the lower forty-eight states, Mount Whitney in the Sierra Nevada (4,417 m; 14,494 ft.), was named after the geologist who measured it. Another major "14,000 footer" is Mount Rainier (4,392 m; 14,410 ft.) in the Cascade Range, climbed in 1870 by Stevens and Van Trump.

But none of those mountains can serve as the basis for a history of mountaineering in a region where, in fact, there was no proper mountaineering movement to speak of, given the immensity of the area and the hundreds of miles between main summits. Thus almost nothing jelled until 1930, when a new type of mountain climbing emerged—a bold, sporting approach that managed to get the jump on European techniques.

The mountainous western part of the United States is dotted with volcanic remnants that rise like towers above the high plateaux, not unlike a gigantic version of the Hoggar Range in Algeria. Certain

Three scenes from the conquest of the south face of Aconcagua: (from left to right) Robert Paragot; a bivouac on the face; scaling the séracs. Bottom: John Charles Fremont, who climbed Fremont Peak in 1842 in the company of a scout named Kit Carson.

other regions feature granite needles or smooth cliffs. All appear impossible to climb and yet ultimately fell to the extremely bold methods employed by American climbers. Indeed, it was here that expansion pitons, or bolts, were first used to scale certain absolutely smooth rockfaces.

It is America that holds the record for the longest time taken to tame a mountain, namely Sentinel Rock in the Sierra Nevada. Its north face, some 900 meters high (3,000 ft.) overlooks Yosemite Valley. The ascent began in 1936, when Morgan Harris, William Horsfall, and Olive Dyer reached a ledge at 500 meters. Not much more height had been gained by 1940. During the Second World War, Robin Hansen, Jack Arnold, and Fritz Lippmann eked out another 50 meters, then, in 1948, Jim Wilson and Phil Bettler another 30. In 1949, Wilson, Bettler, Bill Long, and Allen Steck scaled a further 137 meters in twenty hours of continuous climbing. Then in May of 1950, Long and Bettler reached the top of the buttress some 244 meters above the initial ledge at 500 meters. Finally, from 30 June to 3 July 1950, John Salathé and Allen Steck made the crucial traverse over to the chimney and from there went all the way to the top. The total ascent lasted fourteen years.

In Central America, a historic detail worth recalling concerns the first ascent of Popocatépetl (5,465 m; 17,930 ft.), made in 1519 by Diego de Ordás and his conquistadors. Orizaba (5,610 m; 18,406 ft.), meanwhile, was not conquered until 1848 by American officers Reynolds and Maynard.

The real story of North American mountaineering, however, was grandly written on the icy Alaska Range and the Canadian Rockies. No longer was it a question of scorched summits rising above easily accessible high plateaus. Even in the lower regions, as in the southern Columbia Range, the mountains present serious glacier problems, in addition to difficult rockfaces and uncertain weather conditions. And in the far north, the mountains attain exceptional altitudes. Two enormous groups rise above 6,000 meters in an arctic climate with terrible blizzards. Climbing such peaks entails organizing a full-scale polar expedition, in addition to all the difficulties posed by altitude and by the ascent itself.

It is easy to see, then, why North American mountain climbing involved the organization of veritable expeditions that, like Himalayan expeditions, marked a major stage of international mountaineering. Whereas in the Andes, the expeditionary, indeed exploratory, aspect only came to the fore in the southern reaches of Patagonia, all the mountains of Alaska, the Yukon, and the Canadian Rockies are located beyond normal routes of access; in the north there is the taiga (dense

Above, left: Lionel Terray and Guido Magnone during the Fitz Roy expedition. Above, right: Fitz Roy's two summits, scaled by Terray in 1956 and 1962. Bottom: Major Powell, who made the first ascent of Longs Peak in Colorado in 1868.

evergreen forest), the lethal tundra, and the endless polar night or never-setting summer sun. The Columbia Range is thick with primeval forests and glacier-barred valleys—traveling through this Quaternary landscape required hiring trappers as guides.

The exploration of Alaska can be broken down into two phases: the historic period, when the two main giants were conquered (Mount Saint Elias and Mount McKinley), and the modern era, which began with the 1925 victory over Mount Logan. During both phases, the exploration of North American ranges yielded precious lessons and refined techniques then in use elsewhere.

Thanks to its location near the coast, Mount Saint Elias (5,489 m; 18,009 ft.) is visible far out to sea. It is a gigantic volcano, which implies a relatively easy ascent. But there is extensive glaciation in the region, with enormous glaciers likes those of Greenland and Spitzberg, running right to the ocean. And so a veritable expedition had to be mounted in order to reach Saint Elias. Already, in 1888, a British expedition had reached an altitude of 3,600 meters during an ascent that lasted twenty-five days. Then, in 1890, Dr. Russel attained 4,420 meters. But it was not until 1897 that the summit was reached, thanks to one of the largest purely mountaineering expeditions ever organized to date. The man who headed it, the duke of Abruzzi, was both sailor and mountaineer. Ever since his youth, the duke, son of King Amadeus of Spain, had devoted his life to the mountains, the sea, and distant exploration. From the North Pole to Karakoram, from Alaska to the mountains of central Africa, he directed difficult ventures with an energy and decisiveness that were admired and imitated. Up until very recently, the details of Himalayan expeditions tended to be based on Abruzzi's organizations. It was hard to anticipate

Phimister Proctor made the second ascent of Half Dome by lassoing iron stakes left in the rock by his predecessor, George Anderson.

more thoroughly or do better than the duke. His assault on Mount Saint Elias resembled a polar expedition, lasted 154 days, and enabled the entire climbing team to reach the summit on 31 July 1897. The duke of Abruzzi and his friend Cagni were guided by Joseph Petigax from Courmayeur and J.A. Maquignaz from Breuil; Francesco Gonella was led by Laurent Croux and Erminio Botta from Courmayeur; meanwhile, Vittorio Sella, the famous mountain photographer, and Dr. Filippo De Filippi climbed with André Péllissier from Val Tournanche. This felicitous combination of fine climbers and great guides, all well-equipped and well-directed by a remarkable leader, resulted in one of the finest conquests in mountaineering history.

Mount McKinley, at 6,194 meters the highest peak in North America, was the scene of a strange human adventure. First it repelled an attempt by Wickersham in 1903, only to be furtively climbed on 10 April 1910 by three Alaskan gold prospectors who set out from Fairbanks on a bet, having no mountaineering skills whatsoever. Their crazy, if bold, escapade succeeded against all expectations, probably because the "sourdoughs," as northern pioneers were known, were toughened by years spent in the icy wastes of Alaska and the Yukon, were equipped like trappers, and were perfectly accustomed to the cold conditions. Thus Peter Anderson and William Taylor made an almost unhindered ascent to the north summit—very slightly lower than the south peak—while their companion, Charley McGonagall, halted 150 meters below the top. Only chance determined which of the two peaks they picked. If they had chosen the south peak, all controversy might have ended there.

Mount McKinley, however, inevitably became part of the fabulous legend of the far north. An imposter named Frederick Cook claimed to have scaled it in 1906, just as he falsely declared that he had reached the North Pole. And although Anderson and Taylor's ascent was beyond dispute, they had left the main summit untrodden.

So for three years, explorers Parkel, Browne, and Lavoy sought to reach it, almost managing on 29 June 1912, after a 650-kilometer trek in dog sleds. They were stopped just ninety meters below the top by a terrifying blizzard so violent that they could not even see the summit.

It was only the following year, on 9 June 1913, that an expedition of the same type, this time conducted by Stuck, Karsten, Tatun, and Harper, made it to the top of the south peak at last. McKinley would not be climbed for another twenty years. Also at that time, Dora Keen Handy ascended Mount Blackburn (5,040 m; 16,530 ft.). But then the icy wastes fell silent once more.

It was not until 1925 that the second giant of the north, Mount Logan, was conquered. Logan

displayed extraordinary endurance under conditions of extreme cold and meager nourishment.

The modern era of mountaineering in these arctic regions began around 1930. The main problem for previous expeditions had been the long trek, often lasting weeks or months, which required supply bases and numerous personnel. All that changed, however, when Bradford Washburn came along.

Washburn was a true innovator when it came to conceiving an expedition. At a time when aviation was still in its infancy, he was

is in Canada, at the tip of the Rockies, and required another polar-style expedition. After a month and half of trekking across glaciers, Albert H. McCarthy successfully led his team up the slopes.

Exploratory mountaineering in the arctic zones of Alaska and Canada, then, was characterized by the organization of major expeditions of unlimited duration. Dog sleds were used while rivers were still frozen, shifting to bark canoes during thaws, entailing a lot of strenuous lugging and endless bivouacs in icy caves. Food supplies posed almost insuperable problems, and the pioneers needed uncommon determination to overcome both the rigors of a polar expedition and the demands of athletic climbing. The least that can be said is that they

the first to equip planes with skis so that they could land on vast glaciers or on the snowy saddles of the giant mountains of Alaska (giant is an appropriate term when it is realized that the base of a mountain like McKinley is some one hundred kilometers in diameter). Such aircraft made it possible for expeditions headed by Washburn, often accompanied by his young wife, to receive supplies directly at a base camp at the very foot of the target peak.

But other camps higher up the slopes still had to be established. Washburn, ever aware of the latest technology, used small radio transceivers that enabled him to maintain constant contact with every part of the expedition, including the most advanced posts. Thus, even before the Himalayan expeditions were launched, a mod-

Left: The duke of Abruzzi (foreground) approaching Mount Saint Elias in 1897. Right: The south face of Mount McKinley (or Denali) in Alaska.

ern, rapid and scientific approach was being developed. Washburn, Allen Carpé, and other American mountaineers (mainly the leading climbers of the Seattle Mountaineering Club), efficiently conducted long reconnaissance missions and sensational traverses from one end of the coastal ranges to the other, from Saint Elias to Logan and McKinley. As early as 1933, they regularly parachuted vital supplies by airplane.

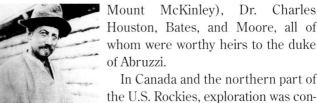

Washburn continued to be an indefatigable organizer of expeditions to Alaska, which he resumed after the Second World War with equal success. But the targets became more difficult and more distant as the main summits of Alaska fell one by one under the repeated assaults of American, Canadian, British, and German climbers—Mount Yukon, Mount Chugach, Mount Wrangell, Mount Saint Elias, and Fairweather Mountain. In addition to Bradford Washburn and Mrs. Washburn, pioneering expeditionary climbers included Wood, Allen Carpé (who was killed during the second ascent of

Mount McKinley), Dr. Charles Houston, Bates, and Moore, all of whom were worthy heirs to the duke of Abruzzi.

In Canada and the northern part of the U.S. Rockies, exploration was conducted by great names of European mountaineering once the railroad arrived—Whymper, Collie, Eccles, and other English and Canadian climbers successfully attacked most of the virgin peaks.

One of the most striking exploits was the ascent of Mount Waddington in British Columbia. This 3,994-meter peak (13,104 ft.) is icy, rocky, and extremely arduous. It was conquered by Wiessner and House in 1936. Sometime earlier, however, a British team, guided by Camille Couttet from Chamonix, had completely crossed the range from east to west via Waddington Pass, tracing an enormous itinerary across imposing glaciers that descend down to the inlet of the Pacific Ocean in a totally desolate region.

Finally, it is worth noting that a small colony of Swiss guides from Oberland settled in the

Above: Frederick Cook, whose purported ascent of McKinley in 1906 was "proven" by a photo taken on another summit. Right: One of the high-altitude camps during an ascent of McKinley, with the threatening séracs of Mount Brooks in the background.

Canadian Rockies, where they were hired by the Canadian Pacific Railway.

One special feature of mountaineering in Alaska and the Yukon is the non-stop daylight (typical of all polar ascents, for that matter): it poses no problem for bivouacs, yet allows for continuous progress and makes for safer returns, often rendered dangerous by falling darkness. This is small compensation, however, for the extreme cold, hard ice, and instability of powdery, wind-driven snow.

Increasingly difficult routes were nevertheless now being sought up the mountains of Alaska. In the summer of 1961, an Italian team headed by Riccardo Cassin (conqueror of the north face of the Grandes Jorasses) managed to scale the awesome south face of McKinley thanks to airborne logistics. The mountaineers had to deploy all their skills as outstanding ice climbers in order to overcome the glacier obstacles they encountered on the way up, and several members of the party suffered severe frostbite.

Above: The"sourdoughs" pose in their Sunday best (from left to right)—Charley McGonagall, Pete Anderson, Tom Lloyd (seated), and William Taylor. Left: Starting in the 1930s, airplanes were used to approach McKinley.

These days, rock climbing on low-altitude massifs like Garet-el-Djenoun in Algeria (pictured here) is no longer considered to be true mountaineering, but that was not the case when Roger Frison-Roche first explored these unknown ranges in 1935.

Africa

In terms of the history of mountain conquest, Africa is limited to three very high peaks in the equatorial zone—Margherita Peak in the Ruwenzori Range bordering Uganda and Zaire (5,118 m), Mount Kenya, (5,240 m), and Kilimanjaro (5,895 m) in Tanzania.

Yet the recent vogue for difficult rock routes has brought back into fashion the little rocky peaks of the Hoggar and Tibesti Ranges in the deserts of Algeria and Chad respectively, as well as mountains in the Moroccan Atlas that had been disdained by mountaineers for years. Morocco has several appealing summits over 4,000 meters high.

The Hoggar Range was practically unknown until 1935, the year in which Swiss climbers Brossart and Hauser made the first ascent of Ilamane, an enormous volcanic spike offering no easy route. Furthermore, a French team comprised of Coche, Lewden, Chasseloup-Laubat, and Ichac, with myself as guide, went prospecting throughout the entire range on camel back. We climbed five peaks, including the notorious Garet-el-Djenoun, a legendary pedestal of granite rising from the sands (2,310 m), plus Ilamane, Iharen, and Saouinan. The expedition confirmed the fact that the Hoggar presented pure rock routes, all fairly tricky and similar to the routes being opened by the new American school in the U.S. Rockies.

In fact, Garet-el-Djenoun would not be scaled again for another twenty-five years, until the days when whole caravans of young climbers from the Club Alpin Français used modern transportation (plane and jeep) to reach the Hoggar and make extremely difficult rock climbs requiring the latest techniques.

The Tibesti Range, in contrast, is visited far less.

Finally, in 1960 I discovered and explored the Gautier Mountains in the middle of the Ténéré region of Niger.

In addition to these "trifles" which, apart from their difficulty, hardly qualify as real mountains, it is worth mentioning the fine routes traced in the

Jurjura hills of Algeria by highly reputed climbers from Algiers, such as Maurice Fourastier.

Returning to the three major mountains in Africa, the first to be explored from a mountaineering standpoint was the tallest and easiest, Kilimanjaro. Thought at the time to rise to a height of over 6,000 meters, it was naturally attractive to mountain climbers. The main peak, Kibo, was reached without difficulty as early as 1889 by Hans Meyer and Ludwig Purtscheller; Mawenzi, a more difficult, rocky secondary peak, had to wait until 1912.

Next it was Mount Kenya that received exploratory visits. A magnificent volcano with twin summits (Batian and Nelion), Mount Kenya is covered by glaciers down to an altitude of 4,500 meters. It also offers splendid rock

cliffs. Its extremely difficult north face was not conquered until 1952, when Maurice Martin and Roger Rangaux climbed it with the aid of numerous pitons.

In the opinion of equatorial mountaineers, however, the greatest difficulty in scaling Mount Kenya (and also Ruwenzori) entails traveling though zones of primeval forest, giant ferns, and dense bamboo thickets in a totally humid atmosphere that makes high-altitude bivouacking very arduous. A path has to be cut with machetes, portage is complicated, and the landscape is strange and hostile—even these days, an ascent necessarily assumes the form of an armed expedition.

Sir Harold Mackinder was the first climber to reach Kenya's Batian peak (5,240 m), on 13 September 1899, via the south face. He was accompanied by guides César Ollier and Joseph Brocherel from Courmayeur. It was not until

In 1889, Hans Meyer (left) and Ludwig Purtscheller scaled Kilimanjaro, the highest peak in Africa. At the time, it still seemed somewhat magical to discover snow-capped summits in the heart of the dark continent. Meyer's book was illustrated with the lithograph of Kilimanjaro seen on the right.

Above, left: Mount Kenya, Africa's "Matterhorn," inevitably became an advertising symbol. Above, right: The strange glacial formations on Kilimanjaro's crater, as discovered by Meyer and Purtscheller.

1929 that a second ascent was made, by the brilliant British climbers Eric Shipton and Wyn Harris, and their partners. The main ridges and secondary peaks, like Nelion and Midget, fell one by one under the assaults by the likes of Eric Shipton and Bill Tilman.

The Ruwenzori is a remarkable range separating the former Belgian and British colonies, today Zaire and Uganda. It is a superb chain of rocky and icy summits between 4,000 and 5,000 meters, the highest peak reaching 5,119 meters. Above 4,500 meters glaciation is heavy, while below that altitude vegetation is overabundant and rain continuous. The tall, mysterious peaks, once known as the Mountains of the Moon, can only rarely be glimpsed from the savannah below. The mountains were long thought to be the source of the Nile.

The Ruwenzori was first explored during a magnificent expedition led by the duke of Abruzzi in 1906. The duke, as the great forerunner to modern expeditions, has already been mentioned above in the context of Alaska. Here again, he masterfully organized a convoy of four hundred people designed to insure the advance, supply, and protection of the lead team, composed of the duke and his guides Joseph Petigax, César Ollier, Joseph Brocherel, and L. Petigax, all from Courmayeur.

The siege laid by these remarkable mountain climbers led to the fall of the highest point,

Margherita Peak (5,119 m), on 18 June 1906. Alexandra Peak on Mount Stanley fell the same day, while Moebius (4,925 m) was climbed by photographer Vittorio Sella on 25 June. The duke of Abruzzi scaled Helen and Savoy Peaks (5,005 m) on 20 June and Emmanuelle Peak on Mount Speke (4,901 m) on 23 June. Semper, Wolasston, Morre, and Baker had been scaled from 10 to 12 June, while it was the turn of Mount Emin on 28 June, Mount Gesi on 16 July, Louis of Savoy on 19 June, and 4 July. All of these peaks were climbed by the duke of Abruzzi and his companions Sella and Roccati in alternation, sharing the double and efficient team of Courmayeur guides.

The methodical conquest of the Ruwenzori Range would be completed later by a 1932 Belgian expedition led by Xavier de Grune, another by Shipton and Tilman, and finally a 1938 assault by the indefatigable Piero Ghiglione.

The main summits of the massive, table-like mountains on the high volcanic plateau of Abyssinia were scaled during the Italian occupation of Ethiopia in the 1930s.

At the southern tip of Africa, Table Mountain and the Drakensberg Range offer some fine rock climbing, including some very high and very difficult routes. They are regularly scaled by climbers from South Africa, but do not seem to attract climbers from other nations, given their distance and modest scope.

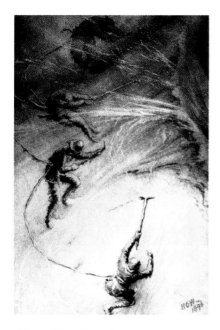

New Zealand

On the opposite side of the earth from the European Alps, separated from the world's other mountain ranges by thousands of miles of ocean, the Southern Alps of New Zealand stretch some 500 miles down the middle of South Island. A set of peaks surpass 3,000 meters which, at that latitude and climate, corresponds to 4,000 meters in Europe—glaciers descend as low as 900 meters, and there is permanent snow at about 1,000 meters. The highest peak, Mount Cook, rises 3,765 meters, flanked by some thirty ice-capped giants. Tasman Glacier, which drains the whole range much as the Mer de Glace does in the European Alps, is eighteen miles long. The area is wilderness, rivers flood dangerously and are sometimes uncrossable, and roads are generally non-existent (except for a few tracks up to the new huts). Expedition tactics are therefore required, with all the complications of portage in an uninhabited region with no resources, and where it is pointless to seek native people for logistical help—the Maoris would not go near the sacred mountains!

New Zealand nevertheless played a true role in mountaineering history as the site of a slow, fifteen-year campaign not only by British climbers and their Swiss guides but also by local climbers who forged their own techniques from top to bottom, becoming amazing ice climbers.

Nor should it be forgotten that New Zealand was the birthplace of mountaineering's most striking modern champion—Edmund Hillary, the peaceful beekeeper who conquered Everest and went on to become one of the heroes of the crossing of the Antarctic continent via the South Pole.

For several years mountain climbing efforts focused on Mount Cook. The first serious attempt nearly succeeded, however. In 1882, the Reverend Green and his Swiss guides Ulrich, Kauffmann, and Boss extensively reconnoitered the immense glacier valleys and attacked long walls of séracs and imposing ridges of snows. They thereby discovered Dom Glacier and the route to the top. They reached a point thought to be just sixty meters below the summit when they were caught in a terrible blizzard with howling winds typical of the region, and were forced to turn back.

Another twelve long years went by. Twelve years of reconnaissance, of unsuccessful attempts which nevertheless contributed further knowledge about the mountain range and made it possible to prepare the approach path, locate base camps, and identify the numerous glacial flows around Tasman and the peaks surrounding Cook. It should not be forgotten that climbers were confronted with slopes of ice some 2,000 to 2,500 meters high, that there was an enormous amount of snow and that, since it was a question of ice routes, conditions varied

Above, left to right: A descent during a storm, as pictured by Edward Fitzgerald; Reverend Green's party bivouacking on Mount Cook, as depicted by an English newspaper of the day; an accident during Fitzgerald's ascent of Mount Sefton.

enormously from one year to another. This created a situation frequently found in the Alps—Mont Blanc du Tacul, for instance, can be an easy climb one year and a far more serious one the next.

Mannering, Dixon, Harper, and Johnson were the protagonists of this gigantic struggle. But it was the New Zealanders Fyfe, Graham, and Clark, spurred by news of the arrival of British climber Edward Fitzgerald and his famous guide Matthias Zurbriggen, who first managed to reach the central peak (3,712 m) on 20 December 1894, followed by the higher north peak on 25 December. They pursued a route, discovered during an earlier ascent, up the west face and north ridge. Fitzgerald arrived too late. Despite a brilliant ascent up the northeast ridge, the disappointed and disgusted British mountaineer did not go all the way to the summit; Zurbriggen continued alone and completed the second ascent on 20 March 1895, just three months after the New Zealanders' exploit.

Zurbriggen and Fitzgerald would nevertheless enjoy a magnificent climbing season, making the first ascent of Mount Tasman (3,497 m) on 5 February 1895, followed by the conquest of Mount Haidinger.

Yet it was not until the 1900–1910 period that most of the island's "3,000ers" were conquered, thanks to the efforts of New Zealand mountaineers, who had become great glacier specialists. A European expedition led by Marcel Kurz in 1929 came back to the old world with specific details on the admirable Southern Alps.

Subsequently, as occurred in Alaska, modern mountain climbers (in the 1930s, and, above all, from 1945 to 1955) used new technology to improve methods of approach and supply. Overland portage was replaced by parachute drops, trekking by ski-planes. Most important, however, high altitude tents were abandoned in favor of cutting caves into the snow itself. This technique, successfully used by Lionel Terray on Mount Fitz Roy in the Andes, seemed par-

Top: Edward Fitzgerald and his party en route for Mount Cook. Bottom: Matthias Zurbriggen in New Zealand. Facing page: The subsidiary peak of Hiunchuli, in the Annapurna group.

ticulary appropriate to glaciers exposed to extremely low temperatures and violent winds, that is to say in the polar regions.

Asia

Asia's great mountain ranges radiate out in different directions from the Pamir Plateau—Tien Shan, Kun Lun Shan, Hindu Kush, and the Karakoram-Himalayas.

The enormity of these ranges is matched only by the mystery that still surrounds them, or at least the first three, since the location of the Himalayas on the edge of the former British empire in India, plus the presence of fourteen peaks over 8,000 meters high—notably Chomolungma (Mount Everest), at 8,848 meters the highest mountain on earth—meant that many expeditions were sent there starting in the early twentieth century. The progressive conquest of the Himalayan range generated a large number of publications, accounts, and remarkable monographs. Indeed, the Himalayas properly speaking certainly boast the most abundant and most accurate mountaineering literature of all.

Tien Shan, Pamir, Kun Lun Shan, Hindu Kush

The Kun Lun Shan range, which separates Tibet to the south from the Chinese Turkestan desert to the north, remains practically unexplored. Nearly two thousand miles long, the range stretches as far as the Karakoram to the west, where Ulugh Mustagh (7,300 m) was explored by the British topographer W. H. Johnson. The western Kun Lun also flows into the Chinese Pamirs, and that is where Mustagh Ata (7,546 m) was attacked by Shipton and Tilman in the company of the Sherpa Gyalzen. They reached an altitude of 7,300 meters before being beaten back by the cold. It was only on 7 July 1956 that Mustagh Ata finally fell to a Sino-Soviet expedition lead by E. A. Beleckij. As to the highest peak in the Chinese Pamirs, Kongur Tagh (7,595 m), it was conquered on 19 August of the same year by six Soviet and two Chinese climbers, who reportedly used oxygen masks and employed artificial aids on certain passages.

The Hindu Kush is an extension of the Himalayas from Kashmir westward. Given its location in Pakistan and Afghanistan, it is still little known. The highest peak, Tirich Mir (7,659 m) was scaled in 1950 by a Norwegian expedition led by Professor Arne Naess; at the time, it was the fourth highest mountain ever climbed, after Annapurna, Kamet, and Nanda Devi. The same range contains Istor-o-Nal, a mountain 7,390 meters high, climbed in 1955 by two students from Princeton.

The Pamirs, often called "the roof of the world," host the highest mountains in the former Soviet Union, notably Communism Peak (7,495 meters). It was climbed for the first time in 1933 by a Soviet team led by the young Evgeni Abolakov and his compatriot Gorbunov, during an expedition commanded by Commissar Krylenko. Eight camps were required to reach the summit.

The second highest mountain in the Pamirs is in the Trans-Alai section to the north: Lenin Peak (formerly Kaufmann Peak, 7,130 m) was scaled as early as 1938 by the German team of Allwein, Schneider, and Wien, who also made the first ascents of the Pamir Breithorn

(6,900 m), Kicker Peak (6,740 m), Tanima (6,000 m), and, in the Trans-Alai, Trapeze Peak (5,100 m).

The indisputable pioneer in this part of the world was Vitali Abolakov, a veteran mountaineer who could be ranked with the best professionals and amateurs in the West. Abolakov notably achieved the second ascent of Lenin Peak in 1934, the first ascent of the granite peak of Ala, and climbed the Breithorn and Mintage in the Alai (5,500 m); his partner Lorenz Saladin succumbed to the conse-

quences of frostbite, suffered during the second ascent of Khan Tengri (6,995 m), the highest point of the Tien Shan range, which had been climbed in 1931 by a Russian team led by Pogrebezky. Abolakov also climbed Pachor (7,154 m) and Karl Marx Peak in 1946.

Equally worthy of note in the Pamirs was the first ascent of Revolution Peak (6,985 m) in 1954 by Ugarow's Soviet expedition, the first ascent of the west face of Communism Peak in 1955 by a Soviet team led by Kahiani, and the conquest of both Unity Peak (6,770 m)

Above: An 1872 watercolor by Henry Haversham Godwin-Austen (1834–1923) showing the Panmah Glacier in Baltistan. Godwin-Austen was the first explorer of the Karakoram range and identified K2, the second highest peak in the world. Left: Soviet mountaineer Vitali Abolakov.

In 1892, Sir Martin Conway organized the first large-scale expedition to the Baltoro Glacier, accompanied notably by artist Arthur David McCormick, who provided a particularly vivid visual record of the expedition.

and Ockjabrski Peak (6,780 m), also in 1955, by a Sino-Soviet group headed by Beleckij.

The Tien Shan range still remained completely shrouded in mystery. For a long time, Khan Tengri was thought to be over 7,000 meters high (now measured at 6,995 m) and was considered the tallest in the group. But in 1956, the indefatigable Abolakov and his ten companions climbed a much higher mountain, Victory Peak (or Pobeda, 7,439 m), henceforth recognized as the second highest Soviet summit. A second ascent was made in seven days in 1958 along the east ridge, some five miles long, by a Czech and Soviet team.

Finally, mention should be made of the Chinese giant to the east, Minya Konka (7,590 m), in the Szechwan range on the eastern edge of Tibet. This mysterious mountain, discovered in 1929, was initially thought to be over 9,000 meters high, and was climbed in 1932 by an American expedition composed of Richard Burdsall, Terris Moore, and Arthur Emmons, with Chinese climber Jack Young. Another ascent was made a few years ago by a group of Chinese mountaineers, success coming at the harsh cost of human lives.

Karakoram and the Himalayas

The "Himalayas" can be divided into two distinct ranges, the Karakoram and the Great Himalayas. The former runs northwest to con-

nect the Great Himalayas to the Pamirs, which serve as a central hub not unlike the Aar in Switzerland but on Asian dimensions. The Himalayas, strictly speaking, are bordered on the west by the Indus and to the east by the Brahmaputra; the two rivers frame the range as perfectly as the Black and Caspian Seas define the Caucasus.

The Himalayas and Karakoram are proud homes to the world's fourteen peaks over 8,000 meters, as well as to hundreds of others over 7,000 meters. The Himalayas stretch some 2,500 kilometers and constitute the southern border of Tibet (invaded by the Chinese Communists in 1950). The Karakoram, meanwhile, is now in the part of Kashmir controlled by the two new countries born of British decolonization in 1947, namely Pakistan and India. The entire Ladakh Valley is controlled by India (although China has laid claim to the southern part), while the Karakoram strictly speaking is controlled by Pakistan. This geopolitical overview is absolutely crucial, because the mountaineering conquest of these peaks has been intimately linked to successive political developments in the region throughout the twentieth century.

Up until 1939, the vast majority of this territory, with the exception of Tibet, was controlled by Britain, so it is hardly surprising that Britain played the biggest role in exploration. True enough, an 800-kilometer stretch of the southern Himalayas belonged to Nepal, a forbidden

kingdom, while at the far end Bhutan opened and closed its borders at will; but the states of Kashmir, Punjab, Garhwal, and Sikkim remained under British influence until 1939. Sikkim, furthermore, was the gateway to Tibet, where the Dalai Lama parsimoniously granted travel permits, most of them to British expeditions. British colonists based at Darjeeling in Sikkim, those marvelous hills so dear to Kipling, preserved Victorian traditions and, in the same spirit, reserved for themselves the right of territorial conquest even in the sphere of mountain climbing. Up until 1950, no foreign expeditions other than British were authorized to enter Tibet, which at that time was the route to Everest.

To assuage the appetite of mountaineers from other countries, authorizations were granted every now and then for secondary goals like the prestigious Karakoram peaks. But Everest was untouchable. Later, given the overwhelming wave of expeditions, the Himalayan Committee based in Darjeeling divided the main summits between certain nations, obviously granting clear priority over Everest to British climbers. No one at the time, despite the desire gnawing at the French, Italians and Germans, thought it wise to tug the lion's tail!

Since a political visa was required, and since embassies at the time had other fish to fry, it is highly probable that everything would have continued as before had not a sudden change occurred in 1950: Tibet, so favorable to the English, was invaded by the Chinese

Communists, thereby closing off the northern route to Everest. Simultaneously, a revolution broke out in Nepal, opening the borders of a practically unknown country that mountaineers had sometimes glimpsed from the summits forming the frontier between Sikkim and Nepal. Suddenly there was a mad, victorious rush on all the mysterious "8,000ers" in Nepal, a peak-rich land where everything remained to be explored. France, Germany, Austria, the United States, Japan, Switzerland, Argentina, and, of course, Great Britain sent expedition after expedition to the upper valleys.

In less than ten years, the conquest of the Himalayas and Karakoram was complete—almost the same time it took to climb all the "4,000ers" during the golden age of the Alps. And just as the conquest of the Alps spurred the training of professional guides selected from among local folk in the upper valleys, so the discovery of the Himalayas and above all attempts on Everest favored recruitment of a particularly well-adapted race of mountain dwellers, the Sherpas. Sherpas were a Tibetan people who settled on the southern slopes of the Himalayas, mainly at Namche Bazar in the Khumbu Valley. During the colonial period, Sherpas emigrated to Darjeeling, where they worked as coolies, that is to say porters. But their physical and human qualities, as well as their profound knowledge of the mountains and capacity for high-altitude portage, soon led to their recruitment for major expeditions. From their start at Everest in 1921 to Tenzing Norgay's victory on

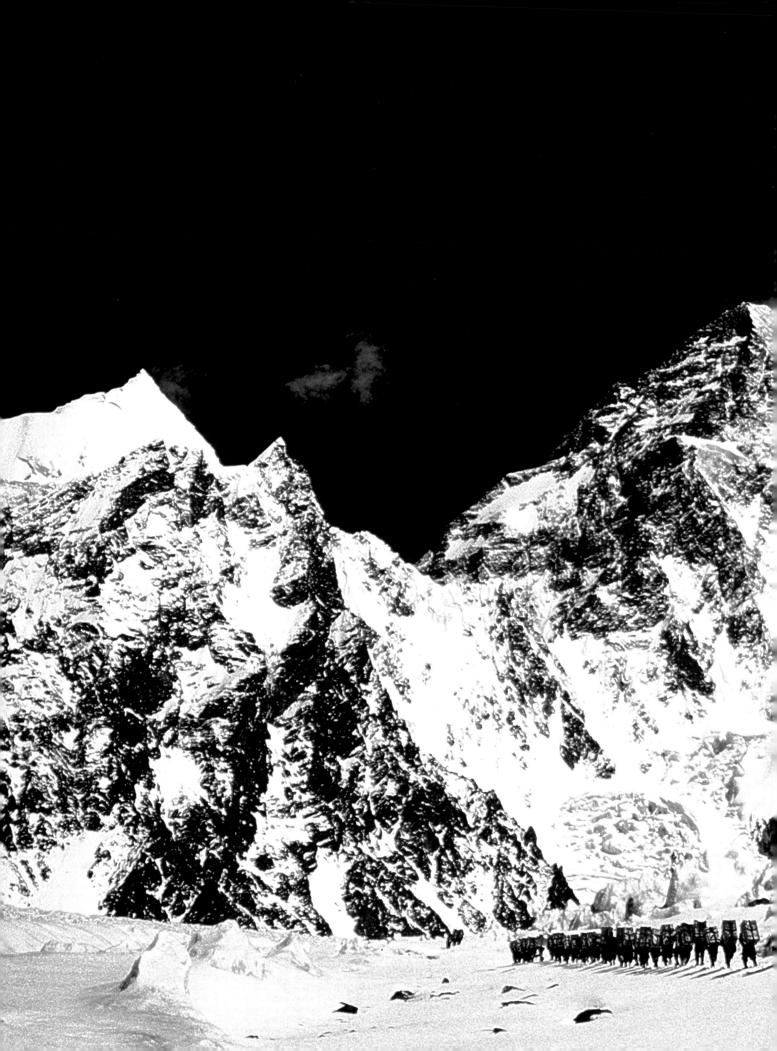

the "roof of the world," there was remarkable similarity between the evolution of Sherpas and the *montagnards* from Chamonix. Just as crystal hunter Jacques Balmat vanquished Mont Blanc, so the humble Sherpa Tenzing became the equal of the greatest mountain conquerors by defeating Everest.

Men such as Shipton and Tilman had already noticed and appreciated the Sherpas' qualities during the interwar period, outside of the context of large, official expeditions. Yet it could be argued that the presence of experienced Sherpas on the lead teams was one of the key elements of victory in the modern conquest of the Himalayas and Karakoram. They very often

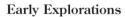

partnered the most famous professionals from the Alps, and men like Franco, Terray, Rébuffat, Tichy, and Lambert were unanimous in their praise of Sherpas.

Sherpas had become mountain guides in the full meaning of the term, and although the type of exploit they were asked to perform did not yet make them fully familiar with Western techniques of aid climbing using pitons on ice and rock, each expedition and each year saw them make progress under the leadership of Norgay Tenzing, the chief (or Sirdar) of their professional association. Sherpas like Tenzing, Pa Norbu, Gyalzen, Ang Dawa, and Nyima, not forgetting Pasang or Pemba, took their place alongside leading European professional dynasties associated with names like Petigax, Croux, Ollier, Maquignaz, Blanc, and Zurbriggen.

But at the very moment that Sherpas were becoming organized and individually recog-

nized (even numbered, to make recognition easier given the similarity in names), thereby offering an unmatched choice of guides to new expeditions, the partition of the subcontinent into two countries based on diametrically opposed religious tenets (Islamic Pakistan and Hindu India) closed the border into the Karakoram and Pakistani ranges to Buddhist Sherpas from Darjeeling and Namche Bazar. Expeditions to those regions henceforth had to recruit porters from among Hunzas, who lived on the northwest edge of the Himalayas, to the south of the Karakoram. The Hunzas turned out to be excellent mountaineers, but their unstable nature led to dissatisfaction, and they lacked the Sherpas' quality of reliability. Here again, however, selection, training, and experience with successive expeditions produced several Hunza guides of great value, and it is highly probable that their positive qualities will blossom in the years to come.

Early Explorations

Just as in the Alps, where officers of the army's topographic service often got the jump on mountaineers (especially in the Pelvoux range), exploration of the Himalayas and Karakoram mountains was begun as early as 1818 by "pundits," learned Indian emissaries responsible for topographic surveys commissioned by the British government. Their secret missions took them far afield, it is claimed, even as far as the Kun Lun Shan. They were backed and seconded by officials from the Survey of India. In 1855, the Schlagintweit brothers launched an attack on the flanks of Kamet (7,755 m), while in 1865 Johnson even scaled a "6,000er" during his geodesic campaign.

Botanists began arriving in 1848 with Hooker, who explored Kangchenjunga, the second highest peak in the world. It was Freshfield who completely circumnavigated the massif in 1889.

But the first veritable expedition was the one led by Sir Martin Conway into the Karakoram in 1892. It was highly organized and included not only British officers serving in the Indian army

Fanny Bullock Workman was an intrepid explorer, along with her husband William Hunter Workman. Her ascent of Pinnacle Peak (6,930 m) in 1906 made her "the highest woman in the world." She is shown above on Biafo Glacier (left) and crossing one of countless Himalayan streams.

Luigi Amedeo di Savoia, duke of Abruzzi, was accompanied on his expeditions by the remarkable photographer Vittorio Sella, who brought back wonderful 30 x 40 cm glass-plate negatives. Here the duke himself (center) can be seen attacking the séracs on Chogolisa Glacier, a tributary of the Baltoro Glacier.

Above: Vittorio Sella took four matching shots to create this "panoramic" view showing the extent of the Baltoro Glacier, one of the largest in the world outside the polar regions. On the left is the pyramidal peak of K2, in the middle is Broad Peak, and on the right is Gasherbrum IV.

and familiar with frontier regions (including the young Lieutenant Charles Bruce, who would later head two expeditions to Everest), but also professionals from the Alps such as Matthias Zurbriggen, so often mentioned in this book. Conway discovered the Baltoro Glacier and explored it; at the end of the gigantic river of ice he scaled a summit 6,900 meters high, called Pioneer Peak, from which he could contemplate hidden "8,000ers" that suddenly came into view, notably the famous K2. But it seems that Conway was most struck by one gigantic, snow-capped tower of rock—a veritable Matterhorn, known as the Mustagh Tower.

It was a strange era, for the Himalayas and Karakoram were the object not only of major, semi-official expeditions like Conway's, but also alpine ventures like Mummery's bold attack on Nanga Parbat in 1895. That extraordinary mountain climber—the vanquisher of the Grépon, the Zmutt Ridge, and the Y-Couloir of Aiguille Verte—went straight for the 8,125-meter giant rising like a sentinel on the western

edge of the Himalayas. Mummery explored its glacier valleys, made an attempt at an ascent, failed, and then disappeared forever with two Gurkhas, probably buried by an avalanche.

This tragic failure by one of the greatest mountaineers of the day made it clear that the Himalayan giants were not about to be conquered without long preparation and substantial resources.

Then, from 1899 to 1912, Mr. and Mrs. Bullock Workman made incessant voyages to the area, sometimes accompanied by guides from Courmayeur, sometimes by the celebrated Zurbriggen. It was Zurbriggen who helped Mrs. Bullock Workman become "the highest woman in the world" at the top of Pinnacle Peak (6,930 m).

International expeditions (all of which had to include British mountaineers and the indispensable Indian army liaison officers) became more systematic, with exploration centering on the Karakoram, Sikkim, and the upper valleys of the Garhwal. There was the Eckenstein expedition to Karakoram in 1902, the Jacot-Guillarmod expedition

to Kangchenjunga in 1905 (which ended with the tragic death of four men), and numerous reconnaissance missions by Kellas to Kangchenjunga from 1907 to 1912. Finally, there was the classic expedition bearing the familiar noble stamp of the duke of Abruzzi in 1909, magnificently completing Conway's reconnoitering mission and attempting to scale both K2 and Staircase Peak (now known as Skyang Kangri, 7,544 m). The duke nearly managed to get to the summit of Bride Peak (now Chogolisa, 7,665 m) in the company of Petigax and the Brocherel brothers. Vittorio Sella, the official photographer as usual, brought back some amazingly precise and beautiful images that remain unequaled to this day.

In 1910, 1911, and 1912, Meade, Kellas, and Morshead attacked Kamet (7,755 m) which, along with Nanda Devi, is the highest peak in Garhwal. Nepal remained unpenetrated. Franz Lochmatter traveled to the Karakoram in 1912 and scaled secondary summits.

But further attempts were temporarily halted by the First World War. Then, in 1919, the veritable battle for the "roof of the world" broke out—the conquest of Everest would last from 1919 to 1953, even as, from 1919 to 1940, the exploration of regions accessible to Westerners—Karakoram, Garhwal, and Sikkim—was pursued with greater precision.

Facing page, bottom: Spencer Chapman scaled Chomolhari in 1937 on an unusually small and bold expedition. Left: R. L. Holdsworth on the summit of Kamet in 1921.

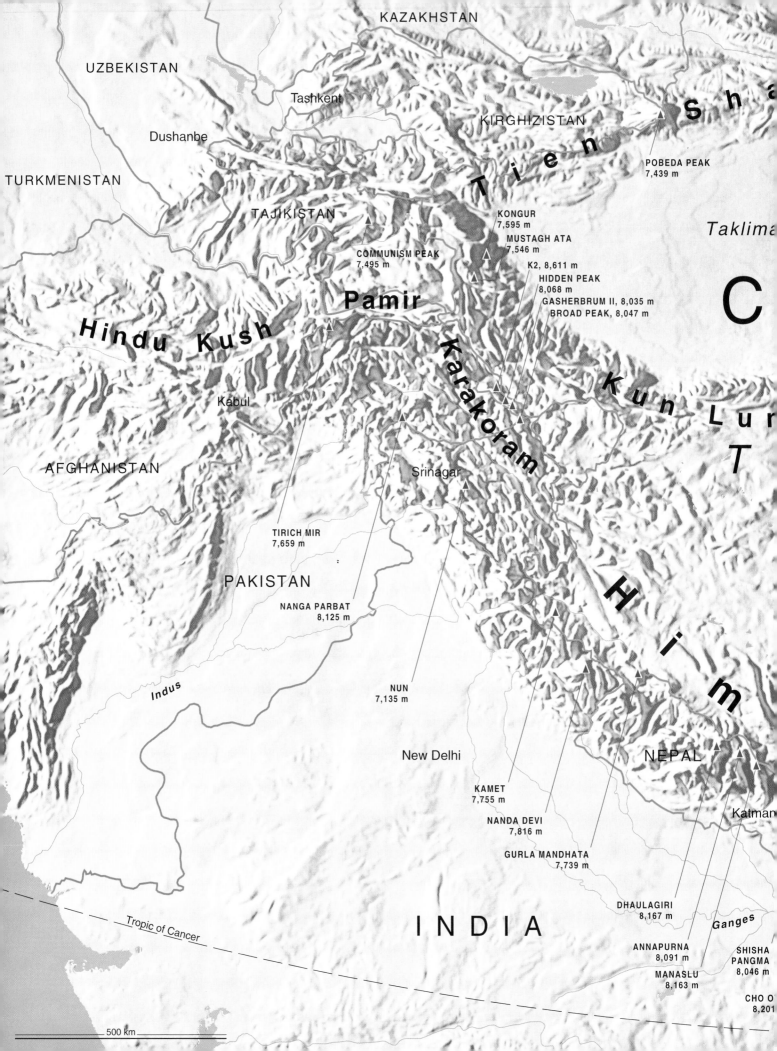

KAZAKHSTAN

UZBEKISTAN

Tashkent

KIRGHIZISTAN

Dushanbe

TURKMENISTAN

Tien Sha

POBEDA PEAK
7,439 m

TAJIKISTAN

Taklima

KONGUR
7,595 m

COMMUNISM PEAK
7,495 m

MUSTAGH ATA
7,546 m

Pamir

K2, 8,611 m

C

Hindu Kush

HIDDEN PEAK
8,068 m
GASHERBRUM II, 8,035 m
BROAD PEAK, 8,047 m

Kabul

Karakoram

Kun Lur

AFGHANISTAN

Srinagar

T

Him

TIRICH MIR
7,659 m

PAKISTAN

NANGA PARBAT
8,125 m

Indus

NUN
7,135 m

New Delhi

NEPAL

Katman

KAMET
7,755 m

NANDA DEVI
7,816 m

GURLA MANDHATA
7,739 m

DHAULAGIRI
8,167 m

Ganges

Tropic of Cancer

INDIA

ANNAPURNA
8,091 m

SHISHA
PANGMA
8,046 m

MANASLU
8,163 m

CHO O
8,201

500 km

MONGOLIA

Desert

H I N A

I B E T

l a y a s

Lhasa

BHUTAN

NAMCHE
BARWA
7,782 m

KANGCHENJUNGA
8,586 m

CHOMOLHARI
7,315 m

Brahmapoutre

MAKALU
8,463 m

HOTSE
8,516 m

EREST
48m

BANGLADESH

BURMA

Slaying the Giants

The tallest peaks on the planet are over 8,000 meters high—but there are only fourteen of them. Attempts to scale these giants date back to 1895, yet they were all vanquished in the space of a single decade, the golden age between 1950 and 1960.

Not a single one of the summits over 8,000 meters high was reached between 1920 and 1940. On the other hand, a multitude of 5,000 to 6,000-meter peaks in the Karakoram and Great Himalayas ranges were climbed, as well as roughly ten "7,000ers," mainly in Sikkim, Garhwal, Kashmir, and Karakoram. Mysterious Nepal was still off limits.

Every assault on Everest, meanwhile, although led roundly by the British, ended in failure. All expeditions approached it via Tibet, a route that the Dalai Lama granted exclusively to the British. The expeditions of other nations, mainly Germany, Switzerland, the United States, Italy, and France, had to content themselves with the goals they were assigned by the Himalayan Club: "Kang" (Kangchenjunga), K2, Nanga Parbat, and three other "8,000ers" in the Karakoram. (None of the nine "8,000ers" in Nepal were accessible to climbers while the region was closed.)

The isolated attempts of the early period—whether private expeditions or scientific voyages—were a thing of the past. "Himalayan Committees" were formed more or less everywhere (Munich, Italy, Paris, Zurich, Geneva) with the express goal of backing powerful expeditions. The composition of such expeditions was sometimes international, like Günther Dyhrenfurth's campaigns and the American expeditions to K2. Professional climbers from the Alps were not yet prominent (as they would be twenty years later), for expeditions retained their amateur image (in the best sense of the term). On the other hand, Sherpas gained a great deal of experience and became an integral part of most assault teams.

In the Karakoram, the international Dyhrenfurth expedition, bringing together excellent Swiss, British, and German climbers in 1934, succeeded in a veritable raid on the "7,000ers," notably Golden Throne (now Baltoro Kangri I, 7,240 m) and the three Queen Mary peaks (now Sia Kangri I—7,422 m—II, and III). A 1938 attempt on Masherbrum (7,821 m) by Harris and Hodgkin got as high as 7,600 meters.

Facing page: Base camp at the foot of the imposing south face of Makalu during the French expedition of 1955. Above, left: A poster for a film of the Italian expedition to K2 in 1954.

An effort to scale Rakaposhi (7,788 m) failed, as did two 1934 attempts on Hidden Peak (8,068 m); the Dyhrenfurth team halted at 7,426 meters, while the first French expedition to the Himalayas, headed by Henri de Ségogne and composed entirely of amateurs, reached 6,800 before it was rebuffed by the monsoon. It would seem that the French climbers lacked, above all, the Himalayan experience acquired by British mountaineers, military personnel, and Crown agents in the preceding twenty-five years. Himalayan chronicles were constantly full of British names, right up to the victory over Everest, ultimately claimed by a new team.

The Himalayas have also worked their magic on artists. Star of Morning *(1932) is by Russian painter Nicholas Roerich, who lived in the Himalayan valley of Kulu.*

K2, the second highest mountain in the world at 8,611 meters, around which the great expeditions of Conway and Abruzzi had orbited, returned to the headlines when U.S. expeditions made two attempts—in 1938, Dr. Charles Houston and Petzoldt reached 7,925 meters on the northeast ridge, while in 1939 a second mixed expedition halted just below the summit, an altitude of 8,370 meters having been attained by Wiessner and Sherpa Pasang Dawa Lama. The experiment ended tragically with three deaths.

In 1935, British climbers Waller, Hunt, and Brotherhood reached one of the peaks (7,470 m) of Saltoro Kangri (7,742 m), bringing to the fore the name of the man who would head the final, victorious expedition to Everest in 1953, Sir John Hunt.

Nanga Parbat, on the western tip of the Great Himalayan range, remained relatively accessi-ble—it will be recalled that its 8,125 meters lured the valiant Mummery to his death, along with two Gurkhas, as early as 1895. With the exception of Everest, no other mountain was the object of such sustained assault between 1932 and 1939. Nor would any other mountain claim so many lives in so short a period.

In 1932, Merkl's German–American expedi-tion to Nanga Parbat reached an altitude of 6,950 meters. In 1934, another Merkl team, this time Austro–German, attained 7,850 meters. But the lead teams were caught in a storm, and nine climbers perished. In 1937, however, the Germans attacked again, this time led by Karl Wien, reaching 6,185 meters before an avalanche swept away the campsites and killed sixteen members of the team. In 1938, Paul Bauer's expedition reached 7,300 meters, as usual along the interminable ridge fringed with dangerous cornices (overhanging shelves of snow). Finally, in 1939, yet another German team, headed by Aufschnaiter, was halted by the outbreak of the Second World War. Aufschnaiter and team member Heinrich Harrer managed to escape from British internment and reach Tibet, where they remained for seven years until the Dalai Lama was exiled in 1949.

Back in 1932, meanwhile, the Germans had successfully conquered Rakhiot Peak (7,070 m) and Leo Pargyal (6,770 m).

The Garhwal region of the Great Himalayas is rich in peaks over 6,000 meters and also boasts several dozen "7,000ers." While the central summit of Satopanth (6,721 m) was scaled as early as 1933, Badrinath Peak (now Chaukhamba I, 7,128 m) continued to hold out even as a dozen peaks between 6,000 and 7,000 meters were being climbed by Scottish, English, German, and Italian mountaineers.

In this region of the Himalayas, the accessibility of mountain valleys made private expeditions feasible and even fashionable. They promoted a fine form of mountaineering that was not overly concerned with the most presti-gious summits, but instead racked up victories over magnificent secondary summits, often quite difficult. This was classic "Alpine" moun-taineering once again.

But even though the Garhwal sector has no peaks over 8,000 meters, it boasts two giants:

Kamet (7,755 m) and Nanda Devi (7,816 m), both of which resisted many assaults before succumbing.

Multiple attempts on Kamet had been made between 1910 and 1914 by the pioneering crew —Meade, Slingsby, Kellas, and Morshead. But the first successful climb was only made on 21 June 1931, by Smythe, Shipton, Holdsworth, and Sherpa Lewa, followed two days later by Birnie, Greene, and Kesar Singh. Smythe distinguished himself again in 1937 when he vanquished Mana Peak (7,272 m) on his own, his partner Oliver having halted below the summit.

Finally, in 1939 the Swiss climber André Roch, a veteran of the Dyhrenfurth expeditions, scaled Dunagiri (7,066 m) with guides Steuri and Zogg.

The most splendid mountain in the Garhwal sector is Nanda Devi. It comprises two summits linked by a very long arête, and came to attention rather late, being hidden from view by a ring of secondary peaks some 6,000 meters high. Nanda Devi was discovered, so to speak, by Longstaff, Shipton and Tilman, the first explorers to penetrate the "sanctuary" of the surrounding cirque.

The first ascent of the main summit was made in 1936 by Odell and Tilman, who thereby broke the record for the highest peak ever scaled, established five years earlier by the British on Kamet. In 1939, a Polish team reached the eastern peak (7,434 m), scaled again in 1951 by French climbers in search of Roger Duplat and Gilbert Vignes, who had disappeared near the main peak while attempting the first grand traversal of a Himalayan ridge.

Another high, but easy, peak, Trisul (7,120 m) was climbed again during this period, although the first ascent had been made back in 1907 by Dr. Thomas Longstaff and the Brocherel brothers from Courmayeur.

Then, heading east, the next 800-kilometer stretch of mountains jealously guarded its secrets, protected by Nepal. Its nine 8,000-meter peaks and hundreds of "7,000ers" remained a mystery.

Mountaineering activity only began again further east, in the choice Sikkim region. Sikkim boasts the third highest mountain on the planet, Kangchenjunga (8,586 m)—commonly known

as "Kang"—whose eternal snows apparently hovering above the clouds are visible from the summer resort of Darjeeling.

Like Nanga Parbat, Kang seemed to carry a curse. The first and most serious attempt, made by Dr. Jacot-Guillarmod in 1905, resulted in four deaths. In 1929, the American climber Farmer was lost on Yalung. Attacks were renewed from 1929 onwards. The first German expedition— Bauer, Kraus, and Allwein—reached 7,400 meters. In 1930, the Dyhrenfurth team attacked the northwest face and climbed as high as 6,400 meters, but at the cost of one man's life. Finally, in 1931, the second Bauer expedition reached

an altitude of 7,800 meters, but had to retreat leaving two dead behind.

The "8,000ers" were not yet ready to yield. Conquering them required improved techniques and, above all, improved equipment: light, warm garments; special food; portable radio gear; and, in particular, oxygen equipment. All these items would be developed during the war. War, it seems, always produces incomparable technical progress—a hollow satisfaction.

Also in Sikkim, Kabru (7,315 m) fell to a solo ascent by Cooke in 1935—the earlier victory claimed back in 1893 by Graham and Boss with Ulrich Almer was the result of an error.

In 1931, Sugarloaf (6,440 m) was conquered by Allwein and Brenner. The Germans also distinguished themselves by climbing various summits of Nepal Peak (7,145 m, by Erwin Schneider in 1930; the north summit, 7,180 m,

Another canvas by Roerich, Dorje the Daring One (1925), is typical of the artist's style, heavily influenced by Tibetan Buddhism.

by L. Wien in 1936), while the west summit (7,145 m) was scaled in 1937 by John Hunt, alone. In 1939, a German team spent seven days on the ridge linking Nepal Peak to Tent Peak (now Kirat Chuli, 7,365 m), scaling the latter.

Jonsong Peak is to Tibet what Mont Dolent is to Mont Blanc: an excellent border marker at the junction of Tibet, Nepal, and Sikkim, some 7,483 meters high. Dr. Kellas launched attacks on it as early as 1912, but it was not scaled until 1930 by the Dyhrenfurth expedition that boasted the fine team of Schneider, Hoerling, M. Kurz, Smythe, and Wieland.

Finally, Siniolchu (6,891 m) was climbed in 1936—like Alpamayo in the Andes, it has been called the most beautiful mountain in the world.

Whereas Panhunri (7,128 m) fell to Kellas in 1911, Chomolhari (7,315 m) on the border between Sikkim and Bhutan held out until 1937. On the far tip of the Himalayas, Chomolhari represented the eastern boundary of mountaineering exploration along this enormous, 2,500-kilometer-long range.

The "8,000ers"

The Second World War came to a close in 1945. But it took several years to heal the wounds and clear the rubble, so it was not until 1947 that new reconnaissance missions to the Himalayas were undertaken. Nor should it be forgotten that India, Pakistan, Tibet, and Kashmir were undergoing profound political changes, and that this led to numerous complications and delays in obtaining visas. British influence was nevertheless sufficiently powerful to sustain the authority of the Himalayan Club in Darjeeling, which continued to control the authorizations issued to foreign expeditions.

Everest, then, remained untouchable—it was still British property! But the opening of the Nepalese borders would shake up all previous forecasts by suddenly delivering eight of the world's "8,000ers" to the assaults of climbers.

Everything was now in place for the acquisition of the finest jewels in mountaineering's crown. Knowledge of the range was far better once giant strides in aviation made it feasible to fly over the Everest area. And technology developed during the war in the spheres of materials, nourishment, and oxygen equipment (a direct by-product of aviation requirements), providing mountaineers with modern, efficient tools. None of that, however, resolved the problem of transporting everything to the base camps—the upper valleys were still accessible only by foot. All accounts include descriptions of the exhausting hikes in the heat or rain of the monsoon, which generally accompanied expeditions on their outward trip and once again welcomed them on their return. And then there were the leeches!

Portage itself was a crucial problem. No confusion should be made between Sherpas, veritable professional guides in the Himalayas, and the coolies, those wretched porters hired from local valley peoples. The latter were greedy, rebellious, and prone to swift enthusiasm or discouragement; their conduct largely depended on the mentality of the "sahib" who was managing them. Every expedition had to contend with a strike or two by porters. Even these new, modern expeditions, then, always had one foot in the past.

Air transport was used mainly in Kashmir, where planes could reach jumping-off points like Gilgit and Skardu, thereby gaining some ground at least. Later, the Swiss would test Pilatus-Porter aircraft on Dhaulagiri, but only at the close of the main period of Himalayan exploration. Expeditions like the French assault on Annapurna and the Swiss attempt on Everest would have gained precious days if planes had been able to land on any saddle of snow—but such feats required the light, powerful planes that only became available around 1960, when Pilatus aircraft were fitted with turbojet engines. Helicopters were not yet up to Himalayan standards—only the French Alouette III could reach the highest peaks.

And yet there they stood, all the "8,000ers": four in the Karakoram range, plus Nanga Parbat on the western tip of the Great Himalayas, eight in Nepal or on the Nepalese–Tibetan border, and Kang (or Kangchenjunga) in Sikkim.

Five plus eight equals thirteen, plus one makes fourteen! Listed not by altitude, but rather in the order they were conquered, that gives: Annapurna (8,091 m) in Nepal, climbed

Facing page: Pinnacles of ice on the Rongbuk Glacier on Everest's north face, photographed at night.

A rare view of the north face of Annapurna. The gusts of snow at the summit indicate the violence of high-altitude winds.

on 3 June 1950, by Maurice Herzog and Louis Lachenal (French expedition); Everest (8,848 m) in Nepal, on 28 May 1953, by Sir Edmund Hillary and Tenzing Norgay (Sir John Hunt's British expedition); Nanga Parbat (8,125 m) in Kashmir, on 3 July 1953, by Hermann Buhl (Karl Herrligkoffer's German expedition); K2 (8,611 m) in the Karakoram, on 31 July 1954, by Compagnoni and Lacedelli (Ardido Desio's Italian expedition); Cho Oyu (8,201 m) in Nepal, on 19 October 1954, by Dr. Herbert Tichy, Sepp Jöchler, and Sherpa Pasang Dawa Lama; Makalu (8,463 m) in Nepal, on 15, 16, and 17 June 1955, by Jean Franco's entire French team (first, second, and third ascents); Lhotse (8,516 m) in Nepal, on 18 May 1955, by Swiss climbers Ernst Reiss and F. Luchsinger; Kang (8,586 m) in Sikkim, on 23 May 1955, by Joe Brown and George Band (British expedition); Manaslu (8,163 m) in Nepal, on 11 May 1956, by Japanese mountaineer Imanishi and Sherpa Gyalzen; Gasherbrum II (8,035 m) in the Karakoram, 7 July 1956, by the Austrian team Fritz Moravec, Sepp Larch, and Hans Willenpart; Broad Peak (8,047 m) in the Karakoram, on 9 June 1957, by the Austrians Marcus Schmuck, Hermann Buhl, F. Wintersteller, and Kurt Diemberger (Buhl was the second man to have scaled two "8,000ers,"

Sherpa Gyalzen having been the first); Hidden Peak (8,068 m, also known as Gasherbrum I) in the Karakoram, on 4 July 1958, by Americans Nevison, Swift, and Clinch; Dhaulagiri (8,167 m) in Nepal, on 13 May 1960, by Swiss climbers Diener, Forrer, Schelbert, and the Austrian mountaineer Kurt Diemberger; and finally the Shisha Pangma (or Gosainthan, 8,046 m), an almost unknown mountain located on Tibetan territory, access to which is denied by Nepal, conquered by a Chinese expedition that reportedly placed a bust of Mao Zedong at the summit!

The fifteenth peak sometimes mentioned, notably by Marcel Kurz, is probably the central (but secondary) summit of Broad Peak, which rises 8,016 meters on the Baltoro orographic sketch and indeed appears to be a summit clearly detached from Broad Peak by a cleft. Up till now, this peak has been considered a mere buttress—on a Himalayan scale, of course. Similarly, during the early period in the Alps, the conquerors of the Aiguille Verte would never have considered the Grand Rocheuse or the Aiguille du Jardin as anything other than buttresses on the ridges leading to the sole summit. Yet much later, with the development of mountaineering, such buttresses came to be considered peaks in their own right!

As will be seen most strikingly in the discussion of the conquest of Everest, the monsoon could play a determining factor in the success or failure of Himalayan expeditions. It is particularly critical in Sikkim and Nepal, but diminishes further westward, thus having less effect on ascents in the Karakoram, where several summer expeditions have successfully attained their objectives. Nepal and Sikkim are another story, however, and ascents are possible only during two periods of the year: spring and autumn. The period of fine spring weather lasts fairly long, but is far less predictable than the shorter fall season; the summer monsoon may arrive fifteen or twenty days early and it is this which has caused most of the mountaineering disasters in the Himalayas. Autumn weather, on the other hand, remains stable right up till December, but the temperatures turn very and it was this cold that partly undid the second Swiss expedition to Everest.

Major expeditions tended to adopt a new approach to the seasons. The fall was used to reconnoiter goals, to climb secondary summits, to establish topographic and photographic surveys, and to study access routes to the giant targeted. This work having been accomplished, the task was then completed in the spring, when the actual ascent was attempted. The French, at least, used this method to topple Makalu, and it was also employed on the difficult 1962 conquest of Jannu (7,710 m).

There was a noticeable increase in expeditions, both private and official, starting in 1949. Naturally, Nepal was the fashionable destination. Sutter and Lohner scaled Pyramid Peak (7,100 m) and Nupsche Peak (7,028 m), Walter made the third ascent of Panhunri (7,128 m) and, most important, the indefatigable Tilman carried out a serious reconnaissance of central Nepal. Listing all the secondary summits scaled, however, is beyond the limited scope of this historical overview.

The year 1950 was a great one not only for the Himalayas but also for French climbers. From April to June, a French expedition headed by Maurice Herzog explored the region around Dhaulagiri (8,167 m), which it had been authorized to climb. It was the first time the French had returned to the Himalayas since the failed 1936 attempt on Hidden Peak. In the preceding five years, however, the training of amateur and professional climbers was extensively developed in France, which henceforth became the leading mountaineering nation in the Alps.

That period has rightly been labeled the golden era of French mountaineering. Herzog's

Nanga Parbat, a magnificent "8,000er" that stands apart from the others, towering above the Indus River.

team included terrific professionals like Lionel Terray, Gaston Rébuffat, Louis Lachenal (all familiar with north face ascents in the Alps), Jean Couzy (who would later become France's leading mountain climber), Marcel Schatz (Couzy's climbing partner), doctor and mountaineer Robert Oudot, and the diplomat Francis de Noyelles. This strong team was selected partly on the basis of natural friendships and teamwork. (Later, other expeditions paid less attention to personal affinities; once France boasted a stable of well-trained Himalayan specialists, climbing teams were arranged on the basis of physical and mental strength rather than friendship.) Only one veteran of the 1936 assault joined that youthful French group, namely film maker Marcel Ichac.

The reconnaissance mission to the upper Kali Gandaki Valley immediately revealed that Dhaulagiri was a formidable mountain—and that the maps being used by the French were remarkably inaccurate. They had thought they could approach Dhaulagiri directly via the north slope, only to discover that a major line of mountains separated them from their goal. They reached a high pass, the French Col (nearly 5,000 m), and made attempts on the east face,

before concluding that it was impossible to scale Dhaulagiri for the moment.

Annapurna

The reconnaissance teams were not idle, however. One had headed over toward Annapurna, on the other shore of the Kali Gandaki. Marcel Ichac circled to the north of the cluster of mountains and discovered a frozen lake; he rectified the faulty maps, but saw that a "great barrier" still separated him from Annapurna. Like Nanda Devi, Annapurna is ringed by a slightly lower crown of peaks. But Couzy and Schatz, meanwhile, discovered an access route to the inner cirque, right up to Annapurna's north glacier.

Only three weeks remained before the scheduled onset of the monsoon. Herzog suddenly decided to focus his attack on Annapurna. Camps were soon installed on the so-called "27 April route" along the icy flanks of the immense mountain. The French climbers did not use oxygen, but apparently were well acclimatized thanks to a month of trekking at altitudes of over 5,000 meters.

On 1 June, Herzog and Lachenal were installed at Camp IVa, some 7,000 meters up.

Calcutta was predicting the arrival of the monsoon for 5 June. On the 3rd, the two Frenchmen left Camp V, set up at 7,400 meters with the help of Ang Tarkey and Sari. The Sherpas redescended, while the climbers headed for the summit, the main difficulties being an exhausting trek through powdery snow and the risk of frostbite, since it was extremely cold. Herzog and Lachenal were carrying a minimum of gear, and climbed in a state of euphoria. Around 2:00 p.m., they reached the top. Photos were taken. But the cold was terrible. On the way down, the drama began. Herzog lost his gloves, of which he seemed almost oblivious. Clouds gathered, the monsoon was about to break. Before reaching Camp V, Lachenal slipped, sliding down the slope alone. Rébuffat and Terray welcomed Herzog to the camp, then went out and found Lachenal.

The next day was fog-bound. They spent the night in a crevasse at 7,000 meters, unable to find Camp IV even though it was right nearby.

By 5 June, they were half-frozen, and were suffering from exhaustion. But the four men's shouts were

heard, and Schatz came to their rescue. Rébuffat and Terray were suffering from snow blindness, while Herzog and Lachenal had frostbite on their hands and feet. They descended slowly, aided by their companions. Just when their suffering seemed over, in the warmth of the late afternoon as they neared Camp III, an avalanche overtook them, spun them around and—miraculously—spit them back out. It was another incredibly close shave.

At Camp II, Dr. Oudot tried to save what he could. Herzog's life hung by a thread—for the first time at that altitude, Oudot carried out a perfusion. The operation was tricky, given the improvised resources, but the doctor managed to save his friend's life. The French had successfully scaled the world's first "8,000er." The sensational victory came at a high cost, however—the amputation of Herzog's fingers and Lachenal's toes.

The ascent received a great deal of attention and, despite the errors that were committed, provided useful lessons. First of all, it demonstrated that speed was of the essence in

Above, left: During the ascent of Annapurna. Above, right: Lionel Terray, suffering from snow blindness, returns to base camp leaning on Sherpa Ang Tharkey, followed by Marcel Schatz. Bottom left: The cover of a children's magazine reflects the enormous impact made by the French conquest of Annapurna.

terms of success and rescue; next, it offered precious information on equipment and on the materials used for shoes and tents. Henceforth, the return route would be marked with flags to avoid becoming lost in the fog; had they used this technique, Herzog and Lachenal obviously would have had an easier time finding their way. Their performance without oxygen seemed satisfactory, but there was no doubt that the euphoria the lead climbers experienced was dangerous—it dulled their normal reactions and induced foolish behavior, like the loss of gloves and the separate descent to Camp V at a time when the two men needed above all to join forces.

From May to October of the same year (1950), Tilman explored the Annapurna sanctuary, nearly reaching the summit of one of the numerous surrounding peaks, Annapurna IV (7,524 m). In July and in September, Dittert's Swiss expedition climbed Abi Gamin (7,355 m) in the Garhwal area. Then Bill Tilman and Oscar Houston made the first autumnal reconnaissance of the southwest face of Everest, that is to say the Nepalese side; once the route through Tibet had been cut off, climbers began exploring the southern slopes of the world's tallest giant.

Above, left: Roger Duplat and Gilbert Vignes, who disappeared on Nanda Devi in 1951. Above, right: The 1953 German expedition to Nanga Parbat. Hermann Buhl is on the far right.

The year 1951 was marked by the tragic attempt of Lyon climbers Roger Duplat and Gilbert Vignes to traverse the ridge separating Nanda Devi's two peaks. This first attempt to cross the huge arête was a sporting feat in the purest mountaineering tradition, concerned more with difficulty than with exploring hidden valleys or conquering virgin peaks. Duplat and Vignes disappeared near the summit of Nanda Devi, never to return.

Also that year, Riddiford climbed Makut Parbat (7,242 m). And above all, Eric Shipton, pursuing the reconnaissance effort begun by Tilman, explored Everest by heading up the Khumbu Glacier and discovering the Western Cwm, which would one day be the route to final victory.

In the spring of 1952, the Swiss reached the south col of Everest, and Raymond Lambert and Sherpa Tenzing pushed as high as 8,600 meters. Shipton made an attempt on Cho Oyu (8,201 m). From September to November, the Japanese, who had been assigned the Annapurna–Manaslu sector, made extensive reconnoitering expeditions to those areas. Then, in September and December, the Swiss made a last desperate attempt at Everest, which had been nearly within their grasp in the spring, before their climbing authorization expired and was transferred to Great Britain. But they were halted by the cold, and got no further than the south col (8,100 m).

Everest would fall the next year, 1953. The long battle conducted by British mountaineers from 1911 to 1953 will be discussed later. Their ultimate success overshadowed every other event that year, notably the Japanese failure on

Manaslu, after having scaled 7,750 of its 8,163 meters, and Lauterburg's attempt on Dhaulagiri (8,167 m).

An extraordinary victory was nevertheless achieved just a few weeks after the conquest of Everest; it concerned the most murderous of the "8,000ers," the notorious Nanga Parbat that Mummery had coveted as early as 1895.

Nanga Parbat

The mountain had already claimed thirty-one victims. And what victims! Alongside obscure Sherpas were the famous names of Mummery, Merkl, Welzenbach, Wieland, and Wien (the cream of Austro–German climbers during the interwar period). Between 1932 and 1939, five German–Austrian and German–American expeditions had met with failure, at a heavy cost in lives. Nevertheless, in 1934 Aschenbrenner and Schneider had reached an altitude of 7,850 meters, not far from the summit. In 1950, a British expedition got no higher than the initial slopes, having added two more names to Nanga Parbat's list of victims. The killer mountain was finally tamed by a solitary Tyrolean climber, the extraordinary Hermann Buhl, who will go down in history as the victor of Nanga Parbat.

His victory was surprising from every standpoint. In particular, it came after Dr. Herrligkoffer had given the signal for retreat—the leader was understandably cautious given the enormous responsibility he was shouldering and the disastrous experience of his predecessors when caught by a storm on the interminable final ridge. But Buhl refused to turn back. He continued on alone, without oxygen, starting at 6,900 meters and climbing the remaining 1,200 meters in a single, seventeen-hour day, covering nearly four miles of dangerous arêtes and cornices.

The expedition was composed of a host of young Bavarian and Austrian climbers determined to avenge the earlier deaths; they ran into bad weather, however, and the monsoon season was forecast to arrive early. On 3 July, Buhl and his partner Kempter nevertheless headed for the summit. Kempter turned back, Buhl carried on. The weather was fine, but the alternation of cold with a warm wind heralded the monsoon—it was his last chance. He scaled the long ridge that had been the undoing of the 1934 assault. He reached Silbersattel, then the subsidiary peak where Aschenbrenner and Schneider had halted. Finally, at 7:00 p.m., Buhl found himself at the summit. He bivouacked upright on a slab, bolstered himself with drugs, awoke more or less frozen, and headed back down. He managed to reach the highest camp, where two climbing partners came out to meet him. The little Tyrolean had shown that he was stronger than the great mountain. He had avenged Nanga Parbat's thirty-one victims.

The summit had held out for no less than fifty-eight years.

Above, left to right: The summit of Nanga Parbat seen from Camp VI—set up at 7,000 meters by the 1934 expedition—showing how much ground remained to be climbed; Hermann Buhl before leaving for the summit in 1953; the historic photo documenting Buhl's victory.

K2

The second highest mountain on earth, the notorious K2, targeted by climbers exploring Karakoram at the end of the nineteenth century, finally fell in 1954. It is part of the Baltoro group, and rises 8,611 meters.

Serious assaults were mounted as early as 1902 by Eckenstein, Crowley, Knowles, Pfannl, Vessely, and Jacot-Guillarmod, who attained an altitude of 6,700 meters on the southeast ridge. Then, in 1909, the duke of Abruzzi's expedition climbed to 6,600 meters on the arête of Staircase Peak (now Skyang Kangri). In 1938, Houston's first American expedition reached 7,925 meters on the northeast ridge. A second American trip, in 1939, enabled Wiessner and Pasang Dawa Lama to get as high as 8,370 meters; but when Wolfe and two Sherpas were killed, it was decided to retreat. In 1953, Houston headed a third American expedition, which again reached a very high altitude, but at the cost of Gilkey's death in the upper camps.

The work begun by the duke of Abruzzi in 1909 was completed by Professor Desio's 1954 expedition, which gave Italy a well-deserved victory. The team included not only a significant number of scientific personnel—the professor himself being above all a man of learning—but also the elite of Italian mountaineering professionals and amateurs: guides Abram, Bonatti, Compagnoni, Lacedelli, Puchoz, Ubaldo Rey, Solà, and Viotto, and amateur climbers Angelino,

Floreanini, and Gallotti. The expedition anchored safety ropes along the "Abruzzi arête" previously followed by American teams (Fritz Wiessner and Pasang Dawa Lama had already reached 8,370 meters in 1939). K2 thus became equipped with safety lines, and camps were set up despite highly unfavorable weather and the death of Puchoz, which provoked temporary confusion. On 28 July, Camp VIII was set up at 7,627 meters and Compagnoni and Lacedelli spent a first night there, joined by Bonatti and Gallotti. On the 30th, Compagnoni and Lacedelli set up another tent at 8,060 meters (Camp IX).

Just at that point, a sensational feat of endurance practically guaranteed ultimate victory. While Compagnoni and Lacedelli were setting up Camp IX, Bonatti and Gallotti devoted their energy to descending halfway down to Camp VII (7,435 m), where they picked up two canisters of oxygen left there the day before—oxygen clearly indispensable to the lead team. By noon Bonatti and Gallotti were climbing back up to Camp VIII, from which Bonatti set off that very afternoon with the Pakistani climber Mahdi, in order to get the equipment and food supplies up to Camp IX. Night fell before they arrived, and they had to bivouac on the spot, at 7,990 meters, with no tent. This exploit was absolutely remarkable, and merits stressing. The young climber from Monza, only twenty-four years old at the time and treated somewhat condescendingly by the veteran mountaineers, showed just what he was made of—indeed, Walter Bonatti went on to become one of the

The 1954 Italian expedition to K2 was state-of-the-art, including oxygen apparatus and specially made fur-lined boots. On the far right is Walter Bonatti during the expedition.

greatest guides and mountain climbers of the modern era, winning universal recognition.

On 31 July, Compagnoni and Lacedelli descended to point 7,990 and picked up the oxygen equipment. Then they headed back up, wading through waist-high snow but powered by the oxygen so lacking until then. Unfortunately, both canisters were empty before they arrived at the summit. The oxygen they breathed nevertheless provided them with enough energy to reach the top at 6:00 p.m. Half an hour later they headed down the dangerous Wiessner Couloir, using the glissade technique to reach their sacks at point 7,990, finally arriving at Camp VIII at 11:00 p.m., where they were greeted by their faithful companions Abram, Bonatti, Gallotti, and the Pakistani climbers Mahdi and Isakhan.

It was a fine collective victory, made possible not only by Professor Desio's meticulous organization but above all by the moral and fraternal support displayed by a team of truly great mountaineers, a team able to deploy its reserves all along the immense ridge of K2. A truly magnificent conquest.

Cho Oyu

Another "8,000er" fell in that auspicious year of 1954—Cho Oyu (8,201 m), right on the Nepalese border. This time, however, victory went to a small, private expedition. Ardito Desio's expedition to K2 reportedly cost 700,000 Swiss francs, whereas the Austrian Dr.

Herbert Tichy was traveling through Nepal the way mountaineers formerly toured the Alps. He managed to win the friendship of a small team of Sherpas, notably Sirdar Pasang Dawa Lama, who looked on Tichy as a brother. Marcel Kurz, known for his accuracy, has informed me that the Tichy expedition cost only 42,000 Swiss francs. Tichy did, of course, have the advantage of his extensive knowledge of Nepal, through which he had led a major trek in 1953.

For Cho Oyu, Tichy was accompanied by Sepp Jöchler, a remarkable mountaineer, and Dr. Heuberger, a geographer. Pasang Dawa Lama, meanwhile, had hired nine Sherpas. On 27 September they were at Nangpa La (5,716 meters), the high pass on the Tibetan border; they set up their camps along the west slope. The difficulty that had stumped Shipton was a glacier cap that presented a frontal wall sixty meters high. On 3 October a camp was installed at the foot of the wall so that a route could be forced up it and equipped with climbing aids. By 5 October they were setting up Camp IV at an altitude of 7,000 meters. The 6th dawned clear but a terrible wind threatened to blow away the tents; in trying to limit the damage, Tichy was seriously stricken with frostbite on both hands. The pain increased. So did the gale, dictating retreat back to Camp II, where Dr. Heuberger treated Tichy's painfully frostbitten hands.

While Pasang went to seek further supplies at Namche Bazar, Tichy nursed his hands, less

National celebrations followed the Italian victory on K2, as witnessed by two posters from the period.

seriously frozen than he had feared. Then, on 11 October, to his surprise who should arrive but the advance party of a Franco–Swiss expedition led by Raymond Lambert. It included, among others, the intrepid French woman climber, Claude Kogan. They had failed to make it up Gauri Sankar, deemed too difficult, and were going to have a shot at Cho Oyu.

Conflict was inevitable. Tichy obviously had a certain claim to Cho Oyu, where he had conducted a highly effective reconnaissance mis-

Top left: The 1954 Austrian expedition—Pasang Dawa Lama, Herbert Tichy, Sepp Jöchler. Bottom left: The members of Claude Kogan's 1959 women's expedition, which ended tragically. Right: The summit of Cho Oyu rising above the handsome pyramid of Pumori.

sion. Claude Kogan suggested that he join their team. Tichy refused, but a few days later the Austrian and Franco–Swiss parties came to a compromise: the latter would equip the first three camps, but would wait for Tichy to either succeed or fail before making their own final assault.

Pasang Dawa Lama hurriedly returned from Namche Bazar, and the battle plans were drawn up. Tichy, unable to use his frostbitten hands, headed up to Camp IV nevertheless; Heuberger would remain behind as backup. On 19 October, Tichy, who could barely hold an ice ax, climbed between Pasang and Jöchler; it was extremely cold and the wind was strengthening. They managed to make it to the shoulder (7,800 m), and from there, in the euphoric state induced by altitude, reached the summit at 3:00 p.m.

On the way down, they met the Franco-Swiss group at Camp III. Dr. Lochmatter (son of the famous climber Franz) treated Tichy's hands once again. Lambert's Franco–Swiss team was thus free to act, but had lost valuable time.

As Tichy had done during his second assault, they cut caves into the hard snow (a technique that has since demonstrated its merits in the Patagonian Andes and in Alaska). The cold became unbearable. One by one, the climbers had to head back down, but the indefatigable Kogan and Lambert remained at Camp IV. On 28 October they pushed on up to 7,700 meters, but the excessive cold and wind drove them back down to the base camp.

It is unfortunate that the fraternal mountaineering spirit was not sufficiently strong to spur Tichy, however good his reasons, to agree to join forces with Lambert and Kogan. Lambert, who had so heroically climbed 8,600 meters of Everest before halting, and Kogan, who held the women's record for altitude, deserved a better fate.

Poor Claude Kogan. In 1959 she returned to the Himalayas in order to make the first women's ascent of Cho Oyu. The expedition included the finest women mountaineers of the day and a few Sherpas. Kogan and the young Belgian climber Claudine van der Stratten formed the lead team; but 500 meters from the summit, they were buried by an avalanche. Kogan remains an example of courage, simplicity, and sporting attitude. She financed her own expeditions to the Andes and the Himalayas, which meant spending nine months of the year in the demanding job of running a company. She was the only woman to equal the best Himalayan climbers, forging the route, cutting steps, belaying like a real professional.

Returning to 1954, it was also a good year for reconnaissance climbs. Although an attempt on Makalu by the American mountaineer William Siri halted around 7,100 meters, an expedition by Edmund Hillary explored the Barun Valley, scaling Baruntse (7,129 m) and Pethangtse (6,730 m). An Argentinean expedition stalled about 8,000 meters up Dhaulagiri (8,172 m), where it lost its young and brilliant leader, Lieutenant F. G. Ibañez.

Makalu

In the fall of 1954, the third French expedition to the Himalayas obtained authorization to explore and attack Makalu. This fine target rises 8,463 meters, making it the fifth highest peak in the world. The expedition was headed by Jean Franco, who was a professional guide and the director of France's national ski and mountaineering school.

It seems to be the rule among French mountaineers that the head of the expedition personally participates in the lead teams, being either a great professional or highly experienced amateur climber. This approach already produced a victory over Annapurna, which certainly would not have occurred had the expedition been directed by a leader who had remained in the valley. The assault teams were too often relegated to a secondary role (especially in the period up to 1940). Operations were directed by the important people down below, who would throw their men into the attack with the goal of conquering, yet who were unable to tell exactly what was happening up above, where the presence of a leader was crucial. The result was slower progress, delays, or even disaster.

The reason often invoked for this system was the importance of the scientific side of the expedition, and it was usually a scientist who commanded. Yet experience has demonstrated that whenever the leader participated in the final assault or was at least present in the advanced camps, victory followed. This was the case with John Hunt on Everest, Maurice Herzog on Annapurna, and Jean Franco on Makalu. Furthermore, as recounted above, Nanga Parbat only fell because Hermann Buhl disobeyed his leader's order to retreat. Finally, the discord that reigned with Ardito Desio's K2 expedition could largely have been avoided if a commander had been present in the advanced camps in order to assign each man a role based on his physical and mental capacities of the moment—Walter Bonatti deserved a better role than the one he played. Looking even further back, I still feel that if a bold professional of the stature of an Armand Charlet had been included in the French attack on Hidden Peak, the outcome would undoubtedly have been completely different, especially if the guide had been given command of the final assaults.

To return to Makalu, however, the French had meticulously planned their expedition. Lucien Devies in Paris had carefully anticipated everything, and the equipment had been perfected thanks to the lessons learned on Annapurna. Furthermore, the official nature of the undertaking and the enthusiasm aroused generally in France by the conquest of the first "8,000er" created a favorable climate that made

it easier to raise funds by fully exploiting the lecture circuit.

Franco enrolled two guides, Pierre Leroux and Lionel Terray, whose reputation has already been discussed. The "amateurs" were made of the same stuff: Jean Couzy (like Terray, a veteran of Annapurna) and Guido Magnone (who conquered Fitz Roy). The scientific wing of the team was composed of Dr. Rivolier, a specialist in polar regions, and a geologist named Bordet.

The French climbers benefited from magnificent autumn weather and acclimatized themselves by trekking up and down the Barun Valley. They were extraordinarily active, dividing themselves into teams to scale the surrounding "6,000ers," which provided wonderful observation posts for studying Makalu. Eight new peaks over 6,000 meters were scaled, and the

Above: A climber heads for the summit during the 1955 Makalu expedition. Following double page: The peaks of Lhotse and Everest (showing its east, or Kangshung, face) as seen from the upper slopes of Makalu.

The French expedition to Makalu in 1955 was the first that managed to get the entire team to the summit of an "8,000er." One of the advance camps is shown on the right.

second ascent of Pethangtse was made. Above all, this preparation revealed that the best route up Makalu rose between Makalu II (now Kangchungste, 7,640 m) and Makalu itself. The expedition even managed to set up its advance camp on the high col at 7,410 meters.

On 22 October, Jean Franco and Lionel Terray climbed Makalu II in the company of Gyalzen Norbu and Pa Norbu. The wind was diabolical on the saddle. But a nearby minor summit intrigued the French—Chomolönzo (7,790 m). Chomolönzo was linked to Makalu by a long ridge whipped by infernal winds that effectively put it out of bounds. Couzy and Terray nevertheless secretly climbed it on 30 October, despite the wind and cold, and were rewarded with a view of the Tibetan face of Makalu, on which they discerned an ascent route up a glacial slide invisible on aerial photographs and unnoticed by previous mountaineers. They took a crucial photo and returned. The expedition kept the news completely under wraps. It was too late to make an attack on Makalu, but future success seemed certain. The photo taken from Chomolönzo would only be published a year later, once Makalu had been conquered.

The team returned to France and spent the winter in preparation. Every detail of equipment was gone over—a great deal of importance was placed on the transceivers establishing contact between the various camps; this enabled the advance camps to keep up to date on monsoon forecasts, and to inform the lower camps of any accident or danger.

But the truly wonderful tool used on Makalu was the oxygen apparatus. It was indisputably the best in the world at the time, and was no longer simply derived from aviation equipment. A specially light mask had been designed for climbers, so that the whole apparatus, including the canister carried in the backpack itself, weighed barely six kilograms (thirteen pounds) yet supplied five and a half hours of oxygen. Furthermore, Franco advocated a revolutionary use of oxygen. Whereas it had previously been employed only for the final assault, Franco had his men in the higher camps sleep with their masks on, reducing the flow from the tanks. This technique eliminated the headaches and distress that had made stays in the advance camps such torture. Henceforth climbers awoke feeling fine; having breathed oxygen during the night, they sometimes no longer needed it during the final ascent.

Thus the French expedition set out for the Himalayas again in March 1955.

On 25 April, the base camp was set up on familiar ground, in the northwest cirque of Barun, at 6,400 meters. All the climbers involved in the previous attempt were on hand, joined by two great mountaineers, Coupé and Vialatte. Lapras replaced Rivolier as doctor, while Bordet was joined by another geologist, Latreille.

Camp IV was set up on 4 May just below the Makalu col, at 7,000 meters. From that point upward, team members used oxygen tanks day and night. On 9 May, Camp V was set up on the north col, at 7,410 meters. The weather cleared. Some 2,500 feet of safety lines had been installed on the long climb up from the base camp.

On 14 May, Couzy and Terray set up Camp VI at 7,400 meters, spending a night in the tent at –33°C (–27°F). But they did not suffer from the cold, thanks to their equipment, and they slept well thanks to a steady if limited flow of oxygen (half a liter per minute). When they set out the next morning, they were as well-rested as any climber in the Alps after a comfortable bivouac. They reached the summit without difficulty in five hours. An easy triumph? No, a triumph of organization and rational ascent. It was the right approach for altitudes over 7,000 meters, as subsequent events would prove.

The next day, 16 May, Franco and Magnone reached the top with Gyalzen Norbu. At the same time, Bouvier, Leroux, Coupé, and Vialatte left Camp III (6,400 m), spent the night at Camp VI (7,800 m), and the following day reached the summit in only four hours—Alpine speed, thanks to the oxygen apparatus.

In 1961, Sir Edmund Hillary, having conquered Everest, attempted another ascent of Makalu. He was determined to do it without the aid of oxygen. After struggling terribly in severe cold, however, the situation became serious and the attempt was finally called off at 8,350 meters—Hillary's partner Mulgrew suffered frostbite on his lower limbs and had to have both legs amputated on his return. It is reasonable to argue that the use of oxygen provides the best defense against frostbite by stimulating the blood and activating the circulation of red blood cells, by permitting sleep at high altitudes without sedatives, and by making it possible to climb without stimulants that make the blood sluggish. Experience shows that a tired or depressed climber can freeze almost unawares, whereas a climber in good condition reacts vigorously. Many guides have thus saved the limbs, nose, or ears of their clients on Mont Blanc or Monte Rosa!

Kangchenjunga

One week later, another giant fell—the terrible Kangchenjunga (8,586 m), the third highest peak on earth. It was finally vanquished by a British team led by Dr. Charles Evans.

The mountain has a dramatic history. The first reconnaissance mission was conducted in 1899 by Douglas Freshfield. "Kang" (to use its nickname) is visible from Darjeeling, so it is hardly surprising that it was one of the first targets of Himalayan pioneers. Its summit constitutes the border between Sikkim to the east and Nepal to the west.

As mentioned above, Nepal was closed to foreigners until 1950, but it would seem that the secluded Yalung Valley on the southwest (and therefore Nepalese) slope of the mountain escaped government control, because that was the route taken by Dr. Jacot-Guillarmod, who headed a mixed expedition which included Crowley. The doctor's attempt was the first truly serious one, and he displayed fine judgment in establishing his base camp on the very

Bottom: Paul Bauer, who headed the 1929 German expedition to Kangchenjunga, where it encountered serious difficulties (above, right and center). Above, left: The slope taken by the current normal route up Kangchenjunga.

spot that Evans would choose in 1955, after multiple reconnaissance missions. Jacot-Guillarmod's own exploratory expedition, however, ended in mourning, when an avalanche killed four members.

In 1907, 1909, 1911, and 1912, Dr. Kellas explored the entire range, and Norwegians Rubenson and Aas also visited the area in 1907; but they were far more concerned with the geographic exploration of Sikkim than with mountain climbing. In 1920, it was the turn of Raeburn and Crawford. In 1929, Farmer, an American climber, died on the Yalung Glacier. That same year, however, the attack on Kang began to take shape with the first German expedition, led by Paul Bauer, which reached an altitude of 7,400 meters on the northeast face (Sikkim). Then, in 1930, the international Dyhrenfurth expedition halted at 6,400 meters on the northwest face, an avalanche having caused one death. In 1931, Bauer's second expedition reached 7,800 meters, but an avalanche took another two lives.

Then the political situation changed. Sikkim, which had been a mountaineering paradise, henceforth multiplied its demands and requirements even as Nepal opened its doors, enabling Kempe to make numerous reconnaissance visits to the southwest slope and Yalung basin. Kempe's reports spurred the formation of a British expedition up the Yalung Valley in the spring of 1955. It was headed by Dr. Charles Evans, an old Himalayan hand, and was carefully chosen—all its members were outstanding mountaineers, notably the New Zealander Norman Hardie (Evans's second-in-command), Tony Streather, McKinnon, and Jackson. Also part of the team were two first-rate young climbers who had distinguished themselves as the best British mountaineers in the Alps—George Band and Joe Brown, twenty-six and twenty-four years old, respectively. The expedition was rounded out by Neil Mather and John Clegg, both of whom

Joe Brown, a remarkable British climber, who reached the summit of Kangchenjunga with George Band. At the request of the maharajah of Sikkim, they respected the sacredness of the mountain by halting a few feet away from the absolute summit.

were under thirty. Sirdar Dawa Tenzing headed a strong team of Sherpas. Oxygen tanks were used, the equipment employed on Everest having been made lighter. Adopting the French technique, Evans had his men sleep with oxygen masks.

Despite all the previous reconnaissance missions, that specific slope of the Yalung was not well known, and the initial results were disappointing. Finally, Hardie found an angle of attack starting from the Jacot-Guillarmod base. The route was entirely over ice up to the final arête—it entailed climbing a long, high hanging glacier, arriving at a large glacial ledge that barred the southwest face of Kang, and then taking a couloir up to the crest that led to the summit. The entire route seemed highly exposed to avalanches and falling rocks, but it was the only feasible one. Camp I was installed at 6,000 meters on 26 April. By 12 May, Evans and Hardie set up Camp IV at 7,160 meters, followed by Camp V. Storms then prevented any assault on the summit until 24 May, when Camp VI was reached by Evans, Mather, and two Sherpas. They blazed the trail, for it had been decided that the final attack team would be comprised of Band and Brown, the two youths, and Evans displayed remarkable leadership by doing all the hard work that would cause them additional fatigue—cutting steps, staking tents, finding the route. Like Franco and Herzog, Evans was a general at the head of his troops. The night was spent at 8,200 meters, with Band and Brown breathing oxygen. The next day, they attacked the final, very difficult climb over rockface as well as ice, not reaching the summit until 2:45 p.m., just as their oxygen ran out. It hardly mattered, though, for they had triumphed. Out of respect for religious tradition in Sikkim, they did not tread on the summit, but remained a short distance away. They returned that night to Camp VI, where Hardie and Streather had arrived. The next day, Hardie and Streather reached the top in only three and a half hours, benefiting from the route blazed the day before yet modifying the itinerary where appropriate, just as the French had done on Makalu.

The giant of giants had fallen. Its conquest had taken half a century, at the cost of fourteen lives, the last being a young Sherpa who died from thrombosis on Evans's expedition.

In that same year of 1955, Annapurna IV (7,525 m) was scaled for the first time when Bavarian climbers in Steinmetz's expedition reached the top on 30 May. But the exploit went unheralded, coming as it did just after the resounding fall of Makalu and Kang.

The slaying of "8,000ers" continued the next year, 1956, when Manaslu, Lhotse, and Gasherbrum II fell one after the other under the climbers' assaults.

Manaslu

Manaslu (8,125 m) had been saved for Japanese climbers, who had been exploring the region for several years. After many reconnaissance missions and attempted ascents, Imanishi triumphed in the company Gyalzen Norbu, who had already climbed Makalu and thereby became the first man to rack up two "8,000ers." They reached the summit on 9 May 1956, and two days later, honoring the new tradition of having several teams from the same expedition attain the summit, Japanese climbers Higeta and Kato repeated the exploit, using oxygen above 7,000 meters.

Meanwhile, another major attack was underway. A Swiss expedition, largely composed of climbers from Zurich, received authorization to attack Lhotse (8,516 m), the mountain facing Everest. The climbers took the south col route, already reconnoitered during Everest attempts made by Lambert and his partners on the Wyss–Dunant expedition, as well as by Genevan mountaineers under Dittert, and by British climbers under Hunt. This time, the equipment had been perfected, oxygen canisters were in full use, and nothing was left to chance. Thus on 18 May 1956, Fritz Luchsinger and Ernst Reiss reached the top of Lhotse.

The weather held that season, and the climbers were in good condition, so on 23 May at 2:00 p.m., Jürg, Marmet, and Schmied completed the sec-

ond successful ascent of Everest, followed the next day, at 1:00 p.m., by Von Gunten and Reist—a startling achievement at the time.

Mustagh Tower

On 7 July 1956, two major events occurred in the Karakoram. First of all, Gasherbrum II (8,035 m) fell to an Austrian team comprised of Sepp Larch, Fritz Moravec, and Hans Willenpart, without the use of oxygen equipment. But the conquest of this major "8,000er" probably had less impact than an exploit accomplished that same day by two small expeditions,

one British and the other French, on a tower of rock simply known as Mustagh (7,273 m).

Ever since it had been discovered fifty years earlier, Mustagh Tower incarnated difficulty. It was an "impregnable peak" par excellence, like the Matterhorn in the Alps. And, like the Matterhorn, overcoming it meant overcoming fear. Up to that point, scaling the great Himalayan summits rarely involved rockface challenges. Most of the time, climbing entailed routes through exhausting snowfields and up glaciers. It was only on Kang that Band and Brown had to resolve tough rock problems, and even then the passage was short, as was the outcrop on Nanga Parbat scaled by Buhl. Mustagh, however, presented sustained difficulties on rock and ice. It was not known whether these problems could be overcome at that altitude—the physical exertion required might simply be beyond human limits.

The summit of Manaslu, an "8,000er" attacked three times by Japanese expeditions before falling in 1956.

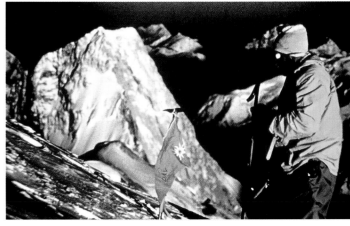

Above, clockwise from left: Mustagh Tower; Hermann Buhl at the summit of Broad Peak; Buhl just prior to disappearing on Chogolisa; Guido Magnone. Bottom: Buhl, once again, just before his disappearance.

By a strange coincidence, two teams attacked the same summit simultaneously, each by a different route.

The British were first in the field. They chose the northwest arête, and on 7 July Joe Brown and Ian McNaught-Davis reached the summit; their partner Hartog was seriously frostbitten and was treated on his return by Dr. Florence, from the French party.

The French team was headed by Magnone, and included guides André Contamine and Paul Keller, plus Robert Paragot and Dr. Florence. They reached the top of Mustagh Tower on 12 July; they had been slowed by poor weather but managed to overcome truly serious glacier difficulties. On their return, they were fraternally greeted by the British, and the double victory was celebrated in typical mountaineer fashion.

Given the technical climbing problems posed by both routes, this fine victory symbolized a turning point in Himalayan mountaineering—the era of conquering 8,000-meter peaks was ending, the age of technical exploits was dawning.

In July and August of that same year of 1956, Beleckij's Sino-Soviet party climbed Mustagh Ata (7,546) and Kongur Tagh (7,595 m), both in the Pamir range in China. Apparently oxygen was used for both ascents (the second included six Russian and two Chinese climbers).

In 1957, Broad Peak (8, 047 m) was conquered by an Austrian team composed of Schmuck, Diemberger, Wintersteller, and Buhl. The extraordinary Hermann Buhl therefore became the second mountaineer to have scaled

two 8,000-meter peaks (the first having been Sirdar Gyalzen Norbu).

The follow year another "8,000er" fell— Hidden Peak (8,068 m). As mentioned earlier, a French expedition had made a first attempt as early as 1936, but it was not until 4 July 1958 that the American team of Nick Clinch, Andy Kauffman, and Pete Shoening finally claimed victory.

Still in 1958, in the distant Tien Shan range, the Russians made the first ascent of the east arête of Pobeda (Victory) Peak, which entailed a route over five miles long on a ridge above 7,000 meters. In that region, too, the age of technical challenges had dawned.

In 1960, the Clinch–Bell expedition to the Karakoram overcame the proud Masherbrum (7,821 m) on 7 July, while Disteghil Sar (7,885 m) fell to the Austrians on 9 July. But the most striking achievement of that year was the

ascent of the thirteenth 8,000er, Dhaulagiri (8,167 m), the initial target of the French Annapurna team in 1950.

Dhaulagiri

This difficult ascent was finally accomplished by a Swiss team. As discussed earlier, poor knowledge of the area and approach routes to Dhaulagiri, complicated by the serious inaccuracies or gaps in the maps of the day, prevented the French from making a serious attack in 1950. Since the west slope of Dhaulagiri seemed too formidable, they had circled it in the hope of attacking straight up the north face, but instead discovered an unknown valley. Dhaulagiri hid behind an impressive mountain chain, the Dhaulagiri Himal. From the French Col, discovered by Lionel Terray and Jacques Oudot, the French took some photographs of the north

Broad Peak, scaled in 1957 by a very small Austrian expedition which was led by Markus Schmuck.

Above, left: Gasherbrum II, vanquished by an Austrian expedition in 1956, is now considered to be one of the easiest "8,000ers." Above, right: Climbing Dhaulagiri in 1960.

face overlooking the Mayangdi Glacier, then changed their goal and scaled Annapurna.

A Swiss attempt, promoted by the Akademische Alpenclub of Zurich (AACZ), explored the north face in 1953, and discovered the arête—or rather, long rib—that rises up the imposing face for over two miles. The team reached an altitude of 7,700 meters.

Then, in 1954, Argentina was given permission to attack Dhaulagiri. The Andean climbers, all accustomed to very high altitudes, were led by Lieutenant F. G. Ibañez. It was a major expedition that employed substantial resources, using explosives to level the ground for campsites on the interminable north slope. Camp VII had been established at 7,500 meters when the monsoon arrived.

Finally, an attack was made on 1 June. In fact, it was not designed to be a final assault; Lieutenant Ibañez was unwell and had remained at Camp VII, while a lightly equipped recon-

naissance group set off, comprised of Watzl, carrying oxygen, and Pasang Dawa Lama (who had climbed Cho Oyu), along with Magnani in partnership with Ang Nyima. They reached 8,000 meters with a great deal of difficulty, then arrived on the crest leading to the summit, which was technically easy but long. They were obliged to make an arduous bivouac, during which a storm came up—and the next morning they were forced to retreat.

They found Ibañez in his tent, still unwell. But he refused to descend. A team had to climb up to get him, by which point he was half frozen. The nightmare of Annapurna occurred all over again: desperate attempts by the team to rescue its leader were followed by a hurried return to the valley and the partial amputation of Ibañez's legs. Unfortunately, he died in a Katmandu hospital on 30 June after nearly a month of dreadful suffering.

In 1958, another attempt by a Swiss expedition failed.

In 1959, an Austrian team arrived at a point 400 meters below the summit before a storm and the merciless monsoon drove them back, taking the life of Heinrich Roiss.

Finally, in 1960, the Swiss mounted yet another attack. This time they used a plane to avoid lengthy portage and save time. Unfortunately, the first aircraft had an accident before the entire team had been flown in; later a second plane had to make an emergency landing. Despite these incidents, however, it was clear that planes could be used.

The airlift problems meant that the first group flown to the site was far ahead of the others. It set up a first camp at Dapa La (or Dambush Pass, 5,182 m) then shifted operations to the northeast col, at 5,650 meters, where the plane had made a second landing. Meanwhile, the rest of the team was at Pokoshi. The plane had nevertheless demonstrated that ground it had taken the French team nine days to cross could be covered in forty-five minutes! On the other hand, the swift change in altitude, with no acclimatization, sorely tried the climbers.

After having vainly awaited the return of the plane, which had meanwhile made a forced landing, the Dapa La team crossed the French Col and climbed to the camp on the northeast col. Then, following the route taken by the Austrians, the Swiss climbers equipped the arête, setting up camps along the way. And on 13 May Diemberger, Forrer, Schelbert, and the Sherpas Nima and Nawang Dorjee reached the summit.

On 23 May, after a long wait in the upper camps until a storm had passed, Michel Vaucher and Hugo Weber also made a victorious run at the summit, then redescended to the northeast col. Dhaulagiri was twice vanquished.

Above: The fine summit of Dhaulagiri, showing the ascent ridge. Left: Kurt Diemberger and Albin Schelbert on the summit of Dhaulagiri in 1960.

The 1962 expedition that conquered Jannu had to overcome unprecedented difficulties in the Himalayas, notably involving a long, complex, and circuitous route.

On 17 May 1960, a British team scaled Annapurna II (7,937 m). That same season saw the Japanese conquer Himalchuli (7,864 m). Finally, on 25 May the north arête of Everest was scaled by a Chinese expedition.

In 1961, Nuptse (7,855 m) was finally tamed by Davis and Sherpa Tashi, followed by another British team. Meanwhile, Nilkanta (6,600 m) in the Garhwal Himalayas, which had been vainly attacked by Smythe and Oliver, fell on 13 June.

In March 1961, the splendid mountain known as Ama Dablam was at last climbed by a party led by Hillary, the conqueror of Everest.

But two tragedies darkened the Himalayan picture. During Hillary's unsuccessful attempt on Makalu, which stalled at 8,350 meters, his partner Peter Mulgrew suffered severe frostbite and ultimately had both legs amputated. Then, at Langtrang Lirung, under attack by a Japanese expedition, an avalanche killed two Japanese climbers and Sirdar Gyalzen Norbu, conqueror of Makalu and Manaslu, one of the most brilliant guides in the Himalayas.

At that point, everything seemed to have been accomplished in the Himalayas. But two major exploits, on Jannu and Nanga Parbat, led Himalayan mountaineering in new directions. Mustagh Tower had set a fruitful example—already numerous "7,000ers" were being climbed. So in 1962 a French expedition, headed by Terray and composed of the best French climbers of the day (Desmaison, Pollet-Villard, Bouvier, Leroux, Lenoir, and Magnone), made an assault on the extremely difficult Mount Jannu (now Kumbhakarna, 7,710 m), the highest peak of an imposing group situated to the west of Kang.

Jannu presented major ice and rock obstacles. Back in 1960, Franco's French team (which included most of the members on the 1962 expedition) had equipped the route up the last steep slope, some 400 meters below the summit. Forced to follow a very long ridge that posed major ice problems, Franco's expedition only failed due to lack of material—the itinerary had been modified at the last moment, an enormous avalanche having swept the glacial cwm that the expedition had initially expected to attack.

Two years later, the second expedition, now headed by Terray (Franco being forced to fulfill obligations as director of the national ski and mountaineering school), took advantage of this experience, vanquished all resistance, and managed to reach the summit of Jannu in May 1962.

On 22 June of that same year, another feat was chalked up on Nanga Parbat. The Herrligkoffer party, in making the second ascent of the peak, was the first to scale the notorious Diamir Face, the one chosen by Mummery. It had been seriously attacked and nearly conquered in 1961 by the same Austrian group that had reached the upper snowfields at 7,100 meters, only to be forced back by bad weather.

Jannu and the Diamir Face of Nanga Parbat had fallen—the era of great athletic accomplishments had arrived.

A similar evolution was occurring elsewhere, beyond the Himalayas. It should not be forgot-

ten that in 1961 Cassin's Italian expedition, composed of Airoldi, Alippi, Canali, Peregan, and Zucchi, conquered the difficult south spur of Mount McKinley in the icy wastes of Alaska.

It is fitting that this summary of the history of mountaineering should terminate with an account of the conquest of Everest, or Chomolungma (8,848 m; 29,028 ft.). I have deliberately chosen to treat it separately, for, like the stories of Mont Blanc, Monte Rosa, and the Matterhorn, it incarnates an entire era, features technical developments, and is essential for understanding, the overall evolution of mountaineering from the days of Jacques Balmat and Dr. Paccard to those of Tenzing and Hillary.

The steep snowy slopes of the Tête de la Dentelle, a subsidiary summit that held the key to the conquest of Jannu in 1962.

Conquering Everest

On 28 May 1953, Sherpa Tenzing and Edmund Hillary stood on the summit of Everest. The highest mountain in the world had finally been scaled! But the British campaign had lasted thirty-two years and cost several lives.

I feel it is time to render this old planet's highest peak the poetic name it had long before Westerners came to the area. It is natural for conquerors to baptize vanquished mountains, especially when, as was often the case in the Alps, they had been ignored for centuries and had no known name. In the case of Everest, however, it is hard to see why the name of a very senior but very obscure civil servant of the British Crown, the Surveyor General of India from 1823 to 1843, should continue to float above the rest of the world's mountains, which he neither visited nor climbed! True enough, Sir George Everest headed a team of cartographers, and dispatched Indian "pundits" and British topographers into the Himalayas. During a routine triangulation conducted some distance away it was realized that Peak 15 was so high that it was the tallest mountain on earth. Yet Peak 15, forming the border between Nepal and Tibet (Nepal being open at the time), was not only venerated throughout the land but also had a marvelous, sacred name: Chomolungma, "Mother Goddess of the World."

From its summit descended the glaciers that fertilized the valleys, serving as source to the major rivers that brought life to the plains. Chomolungma was indeed the mother of all things. Temples were built at her feet, for the mountain was a high pedestal that brought mankind closer to God. Bureaucrats turned her into Mount Everest. The name is so firmly rooted, however, that it will be hard to efface. Such is life. If the mountain must be given some Western name—even though those regions are no longer any of our business—then it should at least be called Hillary and Tenzing Peak.

The first mountaineer who considered climbing Everest may well have been the enthusiastic lieutenant who accompanied Conway to the Karakoram in 1893, but Lieutenant Charles Bruce would have to wait until 1922, when, as a general, he led the second British expedition to Everest. Another Himalayan mountaineer and Tibetan specialist, Dr. Kellas, had conducted an official reconnaissance mission in 1911; his findings were supplemented by those gathered

Facing page: Emerging from the Hillary Step, a climber heads up Everest's final ridge, with Lhotse in the distance. Above: Oxygen equipment tested by the early British expeditions to Everest.

The north face of Everest as seen by the 1921 British expedition. The north ridge —the key to the ascent—is on the left.

by John Noel in 1913. But political complications were already posing problems—both in Nepal and Tibet, entry was subject to authorization by the maharajah or Dalai Lama. Nepal would soon close itself completely to Western influence, which meant that the only route to the foot of Mount Everest was via Tibet, which led to its north face. At that time, the Tibetan route required a veritable expeditionary force, which had to trek for nearly 500 kilometers.

But then the First World War intervened, and it was only in 1919 that the idea of conquering Everest was taken up again. The Royal Geographical Society and the Alpine Club in London proceeded to arrange all the formalities, which took a year, and finally dispatched the first British expedition to Everest in 1921.

Charles Bruce having been promoted to the rank of general, the expedition was placed under the command of Colonel Howard-Bury, who, though not a mountaineer, was a Himalayan soldier and veritable "officer of native affairs." Kellas, Raeburn, Mallory, and Bullock were to form the lead climbing team. A few scientists were also part of the group, which planned above all to make a preliminary reconnaissance of the area.

The long trek lasted five weeks, passing through upper Sikkim and then circling the Himalayas to the north and west, arriving at the monastery of Rongbuk. It established its base camp at the foot of the famous double glacier descending both sides of the north col, known as

Rongbuk Glacier. Mallory and Bullock immediately performed a key task by climbing up to the north col (7,000 m), which gave them a good view of the entire north face of Everest, with its ridge of rocky tiers. The sight warmed their hearts, for they felt that they had discovered a route that day. The expedition concluded with a complete reconnoitering of the three Rongbuk Glaciers and a climb up to the Lho La col, which overlooked the Khumbu Valley and the glaciers on the south face of Everest. George Mallory studied at great length the strange glacial combe that he named Western Cwm, using the Welsh term for glacier-carved valley. Could he have suspected that one day this apparently impregnable heap of séracs would provide a route to the summit?

The expedition was fruitful, and Mallory would have liked to continue up the north arête, but he was inadequately equipped. He was dressed like an Alpine Club mountaineer, in gentlemen's tweed that provided no protection whatsoever from the terrible Tibetan winds that they were encountering for the first time.

The Howard–Bury mission having been deemed a success, it was decided to mount a true assault the following year. Lengthy formalities with the Dalai Lama had to be completed once again, but on 1 May 1922, a long caravan left Rongbuk and climbed toward the glacier. It was a strong team, headed by General Charles Bruce, a true leader and mountaineer, henceforth freed from other duties. His second in command was Colonel Strutt, while a scientific

Surveyor General Sir George Everest supervised triangulation of the Indian subcontinent, a gigantic task that made it possible to calculate the height of the main Himalayan summits.

team of Crawford, Morris, and Morshead backed up the assault crew composed of Mallory, Norton, Somervell, Finch, and Wakefield; John Noel was the photographer, and Captain Geoffrey Bruce also joined the party, thereby following in his uncle's footsteps. The veteran Dr. Thomas Longstaff contributed his medical skills and Himalayan experience.

The composition of the team had sparked lively debate within the organizing committee, yet the most serious question was whether the climbers would use oxygen or not. Just as it opposed the recruitment of professional guides for an expedition that it wanted to be entirely British, the Everest committee was against the use of oxygen. It arrived at a compromise that seems exquisite today: those members who were to blaze the trail, make the route, and install camps could use oxygen, but the final assault team had to advance without oxygen masks, out of a sense of fair play!

Given the previous year's experience, Mallory climbed to the north col via the east slope, which was icy and in far different condition from the year before. Camp IV was set up on the col. On 19 May, Morshead, Norton, Somervell,

and Mallory attacked the north ridge for the first time. Although the terrain was not difficult, the wind and cold were dreadful for men dressed as they were, with sweater piled on top of sweater and stockinged calves wrapped in puttees—they had neither anoraks nor down jackets. Morshead, followed by Mallory, climbed painfully, cutting steps away from the wind on the north face. Finally they built two little bivouacs out of stone on sloping slabs that offered no truly convenient site. After a most uncomfortable night, they started out again and slowly climbed, discovering just how difficult it is to walk at such lofty altitudes. Morshead gave up and returned to Camp V; Mallory and three others carried on, having to halt for breath every three steps. At 2:15 p.m. the summit still seemed far away. They looked around and realized that the highest peaks on the planet were all beneath them—for the first time, they had broken the 8,000-meter barrier! Without oxygen, they had reached 8,225 meters. But they were obliged to descend, which was dangerous on the icy rock; Mallory successfully halted a fall by this three partners. They arrived at Camp IV at 10:00 p.m.

Above: George Mallory.
Right: The 1921 expedition
(standing, left to right):
Wollaston, Howard-Bury,
Heron, and Raeburn;
(seated): Mallory, Wheeler,
Bullock, Morshead.

Finch, meanwhile, "tinkered" with the expedition's breathing apparatus and managed to make it work. On 25 May he set off to make an attempt using oxygen, accompanied by Geoffrey Bruce, a mountaineering novice, and a Gurkha who was also new to such high altitudes. Finch sent porters up from the north col to prepare an upper camp in advance, then  set off himself an hour and a half later. He climbed easily, despite carrying some forty pounds of breathing equipment. The camp was installed at 7,800 meters. A fierce wind rose that night, almost blowing the tent away; it finally calmed about 1:00 p.m. the next day, and the climbers decided to wait for the morrow, rationing their supplies. Porters arrived that evening with additional provisions.

The second night was wretched, for they were all unwell. Finch had the bright idea of inhaling some of the oxygen, which immediately did him and his companions a great deal of good. Thus they discovered the usefulness of oxygen while sleeping, thirty-two years before it became a technique advocated and systematically applied by Franco on Makalu. One wonders why these early promising experiments were not immedi-

ately imitated—perhaps mountain climbers of the day felt some secret shame on using what they thought was an "unfair" advantage.

The next day, the Gurkha turned back at 8,000 meters, but Finch and Bruce carried on. They left the north ridge and headed up the face below the northeast arête, at an altitude of 8,300 meters. At noon they had to turn around, however, one of the breathing devices having jammed. They were back at the north col by 4:00 p.m., which was quite an exploit for a beginner like Bruce.

On 7 June, after a long spell of bad weather, Mallory, Somervell, and Crawford went back up to the north col, but were struck by an avalanche that buried seven porters in a crevasse. Everest had begun to take its toll.

The third British expedition set out in 1924. It was commanded by Colonel Edward Norton (General Bruce having been stricken with malaria on the approach march), and included Theodore Somervell, George Mallory, and Geoffrey Bruce (who, after his brilliant start, had perfected his technique by spending a season in the Alps). The old team was reinforced by new arrivals like Odell, Beetham, Hazard, Shebbeare,

Above: Andrew Irvine, who disappeared with Mallory while heading for the summit of Everest in 1924. Left: The 1922 expedition at breakfast (left to right): Wakefield, Morris, General Charles Bruce, Geoffrey Bruce, a Gurkha, Norton.

Above, left: Bullock tries out snow shoes during the 1921 expedition. Above, right: Camp on the north col in 1922.

Hingston, and Irvine. But once on Rongbuk Glacier, the party ran into terrible weather, and had a great deal of difficulty establishing the three first camps. It returned to base camp having lost two porters to illness and frostbite.

A lot of time had been lost when they finally headed back up to the north col, and the monsoon season was fast approaching. Furthermore, progress was impeded by an enormous bergschrund (deep crevasse at the foot of the slope), across which Mallory, a great glacier specialist, had to hack a route. Then a blizzard struck and Mallory, Somervell, and Norton had to hasten to retrieve four Sherpas who had remained up on the col. The whole party then descended amid a high risk of avalanches.

On 1 June 1924, George Mallory and Geoffrey Bruce finally established Camp V on the north ridge. The cold was severe. The exhausted team of Sherpas refused to climb any higher to set up Camp VI. Everyone descended to Camp IV, encountering Norton and Somervell on their way up. Despite not only the wind but also faulty equipment, Norton and Somervell reached Camp V.

The fatigue was general the following day, yet the remarkable Sherpas agreed to carry equipment higher than had ever been done before, thereby setting up Camp VI at an altitude of 8,200 meters. Then they descended, leaving the two British climbers on their own.

The next morning, Norton and Somervell set out at 6:30 a.m., reaching the 150-meter "yellow band" running below the northeast ridge. By noon, thanks to incredible willpower, the two climbers found themselves on the edge of the large couloir that runs down the east side of the pyramidal summit. Somervell halted there, waiting while Norton continued alone. But the climbing difficulties increased on the icy rocks of the couloir and Norton gave up in turn, having reached 8,573 meters. For many years it would remain the highest point ever attained by a human being. The two men headed back down to the north col, arriving at midnight. Norton was suffering from snow blindness.

Norton and Somervell had eschewed oxygen. Mallory, although he disdained its use, realized that it could be a decisive factor in the final victory and decided to take along devices that, even though improved, still weighed over eleven kilos (twenty-five pounds). Thus he chose Andrew Irvine as his partner, instead of the remarkable mountaineer Odell, for the simple reason that Irvine, though a beginner, was an oxygen specialist.

Mallory and Irvine headed up to Camp V on 6 June; on the 7th, they reached Camp VI, while

Odell climbed up to Camp V as reinforcement. He therefore spent the night alone at an altitude of 7,700 meters, climbing to Camp VI the next morning. Despite the clouds enveloping the mountain, he scrutinized the north face with his geologist's eye and, during a brief break in the clouds, glimpsed the ridge of Everest standing out clearly against the blue sky. There he spied two "tiny black spots" moving and approaching a great rock step. It was noon. Odell knew that Mallory had decided to follow the ridge, but they must already be far above it. At Camp VI, spare parts scattered around the tent showed that the two climbers had tried to repair the oxygen equipment. Odell continued higher. He shouted into the wind. The storm broke, and he returned to Camp VI. Then, obeying Mallory's orders he descended before nightfall; having left at 4:30 p.m., he reached Camp V at 6:00 p.m. and was at the north col an hour later.

The next day, Odell and two porters headed back up to Camp V, then Odell continued on alone to Camp VI, seeking some trace of the missing climbers.

The mystery surrounding the disappearance of Mallory and Irvine was only partly solved when Wyn Harris and Wager, the assault team on the 1933 expedition, found Mallory's ice ax. It was lying on a slab under the east ridge, below the first rock step. A great deal of speculation has focused on whether the accident occurred on the way up or the way down. The question, in fact, remains open to this day: did Mallory and Irvine reach the top of Everest?

The tragedy spawned a legend, for this enigmatic end accorded perfectly with heroic tradition. George Mallory became a god for youthful mountain climbers. It is to be hoped for him that he fell during the ascent, before he fulfilled his dream, while still fully gripped by the quest for victory. Of all those who have climbed Everest after him, he is the only one to have truly won: along with his young companion, the neophyte Irvine, Mallory has been allowed to continue his ascent toward mysterious, non-terrestrial spheres. He never came back to earth.

It was only nine years later that the Dalai Lama agreed to issue another authorization to attempt the impossible ascent. The new expedition was led by Hugh Ruttledge, and included thirteen climbers with a great deal of Himalayan or Alpine experience. Smythe, Shipton, Greene, Birnie, Wood, Boustead, Crawford, and Shebbeare were familiar with the Himalayas, while Wyn Harris, Wager, Longland, Brocklebank, and McLean were excellent Alpinists.

Frank Smythe was the backbone of the team, replacing the great Mallory. They headed up the

Above, left: Heavy and impractical oxygen equipment was of little help to prewar expeditions. Above, right: Norton reached an altitude of 8,573 meters during the 1924 expedition.

ever dangerous north col once more, managing to equip Camp IV with a telephone link via ground cable; thus having learned from Darjeeling that the fateful monsoon was on its way, they decided to go straight for the attack as soon as possible. Smythe and Shipton were already at Camp V, blocked by a terrible snowstorm, and took advantage of a break in the weather to get back to the north col.

Camp VI was installed at 8,350 meters by the "tigers," who had to redescend in a howling storm that suddenly broke upon the team.

But on 29 May, Wyn Harris and Wager were at Camp VI, Eric Shipton and Frank Smythe were at Camp V, and other climbers were waiting in reinforcement on the north col. On the 30th, Wyn Harris and Wager set out for the ridge, fifteen meters below which they found the ice ax used by Mallory (or Irvine). They carried on to the first rock step and were able to skirt around it by remaining below the ridge, which they followed up to the second step. This second step appeared

impregnable. They tried to bypass it via a very steep couloir, but the obstacles were so serious that Wyn Harris wisely backtracked. They moved over to the Grand Couloir and headed up it, but had no more success than Norton did in 1924, reaching the same altitude. On their way back down, Wager managed to reach the very crest of the ridge, enabling him to get a first look at the south face of Everest. The jagged ridge itself proved to be a very difficult climb. They returned with the famous Mallory ice ax to Camp VII, where they found Smythe and Shipton.

After Wyn Harris and Wager headed down, Shipton and Smythe spent two nights in the tent of Camp VI, awaiting favorable weather conditions. On the second morning, at 7:30 a.m., they made their move. The accounts state that, despite donning seven sweaters and a "windjack," the cold went straight through them. (How different was the material twenty-one years later, enabling the French team on Makalu to sleep comfortably at a temperature of –33°C!) Shipton and Smythe

forsook the ridge and attacked the famous yellow band. Shipton, unwell, gave up, but Smythe continued alone. Smythe was in such a feverish state that he was convinced an invisible companion was climbing behind him, spurring him onward. He arrived at the Grand Couloir and reached the Norton-Harris-Wager point, managed to get above it with some difficulty, but then decided to retreat—he was dangerously exhausted. When he rejoined Shipton at Camp VI, Shipton decided to head straight down to Camp V to alert Birnie, the backup climber. But the descent was dangerous. Smythe had risked a potentially fatal maneuver in the Grand Couloir, miraculously held only by his ice ax; now it was Shipton's turn to save himself at the last moment when he stumbled on a slab in the storm. But Shipton managed to reach Camp V.

Up above, Smythe had slept for thirteen hours at a stretch during the blizzard, and awoke beneath the snow that had invaded his tent. He tried to descend the icy north arête; gusts of snow, veritable tornadoes, nearly pushed him

into the void. He approached Camp V just as Shipton and Birnie were leaving it to head back down. He shouted, but the other two neither heard nor saw him. When he arrived at the camp, he realized that the tents had blown down. He had to carry on. Thanks to his superhuman strength, Smythe managed to arrive within sight of the north col, and Longland climbed to meet him. He was in such a state of nervous exhaustion that he could not manage to speak. He broke away from his friends and raced down the slope to Camp III, mumbling incoherently.

The monsoon had indeed arrived early. Another attempt had come to naught.

Foiled Again!

The craziest attempt on Everest occurred in 1934. A former British officer named Wilson, imbued with asceticism, secretly entered Tibet with two porters he had bribed. He reached Rongbuk, and then the Ruttledge expedition's Camp III. From

Above: During the 1922 expedition, Mallory and Norton reached a height of 8,225 meters on Everest's north ridge, without using oxygen equipment.

there he attacked the north col all alone, but failed. He died of exhaustion in his tent, where he was found the following year by Shipton.

That fifth expedition reached the north col (7,007 m) but could get no further. Shipton's small party had arrived on the Rongbuk Glacier late in the season and found the mountain covered in snow. They managed to set up camp on the north col, but were caught by the monsoon, which forced them to redescend. (The same fate awaited the Tilman party of 1938, forced to retreat before the merciless monsoon.) In the meantime,

The Everest Committee found this series of defeats extremely trying; it was finally decided, for financial reasons, to abandon large expeditions in favor of a lighter reconnaissance party led by Tilman, who recruited veteran partners—Shipton, Smythe, Odell, Warren, Lloyd, and Oliver were all experienced high-altitude climbers.

Having arrived early at Rongbuk, the Tilman team set up Camps I and II before persistently foul weather drove them back to the Kharta Valley. On their return to the mountain, every-

an avalanche 400 meters wide had buried all traces of their ascent. Shipton then effected a second reconnaissance mission on Lho La col and the northwest point reached by Mallory, taking a long look at Everest's Western Cwm.

In 1936, Ruttledge mounted another large, powerful expedition. After reaching the north col on 18 May they, too, were surprised by the sudden arrival of the monsoon. During their retreat, an avalanche on the north col nearly cost the lives of Shipton and Wyn Harris.

View of the Rongbuk Glacier from the north face of Everest. The north col can be seen on the lower right.

thing was shrouded in white, and avalanches were crashing down the north col. They reached the col twice, but had to retreat.

Finally, they attacked the west slope, even more dangerous than the eastern one. They set up Camp V, followed by Camp VI at 8,300 meters. Smythe and Shipton, for the second time in their lives, spent a night at that altitude. They slept well, and started out the next morning in excellent condition. But they had to wade through snow up to their waists, and took an hour to advance the length of a single pitch of rope. They turned back. Tilman and Lloyd tried again the next day, with no greater success. A general retreat was ordered. Smythe and Shipton opposed the use of oxygen, for purely sporting reasons, while Lloyd and Warren employed it without a great deal of success, apparently because the devices they used were unsuitable for mountain climbing.

With the outbreak of the Second World War, a sorely tested Britain was in no position to renew the Himalayan expeditions. Then Tibet perma-

with several Sherpas. Larsen did not even have a camping stove to heat his food! His Sherpas refused to go any further, and he was obliged to give up. Such were the attempts of madmen and fanatics!

Tibet, having been invaded by China, was now permanently off-limits to Westerners. The route to Everest seemed barred forever.

Just then, in 1950, Nepal miraculously opened its borders. The move meant sudden access to ten peaks over 8,000 meters high, the most prestigious mountains on earth,

nently closed its borders—not sufficiently tightly, however, to prevent the Canadian climber Earl Denman from repeating Wilson's escapade by secretly entering Tibet in 1947 with two Sherpas. Denman accomplished the sensational feat of getting above the north col, to an altitude of 7,200 meters. But the cold and lack of equipment forced him to retreat.

The Dane K. B. Larsen made an equally foolhardy attempt in 1951, secretly entering Tibet via Nepal and reaching the north col of Everest

reached by completely unfamiliar valleys. One of them was Khumbu Valley on the south side of Everest, the original homeland of the Sherpas who, for the past thirty years, had provided all the porters for Himalayan expeditions. People like Tilman and Shipton immediately remembered the mysterious glacial valley on the south face, Mallory's Western Cwm. Since the northwest route was cut off, it represented the only way to reach the summit of Chomolungma.

The violent winds of the jet stream above the summit of Mount Everest.

A new era of Everest exploration had begun. But it should not be forgotten that the intervening war had provided climbers with technical advances. The idea of Norton or Mallory wading through snow above 8,000 meters dressed in tweed, felt hat, and puttees was a thing of past. Much more suitable equipment had been invented, including windproof outer garments, down jackets, felt shoes, and nylon ropes. In 1950, mankind was almost ready for Everest.

It became clear that the pioneers of the  1920–1938 period had had little chance of success. Above 8,000 meters, conquering a mountain requires a combination of intelligence, bravura, and technology. The natural qualities of endurance, tenacity, and obstinacy no longer suffice. Climbing Everest is a scientific undertaking which requires, at the very least, that science come to the aid of sport. It is now old-fashioned to stubbornly refuse, in the name of fair play, to use oxygen or employ professional climbers (although it is hard to see what other term could be applied to the extraordinary Sherpas who carried the sahibs' heavy loads up to 8,000 meters on previous expeditions). The war changed everything, from the way mountains were climbed to the way they were loved.

But a new factor arose, unsettling the British. Political developments in the Himalayan region meant that their supremacy was no longer assured. Up till then, the Dalai Lama had granted authorizations only to the British, in reward for fifty years of diplomatic relations skillfully nurtured by official and secret agents. Nepal, on the other hand, was a new country that had deliberately and stubbornly closed itself to foreign influence, including British, for twenty-five years. Once the borders were opened, every major nation established relations with the new state. Obviously, the British still enjoyed unmatched prestige, but it was not clear how long that would last. France, the United States, Switzerland, and Japan intended to be present when virgin summits were handed around. Some day soon a non-British expedition would lay siege to Everest; the mere idea made the mountaineers who had trekked the icy trails of Tibet for nearly twenty years shake with indignation. That must not happen! Yet it did, and Britain nearly lost the race to the top.

Let us turn first, however, to the initial attempts of the postwar era.

Above: Nepalese stamps showing Everest, the Western Cwm, and Lhotse. Right: The summit of Everest seen from the séracs of the Western Cwm.

The Nepalese Face

The year 1950 was an auspicious year. Nepal opened up. Its mysterious valleys, leading to the tallest peaks in the world, beckoned foreigners right at the moment that Tibet, invaded by the Chinese, was closing its borders. Even as the road to Everest was cut off, mountaineers were offered new routes.

In October 1950, the American climber Oscar Houston conducted an exploration of the upper Dudh Khosi, which flowed directly from the snows of Everest. At Namche Bazar, the Sherpas' home village, he found Tilman, who was himself returning from an exploratory visit to this unfamiliar area. The two men joined company. Their Sherpas were Gyalzen, Pa Norbu, and Da Namgyal, all valiant "tigers." It was the first time that Westerners had penetrated so far up the valley, and they were welcomed with celebrations. They arrived at the monastery of Tyangboche. Tilman climbed the flanks of Pumori, from which he could see the north face of Everest beyond the curving Tibetan border, as well as the south face, which dropped down to a great valley of ice contained by the ridge from Nuptse to Lhotse. This was Mallory's

famous Western Cwm, connected to Khumbu Glacier by an extraordinary cascade of séracs, a veritable Niagara of snow known as the Khumbu Icefall. Tilman studied the south col and thought he detected a possible route, but returned relatively pessimistic.

The report made by Tilman, one of the recognized masters of Himalayan climbing, brought to light the difficult nature of the undertaking, but nevertheless held out hope for a route up the south face, the only one accessible. He had to act quickly, for the British no longer had exclusive right to authorizations; the new Nepalese government, inclined to display benevolence toward mountaineers from all nations, had established a rota, year by year, and applications were flooding in. Everest, then, was allocated to Britain in 1952, Switzerland in 1953, and France in 1954 should the previous attempts fail. The competition was heating up.

The British Himalayan Committee therefore opted for a small expedition in October 1951. Shipton was placed in command, and he recruited experienced climbers—Hillary and Riddiford from New Zealand, Bourdillon, and Ward. The Sherpa leader, or Sirdar, was Ang Tarkey. A camp was installed on Khumbu

Below, left: The treacherous Khumbu Icefall poses one of the main obstacles on the way to the summit of Everest.
Below, right: The 1951 expedition. Standing, left to right: Shipton, Murray, Bourdillon, and Riddiford. Seated: Ward and Hillary.

Glacier, at the foot of the icefall. The climbers attacked it directly, sensing that if they managed to reach the mysterious cwm, the road to Everest would be open.

The team made a first attempt on 4 October and reached a point high among the séracs before being obliged to turn back. Bourdillon and Shipton struck out again on 28 October and arrived at the edge of the Western Cwm, although still separated from it by a large crevasse. Up ahead, however, a ramp of ice linked the séracs to Lhotse Glacier, while an easy-looking rocky spur led straight up to the south col at 8,000 meters. Hurray—victory seemed within reach! But it was too late in the season, and they had to console themselves by returning with remarkable information and documents that would immediately be used to plan the next British expedition.

That was when the British made a decision that may have seemed strange at that time, and which nearly cost them victory. According to the rota established by the Nepalese government, 1952 was Britain's year. The Himalayan Committee in London, however, felt that it was insuf-

Above, left: The 1952 Swiss expedition found the key to Everest by scaling the Western Cwm, which included a final crevasse that called for acrobatic maneuvers. Above right: Arrival at the south col affords the first view of the ridge to the summit. Right: Tenzing Norgay and Raymond Lambert in 1952.

ficiently prepared. It therefore yielded its turn to Switzerland, and targeted the year 1953. In retrospect, the decision is generally recognized as having been a well-considered move that testifies to phlegmatic British sang-froid.

According to Shipton, the passage up the icefall to the cwm was the only passage that posed technical difficulties. Granted. But the British had had a great deal of experience on Everest by then. On various occasions, their climbers had reached 8,300 or even 8,590 meters on the north ridge. So they knew how crucial equipment was, as well as the composition and training of the team. And finally, they knew that victory depended on the use of oxygen apparatus, which had not yet been perfected for the mountains—produced for high-altitude pilots, the available equipment was too heavy and required respiratory effort, and was therefore unsuited to climbers making strenuous physical effort. The British were the only climbers to have experienced all of that, and it is only normal that thirty years of experience should have influenced their decision. In postponing their attempt,

they were not underestimating Swiss mountaineers, but they knew that the Swiss were beginners in the Himalayas and that success was unlikely.

The Swiss, however, in true sporting spirit, offered to form a mixed expedition with British climbers. In the event of failure, both countries could try again the next year. The response was categorical: if Everest was to be conquered by the British, it would be taken by an exclusively British team.

So the Swiss feverishly prepared to depart. The expedition was headed by Dr. Wyss-Dunant, more of a globe-trotter than a mountaineer, but a man with a great deal of expedition experience. He had the authority required to coordinate the major convoy that set out for Namche Bazar. The actual climbers belonged to the most elite mountaineering club in the world, Androsace of Geneva, which had only forty members. Not just anyone could join. A candidate not only had to be an excellent mountain climber, but above all had to have the right character—he had to be above all a comrade, a brother. So for thirty years Androsace members had been scouring the Alps, performing major feats in the most exquisitely simple *montagnard* style.

René Dittert commanded the assault teams. He took Asper, Aubert, Flory, Hofstetter, André

Roch (who had already made several trips to the Himalayas), Dr. Gabriel Chevalley, and a solid professional guide of French origin, Raymond Lambert, then living in Geneva. Lambert was known for his colossal endurance—he had survived a mid-winter blizzard that lasted several days on Mont Blanc du Tacul, at the cost of frostbitten toes that required amputation. At which point Lambert underwent physical therapy and learned to climb nimbly with orthopedic shoes that endowed him with "elephant feet."

The team was fully manned, its morale solid, its audacity extreme. Their equipment was chosen by real mountaineers accustomed to cold conditions, and it turned out to be very efficient, later requiring only slight modifications based on that initial experiment. Food and supplies were organized with precision. The only point to be resolved was the choice of breathing equipment; they finally opted for light, closed-circuit devices. It turned out that the drawbacks of those devices would cost them, if not victory, at least the prestige of having attained Everest's lower peak (8,760 m), which was within their grasp.

Thus began the long and dangerous climb up the séracs, exposed to avalanches. The Swiss found the glacier in a bad state. They established Camp I on Khumbu Glacier, at the foot of Lho La, an altitude of 5,250 meters. Camp II was erected amid the icefall, at 5,600 meters. Then

Above: Arriving at Everest's south col, with the slopes and ridge of Nuptse in the background.

they reached the lower limit of the fine combe of snow that led to the slopes of the south col—but as the British discovered, it was separated by an enormous crevasse which required hours of step cutting from Asper, the most agile among them. Asper finally managed to get a foothold on the other side, and from there installed a rope bridge and a hauling line for gear. Camp III was set up on the spot. Henceforth, all the loads were transferred upward and Dittert had all the camps placed as high as possible. Camp V was located at the end of the cwm where the Lhotse Glacier began to rise, forming a second, though less formidable, cascade of séracs.

They had reached 6,900 meters, and the unacclimatized team was beginning to feel it. They realized that the oxygen equipment was defective, insofar as it required the climber to make such an effort to breathe that it could only really be used when at rest.

But Dittert, who was directing the attack, now found himself in front of the rocky spur leading straight up to the south col. The rock was particulary dry, presenting a mixed rock and ice route typical of the Alps. Dittert, moreover, was in good condition. He therefore opted for the spur over Lhotse Glacier with its gleaming ice

and risk of avalanche from the slopes above. The spur of rock was 1,000 meters high, however, and with no possibility of establishing a camp on it, the route meant 1,000 meters in a single go. This distance was quite feasible in the Alps—but not in the Himalayas.

Knowing what good climbers the Swiss were, I persist in believing that if they had been able to use the French oxygen devices later employed on Makalu, they would have easily scaled the spur and even Everest. With such devices, ascending and descending the spur in the conditions that they found would have been a straightforward affair.

But they had to struggle and suffer to reach the south col on 15 May after a harsh bivouac on the spur itself. The Sherpas were exhausted. The only members of the team who stayed at Camp VI, situated at an altitude of 7,880 meters and swept by inexorable winds, were Lambert, Aubert, Flory, and Tenzing. Dittert remained with the support group, as befitted his role as leader.

For the first time, men could peer over to the Tibetan slope and, more important, get a good look at the south ridge up Everest. What they saw was far from pleasant—900 meters to scale,

On the Western Cwm, below the glacial slopes of Nuptse's north face.

the same height as the Peuterey arête! After so much effort, they might have hoped to find themselves closer to their goal. Those 900 meters would cause terrible suffering and gasping, sore throats, atrocious headaches, a feeling of suffocation, and pounding hearts. They only found a little respite when they could breathe a bit of oxygen during halts.

However, the proximity of the summit and the certainty that they had found the right path gave them the courage to strike out from the south col after a terrible night. Flory and Aubert would climb as high as possible, deposit equipment and supplies, and then descend. Lambert, the sturdy Genevan who was in the best condition, would carry on with Tenzing, with whom he had formed a friendship. Their friendship was hardly surprising—they were both true *montagnards*, they understood one another perfectly, and there was not the usual distance between a sahib and a Sherpa. Tenzing sensed that right away, and would follow wherever Lambert led.

With difficulty, they set up Camp VII on a tiny terrace at 8,400 meters. Flory and Aubert headed back down, while Lambert and Tenzing bivouacked without sleeping bags or camp stove, but full of hope.

Alas, bad weather arrived the next morning on 28 May. They reached 8,600 meters, but were obliged to turn back due to the terrible wind, the threat of a storm, the piercing cold, and above all the slowness of their ascent caused by inadequate oxygen equipment. But they could be proud, for they had climbed higher than anyone before them—with the possible exception of Mallory and Irvine—on the tallest mountain in the world.

They descended as best they could, running great risks due to exhaustion, cold, and altitude. On the spur they met Dittert on his way up with Chevalley, Roch, Asper, and Hofstetter, for a second assault that would get no further than the south col. Tenzing and Lambert bivouacked a second time under the stars, then finally made it to Camp V.

Dittert was faced with a question of conscience. If the monsoon arrived, they would be trapped in the cwm where avalanches were sure to fall. There was not much time to organize a new assault, and the physical condition of the climbers was sorely affected by the effort made in setting up the advanced camps. Retreat was the only solution. It was a victorious defeat!

Approaching the south col from the slopes of Lhotse.

They returned feverishly to Geneva.

Experience on the Nepalese face had shown that autumn attempts were feasible in Nepal. The weather was invariably fine and stable during that season. The only threat came from the wind and the cold. That is why, knowing that they had just one more shot at victory, the Genevans hastily organized a second expedition for that very autumn. It was headed by Dr. Chevalley and included new members. Lambert was joined by Norman Dyhrenfurth (son of Günther Dyhrenfurth), Spöhel, Reiss, Gross, and Buzio. Gross was a guide from Salvan, the others were members of Androsace.

The camps were established on the same sites as the previous spring. And although the icefall to the cwm posed no new problems, they discovered that the rocky spur—henceforth known as the Geneva Spur—was now covered in ice as they climbed. On their way down, a serious accident occurred when Sherpa Mingma Dorjees was hit by rocks and mortally wounded, while six others tumbled down the slope but survived.

So it was reluctantly decided to follow a route up the Lhotse Glacier, where Lambert and Tenzing, always in the lead, were setting up Camps VI and VII. The latter camp was already on the south col, where Lambert, Tenzing, and Reiss spent the night at –30° C (–22° F) in a terrible wind that threatened to snatch the tents off the ridge at any moment.

On 20 November they struggled up the couloir above the south col. But the wind and cold were so severe that they gave up at 8,100 meters. It is fair to say that the first Swiss expedition was defeated by the lack of oxygen, and the second by excessive cold.

Lambert, Tenzing, and their partners nevertheless accomplished a great deal in the course of their two attempts—the séracs on Lhotse Glacier had been tamed, and all the possible routes up Mount Everest had finally been explored. It was therefore entirely appropriate for John Hunt to address a fraternal telegram to the Swiss the day after the British victory on 29 May 1953: "Half the glory should go to you."

1953: The Victorious British Assault

The extra year of reflection enabled the members of the Himalayan Committee to get things right. Their extensive experience suggested that the leader of the expedition had to fulfill several requirements: he should be familiar with the Himalayas, be a well-known mountaineer, be accustomed to giving orders, and be recognized as leader by all members of the team.

The Swiss had organized a party of friends, and decisions were generally made collectively. But what was possible for climbers from Geneva, thanks to shared attitudes and the spirit of camaraderie that prevailed within Androsace, was hardly appropriate to an expedition that recruited mountaineers from different countries of the Commonwealth. The only difference with prewar expeditions was that henceforth the chief would be a climber capable of directing operations in the advanced camps, even taking part in the assault team if necessary. In short, the leader needed the qualities of a Bruce combined with those of a Mallory.

Leadership therefore fell to John Hunt, colonel in the Indian army and veteran of numerous explorations and ascents in Sikkim, Kashmir, and Garhwal. He called upon a team of experienced Himalayan climbers (Hillary from New Zealand, Bourdillon, Evans, Gregory, and Dr. Ward from Britain), along with some newcomers (Lowe, Wylie, Noyce, Pugh, Westmacott, Band, Stobart). The novelty was that Sirdar Tenzing Norgay was not only leader of the Sherpas, but was to be incorporated from the start into the lead team. A better choice could hardly be made than the man who, with Lambert, had reached an altitude of 8,600 meters via the new route, under technically difficult conditions.

The British, having learned from the Swiss attempt as well as from their own, placed a great deal of importance on equipment that was both light and efficient—overgarments of nylon weighing less than one and a half kilos, shoes that had been extensively tested in the snows of the Oberland at nearly

Above: Hillary and Tenzing savor their victory—and a cup of tea. Left: After conquering Everest, Tenzing became a hero for the people of Nepal and India.

Himalayan temperatures, during training sessions conducted by the full team throughout the summer of 1952. Bourdillon had studied the oxygen question in depth. George Finch's theories finally won out—just as a professional guide, Sherpa Tenzing, had finally been accepted as a leading team member, so it was admitted that oxygen was indispensable above 8,000 meters. The French conquest of Annapurna showed that the euphoria experienced above 8,000 meters could lead to death.

Some 444 human loads of supplies were thus portaged to Tyangboche, the monastery at the south foot of Everest, in the spring of 1953.

Hunt wisely devoted three weeks to getting his troops in shape, setting the example himself by enthusiastically climbing several peaks over 6,000 meters, gazing on the famous cwm from the slopes of Pumori. Then Camp I was established on Khumbu Glacier, at roughly the same spot chosen by the Swiss.

The lower séracs were in much poorer condition than the previous autumn, but the British had learned from the Swiss experience that it was important to have a sufficient supply of rope ladders, metal ladders, poles, ice pegs, and ropes. Thanks to all that—and in spite of all that!—after thirteen days of intensive labor, Camp IV was finally set up above the icefall at the foot of the snowy cwm, near where the Swiss had deposited their supplies.

Having decided against the Geneva Spur, the British installed Camps V, VI, and VIII on the steep slopes of Lhotse Glacier. George Lowe performed the exhausting task of step cutting, spending ten days between Camps VI and VII. But the effort was so exhausting that the team, despite reinforcements, could not go beyond Camp VII.

It was crucial to get to the south col, however, and so Hunt sent Hillary and Tenzing, whom he had held in reserve, as additional reinforcements. That very day, however, Noyce and Sherpa Annulu managed to reach the south col and set up Camp VIII. They were on the doorstep of the heavens, buffeted by the most lethal winds on earth.

From that point onward, the assault operations went as planned, thanks to wonderful weather. On 26 May, Hunt and Da Namgyal set up Camp IX on the south arête, at 8,300 meters, while Evans and Bourdillon continued upward, encountering a slope of snow dangerously liable to trigger an avalanche, which they skirted by the west flank and the rocks. Finally, at 1:00 p.m., they reached the south, or lower, summit of Everest, at an altitude of 8,760 meters. They were already the "highest climbers on earth," but from there they could see that the ridge leading to the real summit was too long—they would never have enough time and perhaps not enough oxygen to make it there and back. They were obliged to turn around. By the time they reached the south col, they were in a state of exhaustion.

A storm on 27 May forced all of the assault teams to keep to their tents. Hunt had planned to remain in the advance camps as reinforcement, and perhaps even form part of an assault team, but when it transpired that Bourdillon proved unable to climb the few meters required to clear the spur and find the route down, Hunt sacrificed himself and helped Evans to get Bourdillon down. On 28 May, two new teams, spurred by the accomplishment of Evans and Bourdillon, left the south col and headed up the henceforth familiar couloir leading to the south ridge. Gregory and Lowe were the support climbers, responsible for helping Hillary and Tenzing set up Camp IX as high as possible. They found the material deposited by Hunt and Da Namgyal and, heavily laden, labored up to 8,590 meters, where they installed a camp on the tiny platform discovered by Tenzing the previous year—the highest camp in the world. There was barely enough space for two, and even then Tenzing's feet stuck out into the bottomless void of the south face! Gregory and Lowe headed back down.

After a relatively comfortable night thanks to the oxygen apparatus, Hillary and Tenzing set off. They soon encountered the tricky slope of snow. But instead of skirting it, as Evans and Bourdillon had done, Hillary—an ice specialist, like all New Zealand mountaineers—decided to head straight up it. They managed to clear it, arriving at the south peak by 9:00 a.m., having left Camp IX at 6:30 a.m. in fine weather and ideal, if very cold, conditions. The thermometer read –27°C (–16°F).

*Looking down on the ridge
and the Western Cwm from
the summit of Everest. In the
distance is Cho Oyu.*

The ridge ahead did not disconcert them. After checking that their breathing gear was functioning well (the intake often became blocked by ice), they scaled the east side of the corniced arête. Then Hillary had to work past a rocky barrier some twelve meters high by sliding between ice and and rock. It was the only technical obstacle they encountered en route. The ridge carried straight on and, in the absence of wind, was easy. They finally arrived at the spot where all the ridges of the pyramid converged: it was 11:30 a.m. and they were on top of the world, on the white summit of Chomolungma.

Hillary lifted his oxygen mask, and found that he could breathe freely. Then he watched as Tenzing kneeled and made an offering to the Mother Goddess of the Snows, burying chocolate, biscuits, and sweets in the snow. Hillary, in turn, deposited the cross that Hunt had given him before he set out. (As mentioned earlier, Chinese climbers would one day supposedly haul a bust of Mao Zedong to the summit!) Everest had become Chomolungma again, throne of gods, altar of beliefs, on which everyone paid homage to their divinity. Fifteen minutes were thus spent. A brief moment, and yet a long time; photos had to be taken, a check had to be made to see if there was any indication that Mallory had reached the summit. Then the masks went back on, and they headed along the lengthy arête, squeezing between rockface and ice, reaching the lower peak, and finally making the steep descent on unstable snow where any glissade or slight avalanche could prove fatal.

They progressively slowed as they descended, picking up some of the material left at Camp IX. Finally they reached the last couloir just above the south col, which had nearly been fatal to Evans and Bourdillon, and which appeared equally dangerous to the exhausted climbers. It is safe to assume that at this altitude, without the use of oxygen, the return route would be very tricky, which only underscores the feat achieved by Tenzing and Lambert in 1952.

From the south col, Lowe and Noyce spotted Hillary and Tenzing and climbed to meet them. Everest had been conquered! It was 29 May 1953, just in time for the coronation of the queen. Her Majesty had triumphed after all

Tenzing on the summit, brandishing the flags of India, the United Kingdom, Nepal, and the United Nations.

those years, all those tragedies, all that stubborn effort. It was only fitting.

Sometime later it was learned that a Russian expedition comprising thirty-five climbers and six scientists, flown into Lhasa from Moscow, had made an attempt on Everest on 16 October 1952. They managed to install their Camp VIII at 8,200 meters, and announced that victory was likely in two days. Then silence fell, once again, on the north ridge. Six men died, including the leader of the expedition. Mystery still shrouds this attempt; it was not until 1960 that a Chinese team finally tamed the north arête.

Everything seemed to be over. Humankind had apparently pulled its last dream down to earth, and it would have been highly appropriate to conclude the history of mountain climbing on that final conquest. Yet nothing would be more misleading—humankind constantly rises to new challenges, and

so climbers immediately began attacking north faces and difficult arêtes. In 1963, an American team scaled the west ridge of Everest, and at the summit met another team that had arrived from the south col. By the time it had been climbed half a dozen times, Everest no longer had any defenses against modern expeditions equipped with modern, light breathing equipment. It remains to be beaten without artificial aids. Hillary attempted Makalu, so welcoming to the French climbers, without oxygen—but he ran into countless difficulties and was forced to retreat.

Given this situation, has Everest really been tamed by man?

Yes, because human intelligence supplied the tools for success. At altitudes above 8,000 meters— and even above 7,000 meters—physical capacity is seriously diminished. While occasional exploits might be pulled off, as at Annapurna and Nanga Parbat, they remain the deeds of supermen. The normal human race is not made to live so high. It was oxygen that conquered Chomolungma, used of course by valiant and tenacious climbers.

But it was also the triumph of teamwork. The great Himalayan summits demand human fraternity and cooperation, self-sacrifice and devotion. In the end, the greatest success of Himalayan mountaineering was the discovery of Sherpas, people who are physically and morally remarkable, and who henceforth formed a constellation of Himalayan guides worthy of their predecessors in the Alps.

Perhaps the finest promise of future brotherhood among the peoples of the earth was joint arrival, on the planet's highest peak, of Tenzing, the Tibetan Sherpa with oriental eyes and sunny heart, and Hillary, the phlegmatic New Zealander, representative of the West.

Sunset on the summit of Everest, looking east toward Chomolönzo, Makalu, and Lhotse Shar.

The Development of Himalayan Mountaineering

Solo climbs, winter ascents, difficult routes and assaults without oxygen—in the Himalayas, too, mountaineering aspired to purity and rigor. At the cost, unfortunately, of greater risks than ever.

It is clear to observers that the main developments in mountaineering over the past thirty years occurred in the Himalayas. There, and only there, did certain slopes remain impregnable, whatever the means employed; there, and only there, did a veritable conceptual revolution take place over an extremely short period. Feats unthinkable just thirty years ago have now been accomplished: an "8,000er" climbed solo, Everest without oxygen, Everest in winter, an assault team remaining in isolated autonomy for fifteen days of ascent, and so on. Better still, some of these exploits, like the ascent, of an "8,000er" by a simple team of two climbers, have become commonplace. The differences that still existed as late as 1970 between Alpine climbs and Himalayan expeditions have slowly diminished to the point where the Himalayas have become part of the standard sphere of mountaineering. Solo climbs, winter ascents and highly difficult routes are now performed everywhere, with one major distinction—high altitude poses its own constraints and dangers, certainly the greatest climbers have ever faced. It is not an exaggera-tion to suggest that mountain climb-ing has never been more dangerous than in the past twenty years.

In 1964, Shisha Pangma, the last "8,000er," was climbed by a Chinese expedition. The peak, in Tibetan ter-ritory, remains off limits to Western climbers to this day. In a surprising repetition of history, one hundred years after all the main Alpine summits were conquered in lit-tle more than a decade, the same phenomenon recurred in the Himalayas. While it is true that the fourteen "8,000ers" are numerically far fewer than the Alpine "4,000ers," it is equally true that considerably greater time and resources are required to scale them.

The Himalayas still seemed like a veritable Eldorado back in the 1960s, able to keep moun-taineers happy for hundreds of years. There were immense faces to conquer, thousands of peaks over 6,000 and 7,000 meters, many of them nameless, of unknown altitude, extremely difficult or impossible to reach. In 1964, Nepal was still a mysterious country, and the Karakoram and Tibet had become off-limits. An expedition was a highly special adventure costing

Facing page: The sheer walls of Trango Towers in the Baltoro, a major field of action for contemporary mountaineers. Above, left: Stephen Venables after making a new route up Everest and bivouacking without oxygen or equipment at an altitude 8,550 meters.

The south face of Annapurna, scaled in 1970 by Chris Bonington's British expedition.

much time and money, an art in which few mountaineers were truly practiced.

Yet within the space of thirty years everything, absolutely everything, has changed. In this respect, two political developments played a key role. In 1974, the Karakoram was opened—or rather, re-opened—to expeditions, after having been closed by the Pakistanis for fifteen years due to border disputes with China and India. And then, starting in 1979, Tibet authorized expeditions, permitting access not only to little known peaks and entire ranges, but also to the Tibetan face of Everest, the site of the great pre-war expeditions.

Conquering Gigantic Walls

Once the "8,000ers" were vanquished, the task at hand was to climb the most gigantic faces and arêtes on the planet (in imitation of what had occurred in the Alps). They obviously represented the most challenging adventures, for not only did extreme altitude impose its own constraints, but climbers also found themselves faced with slopes that rose higher than anywhere else—3,000 or even 4,000 meters in a single go!

The starting signal was given in 1962 with the ascent of the Diamir Face of Nanga Parbat, followed the next year by the conquest of the west ridge of Everest by an American expedition led by Norman Dyhrenfurth. The major date, however, came eight years later when Don Whillans and Dougal Haston, members of Chris Bonington's British expedition, climbed the south face of Annapurna. Never had a face of such size, such steepness, and such height been climbed. After that, hardly a year would go by without a new route being traced up one or another of the "8,000ers."

Another decisive event occurred at the same time. Karl Herrligkoffer's expedition scaled the Rupal Face of Nanga Parbat. The Messner brothers, Günther and Reinhold, found themselves obliged to descend the other face—Diamir—by an unknown route (the route traced up in 1962 is very circuitous). Günther lost his life on the lower part of the descent. It was probably following his survival of this tragic descent that Rheinhold became aware of his fortitude, and he went on to become the greatest living Himalayan climber, and, it goes without saying, one of the greatest mountaineers of all time.

Other major faces would be scaled in the 1970s, starting with the west pillar of Makalu (1971), which represented a degree of technical difficulty still unknown at such an altitude, by Robert Paragot's French expedition; then the south face of Makalu fell in 1975 to Aleš Kunaver's Yugoslav team. But all eyes were focused on the southwest face of Everest, an imposing wall barred by a vertical band of rock looming over the Western Cwm.

Targeting the Southwest Face of Everest

An initial reconnaissance was made as early as 1969 by Naomi Uemura from Japan; in the autumn of that year, Mihashita's expedition reached the 8,000-meter mark. The international expedition of 1971, headed by Norman Dyhrenfurth, was plagued not only by the death of Indian climber Harsh Bahuguna, but also by national rivalries, which also afflicted Karl Herrligkoffer's European expedition of 1972, when "Latins" squared off against "Anglo-Saxons." The two following attempts on the southwest face were British, and both were led by Chris Bonington; the 1975 expedition finally

enabled Doug Scott and Dougal Haston to reach the top of Everest, but only at the end of the day, which forced them to make a daring bivouac on the lesser summit. The next day their feat was copied by Peter Boardman, Pertemba, and Mike Burke (the last at the cost of his life).

Also in 1975, an expedition headed by the veteran mountaineer Riccardo Cassin and notably including Reinhold Messner, attacked the south face of Lhotse, without a doubt one of the most impressive in the Himalayas. The attempt did not get very far, however, and Messner commented that the south face was "a face for the year 2000." In 1978, the French climber Nicolas Jaeger lost his life in a pioneering solo attempt, and expeditions of all kinds, involving the finest mountain climbers in the world, from Messner to Christophe Profit, succeeded one another on Lhotse for fifteen years.

The man who finally climbed the south face, in 1989, was Tomo Cesen—alone. How times had changed since 1970, when all attempts entailed major expeditions, the installation of safety ropes, successive camps, numerous high-altitude porters, and the use of oxygen apparatus! The truth, however, is that Cesen's ascent has been contested. Yet in order to understand what

The 1971 ascent of the west pillar of Makalu by a French expedition entailed overcoming particularly difficult rock passages at extremely high altitudes.

Above, left: The southwest face of Everest, viewed head on. The 1975 route surmounted the far left end of the rock band, then followed the snowy ledges up to the south ridge. Above, right: Everest seen from directly overhead—the southwest face is in the upper right.

was at stake, it is necessary to look back for a moment at the evolution from the era of grand expeditions to the day of ascents by a single climber aided only by what he or she can carry.

Toward "Alpine-style" Ascents

There had to be a limit to the constant increase in number of porters, equipment, and comfort, to the amount of safety lines draping a mountain, to the size of pleasant camps continually supplied by a conveyor-belt of Sherpas, to the almost constant use of oxygen and even planes (the Swiss on Dhaulagiri in 1960) or helicopters (Guido Monzino's 1973 Everest expedition, which also employed two thousand Sherpas). The cost and lack of flexibility of such undertakings represented a drawback in a world where favorable conditions had to be exploited swiftly. A relatively modest expedition could also conquer an "8,000er," as the 1957 ascent of Broad Peak demonstrated. Yet even that expedition had employed a hundred porters during the trek to the site, had installed three high-altitude camps,

and anchored safety ropes. Was it possible to scale an "8,000er" in the same way a peak in the Alps would be climbed, setting out from the base camp with all the necessary material in the climber's backpack? It had to be attempted. Reinhold Messner and Peter Habeler took up the challenge in 1975, with the second ascent of Hidden Peak, via a new route that Messner compared to two north faces of the Matterhorn one after another. Although such feats have now become common, it is worth stressing the impact made by this exploit at a time when classic expeditions seemed to be the only way to conquer an "8,000er." The most amazing thing, in fact, is that what appeared so extraordinary in 1975—reserved for a superhuman elite among mountaineers—now seems so natural!

Without Oxygen

Obviously, using Alpine techniques on an "8,000er" meant forgoing heavy oxygen canisters. It was known that this was possible on "lesser" giants under, say, 8,400 meters (which

did not exclude the use of oxygen for scaling lower, but difficult, summits). But what of the tallest "8,000ers"—Makalu, Kangchenjunga, Lhotse, K2, and, above all, Everest? Even specialists in human physiology doubted that it was possible to make the effort needed to climb at such altitudes without the help of oxygen. Yet three years after their groundbreaking ascent of Hidden Peak, Messner and Habeler repeated the exploit by climbing Everest via the normal Nepalese route, in the context of a classic expedition, without using breathing apparatus. Today, some twenty years later, almost 700 people have made it to the summit of Everest, but merely fifty have managed to do it without oxygen, which shows that it constitutes an exploit at the very limits of physiological possibilities.

Messner's two decisive breakthroughs did not mean that major expeditions were immediately abandoned. Many first ascents, especially up complex routes, continued to use safety ropes. Some extremely bold routes were nevertheless traced using Alpine techniques. In 1981, Yugoslavs Stane Belak, Cene Bercic, Rok Kolar, Emil Tratnik, and Joze Zupan had to bivouac fifteen nights in a row to make it up Dhaulagiri's immense south face (4,000 meters high!); the Spaniards Enrico Luca and Nils Bohigas took nine days to put a new route up the south face of Annapurna in 1984; the Pole Wojciech Kurtyka and the Austrian Robert Schauer bivouacked ten nights on the steep and difficult 2,500-meter wall of Gasherbrum IV in 1985 (a first-rate exploit that did not have the impact it deserved simply because Gasherbrum IV is sixty meters short of the fateful threshold of 8,000 meters).

But these achievements should not be allowed to create the illusion that they are within everyone's reach—they still entail enormous risks. Even as the number of

Above: Dougal Haston on the summit of Everest, photographed by his partner Doug Scott, after the first ascent of the southwest face in 1975. Left: Reinhold Messner and Peter Habeler after their remarkable 1975 ascent of Hidden Peak.

routes up the highest peaks has increased in the past fifteen years, the diversity of techniques employed has prohibited straightforward comparison based on altitude, height, and difficulty. Furthermore, as had occurred earlier in the Alps, climbers were no longer content merely to climb virgin slopes; they introduced new "rules" in an effort to complicate the game.

The Era of Solo Ascents

One of the most obvious novelties was a solo ascent. Although Hermann Buhl's arrival all alone at the summit of Nanga Parbat in 1953 remains a fantastic exploit, he nevertheless benefited from a full-fledged expedition up to an altitude of 7,000 meters. It is something else entirely to scale one of the highest peaks on the planet from the base camp, without any help whatsoever.

Above: The south face of Lhotse, described by Messner as "a face for the year 2000." Right: Nicolas Jaeger, a climber who never returned from a bold solo attempt on that face.

Unsurprisingly, it was Reinhold Messner who came to fore once again. Eight years after the death of his brother on Nanga Parbat, Messner chose that same Diamir slope for the first solo ascent of an "8,000er." He opted for a route near the one Mummery had taken at the dawn of the Himalayan era, in 1895. Messner's route, in fact, was more suitable for a solo ascent than a major expedition, for speed was of the essence to avoid avalanches and toppling séracs.

The truly symbolic event was nevertheless the first solo ascent of Everest, by Messner yet again. He chose the north, Tibetan face, since the icefall on the Nepalese side was not conducive to a solo climb. Messner also chose a period when he was certain to find himself alone on the mountain—namely, during the monsoon. On 20 August 1980, he stood next to the geodesic tripod left on the summit by the Chinese team in 1975, proof without

which the veracity of that inconceivable exploit would certainly have been challenged.

Many other "8,000ers" have been scaled solo, by a fair number of climbers. Yet here again, distinctions must be made. What is the point of climbing a route previously fitted with safety ropes, ascended by several climbers every day, with several supply camps along the way? In the Himalayas and Karakoram, a solo ascent does not simply mean climbing without a partner, it means climbing a route unaided. Some fine examples include Renato Casarotto's first ascent, in seven days, of Broad Peak North (7,550 m, Karakoram) in 1982; Pierre Béghin's first solo ascent of the third highest peak in the world, Kangchenjunga, in 1983; and Marc Batard's conquest of Makalu's difficult west pillar in 1988.

An "8,000er" in a Single Day

Going it alone means going fast. The first "8,000er" scaled in a single day was Broad Peak; in 1984 Krzysztof Wielicki reached the summit seventeen hours after leaving base camp. And yet it was not a completely solo ascent. Nor was Marc Batard's amazing 1988 arrival at the top of Everest, less than twenty-four hours after striking out from camp.

Going fast perhaps means safety more than anything else. In 1986, the team of Erhard Loretan and Jean Troillet accomplished the scarcely believable exploit of climbing Everest by the north couloir in less than forty-three hours all told, including a descent in fewer than four hours. Convinced that the best thing was to remain at high altitude as briefly as possible, the two Swiss climbers lightened their loads to the maximum extent—no rope, no bivouac equipment, barely any food. But this attractively sleek tactic obviously runs up against its limits in technically difficult ascents that require special material (and therefore heavy backpack) and protection maneuvers that take time. And such speed also presupposes total mastery. The following year, Canadian climber Roger Marshall would die on the same route.

The enormous height of the south face of Dhaulagiri rivals that of Lhotse. A 1981 Yugoslav expedition spent fifteen days on the face.

That is why "lightweight" climbs have not totally supplanted heavy expeditions.

Whatever the style adopted, new routes up "8,000ers" have increased to such an extent since 1975 that a "guide book" would prove useful (one indeed exists for Everest). Four different routes rise up the rocky pillars of the southeast face of Dhaulagiri; the southwest face of Everest offers three possibilities; and Annapurna's south and west faces are marked by four routes each. There are two routes up the north face of Kangchenjunga, and K2—probably the most difficult "8,000er" of all—features no less than ten different itineraries. Although some virgin slopes still remain, they are fewer and fewer in number—what inhibits

mountaineering history would have to be rewritten.

Cesen's solo ascent is not inconceivable—and if he really accomplished it, it represents a major feat, one of the greatest ever achieved in the Himalayas. If not, then he has pulled off a feat of another kind, namely making it seem conceivable. The truth will not be known—if ever—until another ascent is made by that route.

For that matter, the uncertainty has not affected the increase in *almost* equivalent firsts, made by very small teams on long, difficult, dangerous routes up the highest summits in the world. One of the most striking was the 1994 ascent of the southwest ridge of Kangchenjunga

Some leading Himalayan mountaineers of the 1980s, left to right: Wojciech Kurtyka, Renato Casarotto, Krzysztof Wielicki, Erhard Loretan, and Tomo Cesen.

ascent is not so much the pure difficulty as the danger of wall-to-wall séracs (as on the formidable Tibetan face of Lhotse). One of the last slopes to remain completely untouched, the daunting north face of Dhaulagiri, was finally scaled in 1993 by Sergei Yefimov's international expedition.

The south face of Lhotse nevertheless remains "the" Himalayan slope par excellence, given its extreme height, sheer steepness, and dramatic aspect when viewed from Sherpa country (somewhat the way the similarly large and complex Eiger appears from the Bernese plain). So did Tomo Cesen climb it alone in 1989 or not? It is hard to say. Some of Cesen's prior ascents had also sparked polemics (the north face of Yalung Kang in 1985, a solo route up K2, the north face of Jannu). No definitive evidence exists, apart from a contested photo. Messner thinks that Cesen was lying, yet Wally Berg and Scott Fischer, who climbed Lhotse, say that his description corresponds to the terrain. Who is to be believed? It is far from being the only Himalayan exploit to be challenged for lack of solid proof, but by that criterion a good part of

South (8,476 meters) by Slovenian climbers Marko Prezelzj and Andrej Stremfelj, who then descended by another route. The main point, then, is that Cesen's ascent is no longer in the realm of the impossible.

Himalayan Winter, the Realm of Wind and Cold

Barely had the highest peaks been conquered than their winter exploration began. Polish mountaineers have written the history of winter ascents practically all by themselves, notably the combative Andrzej Zawada. Dr. Herrligkoffer's expedition, which attempted to climb the Rupal face of Nanga Parbat as early as 1964, managed to get only as high as 5,800 meters. It is easy to imagine that above this altitude, the weather conditions during the winter—understandably little known—are particularly trying. Zawada honed his weapons in the Hindu Kush, making the first winter ascent of a "7,000er" (Noshaq, 7,492 m) in 1973. The next year saw the first attempt on an "8,000er," Lhotse, when Zawada and Zygmunt Heinrich were the first men to get above 8,000 meters in winter. Finally, in 1979–1980 the first winter ascent of Everest was made by the normal Nepalese route, when Leszek Cichy and Krzysztof Wielicki reached the summit on 17 February 1980.

Another stage was reached in 1985 with the forging of a new route in winter, on the southwest face of Cho Oyu, some 3,000 meters high. This was accomplished by, of course, a Polish team—Jerzy Kukuczka, Zygmunt Heinrich, Maciej Berbeka, and Maciej Pawlikowski.

Today, almost all the "8,000ers" have been scaled in winter, usually by Poles: Kangchenjunga in 1986 by Kukuczka and Czok (at the cost of the latter's life), Lhotse in 1989 by Wielicki. Manaslu, Dhaulagiri, and Annapurna

were also Polish winter conquests. Most of the time, major expeditions are involved. The first "8,000er" to have been climbed in winter Alpine-style was Cho Oyu, in 1985, by Czechs Jaromír Stejskal and Dusan Becík. Since that time, as will be discussed below, Cho Oyu was also the object of the first solo winter ascent and the first women's winter ascent—it has almost become a classic! Finally worth noting is the 1993 winter success on the southwest face of Everest (ascended for only the third time) by a Japanese team, probably the toughest Himalayan winter climb accomplished so far.

Yet much remains to be done. The Poles did not manage to succeed on K2. In 1988, Zawada had to halt at 7,350 meters, some 1,300 meters from the summit, which is a long, long way. It is true that logistical problems are enormous on such an isolated peak. Similarly, Everest's west arête, attempted several times in winter, continues to hold out to this day. Winter climbing in the Himalayas still has a bright future ahead of it.

The concept of winter ascents has subsequently been exported to almost all the moun-

tain ranges in the world. In the Tien Shan, Valeri Khrischatyi's Kazakh expedition made the first winter ascent of Khan Tengri in 1992. In the very tough conditions of Antarctic winters in Patagonia, Mount Fitz Roy has been scaled four times (including once by a woman, Erica Beuzenberg, in 1993), while Italian climber Ermanno Salvaterra's 1985 first winter climb of Cerro Torre certainly represented a terrific accomplishment. But it is perhaps in Alaska that winter climbs are the toughest. In terms of weather conditions, at least, the ascent of the classic route up McKinley (Denali) is comparable to an "8,000er." It is generally agreed that Vernon Tejas's first solo winter ascent in 1988 was a truly remarkable exploit (it was while making a similar attempt in 1984, for that matter, that Naomi Uemura died).

New Ski Slopes?

Another way in which Himalayan climbing seems to have copied the Alps entails the use of skis. Early Himalayan expeditions considered employing skis, and back in 1934 André Roch and Piero Ghiglione used them on Baltoro Kangri at an altitude of over 7,000 meters. Yet it long remained unclear whether it would be possible to descend a Himalayan peak entirely on skis. A 1964 German expedition to Cho Oyu with that goal in mind ended tragically. In 1980, American mountaineer Ned Gillette turned Mustagh Ata (7,546 m) into the highest skiable summit; three years later, Jean Afanassieff and Nicolas Jaeger donned their skis at an altitude of 8,300 meters on the south face of Everest. The 1980 descent of Annapurna by Yves Morin (who died in the attempt), followed by the 1982 descent of Hidden Peak by Sylvain Saudan and the "cleaner" one of Gasherbrum II by Wim Pasquier and Patrice

Left to right: Andrej Stremfelj, Andrzej Zawada, Ermanno Salvaterra, Jean Afanassieff, and Hans Kammerlander.

The east, or Kangshung, face
of Everest, up which two
major routes have been
forged.

Bournat in 1984, proved the feasibility of the idea.

In 1990, Hans Kammerlander successfully skied down the very steep Diamir slope of Nanga Parbat, followed four years later by Broad Peak, Kammerlander's ninth "8,000er." Finally, in 1994 Pierre Tardivel donned his skis on the lesser summit of Everest (8,760 m)—the higher, Hillary Peak being too rocky—and skied down to base camp. Although these descents entail very steep slopes, Himalayan skiing has not yet attained the extreme level reached in the Alps. That level will perhaps be matched if Kammerlander successfully executes his plan to ski down the entire north slope of Everest (in 1992, he "only" started from the 7,800-meter mark).

Like it or not, Everest reigns over the Himalayas more than Mont Blanc does over the Alps. While most ascents continue to be made via the normal Nepalese route taken by Tenzing and Hillary, there has been a great deal of competition to resolve the "final problems." The Japanese Couloir on the north face was conquered in 1980, while the east, or Kangshung, face, was climbed by an American expedition in 1982. Meanwhile, the southwest pillar was van-

quished by the Russians (including Balyberdin, Bershov, and Khrischatyi) in 1982, a remarkable ascent not only because it may be the most difficult route but also because it was the first time Russian climbers had passed the 8,000-meter mark. A second route on the east face was opened by a small, bold expedition in 1988.

The route that posed the most problems, however, was the northeast ridge, which killed two of Britain's finest climbers, Peter Boardman and Joe Tasker, in 1982. After numerous attempts, that route—representing one of the last major routes on the highest summit in the world—was tamed in 1995 by a major Japanese expedition using over two miles of fixed safety lines—a tactic some people might consider unfortunate.

For the use of such "heavy" equipment may seem outdated when the number of Alpine-style ascents is increasing. Yet it is important to remain wary of optical illusions. Loretan and Troillet's superfast ascent, cited above, is justly famous, as is a magnificent 1988 performance on the east face. In the latter case, however, only Stephen Venables managed to reach the summit, and he had to bivouac with no equipment on the way down. The tragedy of the first Alpine-

style ascent of the southwest face (only the second ascent in any form) that same year tends to be overlooked: Czechs Josef Just, Dusan Becík, Peter Bozík, and Jaroslav Jasko arrived at the lesser summit, where they made their third bivouac. The next day, only Just was fit enough to make it to the real summit. He then returned to his friends, but all four would die of exhaustion, unable to descend to the south col. It was undoubtedly one of the boldest ascents ever made, yet could hardly be called successful. Everything indicates that a stay of more than just a few hours above 8,000 meters more closely resembles, for the moment at least, a game of Russian roulette than a wisely calculated risk.

In fact, precise statistics reveal that accidents are particularly frequent around the summit of Everest: Yatsuo Kato disappeared during his second winter ascent, his third time up the mountain; Mike Burke also died on the first ascent of the southwest face in 1975; less well known was the Australian climber Michael Rheinberger, who died of exhaustion in 1994 after bivouacking at the highest recorded altitude, 8,830 meters, just below the main summit.

In all, twenty mountaineers have died while descending from the summit. Meanwhile, the most dangerous "8,000er" of all, K2, presents even grislier statistics. As of 1995, this second highest peak in the world had been successfully climbed by 122 people—but 45 never made it back down. A high death rate, to say the least.

The Sensational and the Commonplace

Yet, despite the danger, high-altitude summits draw more climbers than ever. Statistics compiled at the end of 1994 revealed that 677 people had already scaled Everest, and that over 2,600 mountaineers had at least one "8,000er" under their belts. Most of these ascents have been made in the very recent past. On 10 May 1993, some forty people reached the top of the highest peak in the world on a single day! There were more "Everest summiters" in that six-week season than in all preceding years. Just as most expeditions focus exclusively on "8,000ers" at the expense of lesser peaks, so Everest has been drawing an excessive number of mountain climbers. In that same year of 1993, half of all

In 1988, a small expedition put a new route up the Kangshung face of Everest. Above, left: American climber Ed Webster. Above, right: Webster using a Tyrolean rig to cross the crevasse leading to the upper slopes.

expeditions to Nepal targeted the normal route up Everest!

It is not surprising to see new records established. The youngest people ever to climb the highest peak are youths of sixteen and seventeen (Sherpa Shambu Tamang, who was sixteen in 1973, and French teenager Bertrand Roche, who was seventeen in 1990), while an "oldster" of sixty made it to the top in 1993 (Ramon Blanco from Spain). Sherpa Ang Rita has been there nine times, never using oxygen, and several other Sherpas have scaled Everest four, five, or six times. Among Westerners, over twenty people have climbed it twice or more, including a woman climber from India, Santosh Yadev. Yet once again it should be realized that most of these ascents are made by the normal Nepalese route.

Indeed, the other normal route, up the northern Tibetan face, is more difficult. The difficulty stems not from technical climbing problems but from the obligation to make longer stays at high altitude. Statistically, success is rarer. Other routes—there are ten in total, not counting variations and potential combinations—are rarely taken.

Still other signs suggest that high-altitude climbing is becoming commonplace. For instance, a man who had had both his lower legs amputated, Norman Croucher, actually made it up Cho Oyu. Beginning with Dhaulagiri in 1980, tourist expeditions have targeted various "8,000ers." Paid trips up Everest, in particular, have become more common since 1986—people who sometimes have little mountaineering experience can now take a shot at reaching "the roof of the world." It is understandable that the idea of scaling the highest summit on earth attracts people, and that the idea is subsequently sold to them; nor is it surprising that people in excellent physical condition manage—on rare occasions—to make it to the top. But it would be a mistake to think that the risks have therefore diminished. Even if one climbs alongside twenty other mountaineers, once at the summit of Everest physical deterioration is rapid, judgment suffers, and rescue is virtually impossible—the high number of deaths recorded on all the "8,000ers," especially Everest, can be explained by these extreme conditions in which even the most minor incident can swiftly become fatal.

There is a simple and striking way to illustrate the extreme danger of high-altitude climbing. As of 1990, historian Xavier Eguskitza calculated that thirty-eight "Everest summiters" had died. Of that number, twenty-one had died on Everest itself, seven on other "8,000ers," eight in other mountain ranges, and only two in their beds (one of whom was Sherpa Tenzing, who died in Darjeeling in 1986).

The Himalayas Her Way

It is interesting to note that the earliest women's expeditions to the Himalayas took place at a time when they were still highly uncommon in the Alps. But the idea of such expeditions, tested in the 1950s by Antonia Deacock, Joyce Dunsheath, and, above all, Claude Kogan, faded with Kogan's death in 1959. It was not until 1974 that an "8,000er"—Manaslu—was climbed by a team of Japanese women. Masako Uchida, Miyeko Mori, and Naoko Nakaseko (only one of whom used oxygen) completed the ascent, which was marred by the death of Teiko Suzuki. Things then swiftly changed in the Himalayas, for the next year Junko Tabei from Japan made it up the Nepalese slope of Everest, while Phantog from Tibet climbed the north slope. That same year, Halina Kruger-Syrokomska and Anna Okopinska ascended another "8,000er," Gasherbrum II, while the team that first conquered Gasherbrum III (7,952 m) was composed of two women (Wanda Rutkiewicz and Alison Chadwick) and two men (Krzysztof Zdzitowiecki and Janusz Onyszkiewicz, Chadwick's husband). Onyszkiewicz, as a member of the Solidarity movement, would become Poland's minister of defense after the fall of communism. Gasherbrum III, as a "near 8,000er," remains the highest peak whose first ascent was also a women's first, outdistancing Ganesh I (7,429 m, climbed in 1955 by Claude Kogan and Raymond Lambert), Sia Kangri III (7,315 m, climbed in 1934 by Hettie and Günther Dyhrenfurth) and Nun (7,135 m, climbed in 1953 by Claude Kogan and Pierre Vittoz). The French climber Christine Janin was the first woman to participate in an Alpine-style ascent of an "8,000er," namely Gasherbrum II; two years later, Broad Peak was the first "8,000er," climbed by an exclusively women's team, Anna Czerwinska and Krystyna Palmowska, who did it in two days without oxygen and without companions.

The great name among women Himalayan mountaineers is that of another Pole, Wanda Rutkiewicz. Prior to her death on Kangchenjunga in 1992, she had scaled eight "8,000ers," including Everest and K2, and had participated in the conquest of Gasherbrum III. She also climbed the Diamir slope of Nanga Parbat in 1985, with Anna Czerwinska and Krystyna Palmowska, and ascended Hidden Peak in 1990 in the company of Ewa Pankiewicz. Up till now, no other woman has racked up so many conquests. Things may soon change, however, for in 1990 the American climber Kitty Calhoun Grissom scaled Makalu's west pillar (first women's ascent, fourth overall ascent),

while in 1992 French mountaineer Chantal Mauduit reached the summit of K2 all alone. Then, in 1993, Switzerland's Marianne Chapuisat was the first woman to make a winter ascent of an "8,000er," Cho Oyu. Finally, in 1995, for the first time, a women's team unaccompanied by men claimed an absolute "first" on an "8,000er": Takeo Nagao (aged 38) and Yuka Endoh (aged 28) made an important variation to the Kurtyka-Loretan route on Cho Oyu, then descended via the west ridge. For both women, it was their fourth "8,000er."

Once again, the most coveted prize has been Everest without the help of oxygen. A guide from New Zealand, Lydia Bradley, claimed to have accomplished the feat in 1988, but her claim was seriously challenged by testimony from other climbers, and she later made a written retraction. The 1995 ascent by British climber Alison Hargreaves, meanwhile, was beyond dispute; but tragically, Hargreaves died on K2 shortly afterwards. Women, too, have

Top: Changabang, in the Garhwal Himalayas. The Boardman–Tasker route scaled the left edge. Bottom: Joe Tasker on the summit.

Everest's west ridge presents long and difficult rock passages at an extremely high altitude.

paid a heavy tribute in the Himalayas: in addition to Rutkiewicz and Hargreaves, Claude Kogan and Claudine van der Stratten died on Cho Oyu in 1959; Vera Watson and Alison Chadwick-Onyszkiewicz perished on Annapurna in 1978; Halina Kruger-Syrokomska died on K2 in 1982; Liliane Barrard and Julie Tullis never returned from K2 in 1986; and Jekaterina Iwanowa and Jordanka Dimitrova perished on Kangchenjunga in 1994.

In Search of Virgin "7,000ers"

These days, there is a strict hierarchy of Himalayan objectives. There are crowds on Everest, a good number of climbers on the other "8,000ers," a few mountaineers on lesser peaks that are easily accessible or well known (like Ama Dablam and Pumori), but absolutely no one anywhere else. This is cause for rejoicing insofar as "old-style" exploration is still possible,

along with the conquest of virgin summits. The taller the target, of course, the greater the interest. So the altitude of the highest "virgin" summit on the planet is steadily diminishing.

This search is often frustrated by political developments. The "highest war in the world," on the Siachen Glacier between India and Pakistan, has placed the fine Saltoro Kangri group off-limits. For different reasons, Bhutan has closed its doors to expeditions. Thus many fine "7,000ers" are currently out of reach, probably to the greater pleasure of future mountaineers.

Following the 1971 ascent of Kungyang Kish (7,852 m) by Andrzej Zawada's expedition, a key event in the race for the highest virgin summit was the 1992 conquest of Namche Barwa (7,782 m). Namche Barwa is an isolated peak in Tibetan territory, ringed by the Brahmaputra River and protected by dreadful weather and

A snowstorm on the crowning ridge of Anye Machen, a rarely climbed peak in Tibet, in 1993.

The splendid face of Gasherbrum IV, which would be far more famous if it were not twenty meters short of being an "8,000er."

difficult snow conditions—it put up stiff resistance before succumbing to the climbers on Tsuneo Shigehiro's Japanese expedition.

There are approximately 400 peaks on the planet over 7,000 meters high. Most of them are in the Himalayas. In addition, there are some in Tibet, a few others in the Tien Shan and Pamir ranges, and another in China. A good third of these peaks are still virgin (few of the very highest ones, however). Yet even though the glamor of an unconquered peak remains strong, many of those untrammeled "7,000ers" offer no particular difficulty, apart from being out of the way. Therefore, some of the most coveted trophies in the Himalayas do not even attain that altitude, which itself is rather modest in the context of Asian ranges.

The Race for Difficult Peaks

The normal routes up the "8,000ers" and many "7,000ers" could not be described as technically difficult. They generally present snow ramps, arêtes, and passages of rock, or rock and ice, that are relatively simple or, once they become trickier, are swiftly equipped with safety ropes and ladders (as was the case, for instance, with the chimney forced by House and Bates on K2, and the second rock step on Everest's north ridge). The difficulty and risk lie elsewhere, and arise mainly from altitude and length. Of course, on Everest, and especially on the other "8,000ers," climbers have deliberately sought difficult routes—during the complete ascent of the west ridge in 1979, Yugoslav climbers negotiated the two highest grade-five (V) passages in the world (8,500 meters). However, for mountaineers in search of pure difficulty, other, less lofty peaks appear more interesting. As mentioned above, this was the case as early as 1956 with the double conquest of Mustagh Tower.

The true starting signal for extremely difficult climbs in the Himalayas (somewhat similar, perhaps, to Otto Ampferer's conquest of Campanile Basso in 1899) was given in 1976. That was the year British climbers Joe Tasker and Peter Boardman traced a route up the west face of Changabang (6,782 m) in the Nanda Devi group in Garhwal. Their route included passages of free and aid climbing at a level of difficulty then unknown in the Himalayas. It was clearly on such haughty, if less lofty, peaks that climbs of increasing difficulty would be made. The same thing, after all, had occurred in the Alps, where the Grépon and the Petit Dru are modest summits compared to Mont Blanc. It goes without saying that, as soon as altitude is no longer the main draw, the quest for difficulty can be pursued all across the globe.

Several regions are particularly propitious to such climbing. For example, challenging targets that nourish the new approach include the towers ringing the Baltoro Glacier and the lofty peaks of the Biafo Glacier in the Karakoram, the mountains flanking the sources of the Ganges in the Garhwal Himalayas, and the needles in the Paine and Chálten groups (like Mount Fitz Roy) in Patagonia. It might be noted that all these ranges are primarily granitic. There is no certainty that other challenges of equal scope will ever come to light, given that there are a limited number of "reserves," even if access to some of the mountains of Nepal currently remains restricted. Norway can nevertheless boast that it was only in 1994 that the highest peak on its territory was scaled: Ulvetanna (2,931 m) is in fact located in Queen Maud Land, Antarctica. And, as luck would have it, it turns out to be a magnificent, challenging needle, and not some simple nunatak (i.e., rounded hill poking above a glacier).

As to the Peruvian Andes, the scene of so many remarkable ascents in the 1960s, they remained largely in the background. The "last great problem," the south face of Huandoy Sur, held out against numerous expeditions until it was finally scaled in 1975, via three different routes! Subsequently, political events have further marginalized the Cordillera Blanca.

The Saga of the Ogre

Peter Boardman and Joe Tasker's 1976 ascent was perceived as the dawn of a new era. Yet confirmation was required. The next year, a small British expedition attacked the magnificent Baintha Brakk, or "Ogre" (7,285 m), in the Karakoram. The ascent followed a long, complex, and very difficult route, and nearly led to tragedy—while rappelling down from the

Following double page: The Karakoram's wonderful "sea of mountains" flanking the Biafo Glacier. In the center is the "Ogre" (Baintha Brakk), while the Latok group can be seen to the right.

Above, left: With both ankles
broken, Doug Scott was
forced to crawl down from the
Ogre. Above, right: The
impressive face of Bhagirathi
III in the Garhwal
Himalayas. Right: Doug
Scott.

summit, Doug Scott involuntarily swung to one side and broke both ankles. Assisted by his partners Chris Bonington and Tut Braithwaite, he nevertheless managed to reach base camp after further rappels and by crawling on his knees. During the same descent, Bonington also fell and broke his ribs. All climbers managed to survive with their health intact, however.

Other peaks in the area, such as Latok I, II (the highest, at 7,171 m), and III, were also the sites of magnificent first ascents.

Whereas Changabang and Baintha Brakk required mixed rock and ice climbing, the less elevated and more easily accessible faces of the Baltoro "Grand Cathedrals" and Trango Towers in the Karakoram presented primarily rock routes. These superb and compact walls are comparable to Yosemite, but at an altitude of 6,000 meters! Their beauty had been documented early in the century by Vittorio Sella's photographs, but the starting gun was not fired until 1976, when Nameless Tower (6,239 m) was scaled by Mo Anthine, Martin Boysen, Joe Brown, and Malcolm

Howells. The very next year, the central summit of the Great Trango Tower (6,286 m) was conquered by Americans Galen Rowell, John Roskelley, Schmitz, and Morrissey.

Subsequently, climbers would trace routes of a difficulty equal to anything found on California's "big walls," with added altitude and remoteness. In 1984, Norwegians Hans Christian Donseth, Finn Doehli, Dag Kolsrud, and Stein Aasheim took twenty days to open a route dubbed "No Return" on the southeast face of the Great Trango Tower's east summit (6,231 m). The route was indeed one of no return, for all four died during the descent. Since that time, the world's best climbers have been drawn to the area. In 1987, the south face of Nameless Tower was attacked by Slovenian climbers Cankar, Srot, and Knez, who opened an extremely difficult route some twenty-three pitches long, with certain free-climbed passages graded 7b (U.S.: 5.12/13). The west pillar, meanwhile, was climbed by Michel Piola, Stéphane Schaffter, Michel Fauquet, and Patrick Delale.

In 1988, it was the turn of Wojciech Kurtyka and Erhard Loretan to confront the east face of Nameless Tower. Then came Spanish climber Miguel Angel Gallego, Germans Kurt Albert and Wolfgang Güllich, the Italian Maurizio Giordani, and others. In 1992, the Swiss–American team of Xavier Bongard and John Middendort took sixteen days to trace "The Great Voyage" up Great Trango Tower (graded A4 + U.S. 5.10, or 5c). All these routes combined numerous difficulties—free and aid climbing techniques, extreme heights, bivouacs on "portaledges" (that is to say, dangling hammock-like devices). It was all a long way from the "8,000ers" and many of the protagonists were more familiar with the rockfaces of the Alps or Yosemite than with extremely high altitude climbs; but the technical difficulty of the routes is probably greater than anything else that exists at the same altitude.

The Gangotri region also proved fertile. Its summits directly overlook the pilgrims' ashrams at the sources of the Ganges River, which indicates how short and easy the approach is. The local Matterhorn is the magnificent Shivling ("Shiva lingam," or phallus of Shiva), whose

6,543 meters were scaled in 1974 by Indian climbers. More recently, remarkable routes have been forged up the most formidable slopes in the area, entailing difficulties on ice as well as rock. Slovenian mountaineers have been particularly active here, notably on the west face of Bhagirathi III (6,454 m), scaled in 1990 by Silvo Karo and Janez Jeglic, the west face of Bhagirathi II (6,512 m), climbed in 1989 by Andreja Hrastnik and Francek Knez (comprising passages graded 7a, U.S.: 5.12), and the north spur of Shivling by Hans Kammerlander and Christoph Hainz in 1993. Above all, perhaps, the north face of the most difficult peak in the group, Thalay Sagar (6,904 m), was scaled by Hungarian climbers Peter Dékàny and Attila Ozsvàth in 1991. Thalay Sagar has often been attacked, but has succumbed only six times so far!

On the Other Side of the Planet—Patagonia

The high-altitude ranges, however, do not have a monopoly on extreme difficulty as conceived by late twentieth-century mountaineers. On the other side of the planet, the thrusting, compact

Above, left: On the west pillar of the Nameless Tower in the Trango group. Above, right: The "Return of Flame" route on the same Nameless Tower.

peaks of Patagonia are equally difficult to climb, and have now become one of the main destinations of cutting-edge climbing. Their altitude may not be as lofty, but they make up for this "failing" with wretched weather and violent winds, which, apart from their intrinsic drawback, drape the rockfaces with incrustations of ice that pose enormous difficulties, like the famous "mushroom" that crowns Cerro Torre. This means that climbers must have perfect ice as well as rock skills.

The first certified ascent of Cerro Torre, probably the most pointed peak on earth, was made by Casimiro Ferrari's expedition in 1974. The controversial story behind this peak nevertheless requires explanation. In 1959, two outstanding mountain climbers, Cesare Maestri from Italy (known for solo ascents of a boldness rivaling those of Hermann Buhl) and Toni

Egger from Austria, climbed the mountain. Egger was killed during the descent. When Cerro Torre was later attacked by other climbers, inconsistencies in Maestri's account emerged; then, when further ascents were attempted, it appeared unlikely to many people that the extreme glacial difficulties of the purported route could have been overcome with the equipment available at the time. Indignant at such criticism, Maestri returned to the foot of Cerro Torre in 1970—armed with an electric drill and a compressor weighing fifty-nine kilos! He chose the southeast arête (now the normal route), but despite an orgy of bolts, he could not vanquish the mushroom of ice at the top. Unlike Maestri, Casimiro Ferrari attacked the west face, and managed to arrive at the summit of what is reputed to be the most difficult mountain on earth.

Cerro Torre with, to its right, two satellite peaks of Torre Egger and Cerro Stanhardt. In the distance is the glacial cap of Hielo Patagonico Sur.

It is perhaps this complicated history that has drawn so many Italian climbers to Patagonia. Whatever the case, conquest of the range can be broken down into three stages. Most notable was Renato Casarotto's first ascent, in 1979, of the north pillar of Fitz Roy in eight days, all alone—only Bonatti accomplished comparable feats. Then, in 1985, Ermanno Salvaterra, an extremely good Italian climber who has made Patagonia his specialty, managed to scale Cerro Torre in winter; that same year, Marco Pedrini from Switzerland repeated the feat, all on his own.

Another important event, which occurred the same year Cerro Torre was first definitively climbed, was the ascent of the vast east face (1,500 m) of the central peak of Paine by Faul Fatti's South African team. These days, the compact, vertical wall boasts five different routes. In 1976, Americans John Bragg, John Donini, and Jay Wilson scaled a satellite of Cerro Torre, called Torre Egger (2,900 m), including the dangerous mushroom of ice that had foiled the British team of Martin Boysen and Tut Braithwaite the previous year. Finally, one of the last virgin peaks, Cerro Stanhardt, fell in 1988 to Americans Bridwell, Jay Smith, and Greg Smith. Three years later, Italians Salvaterra, Ferruccio Vidi, and Adriano Cavallero made the traverse from Stanhardt to Punta Herron. One awaits a complete traversal of the Cerro Torre group—Torre Egger, Cerro Stanhardt, Punta Herron.

The two most remarkable ascents, however, were accomplished by Slovenian climbers, who successively opened the east face of Cerro Torre in 1986 (Janez Jeglic, Francek Knez, Pave Kozkjek, Peter Podgornik, Matjaz Fistrovec) and the southeast face of Torre Egger (Jeglic, Knez, Silvo Karo), followed in 1988 by the south

Below: The fine spire of Fitz Roy with, to its left, Aguja Poincenot. Following double page: Vincent Sprungli on a subsidiary peak of the south tower of Paine, seen against the fantastic shadows of Paine's three towers stretching across the Patagonian pampa.

Top left: Francek Knez, Silvo Karo, and Janez Jeglic after ascending the west face of Fitz Roy. Bottom left: "The box," a portable hut that enabled Ermanno Salvaterra and his companions to spend twenty-four straight days on the south face of Cerro Torre. Right: The fine south face of Paine's southern tower.

face of Cerro Torre (Jeglic, Karo). This last route (on the equivalent of a north face in the Alps), combining extreme difficulty with danger, constituted one of the major accomplishments of the day. In 1994, Jeglic returned with Marko Lukiz and Mika Praprotnik to open a second, even more difficult route up the south face. A list of all the new routes in Patagonia, however, would go on indefinitely.

Mountaineering, a Worldwide Sport

A perusal of the preceding paragraphs brings to light a new phenomenon—the arrival of "non-Alpine" countries in worldwide mountaineering. It was a Norwegian, Donseth, who first climbed the north pillar of Thalay Sagar (and later died after ascending Trango Tower); the final challenge of Thalay Sagar—its north face—was ultimately met by Hungarians. Europe, unfortunately, often remains oblivious

to the exploits by the likes of Carlos Carsolio, a Mexican with thirteen "8,000ers" under his belt, or the numerous expeditions organized by Koreans and climbers of other nations. Mountaineering has now become a worldwide sport, and distinctions between national schools or trends are becoming less and less marked. Things have changed a great deal since the 1960s when the arrival in the Alps of American climbers such as Harlin, Hemming, and Robbins forced French mountaineers to rethink their approach to climbing.

Two countries, in fact, long ago challenged the primacy of Alpine nations. Both countries have had a long tradition of mountaineering, and in the case of Poland, climbing was perhaps a way of compensating for political frustration. It is well known that the Tatra range in Poland produced a school of "Tatranism" as venerable as Alpinism, and that mountain climbing is still a popular activity there. Polish "Tatraniks" were not totally absent from the Alps, but since leaving

Poland was usually complicated, whenever they had the opportunity they tended to head straight for the Himalayan ranges. This they did for many years, mobilizing a wealth of energy and ingenuity, going so far as to set up a truck transportation and barter system to finance their expeditions. Initially specialized in exploratory mountaineering, notably in the Hindu Kush, the Polish began innovating in the 1970s. Word got back to Europe of exploits that seemed incredible at the time: Krzysztof Zurek made a solo ascent of Noshaq (7,492 m) in only eleven hours, while Dina Sterbova made the first women's solo ascent of a "7,000er" (Noshaq again). The Polish, as we have seen, subsequently went on to play a leading role in the development of Himalayan mountaineering, notably by conquering some of the highest virgin summits: Kangbachen (7,902 m, 1974), Kangchenjunga South (8,476 m,

1978) and Central (8,482 m, 1978), Broad Peak Central (8,016 m, 1975), Gasherbrum III (7,952 m, 1975), and Kunyang Kish (7,852 m, 1971). In the 1980s, Polish mountain climbers were preponderant in the Himalayan zones. Wojciech Kurtyka has recently calculated that of all the "firsts" racked up on "8,000ers," Poles have accounted for twenty-three, Japanese for fifteen, Austrians for thirteen, Yugoslavs for nine, and Italians and British for eight each. Furthermore, almost every one of the "winter firsts" was Polish.) France then follows with seven "firsts"—it is no secret that French climbers are criticized abroad for favoring media events over demanding firsts; the reputations of French mountaineers who break that rule, like the late Pierre Béghin, are therefore all the greater.

Polish mountain climbers are less predominant these days, if only because many of the protag-

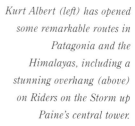

Kurt Albert (left) has opened some remarkable routes in Patagonia and the Himalayas, including a stunning overhang (above) on Riders on the Storm up Paine's central tower.

Wolfgang Güllich
bivouacking on the central
tower of Paine while forging
Riders on the Storm.

onists are dead. Wroz, Chrobak, Czok, Heinrich, Kukuczka, Piotrowsky, and others are gone. The same phenomenon explains the relative modesty of British mountaineering in the Himalayas following the great expeditions of the 1970s: Tasker, Boardman, Estcourt, Burke, Clough, Fanshave, MacIntyre, and Rouse have been killed, making Doug Scott and Chris Bonington appear like survivors.

In Poland's wake, other Eastern European countries came to the fore, none more so than the former Yugoslavia. Some of today's most enterprising climbers are from Slovenia (a land that, like Poland, boasted a solid mountaineering tradition acquired on the fine slopes of the Julian Alps). Yugoslavia earned its Himalayan stripes as early as 1960, thanks to Aleš Kunaver's expedition to Trisul (7,120 m). Their true strength and boldness, however, only emerged in the late 1970s and early 1980s. In 1979, they made a complete ascent of the west ridge of Everest (Jernej Zaplotnik, Andrej Stremfelj, Stane Belak, Stipe Bozik, and Ang Phu Sherpa, who was killed during the descent). Three years later, a route was traced up the south face of Aconcagua, straight to the south summit, by Peter Podgornik's team, while in 1985 the north face of Yalung Kang was conquered by Tomo Cesen and Borut Bergant (who died on the way down). Ever since, the number of extremely difficult new routes opened by Karo, Knez, and Jeglic, not to mention the controversial Cesen, has kept the former Yugoslavia in the limelight.

Also worth mentioning is the Czech Republic, which also used the Tatras as a training ground. One Czech specialty is the south face of Dhaulagiri, where they have put up no fewer than four new routes!

Japanese Mountaineers, Champions of Exploration

The thoroughly crucial role long played by Japan in the exploration of the Himalayas is rarely stressed. Yet of the 261 peaks over 7,000 meters scaled up to 1989, seventy-seven were first climbed by Japanese expeditions (starting in 1958), against thirty-nine by Austria, thirty-two by Great Britain, twenty-three by Germany, fifteen by Italy, twelve by Poland, and twelve by

France. Such figures speak for themselves. True enough, Japanese mountaineers have long preferred large expeditions, but outstanding individuals like Naomi Uemura (who died on Mount McKinley in 1984) and Yatsuo Kato (killed on his third ascent—and second winter ascent—of Everest, in 1980) were first-rate climbers, although little known in the West. Uemura was one of the greatest mountain explorers of all time. By 1970 he had climbed all of the "Seven Summits" except for the Carstensz Pyramid in Indonesia and Vinson Massif in Antarctica, which were difficult to reach at the time. Uemura's polar crossings, notably the first north-south traverse of Greenland's Inland Ice (alone, at that!) were not mountaineering feats but nevertheless count as some of the greatest exploits ever accomplished.

In fact, national expeditions are no longer in fashion. Worldwide travel has broken down many old barriers, so that modern expeditions are organized around shared interests or affinities. Thus in 1980, René Ghilini from France, Alex MacIntyre from Britain, and Kurtyka and Wilczynski from Poland teamed up to conquer the east face of Dhaulagiri. Many expeditions to Everest are now motley affairs composed of many nationalities.

The same internationalization has occurred in terms of target ranges. While most mountaineering developments still take place in the Himalayas, followed by a few special regions, the worldwide development of the sport has greatly increased the potential field of action (accompanied by the inevitable vagaries of fashion that tend to undervalue or overestimate certain sites). The mountain climbers of today (and of the future) can choose from ranges scattered across the globe: the cliffs of the Hombori range in Mali; the

A trio of Slovenians whose names often crop up in Patagonia and the Himalayas (left to right): Francek Knez, Janez Jeglic, and Silvo Karo.

canyons of Wadi Rum in Jordan; the *tepuys* (table-top summits) of Venezuela; the peaks of Baffin Island, where the magnificent Mount Asgard reigns; the superb slopes in southern Greenland, notably the elegant Ketil; the Sigunian range in China; the Ak-Su group in the Pamirs; and so on. But are there still any unknown reserves of peaks liable to satisfy top-notch climbers? It seems unlikely, even if the amazing performance of Alaskan climber Mugs Stump seemed to open

new doors when he traced a solo route up the west face of Mount Tyree (2,500 m) in Antartica (Stumps would die in 1992, after having made a solo ascent of the Cassin Spur of McKinley and the first ascent of the Emperor Face of Mount Robson). Antarctica is the least well explored continent from a mountaineering standpoint.

Conquering the "Seven Summits"

Just as Karl Blödig had racked up all the 4,000-meter peaks in the Alps, mountaineers came up with the idea of "bagging" the highest peaks on all seven continents. In 1985, Dick Bass, from the United States, was the first to scale the peaks of all seven continents: McKinley (6,194 m, North America), Aconcagua (6,960 m, South America); Everest (8,848 m, Asia); Elbrus (5,642 m, Europe); Kilimanjaro (5,895 m, Africa); Vinson Massif (4,897 m, Antarctica); and Mount Kosciusko (2,228 m, Australia). But the list has been subject to dispute. Some people thought Mont Blanc was more naturally the highest point in Europe, especially since many geographers situated the Caucasus in Asia. As to Australia, it could be considered just a part of the fragmented continent of Oceania, leading Canadian climber Pat Morrow to reject the modest Kosciusko in favor of the Carstensz Pyramid (4,884 m, Indonesia) when he did his own tour in 1986. Morrow was followed by Messner, then by many others, including two women (the first being Junko Tabei from Japan, with Christine Janin from France just behind). Although a powerful symbol, this circuit provides no mountaineering interest whatsoever; for a modern climber, only the ascent of Everest poses any difficulty. The rest is above all a question of time—and money.

Infinitely more serious is the complete series of fourteen "8,000ers," far more difficult to accomplish. And here again, the historical list merits review. Yalung Kang (8,505 m) and Lhotse Shar (8,400 m), for example, are not included because they are seen as satellite peaks of Kangchenjunga and Lhotse, respectively, yet they are no less independent than Mont Maudit is of Mont Blanc. A truly exhaustive list of "8,000ers" would in fact include some twenty peaks. Whatever the case, completing that particular collection requires a Himalayan experience that is still—and will perhaps remain for a long time—the realm of exploit. It is no coincidence that two of the greatest Himalayan mountaineers of modern times (if not *the* two greatest) were the first to pull it off: Messner in 1986, followed by Jerzy Kukuczka the next year in a blaze of impressive ascents (nine new routes, four winter ascents, one solo, five ascents Alpine-style). Kukuczka died in a 1989 attempt to climb the south face of Lhotse. The same fate awaited several others who were on their way to collecting all fourteen peaks, including Benoît Chamoux, who died in 1995 just a few meters

Clockwise, from top left: Naomi Uemura, Benoît Chamoux, Reinhold Messner, Jerzy Kukuczka. Four great Himalayan climbers—all except Messner have died in the mountains.

from his last summit, Kangchenjunga, on the very day that his rival Erhard Loretan became the third person to have successfully scaled all of them. This only goes to show the extent to which Himalayan mountain climbing, even when practiced on the "normal routes," remains an extremely dangerous game. One thing is sure, however: Loretan will not be the last. Carlos Carsolio from Mexico already has thirteen "8,000ers" under his belt (including a new

The Latest Challenge—Traverses

Successfully completing such collections is largely a question of perseverance and luck. It is probably more interesting and trickier to accomplish major traverses, as has long been done in the Alps and Caucasus. That is the sphere for future exploits. Steps have obviously been taken in this direction, with Reinhold Messner leading the way once again. It may be tiring to find

route traced, all alone, up Broad Peak in 1994), and behind him comes the Pole Krzysztof Wielicki, the Slovenian Victor Groselj, the American Ed Viesturs, the Austrian Hans Kammerlander, and other climbers who have already bagged ten or twelve summits. Some day, a woman will join this highly elite club. And some day, perhaps, a mountaineer will climb them all in the space of a single year. After all, in 1983, Loretan and his Swiss partner Marcel Ruedi (who later died on Dhaulagiri) managed to scale three "8,000ers" in just two weeks (Gasherbrum II, Hidden Peak, Broad Peak).

Messner's name on every page of this chapter, but that frequency merely reflects his importance. Along with Hans Kammerlander, in 1984 Messner took four days to complete the first traverse—which could also be called the first linkage—of two "8,000ers," Hidden Peak and Gasherbrum II. The same year, the Kurtyka–Kukuczka team traversed the three summits of Broad Peak (main summit, 8,047 m; central summit, 8,016 m; north summit, 7,550 m). Both of these fine feats were accomplished Alpine-style.

It is not certain, however, that all traverses can be accomplished in that manner. In an attempt

The Carstensz Pyramid, considered the highest point in Oceania, is now one of the Seven Summits crowning the seven continents.

that proved to be too risky for the time, French mountaineers Duplat and Vigne died while trying to link the two summits of Nanda Devi, a traverse that was not successfully completed until 1976 by an Indo-Japanese expedition. In 1989, when Kangchenjunga's four peaks succumbed to a double traverse (two teams, one traveling in each direction), it was a major Soviet expedition that pulled off the operation; it is not certain that a pure Alpine-style team could have negotiated several miles of rocky ridge at an altitude of 8,000 to 8,500 meters. Sergei Bershov and his companions spent five days above 8,000, some of them without oxygen, to make the highest ridge

Pierre Béghin arriving at the summit of Jannu, with Kangchenjunga in the background.

traverse ever completed, which probably constitutes a survival record at that altitude. The performance was amazing from every point of view.

The same problem arises with the traverse from Lhotse to Lhotse Shar, one of the last great remaining challenges posed by the Himalayas, all the more attractive for entailing the conquest of the highest virgin peak on the planet, Lhotse Central (8,430 m). Other climbers already envisage a grand traverse from Nuptse to Lhotse to Everest, which still appears to be a utopian project. Another tricky ridge is the one between Mazeno and Nanga Parbet; although much lower in altitude, it is a colossal thirteen kilometers long.

Nearing the Final Frontier

As mentioned above, the Himalayas still present challenges. Elsewhere, on the other hand, things are less open. It is easy to envisage future routes that will pose novel difficulties, but it is equally obvious that no one will ever discover a mountain more difficult than Cerro Torre, all the faces of which have been scaled. The reserves of extremely difficult "firsts" are beginning to look depleted. The mountaineers of tomorrow will have to invent something. Who in 1964, for that matter, could have predicted the developments that have occurred since that time?

Now, as the year 2000 approaches, mountaineering has little in common with what it was just thirty years ago. All the mountain ranges in the world have been explored, mapped, and documented, even if such information is not always easy to come by. There are many routes on even the most distant mountains, and virgin summits are increasingly rare. Beyond the now tricky evolution toward increased difficulty, an entire dimension of traditional mountaineering—namely, exploration—is vanishing. The drive to explore, present since the dawn of mountain climbing, was the impetus for some of its greatest figures.

Perhaps people will come to realize that unexplored territory is, in a way, valuable in itself. Bhutan, which despite its tiny size probably harbors more untrammeled peaks—including numerous "7,000ers"—than all other countries combined, has closed its borders to all expeditions for an indefinite period. Bhutan's move almost certainly represents a shrewd investment, because twenty years from now those summits will be worth a great deal more. Altitude has a price, and it is swiftly rising. As mountaineering enthusiasts rush toward 8,000-meter peaks, the few countries concerned (Nepal, Pakistan, China) have realized that they can cash in, and therefore constantly increase the level of their permit fees.

Does this mean that true mountaineering adventure has actually come to an end? Probably not, but Mummery's notion of "fair means" probably entails, now more than ever, a limiting of technological resources available to mountain climbers. In recent years, the opposite impression has been created by expeditions concerned with media coverage—fax machines, computers, radios, and telephones all above 7,000 meters! It is now possible to make a telephone call from the summit of Mount Everest, and it is a safe bet that this development will soon be vaunted as "progress." Environmental issues, ethics, and purity of style are often invoked when they make good advertising copy, only to be discarded when no longer perceived as being profitable.

For that matter, one of the crucial issues that the future will have to resolve stems from the increasing number of expeditions to the same old sites—pollution is afflicting not only base camps, but the mountains themselves. The south col of Everest, at 8,000 meters, is now dubbed "the world's highest garbage dump" thanks to some 2,000 oxygen canisters awaiting the rather unlikely arrival of a garbage truck. Since 1984, several expeditions have tried to clean up Everest, but none has really managed. Although cleaning the base camps is simple enough, higher altitudes are another problem entirely—at 8,000 meters, it is hard enough to climb down without a load! In 1900, the "Free K2" expedition organized by Mountain Wilderness cleaned the giant mountain only up to an altitude of 7,100 meters. Since "pressure" is increasingly concentrated on just a few summits, some remedy will have to be found. Otherwise, referring to the "purity" of the mountains will be nothing other than pure hypocrisy.

Since Mummery's day, there has been endless debate in mountaineering circles about "means," whether fair or not. In the Alps, the issues focused chiefly on ropes, rappelling, pitons, bolts, and electric drills; for more distant expeditions, the use of oxygen, fixed lines, and Sherpas have all been challenged. At the same time, other techniques and aids have been tacitly accepted—mountain rescue techniques (which sometimes require guides to maintain radio links), exhaustive documentation, and, above all, communications and media technology have never been contested. In the near future, the now operational Global Positioning System will probably eliminate entirely the risk

of getting lost, and it is not impossible that some medical remedy will minimize the current risks of high-altitude mountain climbing.

But is all of this truly desirable? When Mount Everest is as easy to reach as the summit of Mont Blanc—given that no other remoter or more difficult Mount Everest exists (unless we consider scaling the 11,000-meter Maxwell Montes range in the Ishtar Terra region of Venus)—then mountaineers will have lost more than they have gained. Cliff climbers have developed the concept of "unseen" rock climbs (climbing a previously established route without any previous knowledge of it), but this idea

has never really been adopted for mountain climbing.

Nevertheless a certain form of "technological ecology" would be welcome these days, at least if mountaineering hopes to retain its authentic spirit. As Jacques Lagarde wrote some sixty years ago, "It is strange to observe that ever since man has been drawn to the mountains by a love of wild nature, rigor, solitude, and the unknown, all of which he found in that final refuge, he has done everything to eliminate precisely what he sought there." It is worth meditating on Lagarde's comment, if we wish to avoid destroying the very essence of the wonderful activity of mountaineering.

Above: The Biafo Glacier seen from the summit of Lukpilla Brakk. Following double page: Jean-Noël Roche arriving on the summit ridge of Dhaulagiri.

50 Great Names in Mountaineering

There are far more than fifty climbers who have left their mark

on history—the following selection, if unavoidably limited, at

least has the merit of reflecting the wealth and diversity of

those who dedicated their lives to the mountains.

Facing page: The Petit Dru as seen from
the Mer de Glace, in a photo taken
by Adolphe Braun circa 1880.

Abruzzi (Luigi Amedeo di Savoia, duke of)
Italian explorer and mountaineer
(1873–1933)
Perhaps the greatest mountaineering explorer of all time, the duke of Abruzzi conquered Mount Saint Elias (Alaska, 1897) as well as the main summits of the Ruwenzori range ("Mountains of the Moon") in Africa (1906). He failed to reach the North Pole (1899), and also failed to reach the summit of K2 (1909), although he broke the altitude record of the day by attaining a height of some 7,500 meters (24,500 ft.). Furthermore, the duke accomplished some fine "firsts" in the Alps (Pointe Marguerite and Pointe Hélène on the Grandes Jorasses, 1898). He was accompanied on his expeditions by the talented photographer Vittorio Sella.

Allain (Pierre)
French mountain climber and inventor
(1904)
Pierre Allain was one of the "Bleausards" who trained on the boulders in the Forest of Fontainebleau outside of Paris. Along with Raymond Leininger, he attained a new threshold of difficulty in rock climbing by scaling the north face of the Petit Dru in 1935. Allain also played a notable role in the development of equipment, having designed the first modern-style rock boots, down jackets, and lightweight carabiners. In addition to numerous firsts, he participated in the first French expedition to Hidden Peak (1936) and published a classic text on mountain climbing titled *Alpinisme et Compétition*.

Almer (Christian)
Swiss guide (1826–1897)
Christian Almer's name is intimately linked to the golden age of mountain climbing. He accompanied Edward Whymper up the Barre des Ecrins (1864), the Aiguille Verte, and the Grandes Jorasses (1865), then was the faithful climbing companion of W. A. B. Coolidge until 1885. Almer probably racked up more major firsts than any other guide of the day—some forty in all. Even more extraordinary for the times was his knowledge of almost all the Alpine ranges, from Dachstein to the maritime Alps. In 1896, at the age of seventy, Almer celebrated his fiftieth wedding anniversary by climbing the Wetterhorn in the company of his wife!

Anderegg (Melchior)
Swiss guide (1828–1914)
Having started as a shoe-shine boy at the Grimsel hospice, then working as a wood-carver, he became "the great Melchior" by the end of an outstanding climbing career. He regularly accompanied the finest British Alpinists, such as brothers Horace and Frank (and Lucy, Frank's daughter), Francis Tuckett, Leslie Stephen, Charles Edward Mathews, and so on. Anderegg was remembered as an intelligent man with a sense of humor. If one ascent in his career were to be singled out, it would certainly be the Brenva Spur on Mont Blanc (1865), a route without equal at the time, where his mastery was admired by clients F. and H. Walker, A.W. Moore, and Graham S. Mathews.

Balmat (Jacques)
Guide and crystal hunter from Savoy (1762–1834)
Although he entered the lists rather late, Jacques Balmat made the first successful ascent of Mont Blanc, in the company of Dr. Michel Gabriel Paccard. The respective parts played by the two men during the ascent has long sparked polemical debate, but there is no doubt that Balmat had an energetic role. After his initial victory in 1786, Balmat returned to the summit six times (once as a guide to Horace Bénédict de Saussure in 1787), thereby winning a certain fame, if not fortune. His death remains as mysterious as it was tragic—at the age of seventy-two, he disappeared in the Sixt Valley while searching for gold.

Boivin (Jean-Marc)
French mountaineer (1951–1991)
Among the recent generation of mountain climbers, Jean-Marc Boivin was one of those most attached to a constant search for novelty and a pronounced taste for distinct risk. After his initial "classic" routes, he won recognition for his bold ice routes (the Supercouloir on Mont Blanc du Tacul); astonishing solo climbs (the Shroud on the Grandes Jorasses in only three hours); extremely difficult descents on skis, by hang-glider, and later by paraglider (the first from the summit of Everest); and amazingly masterful marathon linkages. He died from wounds incurred in a paragliding accident on Salto Angel in Venezuela.

Bonatti (Walter)
Italian guide and mountaineer (1930)

In the second half of the twentieth century, Bonatti's dominant stature has been rivaled only by Reinhold Messner (and for different reasons). While Bonatti's first ascent of the east face of the Grand Capucin (1951) marked the introduction of artificial aid climbing in the western Alps, his first solo ascent, lasting five days, of the southwest pillar of the Petit Dru (1955) was one of the great (if not the greatest) mountaineering exploits of all time. Bonatti also left his mark with other solo firsts, winter ascents, and numerous routes up Mont Blanc, the Brouillard Pillars, and the Grand Pilier d'Angle. In 1965, he brought his career to a magnificent close by tracing a new route, alone and in winter, up the north face of the Matterhorn on the hundredth anniversary of the first ascent.

Bonington (Sir Christian)
British Alpine and Himalayan specialist (1934)

After training on British crags and making a number of important Alpine ascents (he was the first up the Frêney Pillar on Mont Blanc, 1961), Bonington headed first for Patagonia (Central Tower of Paine, 1963) and then became a first-rate Himalayan expert and expedition leader. His Himalayan ascents include the south face of Annapurna (1970), southwest face of Everest (1975), and Baintha Brakk (1977) to name only a few. As a highly appreciated speaker and prolific author (a three-volume autobiography!), Bonington is now Britain's most famous mountain climber. He was recently knighted in recognition of his mountaineering exploits.

Buhl (Hermann)
Austrian mountaineer (1924–1957)

Hermann Buhl, who died too young, seems to have been well ahead of his time. He was an amazing pioneer in every sphere— exceptional firsts, solos ascents in record times, difficult winter climbs. He came fully into his own in the Himalayas with the first ascent of Nanga Parbat, which he completed in an astonishing solo climb after ignoring the orders of his expedition leader. In 1957, on reaching the summit of Broad Peak, Buhl became the second person to have scaled two "8,000ers" (after the Sherpa Gyalzen Norbu). Unfortunately, he died shortly afterward when a show cornice collapsed as he was progressing, unroped, along the ridge of Chogolisa in the company of Kurt Diemberger.

Cassin (Riccardo)
Italian mountaineer (1909)

Cassin forged two epoch-making routes in the 1930s—the north face of Cima Ovest di Lavaredo in the Dolomites (1935), and the northeast face of Piz Badile (1937), a granite peak in the Bregaglia Valley. Most importantly he conquered the Walker Spur of the north face of the Grandes Jorasses (1938) with Ugo Tizzoni and Luigi Esposito, encountering little difficulty even though none of the three were familiar with the Mont Blanc range. After having created his own brand of mountain equipment, Cassin became a skilled expedition leader in the postwar period, notably conquering Gasherbrum IV (7,980 m) in 1958 and the south spur of Mount McKinley in 1961.

Facing page: The incredible Alpine atmosphere, as experienced on the Rochefort Ridge in the Mont Blanc range.

Charlet (Armand)
Guide from Chamonix, born in Argentière
(1900–1975)
Charlet's name is closely associated with the Aiguille Verte, which he climbed some hundred times, tracing several new routes. Unlike most of his professional colleagues, Charlet also made "amateur" ascents. He is remembered for his remarkable skills on ice and rock (his 1928 route up the Isolée on the Aiguilles du Diable remains a highly exposed passage to this day), as well as for his legendary speed. However, his old-fashioned conception of mountaineering (eschewing bivouacs and pitons) probably prevented him from playing a role worthy of his talent during the siege of the north face of the Grandes Jorasses.

Charlet (Jean Estéril)
Chamonix guide
(1840–1925)
Jean Charlet is remembered for his endearing personality and his unusual career. After numerous attempts, some of them solo, he managed to conquer the Petit Dru in 1879 in the company of two other guides whom he hired (a rather paradoxical move for a guide). During that ascent, Charlet perfected the rappel (or abseil) method of roping down, which he had devised during a solo attempt in 1876. In 1871, Miss Isabella Straton was his client during the first ascent of the Aiguille du Moine; five years later, Charlet made the first winter ascent of Mont Blanc in her company, and married her the following year. He was the first guide to join the Club Alpin Français.

Comici (Emilio)
Italian guide and mountaineer
(1901–1940)
Comici's first ascent, with the Dimai brothers, of the unvanquished north face of Cima Grande in 1933 represented the most spectacular victory of piton climbing, which was then in its early phase. Comici racked up some two hundred firsts, having guided climbers to the most exotic ranges (Olympus, Sinai). He is remembered as a warm and human climber, sensitive not only to the difficulty but also to the aesthetic appeal of his chosen routes. In 1937, Comici's solo ascent of the north face of Cima Grande was widely publicized. The climber died on the training cliffs in Val Gardena.

Conway (Sir William Martin)
British art critic and mountain climber
(1856–1937)
Somewhat in the spirit of the duke of Abruzzi, Sir Martin Conway was above all a great mountain explorer. He attempted very few Alpine ascents, despite having made the first entire traverse of the range in 1894. Two years earlier, his expedition to the Karakoram represented the first Himalayan expedition worthy of the name, attaining the altitude record for that period. Conway later organized expeditions to Spitzberg, and then to the Andes, from Peru (where he made the first ascent of Illimani) to Chile (Cerro Aconcagua) and down to Patagonia (an attempt on Sarmiento).

Coolidge (William Augustus Brevoort)
American minister and mountain climber (1850–1926)

The Reverend Coolidge played a significant role in the development of Alpine mountaineering. Often accompanied by his aunt, Miss Meta Brevoort, sometimes by his dog Tschingel, and almost always by guide Christian Almer, Coolidge spent thirty-three years in the Alps without missing a single season, carrying out campaigns from one end of the range to the other. He climbed some 2,500 summits, often for the first time, including Piz Badile and the central peak of Meije. He assembled a unique library (bequeathed to the Schweizer Alpen Club on his death) and conducted irreplaceable scholarly research into the history and prehistory of mountaineering.

Desmaison (René)
French guide and mountaineer (1930)

After having trained under the outstanding climber Jean Couzy, Desmaison became the leading French mountaineer. His sole rival was Walter Bonatti, and once Bonatti retired Desmaison had a clear field. He bagged of the great exploits of the 1960s and 1970s, notably in the sphere of solo and winter climbs, including a direct route up the north face of Cima Ovest (1959, in memory of Jean Couzy); a winter ascent of the Frêney Pillar (1967); the Shroud on the Grandes Jorasses (1968); and a solo climb of the entire Peuterey Arête. Desmaison remained aloof from Himalayan ascents, although he climbed a great deal in the Andes. The outspoken Desmaison has often found himself in polemical disputes with Chamonix guides.

Dibona (Angelo)
Italian guide (1879–1956)

Angelo Dibona was the most famous of a long line of Dolomite guides. He was the first to use pitons for protection on the big Alpine walls, notably Cima Una (1911) and especially Laliadererwand (or Karwendel, 1911). His clients, the Mayer brothers, hired him to guide them in the western Alps, where an outstanding campaign took the group up several historical routes on the Ecrins and Mont Blanc ranges. Among them were the Coste Rouge Ridge on Ailefroide, the Aiguille Dibona, and the Aiguille du Requin.

Dülfer (Hans)
Bavarian mountaineer (1893–1915)

Dülfer's historic ascents focused on the small Kaisergebirge group, where he notably made two pioneering routes up the faces of Fleischbank. The east face route (1912) employed numerous pitons, pendulum movements, and other subtleties of the emerging aid technique. The Dülferriss route (1913), climbed solo, included passages of free climbing of a difficulty unequaled at the time. Dülfer was a complete climber and theorist, notably developing the "layback" technique, still called a "dülfer" in France.

Gaspard (Pierre)
Guide from Saint-Christophe-en-Oisans (1834–1915)

As a poor mountain dweller in the Oisans region of France, Pierre Gaspard was almost forty years old when he began his career as a guide. His partnership with Emmanuel Boileau de Castelnau, and their joint victory over the Meije (1877), turned Gaspard into a famous figure and active, respected guide. While professional guiding had long existed in the valleys of Chamonix and Switzerland, at that time there was no such tradition in the Oisans range. Gaspard continued guiding clients into his old age, and founded a family of guides—no fewer than five of his children took up the trade.

Gervasutti (Giusto)
Italian mountaineer (1909–1946)

Gervasutti's long association with French climber Lucien Devies was one of the rare examples of an international team at a time when climbing was poisoned by nationalism. Several failures on the north face of the Grandes Jorasses, were offset by success on the northwest face of Ailefroide (1936), the Olan, and the north pillar of Frêney, not to mention the Gervasutti Couloir and the east face of the Jorasses. Pugnacious, he attacked Ailefroide after having broken two ribs while hiking to the face. Gervasutti died in a rappel maneuver during an attempt on what is now known as the Gervasutti Pillar on Mont Blanc du Tacul.

Hacquet (Belsazar)
French-born naturalist (1740–1815)

Belsazar Hacquet was the "Saussure" of the eastern Alps. He led an adventurous life, traveling to all the ranges in eastern Europe, playing a role similar to that of Ramond de Carbonnières in the Pyrenees. Although born in France, Hacquet published many books in German. In 1777, he scaled one of the peaks of Triglav, reaching the highest summit several years later. Hacquet's work and travels drew attention to the eastern Alps, notably their highest point, the Glockner, which inspired Cardinal von Salm to scale it in 1800.

Hiebeler (Toni)
German mountaineer (1930–1984)

Hiebeler's name is linked to the masterful winter ascents of the 1960s, in particular the north face of the Eiger (1961) and, perhaps even more difficult, the north face of Civetta. These lengthy ascents (requiring up to a week of complete autonomy) represented the ultimate level of audacity and commitment at the time. Highly attached to promoting contacts between climbers throughout the entire world, in 1963 Hiebeler founded an innovative review called *Alpinismus*, which tried to strengthen ties with climbers from the East. Hiebeler, who also published numerous books, died in a helicopter accident.

Facing page: The fantastic form of Devil's Tower in Wyoming, as seen from an airplane.

King (Clarence)
American geologist (1842–1902)

King's exploration of California's Sierra Nevada made him the father of American mountaineering. His 1872 book, *Mountaineering in the Sierra Nevada*, is viewed as a founding document, even though with a very colorful style he sometimes embellished the facts. While carrying out his geological exploration of the Sierra range, King discovered its highest point, Mount Whitney (1864)—along with an arrowhead. He also scaled Mount Tyndall naming it in honor of another scientific mountaineer. King's book and his articles for the *Atlantic Monthly* rivaled the writings of John Muir and did a great deal to popularize California's mountains.

Kogan (Claude)
French mountain climber (1919–1959)

Kogan was one of the first women to climb on equal terms with men, notably in the Himalayas. As early as 1949, she lead-climbed the south ridge of the Aiguille Noire de Peuterey, an extremely rare feat for a woman at the time. In 1951, she scaled Alpamayo and, in partnership with Nicole Leininger, Quitaraju in the Peruvian Andes. Then came her conquest of Salcantay (Peru) and Nun (India). In 1954, she nearly made the first ascent of Cho Oyu with Raymond Lambert, and the following year successfully climbed Ganesh I (7,420 m), which made her "the highest woman in the world." She died in 1959 while leading the international women's expedition to Cho Oyu.

Kukuczka (Jerzy)
Polish Alpine and Himalayan mountaineer (1948–1992)

As the second man, after Reinhold Messner, to have scaled all the "8,000ers" on the planet, "Jurek" Kukuczka had a first-rate list of Himalayan victories to his credit—nine new routes on "8,000ers," four winter ascents, one traverse, one solo, and five Alpine-style ascents. The southeast face of Cho Oyu (1985), was the first new route opened in winter in the Himalayas; his companion Piotrowsky died while attempting to open a new route on the south slope of K2 . A leading figure of Polish mountaineering with a legendary resistance and tenacity, Kukuczka died while attempting the south face of Lhotse, the "great problem" then being attacked by Himalayan specialists.

Lochmatter (Franz)
Swiss guide (1878–1933)

Lochmatter began to come to the fore in 1903 in association with the curious figure of Valentine J. E. Ryan, a meteoric mountaineer who never bothered to write a single line concerning his ascents. The team's masterpiece was the east ridge of the Plan, a route of unequaled difficulty for the day, as well as the south face of Täschhorn, where, in conjunction with the Young–Knubel team, Lochmatter forced an exceptional passage during a blizzard. But when Ryan gave up climbing, Lochmatter never found another client worthy of his talents. Starting in 1912, he joined in several expeditions to the Himalayas, notably Meade's to Kamet, and the Karakoram expedition of Dutch diplomat Philips Visser and his wife Jenny van't Hooft. Lochmatter fell to his death on the Weisshorn, above his home village of Sankt Niklaus.

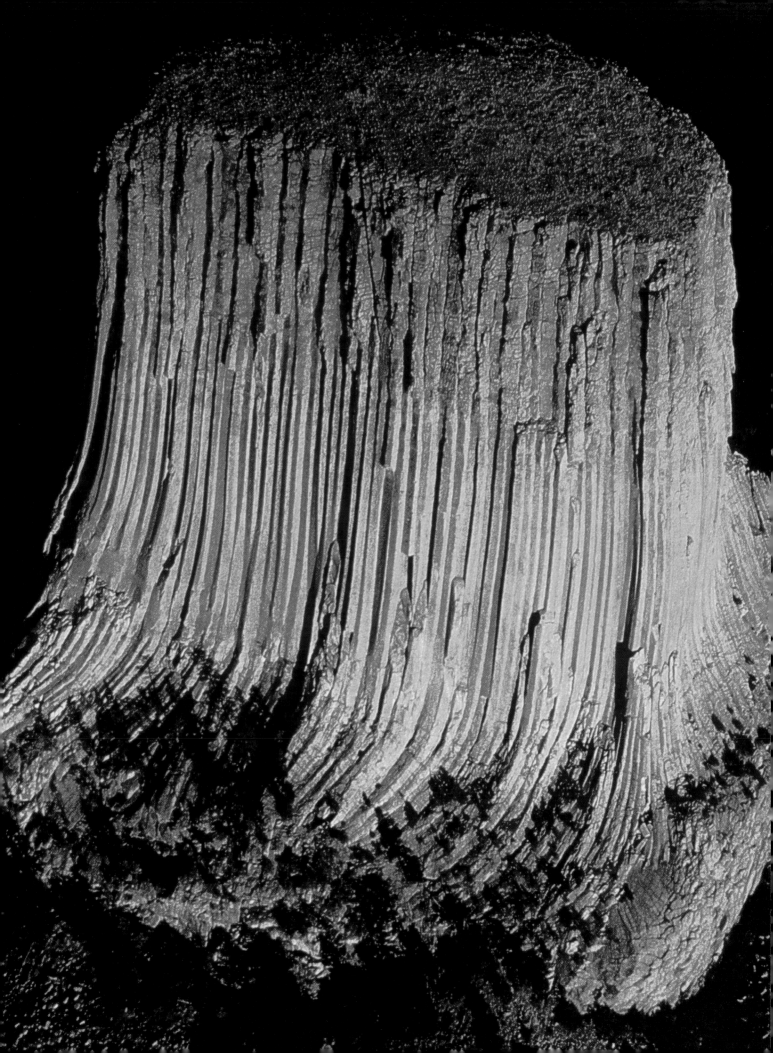

Messner (Reinhold)
Italian mountaineer (1944)

The greatest Himalayan mountaineer of all came to attention in 1968 thanks to his solo firsts of two routes then considered to be among the most difficult—the Philipp–Flamm dihedral on Punta Civetta and the north face of Les Droites. In 1970 he made the first ascent of the Rupal face of Nanga Parbat, followed by the first descent of the Diamir slope. Almost all the major Himalayan advances since have been due to Messner: the first Alpine-style ascent of an "8,000er" (Gasherbrum I, 1975); the first solo ascent of an "8,000er" (Nanga Parbat, 1978); Everest without oxygen (1978); Everest solo (1980); and the first linkage of two "8,000ers" (1984). Messner was, naturally, the first man to have scaled all the "8,000ers" on the planet.

Mummery (Albert Frederick)
English businessman and mountain climber (1855–1895)

Mummery came to mountaineering somewhat late, but soon linked up with the famous guide Alexander Burgener (1846–1910), in whose company he made the first ascent of the Zmutt Arête of the Matterhorn and the Y-Couloir of the Aiguille Verte. After a few lean years, he took up mountaineering again in a radically different manner: without a guide, and in increasingly bold climbs that culminated, after several ascents of the Grépon (first ascent, first traverse, first women's ascent in the company of Lily Bristow), with an attempt on the north face of the Plan. Having decided to have a shot at the Himalayas, Mummery targeted Nanga Parbat, but seems to have underestimated its true difficulty—he died there along with two Gurkha porters.

Piaz (Tita)
Italian guide (1879–1948)

Tita Piaz's career spanned nearly fifty years, and covered most of the major climbing developments in the eastern Alps. His numerous first ascents took place between the years of 1899 and 1933. Nicknamed the "Dolomite Devil," the independent and original Tita Piaz advocated a socialism bordering on anarchism, which often landed the Italian guide in prison. His political views, however, did not prevent him from having King Albert I of Belgium as a client. Piaz was killed in a bicycling accident.

Placidus a Spescha
Swiss priest and mountaineer (1752–1833)

It would be an understatement to assert that Father Placidus was not a typical mountain climber. He was not a man of science like Saussure and Hacquet, and nothing disposed the humble monk from the abbey of Disentis to frequent the little-known mountains of the central Alps so assiduously. Yet he climbed a great number of them, often alone or with the help of shepherds, including the Rheinwaldhorn in 1782. In 1824, during his sixth attempt on Tödi, his partners managed to make it to the top of that fine summit, even though the seventy-two-year-old Placidus could not follow them all the way.

Preuss (Paul)
Austrian mountain climber (1886–1913)
Famous for a particularly bold 1911 ascent of the east face of Campanile Basso in the Brenta Dolomites, which Preuss scaled alone and without pitons. The first team that tried to repeat his feat died in the attempt, and the route is still considered difficult today. Preuss adhered to a strict ethical philosophy (he rejected the use of pitons and felt that a passage should only be climbed if it could also be descended), and participated in every sphere of mountaineering, from winter ascents and solo climbs, to ski ascents and grand Alpine routes (the first ascent of the southeast arête of the Aiguille Blanche de Peuterey). Preuss died during a solo attempt on Mandlkogel in the Dachstein range.

Ramond de Carbonnières (Louis)
French naturalist and writer (1755–1827)
The "inventor" of Pyrenean mountaineering admitted that his life was like a novel. He started out as a pre-romantic poet, a friend of Lenz and Goethe, then became secretary to Cardinal Rohan, whom he followed in exile to the Pyrenees. Comparing the Pyrenees to the Alps, Ramond was the first writer to render them homage. He long sought a way up Mont Perdu (Monte Perdido), thought at the time to be the highest in the Pyrenees, and his guides made the first successful ascent in 1802. Named prefect of the Puy-de-Dôme region, Ramond spent the final part of his life refining Laplace's barometric formula, thereby increasing the accuracy of altimeters.

Rébuffat (Gaston)
French guide and mountaineer (1921–1985)
Born in Marseille, Rébuffat was one of the first city dwellers to be admitted to the Compagnie des Guides in Chamonix. He won recognition for his ascents of the great Alpine routes (the north face of the Eiger, the Grandes Jorasses, Piz Badile), often with clients, which was rare at the time. One of his firsts, the south face of the Aiguille du Midi (1956), went on to become a highly popular climb. Rébuffat was above all an excellent ambassador of classic mountaineering, its values and its delights; his books, photos, films, and lectures were not designed to promote his own exploits, but rather a type of mountaineering that everyone could appreciate. This rare talent made Rébuffat one of the world's best-known mountain climbers.

Rey (Guido)
Italian mountaineer (1861–1935)
Guido Rey's name is linked to the Furggen Arête on the Matterhorn, which he only managed to scale in 1899 with the help of an artificial aid, namely the use of a rope ladder. Like several other climbers of the day, however (for example, Julius Kugy and Eugen Guido Lammer), Guido Rey's writing had as much if not more influence than his actual ascents (which might be considered minor today). In his two main books, *The Matterhorn and Peaks and Precipices*, Rey advocated a humanist approach to mountain climbing that has more in common with other cultural activities than with athletic accomplishments.

*Facing page: The south ridge of the
Aiguille Noire de Peuterey, during
the first winter ascent of the entire
Peuterey Ridge.*

Rey (Emile)
Guide from Valle
d'Aosta (1846–1895)
One of the greatest
guides of his day, Emile
Rey is remembered for
his famous Peuterey
trilogy, having
successively conquered
the Aiguille Noire (1877),
the Aiguille Blanche
(1885), and the Arête de
Peuterey (1893) in the
Mont Blanc group; this
last climb, in the company
of the German Paul
Güssfeldt, turned out to
be an eighty-eight-hour
odyssey. After have succeeded in the second, third, and fourth
ascensions of the Grand Dru, he led the fifth at lightning
speed—only fourteen hours starting from Montenvers! A highly
appreciated guide, Emile Rey died in a rather inexplicable
accident while descending the Dent du Géant.

Robbins (Royal)
American climber
(1935)
Robbins name is
intimately linked to
Yosemite's "Big Walls."
He participated in the
first or second ascents of
practically all the major
routes opened in the
1960s, notably the first
ascent of the famous
Salathé Wall (1961) and a
solo climb of Muir Wall
(1968). Furthermore,
Robbins opted for Alpine-
style climbing rather than
the expedition tactics
employed on the Nose in 1958. Robbins's arrival in the Alps
alongside Gary Hemming and John Harlin yielded two major
new routes on the Petit Dru, the Robbins–Hemming Direct and
the Robbins–Harlin Direttissima. In 1975, Robbins founded his
own mountaineering garment firm.

Russell-Killough
(Henry, Count of)
Franco-Irish explorer
of the Pyrenees
(1834–1909)
Along with Ramond de
Carbonnières, Russell-
Killough is the most
respected Pyrenees
enthusiast. After having
traveled across the world,
he settled in Toulouse
and devoted his life to the
Pyrenees, which he
explored up and down
with precision and
passion. Russell-Killough
took a particular shine to
Mont Vignemale, to the extent of becoming a lifelong resident
of the mountain, having had grottoes carved into it where he
was able to have the Mass celebrated as well as receive his
friends! Russell-Killough's well-written books and articles did a
great deal to give Pyrenean specialists their own identity,
distinct from that of Alpine mountaineers.

Saussure (Horace
Bénédict de)
Naturalist from Geneva
(1740–1799)
Saussure played a key
role in the exploration of
the Alps. During his first
trip to Chamonix, he
offered a reward to the
first person to find a route
to the top of Mont Blanc.
It took a quarter of a
century and numerous
attempts before Jacques
Balmat and Michel
Gabriel Paccard stood on
the summit in 1786.
Saussure followed in their
footsteps the following year, guided by Balmat. Saussure's
primordial role did not stop there, however, for he was the first
person to make an extended stay at high altitude (the Col du
Géant) and to systematically study every aspect of the
mountain. Although his modesty inhibited him from elaborating
a coherent geological theory, historians now recognize the
novelty and fertility of his ideas.

Facing page: Pierre Béghin arriving at the summit of Jannu.

Shipton (Eric)
British mountaineer and explorer (1907–1977)
Shipton's climbs took him to the four corners of the earth, often in the company of H. W. "Bill" Tilman (1898–1978), who shared Shipton's approach to mountaineering—simple to the point of austerity. Shipton is remembered above all for his conquest of Kamet (7,755 m). It was Tilman, meanwhile, who claimed Nanda Devi (7,816 m), the highest summit scaled prior to 1950. Shipton served for a while as consul general at Kashgar, which enabled him to explore the little-known ranges of Central Asia, such as the Bogdo Ola range in the Tien Shan. He also led no fewer than six expeditions to Patagonia. Tilman, meanwhile, pursued his explorations aboard a simple boat that took him to the most distant mountains of the earth.

Schneider (Erwin)
Austrian mountaineer and cartographer (1906–1987)
Although little known to the general public, Schneider was one of the people who most contributed to accurate knowledge of non-European mountain ranges. After making the first ascent of Lenin Peak in the Pamirs in 1928, followed by Huascarán in Peru in 1932, Schneider participated in the expedition to Nanga Parbat in 1934. He drew up maps of mountains as varied as the Huayhuash Cordillera, Mount Everest, Mount Kenya, and various groups in the eastern Alps. In each case his precise information on mountain geography, place names, and altitudes proved indispensable to the climbers who followed him.

Solleder (Emil)
Bavarian guide and mountaineer (1899–1931)
After having tested his luck in America as a gold prospector, he later worked as a manual laborer and a mountain guide. Among Solleder's twenty firsts, three were of the highest class, becoming the most difficult routes in the Dolomites. Achieved in 1925 and 1926, they were: the north face of Furchetta in the company of Fritz Wiessner; the east face of Sass Maor with F. Kummer; and, most importantly, the north face of Punta Civetta, which he scaled with Gustav Lettenbauer, employing some twenty pitons on a face one thousand meters high. Solleder died while descending the Meije with a client, probably before truly coming into his prime.

Terray (Lionel)
French guide and mountain climber (1921–1965)
Terray formed a legendary partnership with Louis Lachenal, notably tracing a second route up the formidable north face of the Eiger in 1947. Following an expedition to Annapurna (1950) and Lachenal's death (1955), Terray concentrated on foreign expeditions that brought French mountaineering to the fore. He made the first ascents of Fitz Roy (1952), Huantsan (1952), Makalu (1954), Chacraraju West (1956), Jannu (1962), and Mount Huntington, Alaska (1964). At the same time, Terray also pursued a career as a traditional guide, which is described in his book, *Borders of the Impossible: From the Alps to Annapurna.* He died on the Vercors cliffs of France.

Tyndall (John)
Irish scientist and mountain climber (1820–1893)

A celebrated physicist, Tyndall was drawn to the Alps by glaciology, a subject that brought him into competition with another scientific mountaineer, James David Forbes. Tyndall made several attempts on the Matterhorn, and successfully scaled the Weisshorn (1861). In 1868 he was the first person to dare to confront the Hörnli Ridge of the Matterhorn following the tragedy of 1865, in order to make the first complete traverse of the mountain. Tyndall, however, felt that mountaineering could not be divorced from its scientific purpose, which brought him into conflict with other climbers of the day, including Edward Whymper and Leslie Stephen. His quarrel over the subject with Stephen led Tyndall to withdraw from the Alpine Club.

Welzenbach (Willo)
Bavarian mountaineer (1900–1934)

Of the illustrious group of German climbers of the 1930s, Welzenbach was the one who most clearly displayed an attraction for great, icy north faces. He vanquished a great number of them, often with a sovereign contempt for bad conditions. Particularly important was his conquest of the north face of the Gross Wiessbachhorn, where, for the first time, ice pitons were used (1924). In 1932, Welzenbach scaled no fewer than four north faces around Lauterbrunnen in the Bernese Oberland: Grosshorn, Gspaltenhorn, Gletscherhorn, and Lauterbrunnen Breithorn. After conquering the north face of Nesthorn (1933)—a climb that still inspires respect today—Welzenbach died on Willi Merkl's expedition to Nanga Parbat.

Whillans (Don)
British mountain climber (1933–1985)

Whillans got his start on the crags of Derbyshire, thereby becoming a terrific rock climber like his friend Joe Brown. In 1954, the British route up the west face of the Blaitière, opened up by the Brown–Whillans duo, included an exceptionally difficult passage. Whillans took part in the conquest of the Frêney Pillar (1961), then concentrated on distant expeditions to Patagonia (first ascent of the Aiguille Poincenot in 1962) and the Himalayas (paticipating in climbing a new route up the south face of Annapurna in 1970 as a member of Chris Bonington's British expedition). Don Whillans was notorious for his joviality that so contrasted with the asceticism of many modern climbers; anecdotes concerning Whillans have transformed him into something of a legend.

Whymper (Edward)
British engraver and mountain climber (1840–1911)

Whymper went to the Alps at the age of twenty-one in order to do engravings of them. He developed a passion for the Matterhorn, which he attempted to scale nine times, all the while climbing other peaks, including the Barre des Ecrins, Mont Dolent, the Aiguille d'Argentière, and the Aiguille Verte. The well-known tragedy that accompanied his ultimate victory over the Matterhorn (1865) seems to have marked him for life. He forsook the Alps to become the first mountaineering explorer in Greenland, the Andes, and the Canadian Rockies. His major accomplishment from that period was the 1880 ascent of Chimborazo in Ecuador (6,310 m), which thereby became the highest peak ever scaled. Whymper illustrated his numerous books on mountains with his own engravings.

Following double page: Christine Janin reaching the summit of Mount Everest.

Wiessner (Fritz)
German-born American mountaineer (1900–1988)

Fritz Wiessner had an exceptionally long and rich career. Starting in the 1920s, he was one of the greatest climbers in the eastern Alps (accompanying Emil Solleder on the Furchetta). After having emigrated to the United States, he discovered the outstanding East Coast cliffs known as the Shawangunks, and played a major role in the development of American mountaineering. He nearly managed to reach the summit of K2 in 1939, accompanied by the Sherpa Pasang Dawa Lama. His two major ascents in the United States were Devil's Tower in Wyoming (1937) and Mount Waddington in Washington (1939).

Young (Geoffrey Winthrop)
British mountaineer (1876–1958)

Young was the most remarkable climber of the early twentieth century. Often in partnership with guide Josef Knubel, Young inaugurated highly aesthetic routes in the Alps, notably the Mont Blanc and Valais ranges, along what are now known as the Young Ridges on the Breithorn and the Weisshorn. He nevertheless always remained fond of the mountains in Wales. As an ambulance driver during the war, Young lost a leg, but nevertheless took up climbing again. Despite a rigid wooden leg and his advancing age, he managed to climb the Matterhorn and Monte Rosa. Young was also a highly talented poet and writer.

Zsigmondy (Emil)
Austrian physician and mountaineer (1861–1885)

Along with his brother Otto Zsigmondy (1860–1918) and Ludwig Purtscheller (1849–1900), Zsigmondy represented the "new spirit" that blew across the eastern Alps around 1880. The young men's bold routes, their refusal to rely on professional guides, and their solo ascents appeared to be madly audacious at the time. Emil Zsigmondy's death in an attempt to force a direct route up the south face of the Meije (shortly after the summit was first conquered by the two Zsigmondy brothers and Ludwig Purtscheller), helped to convince advocates of the classic approach that things should not be pushed too far.

Zurbriggen (Matthias)
Italian guide (1856–1917)

After working at various trades, Zurbriggen began his career as a guide by specializing in routes up the east face of Monte Rosa. His big chance came in 1892, when he accompanied Conway to the Karakoram, breaking the altitude record of the day on Pioneer Peak. Hired by the British climber Edward Fitzgerald, he reached the summit of Mount Cook in New Zealand on his own. Fitzgerald also took Zurbriggen to the Andes, where the guide scaled Aconcagua, once again on his own, thereby breaking the altitude record for a second time. Later hired by the Bullock Workman couple, Zurbriggen returned to the Karakoram. His outstanding career as explorer-guide turned Zurbriggen into a kind of celebrity—he was the first guide to publish an autobiography.

633   The Japanese monk En no Shokaku made the first known ascent of Mount Fuji (3,776 m), the highest summit in Japan. His feat represents the first recorded climb of a high-altitude mountain.

1334–1336   Just a few years apart, philosopher Jean Buridan and poet Petrarch ascended Mont Ventoux (1,909 m) in the south of France. The former was motivated by cosmological concerns, the latter by philosophical considerations.

1358   Boniface Rotario climbed Rochemelon (3,537 m), which would become a pilgrimage site. This was the first known ascent of a 3,000-meter peak in the Alps.

Circa 1400   The Incas climbed Llullaillaco (6,723 m) and many other tall Andean peaks, leaving vestiges and mummies. It is likely that even Cerro Aconcagua was scaled. An equivalent altitude would not be attained by modern mountaineers until 1855.

1492   Antoine de Ville and his companions climbed Mont Aiguille (2,806 m) at the request of the king of France, accomplishing the first "technical" ascent of a difficult peak (employing ladders, ropes, and other scaling techniques).

1582   Edmund Scory scaled Tenerife Peak (now Teide Peak; 3,176 m) in the Canary Islands, then considered to be "the highest part of the earth." Although the summit was thought to be the highest point on the planet, this ascent—often repeated—had little impact on public opinion.

1648   Florin Perrier, Blaise Pascal's brother-in-law, climbed Puy de Dôme (1,465 m) in order to demonstrate barometric pressure. The invention of the barometer would slowly but surely lead to increased interest in altitude and its effects.

1738   On 20 July, Bouguer and La Condamine scaled Corazon (4,791 m) in Ecuador, commenting that "probably no one has ever climbed to such a height—we were at 2,470 fathoms [4,814 m] above sea level."

1770   While carrying out research into the atmosphere, the Duluc brothers climbed Mont Buet (3,109 m), at the same time making the first recorded high-altitude bivouac.

1778   In search of a "Lost Valley," the inhabitants of Gressoney climbed Entdeckungsfelsen (4,366 m) on the flanks of Monte Rosa. It is the first time that an altitude of 4,000 meters in the Alps was incontrovertibly surpassed.

1779   Belsazar Hacquet, the "Saussure of the eastern Alps," made an ascent of Triglav (2,863 m), the highest summit in the Julian Alps on the Austro–Italian–Slovenian border.

1786   Mont Blanc was first scaled by Jacques Balmat and Michel Gabriel Paccard from Chamonix, at the prompting of Genevan scientist Horace Bénédict de Saussure, who would climb the mountain himself the following year.

1799   Cardinal von Salm and his entourage climbed Kleinglockner (3,783 m), the first truly high summit in the eastern Alps to be scaled. Grossglockner (3,798 m) would be climbed the following year.

1802   Rondo and Laurens, guides to Ramond de Carbonnières, climbed Mont Perdu (Monte Perdito; 3,353 m) in the Pyrenees, thereby inaugurating mountaineering in that Franco–Spanish range.

1803   German naturalist Alexander von Humboldt climbed to an altitude of 5,800 meters on Chimborazo in Ecuador, observing the effects of altitude sickness.

1811   The Meyer brothers from Aarau, Switzerland, made the first ascent of Jungfrau in the Bernese Oberland, in the company of two chamois hunters from Lötschental.

1820   Ed James and his partners scaled Pikes Peak (4,310 m;14,110 ft.), making the first recorded ascent of a high summit in the Rocky Mountains.

1829   A Russian scientific expedition led by General Emanuel attempted to scale Elbrus in the Caucasus. Although geologists Lenz and Kuppfer halted some 200 meters below the summit, it would appear that Killar Hashirov, from Cherkessk, continued to the top.

1829   Jakob Leuthold and Johannes Währen, guides to Professor Franz Joseph Hugi, conquered Finsteraarhorn (4,275 m), the highest peak in the Bernese Oberland.

1830   Captain Durand climbed Mont Pelvoux (3,946 m) with chamois hunters Mathéoud and Liotard, as part of his surveying campaign.

1850   Johann Coaz climbed Piz Bernina (4,055 m), the easternmost "4,000er" in the Alps.

1855   James and Christopher Smyth, Charles Hudson, John Birbeck, and E. J. Stevenson, with guides Ulrich Lauener, Johann Zumtaugwald, and Mattias Zumtaugwald, arrived at the Dufourspitze, the highest point on Monte Rosa (4,638 m).

1861   Weisshorn (4,512 m), one of the highest peaks in the Valais Alps, was scaled by Professor John Tyndall with guides Johann-Josef Bennen and Ulrich Wenger.

1864   A. W. Moore and Edward Whymper, guided by Michel Croz and Christian Almer senior and junior, ascended the Barre des Ecrins (4,101 m).

1865   The first ascent of the Matterhorn is made by Edward Whymper, Lord Francis Douglas, Charles Hudson, Robert Hadow, and guides Michel Croz and Peter Taugwalder senior and junior. The event received enormous publicity due to the deaths of Douglas, Hadow, Croz, and Hudson during the descent.

100 Key Dates

1875 Henri Cordier, Thomas Middlemore, and John Oakley Maund, with guides Jakob Anderegg, Johann Jaun, and Andreas Maurer, climbed the north face of the Aiguille Verte (Cordier Couloir). This route, highly advanced for the day, would not be repeated until 1924.

1877 Emmanuel Boileau de Castelnau and guides Pierre Gaspard senior and junior conquered Meije (3,983 m), the last great virgin summit in the Alps.

1880 Edward Whymper inaugurated mountaineering outside of Europe by climbing Chimborazo in the Andes (6,272 m).

1882 The Sella brothers climbed the Dent du Géant—which Mummery declared "inaccessible by fair means"—by employing the Maquignaz family of masons to equip the mountain with cables and ropes. The issue of "fair means" in mountain climbing had been raised.

1885 The last great independent summit in the Mont Blanc chain, the Aiguille Blanche de Peuterey, was conquered by H. Seymour King with guides Emile Rey, Ambros Supersaxo, and Aloys Anthamatten.

1897 Wilhelm Paulcke, Wilhelm Lohmüller, and their companions first used skis in mountaineering to cross the Oberland from Grimsel to Belalp, climbing to 3,780 meters on the flanks of Jungfrau.

1898 Guide Matthias Zurbriggen arrived alone at the summit of Aconcagua (6,960 m), the highest peak in the Americas.

1899 The first ascent of Campanile Basso (2,877 m) in the Brenta Dolomites was made by Otto Ampferer and Karl Berger, probably representing the most difficult climb of the day.

1903 The first traverse between the two summits of Ushba (4,698 m) in the Caucasus was made by Georg Leuchs, Hans Pfann, and Ludwig Distel. It constituted an enormous undertaking at the time, with no fewer than four bivouacs.

1904 By scaling the north spur of Finsteraarhorn, Gustav Hasler, and Fritz Amatter tamed one of the great north faces in the Alps. They needed to bivouac twice.

1906 An expedition led by the duke of Abruzzi to Africa's Ruwenzori range (Mountains of the Moon) successfully climbed seventeen summits, including the main peak, Margherita (5,119 m). The second ascent would take place twenty years later.

1906 Valentine Ryan and guides Franz and Josef Lochmatter climbed the East Ridge of the Aiguille du Plan, one of the most difficult rock routes of the prewar era.

1907 For the first time, a summit over 7,000 meters high was scaled when Tom Longstaff, with guides Alexis and Henri Brocherel and porter Kabir, arrived at the summit of Trisul (7,120 m) in the Garhwal Himalayas.

1909 The duke of Abruzzi's expedition to the Karakoram did not manage to scale K2, but climbed to a height of 7,500 meters on Bride Peak (Chogolisa), the highest altitude ever reached by mountain climbers.

1910 Peter Anderson, William Taylor, and Charles McGonagall—Alaskan gold prospectors known as "sourdoughs"—climbed the north summit of Mount McKinley (6,187 m; 20,298 ft.) and perhaps the main summit (6,194 m; 20,320 ft.) in an extremely bold ascent.

1911 On the north face of Lalidererwand (Karwendel), guide Angelo Dibona led Guido and Max Mayer up a route on which pitons were employed for the first time on a great Alpine face.

1911 One of the greatest mountaineering feats of all times was accomplished by Paul Preuss from Munich when he took just two hours to climb, without a rope, the east face of Campanile Basso in the Brenta. Italian climber Pino Prati would be killed attempting to repeat the exploit, which would only be successfully repeated (by a roped party) in 1928.

1912 Hans Dülfer and Walter Schaarschmidt successfully scaled the east face of Fleischbank (Kaisergebirge) by employing all the modern techniques of climbing—pitons, carabiners, double rope, and pendulums, although they did not use the drill they had taken along.

1922 New altitude records were broken when George Mallory and Theodore Somervell reached 8,230 meters on the north face of Everest, without oxygen; it was the first time the 8,000-meter threshold had been passed. George Finch and Charles Bruce, using oxygen apparatus, attained 8,326 meters.

1924 One of the greatest mysteries in the history of mountain climbing was born when Mallory and Irvine disappeared above 8,500 meters, while heading for the summit of Everest. Even today, there is no definitive proof that they never reached the top. Edward Norton, meanwhile, reached an altitude of 8,573 meters without oxygen.

1925 By taming the northwest face of Punta Civetta, employing fifteen pitons on a route 1,000 meters long, Emil Solleder and Gustav Lettenbauer pulled off one of the earliest triumphs of "modern" climbing.

1927 The famous guide Adolphe Rey used three pitons (but no carabiners) on the Hirondelles Ridge of the Grandes Jorasses. Giusto Gervasutti would give the passage a grade of 6.

1928 Americans Robert Underhill and Myriam O'Brien (the future Mrs. Underhill), guided by Armand Charlet and Georges Cachat, made the first successful traverse of the Aiguilles du Diable. Armand Charlet negotiated the Isolée Passage without the use of pitons.

1929 The first ascent of the Couturier Couloir on the north face of the Aiguille Verte was made by American Bradford Washburn with guides Georges Charlet, Alfred Couttet, and André Devouassoux. Dr. Marcel Couturier would make a second, more direct ascent in 1932 with Armand Charlet and Jules Simond.

1930 Karl Brendel and Hermann Schaller successfully climbed the south ridge of the Aiguille Noire de Peuterey, which Willo Welzenbach had fruitlessly attempted.

1931 Eric Shipton, Frank Smythe, R. L. Holdsworth, and the Sherpa Lewa climbed Kamet (7,755 m) in the Garhwal Himalayas. It was the highest peak ever scaled, the first "25,000 footer," and the first time that a Sherpa had participated in a major first ascent.

1931 The north face of the Matterhorn yielded to the Schmid brothers, who had arrived from Munich by bicycle.

1933 In the Dolomites, Emilio Comici and the Dimai brothers finally managed to scale the north face of Cima Grande di Lavaredo. Eighty pitons were driven into the rock.

1935 By successfully climbing the north face of the Petit Dru, Pierre Allain and Raymond Leininger forged what would long be the toughest route in the western Alps—the Allain Fissure.

1935 Riccardo Cassin and Vittorio Ratti required three days and sixty pitons to conquer the north face of Cima Ovest di Lavaredo in the Dolomites, entailing a highly spectacular traverse among a series of overhangs.

1936 By successfully scaling Nanda Devi (7,817 m), Noël Odell and Bill Tilman broke the record for the highest peak ever climbed.

1936 The two most difficult routes of the interwar period were opened: up Marmolada, forged by Giovanbattista Vinatzer and Ettore Castiglioni in twenty-seven hours, and Death Corner between Rosskuppe and Dachl in Gesäuse (Austria), climbed by Raimund Schinko and Fritz Sikorowsky in four days.

1938 Two of the greatest problems in the Alps were finally solved: the north face of the Eiger was climbed by two teams—Anderl Heckmair with Ludwig Vörg and Heinrich Harrer with Fritz Kasparek—while the north face of Pointe Walker on the Grandes Jorasses was scaled by Italians Riccardo Cassin, Ugo Tizzoni and Gino Esposito.

1950 Maurice Herzog and Louis Lachenal were the first men to tread the summit of an 8,000-meter peak, Annapurna. But it cost them serious frostbite requiring amputations, and they barely escaped a worse fate.

1950 Allen Steck and John Salathé finally climbed the north face of Sentinel Rock in Yosemite, after a decade of attempts. They spent four nights on the face. The last 500 meters required 150 pitons and nine expansion bolts. Yosemite's first "big wall" had fallen.

1951 By ascending the east face of Grand Capucin in the Mont Blanc range, Walter Bonatti and Luciano Ghigo demon-strated the usefulness of the piton techniques developed in the eastern Alps.

1952 A Parisian party—Adrien Dagory, Lucien Bérardini, Guido Magnone, and Marcel Lainé—successfully climbed, in two stages, the west face of the Petit Dru, which in 1935 Pierre Allain had described as "the very prototype of the impossible."

1952 Guido Magnone and Lionel Terray, members of the French expedition, climbed the extremely difficult Mount Fitz Roy (now Chaltén, 3,405 m) in Patagonia.

1953 The two most coveted "8000ers" fell in the same year: Everest, climbed by New Zealander Edmund Hillary and Tenzing Norgay (members of John Hunt's British expedition), and Nanga Parbat, whose summit was reached by Hermann Buhl after a final and extraordinary solo "sprint."

1954 The first ascent of K2 (8,611 m), the second highest peak in the world, was made by Achille Compagnoni and Lino Lacedelli (members of Ardito Desio's Italian expedition). Walter Bonatti and the porter Mahdi were obliged to bivouac, with no material, at an altitude of nearly 8,000 meters.

1954 At the conclusion of an extremely bold ascent, Lucien Bérardini, Robert Paragot, Edmond Denis, Adrien Dagory, Guy Poulet, and Pierre Lesueur triumphed over the immense south face of Aconcagua, at the cost of serious frostbite for several members of the team.

1955 In one of the greatest exploits in the history of mountaineering, Walter Bonatti climbed the southwest pillar of the Petit Dru during a five-day epic.

1955 Maurice Davaille and Philippe Cornuau took five days to tame the north face of Les Droites, an ascent that went almost unnoticed at the time but that continued to grow in repute.

1957 Hamish MacInnes, Tom Patey, and G. Nicol climbed Zero Gully on Ben Nevis, one of the great challenges of Scottish ice climbing.

1957 Walter Philipp and Dieter Flamm open a route up the northwest dihedral (corner) of Punta Civetta, long considered one of the toughest climbs in the Dolomites.

1958 Warren Harding, George Whitmore, Wayne Merry, Allen Steck, et al. complete their ascent of the Nose, the first route up El Capitan in Yosemite. It took them forty-five days of climbing over an eighteen-month period; 675 pitons and 125 bolts were used.

1958 On the north face of Cima Grande in the Dolomites, Lothar Brandler and Dietrich Hasse put a route directly up the huge central overhangs.

1961 From 6 to 12 March, Toni Hiebeler, Walter Almberger, Toni Kinshofer, and Anderl Mannhardt accomplished the most coveted of winter ascents, namely the north face of the Eiger.

1961 Belgian climber Claudio Barbier made successive solo ascents, all in a single day, of the five north faces of Tre Cime di Lavaredo in the Dolomites—the Cassin route on Cima Ovest, the Comici route on Cima Grande, the Preuss route on Cima Piccola, the Dülfer route on Cima Piccolissima, and the Innerkofler route on Punta di Frida.

1962 The conquest of Jannu (or Kumbhakarna, 7,710 m) in the Nepalese Himalayas inaugurated a new phase of Himalayan climbing, namely the ascent of less lofty but highly difficult peaks.

1963 Michel Darbellay, from Valais, pulled off the most coveted of solo firsts—the north face of the Eiger. In the same year, Walter Bonatti and Cosimo Zapelli accomplished the most sought-after winter ascent, namely the Walker Spur on the Grandes Jorasses.

1963 One of the last virgin faces of the Mont Blanc chain fell to the tact and technique of Californian climbers when the south face of the Fou was scaled by Tom Frost, Stewart Fulton, John Harlin, and Gary Hemming.

1965 Walter Bonatti capped his mountain climbing career by opening a direct route, alone and in winter, up the north face of the Matterhorn, 100 years after the mountain was first conquered.

1967 Swiss mountaineer Sylvain Saudan's descent of the Spencer Couloir on the Aiguille de Blaitière (average gradient of 51°) heralded the beginning of "extreme skiing" in the Alps.

1968 The Shroud on the Grandes Jorasses, which the finest teams of climbers had been vainly attacking for years, finally fell (in January) to René Desmaison and Robert Flematti.

1970 A British expedition led by Chris Bonington climbed the south face of Annapurna, conquering the first Himalayan big wall of great technical difficulty.

1973 After multiple attempts by the finest mountaineers of the day, Walter Cecchinel and Claude Jager managed to scale the north couloir of the Petit Dru during an ascent that lasted four days, ending on 31 December. This feat was made possible by advances in ice-climbing equipment, notably the ice axes and crampons developed by Cecchinel for the Simonds firm.

1974 The first clean and indisputable ascent of Cerro Torre, the "most difficult peak in the world," was made by Casimiro Ferrari's Italian expedition (which, unlike Cesare Maestri in 1970, managed to scale the mushroom of ice on the summit). The authenticity of the 1959 ascent by Maestri and Toni Egger (during which the latter died) has been strongly contested.

1975 A new era opened in the Himalayas when Reinhold Messner and Peter Habeler made the second ascent of Hidden Peak, not only via a new route but also in a pure "Alpine style" (no high-altitude porters, no intermediate camps, no fixed lines, and in a single go).

1975 The ascent of the southwest face of Everest, attempted since 1968, was finally accomplished by Chris Bonington's British expedition. Dougal Haston and Doug Scott were the first to reach the main summit. They then bivouacked on the southern summit.

1976 The British climbing team of Joe Tasker and Peter Boardman took Himalayan mountaineering into the sphere of extreme difficulty by scaling the west face of Changabang (6,864 m) in the Garhwal.

1978 Reinhold Messner and Peter Habeler were the first men to successfully climb Everest without oxygen.

1980 Andrzej Zawada's Polish expedition made the first winter ascent of Everest, via the Nepalese face.

1980 Reinhold Messner climbed Everest alone, without oxygen, via the north face—a feat considered absolutely impossible just ten years earlier.

1981 On Marmolada, Czech climbers Igor Koller and Jndřich Šustr blazed a route ("A Travers le Poisson") typical of the new level of difficulty being attained.

1983 The greatest Alpine routes were free-climbed: Swiss climber Marco Pedrini scaled the "superdirect" route on the Drus (using nuts) and Eric Escoffier from France freed the south face of the Fou.

1984 Reinhold Messner and Hans Kammerlander made the first traverse between two "8,000ers," Hidden Peak and Gasherbrum II, in four days.

1984 Norwegians Hans Christian Donseth, Finn Doehli, Dag Kolsrud, and Stein Aasheim took twenty days to complete their route No Return on the southeast face of the east summit (6,231 m) of the Great Trango Tower. Although two climbers were killed during the descent, it represented an important stage in ever-increasing difficulty in the Himalayas.

1985 By successfully climbing the west face of Gasherbrum IV, Wojtech Kurtyka and Robert Schauer accomplished one of the boldest feats of contemporary mountaineering in the Himalayas, which was completely ignored by the media since both the peak and the climbers were unknown.

1986 With his ascent of Lhotse, Reinhold Messner became the first man to have climbed all of the planet's fourteen "8,000ers"—Annapurna, Broad Peak, Cho Oyu, Dhaulagiri, Everest, Gasherbrum II, Hidden Peak, K2, Kangchenjunga, Lhotse, Makalu, Manaslu, Nanga Parbat, Shisha Pangma.

1989 Tomo Cesen, from Slovenia, racked up two impressive firsts: the north face of Jannu and the south face of Lhotse. The veracity of these ascents has nevertheless been contested.

1991 The first major high-altitude route to be forged by a woman was the work of Catherine Destivelle from France, on the Petit Dru, in nine days.

1991 The north face of Thalay Sagar (6,904 m), one of the most difficult peaks in the Garhwal Himalayas (and, with Cerro Torre, one of the most difficult in the world), was climbed by Hungarians Peter Dékàny and Attila Ozsvàth.

1993 The American Lynn Hill free-climbed the Nose on El Capitan, a feat that had defied the best men climbers in the world.

1995 The Briton Alison Hargreaves was the first woman to reach the summit of Everest without oxygen equipment (she was killed a few months later on K2).

*Preceding double page: An
advanced base camp at the foot
of the south face of Annapurna,
with Machapuchare visible
in the background.*

1. Mountaineering Classics

Allain (Pierre). *Alpinisme et compétition.* Paris, 1949. Reprint, Geneva, 1978.

Azéma (Marc-Antoine). *The Conquest of Fitz Roy.* Trans. from the French by Katherine Chorley and Nea Morin. London, 1957.

Barth (Hermann von). *Gesammelte Schriften.* Munich, 1926.

Béghin (Pierre). *Hautes Altitudes. Voyage dans l'oxygène rare.* Grenoble, 1991.

Blödig (Karl). *Die Viertausender der Alpen.* Munich, 1923.

Boardman (Peter). *The Shining Mountain: Two Men on Changabang's West Wall.* London, 1978.

Bonatti (Walter). *On the Heights.* Trans. from the Italian by Lovett F. Edwards. London, 1964.

Bonington (Christian). *Annapurna South Face.* New York, 1971.

————. *Everest the Hard Way.* New York, 1976.

Bourrit (Marc-Théodore). *A Relation of a Journey to the Glaciers in the Duchy of Savoy.* Trans. from the French by Cha. and Fred Davy. Norwich, 1775.

Brown (Thomas Graham). *Brenva.* London, 1944.

Buhl (Hermann). *Nanga Parbat Pilgrimage.* Trans. from the German by Hugh Merrick. London, 1956.

Cesen (Tomo). *Solo.* Milan, 1991.

Charlet (Armand). *Vocation alpine. Souvenirs d'un guide de montagne.* Neuchâtel, 1949.

Cichy (Leszek), Wielicki (Krzysztof), Zakowski (Jacek). *Rozmowy o Everescie.* Warsaw, 1987.

Clinch (Nicholas). *A Walk in the Sky.* Seattle, 1983.

Comici (Emilio). *Alpinismo eroico.* Bologna, 1961.

Conway (Sir William Martin). *Mountain Memories: a Pilgrimage of Romance.* London, 1920.

————. *Climbing and exploration in the Karakoram Himalayas.* With 300 illustrations by A. D. McCormick. 2 vols. London, 1894.

Dalloz (Pierre). *Zénith.* Paris, 1951.

Dent (Clinton T.). *Above the Snow Line: Mountaineering Sketches between 1870 and 1880.* London, 1885.

Desmaison (René). *Total Alpinism.* Trans. from the French by Jane Taylor. New York, 1982.

Desor (Edouard). *Excursions et séjours dans les glaciers.* Neuchâtel, 1844.

Desio (Ardito). *Ascent of K2.* Trans. from the Italian by David Moore. London, 1955.

Diemberger (Kurt). *Summits and secrets.* Trans. from the German by Hugh Merrick. London, 1971.

Dittert (René), Chevalley (Gabriel), Lambert (Raymond). *Forerunners to Everest.* English version by Malcolm Barnes. London, 1954.

Eggler (Albert). *The Everest–Lhotse Adventure.* Trans. from the German by Hugh Merrick. London, 1957.

Eiselin (Max). *The Ascent of Dhaulagiri.* Trans. from the German by E. Noel Bowman. London, 1961.

Evans (Sir Robert Charles). *Kangchenjunga, the Untrodden Peak.* London, 1956.

Fellenberg (Edmund von). *Der Ruf der Berge. Die Erschliessung der Berner Hochalpen. Gesammelt und mit Lebensbild.* Zürich, 1925.

Ferlet (René), Poulet (Guy). *Aconcagua: South Face.* Trans. from the French by E. Noel Bowman. London, 1956.

Filippi (Filippo de). *Karakoram and Western Himalaya 1909: an Account of the Expedition of H.R.H. Prince Luigi Amedeo of Savoy, Duke of the Abruzzi.* Trans. from the Italian by Caroline de Filippi and H. T. Porter. New York, 1912.

Franco (Jean). *Makalu.* Trans. from the French by Denise Morin. London, 1957.

Franco (Jean), Terray (Lionel). *At Grips with Jannu.* Trans. from the French by Hugh Merrick. London, 1967.

Frendo (Edouard). *La face nord des Grandes Jorasses.* Paris, 1950.

Freshfield (Douglas William). *Travels in the Central Caucasus and Bashan: Including Visits to Ararat and Tabreez and Ascents of Kasbek and Elbruz.* London, 1869.

Gervasutti (Giusto). *Gervasutti's Climbs.* Trans. from the Italian by Nea Morin and Janet Adam Smith. London, 1957.

Grohmann (P.). *Wanderungen in den Dolomiten.* Vienna, 1877.

Güßfeldt (Paul). *In den Hochalpen.* Berlin, 1886.

Habeler (Peter). *The Lonely Victory: Mount Everest '78.* New York, 1979.

Heckmair, (Anderl). *Die Drei Letzten Probleme der Alpen.* Munich, 1949.

Herzog (Maurice). *Annapurna.* Trans. from the French by Nea Morin and Janet Adam Smith. New York, 1953.

Hillary (Sir Edmund). *High Adventure.* New York, 1955.

Horbein (Thomas). *Everest: the West Ridge.* San Francisco, 1965.

Hudson (Rev. Charles), Kennedy (Edward Shirley). *Where There's a Will There's a Way: an Ascent of Mont Blanc by a New Route and without Guides.* London, 1856.

Hugi (Franz-Joseph). *Naturhistorische Alpenreise.* Solothurn, 1830. Reprint, Solothurn, 1995.

Hunt (John). *Conquest of Everest.* New York, 1954.

King (Clarence). *Mountaineering in the Sierra Nevada.* Boston, 1872.

Bibliography

Koenig (Erich). *Empor! Georg Winklers Tagebuch.* Munich, 1910.

Kukuczka (Jerzy). *De la mine aux sommets.* Paris, 1990.

Lachenal (Louis). *Carnets du Vertige.* Paris, 1963.

Lambert (Raymond). *A l'assaut des "Quatre Mille."* Geneva, 1946.

Lammer (Eugen Guido). *Fontaine de Jouvence.* Chambéry, 1931.

Lépiney (Jacques and Tom de). *Climbs on Mont Blanc.* Trans. from the French by Sydney Spencer. London, 1930.

Livanos (George). *Au-delà de la Verticale.* Paris, 1958.

————. *Cassin: il était une fois le sixième degré.* Paris, 1983.

Longstaff (Thomas). *This My Voyage.* New York, 1951.

Maestri (Cesare). *Arrampicare è il mio mestiere.* Milan, 1960.

Magnone (Guido). *West Face.* Trans. from the French by J. F. Burke. London, 1955.

Messner (Reinhold). *The Seventh Grade.* New York, 1974.

————. *Everest: Expedition to the Ultimate.* Trans. from the German by Audrey Salkeld. New York, 1979.

————. *Solo Nanga Parbat.* Trans. from the German by Audrey Salkeld. New York, 1980.

————. *The Crystal Horizon.* Seattle, 1989.

————. *All Fourteen Eight-Thousanders.* 1988.

————. *Free Spirit: A Climber's Life.* Seattle, 1991.

Meyer (Rudolf). *Reise auf die Eisgebirge des Kantons Bern und Besteigung Ihrer höchsten Gipfel.* Aarau, 1811.

Moore (Adolphus Warburton). *The Alps in 1864: a Private Journal.* London, 1867.

Mummery (Albert Frederick). *My Climbs in the Alps and Caucasus.* New York, 1895.

Moravec (Fritz). *Weisse Berge, schwarze Menschen.* Innsbruck, 1957.

Newby (George Eric). *A Short Walk in the Hindu Kush.* London, 1958.

Paragot (Robert), Bérardini (Lucien). *Vingt ans de cordée.* Paris, 1974.

Patey (Thomas). *One Man's Mountains: Essays and verses.* London, 1971.

Peaks, Passes and Glaciers: a Series of Excursions by Members of the Alpine Club. 1st series, London, 1859; 2nd series, London, 1862.

Petrarch. "The Ascent of Mount Ventoux." In *Petrarch: A Humanist Among Princes.* Edited by David Thompson. New York, 1970.

Piaz (Tita). *Le diable des Dolomites.* Paris, 1963.

Purtscheller (Ludwig). *Über Fels und Firn.* Munich, 1901.

Ramond de Carbonnières (Louis-François Elizabeth). *Travels in the Pyrenees.* Trans. from the French by F. Gold. London, 1813.

Rébuffat (Gaston). *Starlight and Storm.* Trans. from the French by Wilfred Noyce and Sir John Hunt. London, 1956.

Rébuffat (Gaston). *La montagne est mon domaine.* Paris, 1994.

Rey (Guido). *The Matterhorn.* Trans. from the Italian by J. E. C. Eaton. London, 1907.

Roper (Steve). *Camp 4.* Chamonix, 1996.

Russell-Killough (count Henry). *Souvenirs d'un montagnard.* Pau, 1888.

Saussure (Horace-Bénédict). *Voyage dans les Alpes.* Neuchâtel, 1779–1796, 4 vols. Reprint, Bologna, 1970. Reprint, Geneva, 1978.

Saussure (Horace-Bénédict). *Lettres de Saussure à sa femme.* Chambéry, 1937.

Schmuck (Markus). *Broad Peak, 8047 m. Meine Bergfahrten mit Hermann Buhl.* Stuttgart, 1958.

Shipton (Eric). *The Six Mountain-Travel Books.* Seattle, 1985.

————. *That Untravelled World. An Autobiography.* New York, 1969.

Stephen (Sir Leslie). *The Playground of Europe.* London, 1871.

Studer (G.). *Ueber Eis und Schnee. Die höchsten Gipfel d. Schweiz u. d. Geschichte ihrer Besteigung.* 3 vols. Bern, 1869.

Tasker (Joe). *Savage Arena.* New York, 1982.

Terray (Lionel). *Conquistadors of the Useless.* Trans. from the French by Geoffrey Sutton. London, 1963.

Tézenas du Montcel (Robert). *Ce monde qui n'est pas le nôtre.* Paris, 1965.

Tichy (Herbert). *Cho Oyu: by Favour of the Gods.* Trans. from the German by Basil Creighton. London, 1957.

Tilman (Harold William). *The Seven Mountain-Travel Books.* Seattle, 1983.

Tyndall, Haute Montagne. Neuchâtel, 1942.

Whillans (Donald Desbrow), Ormerod (Allick). *Don Whillans: Portrait of a Mountaineer.* London, 1971.

Whymper (Edward). *Scrambles amongst the Alps.* London, 1871.

————. *Travels amongst the Great Andes of the Equator.* London, 1892.

Young (Geoffrey Winthrop). *On High Hills: Memories of the Alps.* London, 1927.

Zsigmondy (Emil). *Im Hochgebirge.* Leipzig, 1889.

Zurbriggen (Matthias). *From the Alps to the Andes: Being the Autobiography of a Mountain Guide.* London, 1899.

2. The Mountains in Fiction and Humor

Aldebert (Max). *Les îles désertes.* Paris, 1957.

Auden (Wystan Hugh), Isherwood (Christopher). *The Ascent of F6.* London, 1936.

Bowman (William E.). *Ascent of Rum Doodle.* New York, 1956.
Bruhl (Étienne). *Accident à la Meije.* Hoëbeke, Paris, 1996.
Buzzatti (Dino). *Barnabé des montagnes.* Paris, 1989.
Cendrars (Blaise). *Le Plan de l'Aiguille et les confessions de Dan Yack.* Lausanne, 1987.
Coxhead (Elizabeth). *One Green Bottle.* Philadelphia, 1951.
Daudet (Alphonse). *Tartarin sur les Alpes.* Paris, 1888.
Daumal (René). *Mount Analogue.* London, 1959.
Frison-Roche (Roger). *First on the Rope.* London, 1949.
Höhl (Ludwig). *Une ascension.* Paris, 1980.
Labiche (Eugène), Martin (Edouard). *Le voyage de Monsieur Perrichon. Comédie en quatre actes.* Paris, 1860.
Mason (Alfred Edward Woodley). *Running Water.* New York, 1907.
Morin (Jean). *Les royaumes du monde.* Paris, 1954.
Peyré (Joseph). *Matterhorn.* Paris, 1992.
Sauvy (Anne). *Les Flammes de pierre.* Grenoble, 1993.
Silverberg (Robert). *Les royaumes du Mur.* Paris, 1993.
Toulouse (Gilbert). *Mont Perdu.* Paris, 1977.
Twain (Mark). *A Tramp Abroad.* Hartford, 1879.
Zöpfli (Emil). *Die Wand der Sila.* Zürich, 1986.

3. Useful Reference Works

Anderson (J. R. L.). *High Mountains and Cold Seas: a Biography of H. W. Tilman.* Seattle, 1980.
Angelini (G.). *Civetta per le vie del passato.* Belluno, 1977.
Anker (Daniel). *Jungfrau, Zauberberg der Männer.* Zürich, 1996.
Annan (Noel). *Leslie Stephen. The Godless Victorian.* London, 1984.
Ballu (Yves). *Gaston Rébuffat.* Paris, 1996.
Bauer (Paul). *The Siege of Nanga Parbat 1856–1953.* Trans. from the German by R. W. Rickmers. London, 1956.
Baume (Louis). *Sivalaya. Explorations of the 8000-meter Peaks of the Himalayas.* Seattle, 1979.
Béraldi (Henri). *Cent ans aux Pyrénées.* 7 vols. Paris, 1898–1904. Reprint, Pau, 1977.
———. *Le passé du pyrénéisme. Notes d'un bibliophile.* 10 vols. Paris, 1911–1927.
Birkett (Bill), Peascod (Bill). *Women Climbing: 200 Years of Achievement.* Seattle, 1990.
Boy (G.), Allan (I.), Ward (C.). *Snowcaps on the Equator.* Bodley Head, 1988.
Broc (Numa). *Les montagnes au siècle des Lumières.* Paris, 1991.
Brunhuber (Sepp). *Wände im Winter.* Munich, 1951.
Camena d'Almeida. *Les Pyrénées, Développement de la connaissance géographique de la chaîne.* Paris, 1893. Reprint, Amsterdam, 1969.
Cameron (Ian). *Mountains of the Gods. The Himalayas and the Mountains of Central Asia.* London, 1984.
Cammani (Enrico). *La letteratura dell'alpinismo.* Bologna, 1985.
Canac (Roger). *Gaspard de la Meije.* Grenoble, 1992.

Casara (Severino). *Preuss, l'alpinista leggendario.* Milan, 1970.
Chamson (Max). *Le roman de la montagne.* Paris, 1987.
———. *Whymper, le fou du Cervin.* Paris, 1986.
Clark (Ronald). *The Day the Rope Broke: the Story of a Great Victorian Tragedy.* New York, 1965.
———. *The Early Alpine Guides.* London, 1949.
———. *An Eccentric in the Alps: the Story of the Rev. W. A. B. Coolidge.* London, 1959.
———. *Men, Myths, and Mountains.* New York, 1976.
———. *The Splendid Hills: The Life and Photographs of Vittorio Sella.* London, 1948.
———. *The Victorian Mountaineers.* London, 1953.
Coolidge (William Augustus Brevoort). *The Alps in Nature and History.* New York, 1908.
Cunningham (Carus Dunlop), Abney (Sir William de Wyveleslie). *The Pioneers of the Alps.* London, 1887.
De Beer (Sir Gavin Rylands). *Alps and Men.* London, 1932.
———. *Early Travellers in the Alps.* London, 1930.
———. *Travellers in Switzerland.* London, 1949.
De Beer (Sir Gavin Rylands), Brown (T. Graham). *The First Ascent of Mont Blanc.* New York, 1957.
Dübi (Heinrich). *Paccard wider Balmat. Die Entwicklung einer Legende.* Berne, 1913.
Dumler (Helmut). *Drei Zinnen. Berge, Menschen, Abenteuer.* Munich, 1968.
Durier (Charles). *Le Mont Blanc.* Chamonix, 1897. Reprint, Fayence, 1982.
Dyhrenfurth (Günther Oskar). *Das Buch vom Kantsch. Die Geschichte seiner Besteigung.* Munich, 1955.
Engel (Claire Eliane). *A History of Mountaineering in the Alps.* New York, 1950.
Engel (Claire Eliane), Vallot (Charles). *Mont Blanc.* 1965.
Fantin (Mario). *Le Ande (Un secolo di alpinismo).* Turin, 1979.
———. *Cervino 1865–1965.* Bologna, 1965.
———. *I quattordici " 8000," Antologia.* Bologna, 1964.
Fini (F.). *Il Monte Rosa.* Bologna, 1979.
Freshfield (Douglas W.). *The Life of Horace-Bénédict de Saussure.* London, 1920.
Girdlestone (Cuthbert). *Louis-François Ramond (1755–1827). Sa vie, son œuvre littéraire et politique.* Paris, 1968.
Gogna (Alessandro). *Grandes Jorasses sperone Walker. 40 anni di storia alpinistica.* Bologna, 1969.
Gos (Charles). *Alpine Tragedy.* Trans. from the French by Malcolm Barnes. New York, 1948.
———. *Le Cervin.* 2 vols. Neuchâtel, 1948.
Gramminger (Ludwig). *Das gerettete Leben: aus der Geschichte der Bergrettung. Einsätze, Einwicklungen, Ausbildung, Episoden.* Munich, 1986.
Grand-Carteret (John). *La montagne à travers les Ages.* 2 vols. Grenoble, 1904. Reprint Geneva, 1980.

Guichonnet (Paul). *Histoire et civilisation des Alpes.* 2 vols. Toulouse/Lausanne, 1980.

Harding (Warren). *Downward Bound. A Mad! Guide to Rock Climbing.* Englewood Cliffs, New Jersey, 1975.

Harrer (Heinrich). *The White Spider.* Trans. from the German by Hugh Merrick. London, 1959.

Haston (Dougal). *In High Places.* London, 1972.

Hiebeler (Toni). *North Face in Winter.* Trans. from the German by Hugh Merrick. London, 1962.

————. *Zugspitze. Von der Erstbesteigung bis heute.* Pawlak Verlag, 1985.

Holzel (Tom). Salkeld (Audrey). *The Mystery of Mallory and Irvine.* London, 1986.

Houston (Charles). *Going Higher. The Story of Man and Altitude.* Burlington, Vermont, 1983.

Isselin (Henri). *Les Aiguilles de Chamonix.* Paris, 1980.

————. *Du côté de l'aiguille Verte.* Paris, 1972.

————. *La Meije.* Grenoble, 1956.

Jantzen (René). *Montagnes et symboles.* Lyon, 1988.

Jones (Christopher). *Climbing in North America.* Berkeley, 1976.

Joutard (Philippe). *L'invention du mont Blanc.* Paris, 1986.

Julyan (Robert Hixson). *Mountain Names.* Seattle, 1984.

Kearhey (Allan). *Mountaineering in Patagonia.* Seattle, 1993.

Kurz (Marcel). *Chronique himalayenne.* Zürich, 1959. Supplement, Zürich, 1963.

Lehner (Wilhelm). *Die Eroberung der Alpen.* Leipzig/Zürich, 1924.

Lejeune (Dominique). *Les "alpinistes" en France (1875–1919).* CTHS, Paris, 1988.

Mantovani (Roberto), Diemberger (Kurt). *The Endless Knot: K2, Mountain of Dreams and Destiny.* Seattle, 1991.

Martina (E.). *Alpinismo invernale. Delle origine ai giorni nostri.* Milan, 1968.

Mason (Kenneth). *Abode of Snow. A History of Himalayan Exploration and Mountaineering.* Seattle, 1987.

Mazel (David). *Pioneering Ascents: the Origins of Climbing in America, 1642–1873.* Harrisburg, 1991.

Melucci (E.). *Breve storia dell'alpinismo dolomitico.* Florence, 1960.

Motti (Gian Piero). *La storia dell'alpinismo.* 2 vols. Turin, 1994,

Müller (C. C.), Rauning (W.). *Der Weg zum Dach der Welt.* Innsbruck, 1982.

Mumm (Arnold Louis). *The Alpine Club Register.* 3 vols. London, 1923-1928.

Neate (Jill). *Mountaineering in the Andes.* London, 1987.

Neate (Jill). *High Asia. An Illustrated History of the 7,000-Meter Peaks.* Seattle, 1989.

Nicholson (Marjorie Hope). *Mountain Gloom and Mountain Glory: the Development of the Aesthetics of the Infinite.* Ithaca, 1959.

Pascoe (J. D.). *Great Days in New Zealand Mountaineering.* Wellington, 1958.

Payot (Paul). *Au royaume du mont Blanc.* Paris, 1978.

Reinisch (Gertrude). *Wanda Rutkiewicz. Karavane der Traüme.* Munich, 1995.

Richter (E.). *Die Erschliessung der Ostalpen.* 3 vols. Berlin, 1893–94.

Roberts (Eric). *Welzenbach's Climbs.* Seattle, 1981.

Salkeld (Audrey). *On the Edge of Europe, Mountaineering in the Caucasus.* London, 1993.

Savenc (Franci). *Na Vrhovih Sveta. Od prvih pristopov do najvisjih sten.* Ljubljana, 1992.

Schmitt (Fritz). *Hans Dülfer.* Munich, 1985.

Scott (Douglas). *Big Wall Climbing.* New York, 1974.

Ségogne (Henri de), Couzy (Jean). *Les alpinistes célèbres.* Paris, 1956.

Senger (Max). *Wie die Schweizer Alpen erobert wurden.* Zürich, 1945.

Sircar (S. Joydeep). *Himalayan Handbook.* Calcutta, 1979.

Steinitzer (Alfred). *Der Alpinismus in Bildern.* Munich, 1924.

Tursky (Franz). *Der Grossglockner und seine Geschichte.* Vienna, 1922.

Unsworth (Walter). *Encyclopaedia of Mountaineering.* London, 1993.

————. *Everest. A Mountaineering History.* London, 1991.

————. *Hold the Heights. The Foundations of Mountaineering.* London, 1994.

————. *Savage Snows: the Story of Mont Blanc.* London, 1986.

————. *Tiger in the Snow. The Life and Adventures of A. F. Mummery.* London, 1967.

Varale (Vittorio). *La battaglia del sesto grado (1929–1938).* Milan, 1965.

Zhou Zheng. *Liu Zhenkai, Footprints on the Peaks. Mountaineering in China.* Seattle, 1995.

Ziak (Karl). *Der Mensch und die Berge. Eine Weltgeschichte des Alpinismus.* Salzburg/Stuttgart, 1965.

4. Specialized Bibliographies

Alpine Club. *Catalogue of books and periodicals.* London, 1982.

Durio. Bibliografia alpinistica storica e scientifica del gruppo del M. Rosa (1527-1924). Novara, 1925. Reprint 1972.

Imhof (Viola). *Katalog der Zentralbibliotek des Schweitzer Alpenclub.* Zürich, 1986.

Labarère (Jacques). *Essai de bibliographie pyrénéiste (des origines à nos jours).* 2 vols. Pau, 1986.

Meckly (Eugene P.). *Mont Blanc, The Early Years: A Bibliography of Printed Books from 1744 to 1860.* Asheville, 1995.

Mountaineering. Catalogue of the Graham Brown and Lloyds Collections in the National Library of Scotland. Edinburgh, 1994.

Neate (Jill). *Mountaineering Literature.* Seattle, 1986.

Salkeld (Audrey), Boyle (John). *Climbing Everest. The bibliography.* Clevedon, 1993.

Yakushi (Yoshimi). *Catalogue of Himalayan Literature.* Tokyo, 1995.

Index

Photograph credits